THE STORY OF ALICE

ALSO BY ROBERT DOUGLAS-FAIRHURST

Becoming Dickens: The Invention of a Novelist
Victorian Afterlives: The Shaping of Influence in
Nineteenth-Century Literature

THE STORY OF
ALICE

*Lewis Carroll
and the Secret History
of Wonderland*

ROBERT
DOUGLAS-FAIRHURST

Harvill *Secker*

LONDON

1 3 5 7 9 10 8 6 4 2

Harvill Secker, an imprint of Vintage,
20 Vauxhall Bridge Road,
London SW1V 2SA

Harvill Secker is part of the Penguin Random House group of companies
whose addresses can be found at global.penguinrandomhouse.com.

Penguin
Random House
UK

First published by Harvill Secker in 2015

www.vintage-books.co.uk

A CIP catalogue record for this book is available from the British Library

ISBN 9781846558610 (hardback)
ISBN 9781846558627 (trade paperback)

Picture research by Caroline Wood
Text designed by Lindsay Nash

Typeset in Dante MT by Palimpsest Book Production Limited,
Falkirk, Stirlingshire

Printed and bound in Great Britain by Clays Ltd, St Ives PLC

Penguin Random House is committed to a sustainable future for our
business, our readers and our planet. This book is made from Forest
Stewardship Council® certified paper.

MIX
Paper from
responsible sources
FSC
www.fsc.org FSC® C018179

In Memoriam
Conor Michael Francis Robinson
18 September 1992 – 15 October 2013

Contents

PROLOGUE

'I'm not myself . . .'

Lewis Carroll, *Alice's Adventures in Wonderland*

Alice Hargreaves photographed in New York (1932)

Snap

Hidden away inside a plain cream folder in the Beinecke Library at Yale there is a black-and-white photograph with the hand-written caption 'Alice P. Hargreaves 1932'. It was taken on the thirty-first floor of New York's Waldorf-Astoria Hotel, in a large suite with views across the city's jagged skyline, and it marked the start of a visit to celebrate the centenary of someone the sitter still referred to with Victorian propriety as 'Mr Dodgson'. To the rest of the world he was better known as Lewis Carroll, the author of *Alice's Adventures in Wonderland* (1865) and *Through the Looking-Glass, and What Alice Found There* (1872), two of the most popular and influential stories in the history of children's literature. But he was not the only person involved in their creation whose real identity had become bundled up with a literary one in the public mind. For the past seven decades, Alice P. Hargreaves had also been living a double life.

I first came across this photograph in the autumn of 2013. After leaving a gloomy Oxford at the start of October, I had already spent a couple of weeks travelling across America in the search for material that would help me make sense of Lewis Carroll's life. In some ways it was also an attempt to make sense of my own. Like many people, I first read the *Alice* books as a young child, and the mixture of feelings they produced in me at the time – an emotional scramble of amusement, fear, bewilderment and sheer unexamined joy – had never gone away. But it was only now that I found myself wanting to know why. I was approaching middle age, and although there was no sign yet of a full-blown midlife crisis, I was getting used to discovering new sources of niggling anxiety. Would I ever be able to read anything again with the unalloyed passion I had once devoted to books like *Alice's Adventures in Wonderland*? The brightness of Carroll's dreamworld also seemed to sharpen certain forms of loss. How had Carroll managed to create something I still remembered so intensely, when the rest of my childhood had faded to a distant blur?

Every few days I arrived in a new city, checked into a budget hotel, and then hunkered down in an archive with no company other than a handful of academics tapping away at their laptops like eager woodpeckers. The life of a travelling researcher is not a glamorous one, and so far it had been a predictably depressing experience. Each morning involved the same routine: rubbery breakfast eggs ('table for one, sir?'), a short walk, a polite exchange with a librarian, and then long hours working through scraps of writing that gave the illusion of order, as they arrived in their neat cardboard boxes, but stubbornly refused to settle into a meaningful pattern. There had been a few highlights. In New York, I was shown a game Carroll had invented for one of his child-friends, and on the other side discovered some doodles that included a fragile stick man and three attempts at a bird flapping its wings; in Texas, I was allowed to turn the pages of Carroll's first photograph album, where it was still possible to see pale brown traces of the gum he had used to fix his original albumen prints in place.

But it wasn't until I arrived at the Beinecke Library, on a crisp sunny morning towards the end of October, that I saw pieces of Carroll's biographical jigsaw that allowed many more to slot into place. Inside one box was Alice Hargreaves's passport. Another contained a fat scrapbook of newspaper clippings labelled 'A. P. H.' and an academic hood. And linking everything together were hundreds of references to the little girl who first inspired Carroll to create his most famous literary character, and then spent the next seventy years living in her shadow. Alice Pleasance Hargreaves was the original Alice in Wonderland.

Although she had become a minor literary celebrity herself in the years immediately before this photograph was taken, there were occasions when she found the constant thrusting of microphones and flaring of flashbulbs something of an ordeal. 'She disliked having her photograph taken all her adult life,' one of her neighbours later recalled, and although

4

Carroll's photographs of her as a girl are among the most popular of Victorian images, later examples 'are extremely rare'. On her return to England she wrote to her son Caryl (an interesting choice of name) confessing 'oh, my dear I am tired of being Alice in Wonderland! Doesn't it sound ungrateful & *is* – only I do get tired.' Sometimes it showed: in other photographs taken on the same day she appears crumpled and confused. But in this one she holds her pose with steely determination: her hands are clasped tightly in her lap; a faint smile plays across her mouth, as if she is amused by the attention, or perhaps bemused by the fuss; her favourite velvet bow – a variation on the newly fashionable 'Alice band' – is perched at a jaunty angle on her head. Meanwhile, just visible in the background is another Alice: a pert little girl in a crisp pinafore dress, who gazes off into the distance with her arms folded in a mocking echo. It is as if the screen on which she was painted was really a magic mirror in which old people could become young again, the tedious business of adult life transformed into a children's game.

It was a game many people wanted to play. In the opening pages of *Alice's Adventures in Wonderland*, Carroll tells us that his heroine 'was very fond of pretending to be two people', but throughout her visit to America the newspapers were keen to present the widowed Alice Hargreaves as one person rather than two. Not only had she previously been Alice Liddell, the little girl who first persuaded Lewis Carroll – Mr Dodgson – to write down his fairy tales, but the real Alice was widely assumed to be identical to the fictional Alice. As a result, the arrival of an old lady in New York soon became a story about Alice exploring a new Wonderland.

On Friday 29 April, a scrum of thirty or forty reporters surrounded her on the sun deck of the Cunard liner *Berengaria*. In a short Paramount newsreel entitled 'Alice in U. S. Land!' she reflected on her childhood, speaking in an upper-class drawl that was spiced with hints of quiet mockery. Nothing she said in this crackly recording was very unusual – 'It is a great honour and a great pleasure to have come over here, and I think now my adventures overseas will be almost as interesting as my adventures underground were' – but the next morning 'Alice' was splashed across the local newspapers. 'Yesterday she came into her new wonderland,' cooed the *Herald Tribune*, 'still wide-eyed but undaunted . . . She will be eighty years old on Wednesday, but she appeared many years younger than that, a slender, erect little figure in a black fur coat.' 'Her skin', observed the *New York Sun*, was 'as clear as in her childhood', while the *New York World Telegram* informed its readers that her 'lively little figure' was dressed 'in a frilled and beflowered frock, a relic of a period known as mid-Victorian', like a child who had been let loose in her grandmother's dressing-up box. The *New York American* ventured further into fictional territory, reporting that 'her big blue eyes were as bright as they must have been that afternoon so long ago', and her reception 'drew from her the comment, "Curiouser and curiouser"'.

Later events were taken as the strongest evidence yet that New York was entertaining the real Alice in Wonderland. A photograph of her in the *Evening Post*, which showed her gamely cutting a cake covered in dozens of intricate pastry characters, was accompanied by the explanation that 'She was as pleased as a child when Oscar, maître d'hôtel, presented a large birthday cake to her.' A ceremony at Columbia University to award her with an honorary degree was designed, her host declared, 'to honor the little girl whose magic charm elicited from [Carroll] seventy years ago the story that has brought such delight to humanity'. Even photographs of her wearing a mortar-board were reproduced like distorted reflections of the climax to *Through the Looking-Glass*, in which 'Queen Alice' receives a golden crown. No matter how frail she appeared, everyone was determined that 'Alice' should still be the endlessly curious small child from the stories, like an illustration that had somehow wandered off the page and entered real life.

The only note of mild dissent came from Alice herself. In a speech she drafted on *Berengaria* notepaper, which probably formed part of a teatime radio broadcast over the WABC-Columbia network on 1 May, she apologized for not replying to letters and requests for autographs, and warned that 'If the children expect to see a girl like the one in the books, I am afraid that they will be disappointed.' Such quiet realism was quickly drowned out by the sound of ringing cash registers. Caryl, who had come to New York as her secretary and tour manager, noted in his diary that 'My friends here are much annoyed because I only asked $400' for the broadcast, whereas 'I should have asked $1000', and for the rest of their stay he was careful to give the American public the Alice they wanted: a wide-eyed innocent marvelling at another new world, rather than a reluctant celebrity being shepherded through hotel lobbies by her ambitious son.

Accordingly, on the same day as her radio broadcast, the *New York Times Magazine* carried a feature on 'The Lewis Carroll that Alice Recalls' (a subtitle revealed who was guiding her pen: 'Her Vivid Memories of the Inspired Author of Nonsense Tales, Told by Her Son'), which tried to convince its readers that, regardless of her actual age, Alice Liddell remained young in Lewis Carroll's eyes. 'Even when she was past 40,' Caryl affirmed, 'she was still, to Mr Dodgson, the "child of the pure unclouded brow and dreaming eyes of wonder" to whom he had dedicated the "Looking Glass."' A second article, 'Alice in a New Wonderland', published a month later in the *New York Herald Tribune*, left its readers in even less doubt about 'Alice's' true identity. 'The Same "Alice" Who Fell Down a Rabbit Hole 70 Years Ago and Landed in "Wonderland" Has Visited America and Written This Added Chapter on Her New Adventures,' trumpeted the headline, followed by an explanatory byline, 'By Alice Hargreaves – the Alice of "Alice in Wonderland"', and finally, in much smaller font, 'As Told to Her Son, Captain C. L. Hargreaves'. What follows is an attempt at wit that rarely escapes whimsy. '"Beautifuller and beauti-fuller!"' Alice cries as her ship comes into dock, '"Now the buildings are opening out like the largest telescopes that ever were!"' Later, travelling in a hotel elevator, she questions 'whether they would soon reach heaven', and on arriving at the thirty-first floor she recalls how '"When I was young . . . I had to grow my neck long in order to get up to these heights."' (Here Caryl may have been influenced by the *New York World Telegram*, which noted that on the *Berengaria* his mother asked a question about sky-scrapers 'with the earnestness of a little girl suddenly transported into an unfamiliar realm and trying to hold fast to reality'.) Even her experience of being hounded by a pack of photographers was turned into a modern comedy of manners, with an illustration that depicted the fictional Alice being surrounded by camera lenses as a set of huge unblinking eyes.

7

It isn't hard to explain the contemporary appeal of these articles. A reader who came across 'Alice in a New Wonderland' in the *Herald Tribune* would only have had to turn to the front page to see why an innocent abroad might have been an attractive figure in Depression-era America. The leading article, 'Shall the Underworld Rule?', warned in lurid detail of the increasing threat posed by gangsters, described as 'the spawn of the brothels, the gambling dens and the corrupt political machines of the big cities', under an illustration of the Statue of Liberty bound by ligatures labelled 'Racketeer', 'Greed', 'Bootlegging', 'Dope' and 'Vice'. Childhood seemed to be of little advantage in this world: the same article pointed out that Charles Lindbergh and his wife had recently employed 'two underworld characters to aid in the hunt for their baby', who had been kidnapped at the beginning of March and was later found a short distance from the family home with his skull smashed in like an egg. Even Caryl Hargreaves, whose diary largely reports his New York experiences with a sturdy indifference to surprise, seems to have been shocked at the sight of people brawling in the streets over tickets for a late-night screening of the grisly new gangster movie *Scarface*.

The role that children should play in a rotten society was also being investigated in other ways. *Runt Page*, released in April 1932, was the first of a series of cheaply produced comedies under the general title 'Baby Burlesks' that showed very young children, many of them still in nappies, acting out comic versions of hard-boiled adult dramas. Even as a ten-minute short *Runt Page* is probably nine minutes too long, although it is still remembered today as the professional debut of a three-year-old Shirley Temple, who falls asleep and dreams the main action sequence. However, for many people the survival of childhood innocence was inextricably bound up with the dreams of a much older character. A leader in the *Herald Tribune* summed up the popular mood: 'Is it inconceivable that [Alice Hargreaves's] presence might remind a host of worried Americans of how much more there is in the world than economics,' it asked hopefully, 'and how scant a relationship wealth has to fun?' Or, as a fictional newspaper reporter explains to Alice in the 1985 film *Dreamchild*, which depicts her visit to New York as a sequence of real events muddled up in

8

her mind with far darker fantasies: 'People want to make-believe . . . Sometimes we have to dream a little.'

It seems that the real Alice sometimes enjoyed playing the role assigned to her, or at least willingly accepted its demands. A scrap of paper survives in her handwriting that concludes '. . . is the fervent wish of Alice in Wonderland', a signature created with the tentative flourish of someone practising her autograph. Some of her recorded memories went even further. Asked to reflect on her childhood, she was happy to flatten out real life until it fitted the simple and reassuring outlines of a fairy tale. A set of handwritten notes for the article 'Alice's Recollections of Carrollian Days' ('As Told To Her Son, Caryl Hargreaves'), published later that year in the *Cornhill Magazine*, begins: 'In the early sixties [in] the old grey stone built Deanery at Christchurch there lived three little sisters, Ina, Alice & Edith, happy little maidens they.' The only missing words are 'Once upon a time'. Another draft, which describes some of their Thames excursions with 'Mr Dodgson', experiments with 'Such is the fairy godfather who helps row', a character sketch that was fluently written in fountain pen before being crossed out in pencil.

She was hardly unusual in wanting to view her life as a story. As many writers have pointed out, narrative provides an attractive set of models to follow when we want to make sense of life's uncertainties. The narrator of Julian Barnes's novel *Flaubert's Parrot* explains why: 'Books say: she did this because. Life says: she did this. Books are where things are explained to you; life is where things aren't. I'm not surprised some people prefer books.' A story reflects life but also redeems it: assembled on the page, even unpredictable events can be plotted, their random scatter made part of a meaningful design.

In the case of Alice Hargreaves's childhood river trips, this narrative pull was far too powerful to be satisfied by a light sprinkling of fairy-tale language. That was especially true when she tried to remember what had happened on 4 July 1862, the day Carroll and his colleague Robinson Duckworth had rowed her and two of her sisters up the Thames to a picnic spot near Oxford. Some of the details in her account may be unfamiliar to modern eyes – for example, she refers to *Alice's Adventures Underground* rather than *Alice's Adventures in Wonderland*, because that is the original title of the story Carroll invented for them that afternoon – but otherwise her version of events slipped easily into a well-worn narrative groove. 'Nearly all of "Alice's Adventures Underground" was told on an afternoon under the haystack at Godstow', she explained in a later typed draft of the *Cornhill* article, 'which has since become famous.' Then she added and crossed out a detail about having tea, and finally 'afternoon under the' was replaced by a short burst of purple prose in her son's handwriting that ballooned out into the margin: 'blazing summer afternoon with the heat haze shimmering over the meadows where the party landed to shelter for a while in the shadow cast by the'.

Perhaps Caryl was simply prompting her memory. 'Unfortunately nowadays my mother's memory is so bad,' he warned a correspondent in 1932, and he would have known that more than thirty years earlier she had supplied a very similar version of events for the first full biography of Carroll, recalling a 'summer afternoon when the sun was so burning that we had landed in the meadows down the river, deserting the boat to take refuge in the only bit of shade to be found, which was under a new-made hayrick'. Perhaps he wanted to ensure that her account did not contradict the poem that had opened *Alice's Adventures in Wonderland*: 'All in the golden afternoon . . . Beneath such dreamy weather.' Or perhaps he hoped that his choice of language – slightly archaic, slightly arch – would blend seamlessly with Carroll's 1887 essay '"Alice" on the Stage':

Many a day had we rowed together on that quiet stream – the three little maidens and I – and many a fairy tale had been extemporised for their benefit – whether it were at times when the narrator was 'i' the vein', and fancies unsought came crowding thick upon him, or at times when the jaded Muse was goaded into action, and plodded meekly on, . . . yet none of these many tales got written down: they lived and died, like summer midges, each in its own golden afternoon.

From 'three little maidens' (a tangled memory of the 'three little maids' in Gilbert and Sullivan's operetta *The Mikado*, which Carroll had seen at least five times since its opening two years earlier) to the summer midges (a mournful echo of the gnats in Keats's poem 'To Autumn', 'borne aloft | Or sinking as the light wind lives or dies'), the whole passage is a hazy mixture of earlier stories and songs, the daydream of a creative writer. It is all rather different to official meteorological reports, which record the day's weather as dreary rather than dreamy: 'cool and rather wet', with total cloud cover and a maximum temperature of 67.9°F. But for Carroll, a story-teller keen to forge a creation myth for his character, fact was much less powerful than fiction. Memory could create a microclimate that was as fixed as a painted sunset. And Alice Hargreaves, it seems, was content for her recollections to fall into line, either because, as the cultural historian Will Brooker has suggested, as she got older 'she may actually have begun to rely on the fiction in place of her own memories', or because, working alongside her canny son, she recognized that her status as Carroll's muse would not be strengthened by anyone rocking the boat.

Carroll's version of events has usually been accepted without question. As Brooker notes, although a few critics have raised sensible questions about what this account omits ('Taking children on river expeditions', the authors of *The Alice Companion* point out, inevitably involves moments when 'they have to pee' or are 'stung by insects and nettles'), most simply repeat the same details, replacing the shifting moods of real life with an afternoon of permanent sunshine. Nor is this a recent phenomenon. As early as 1932, the 'golden afternoon' was being interpreted as a fitting emblem for a lost golden age. The scrapbook of newspaper clippings put together by Alice and Caryl Hargreaves after their trip to New York includes a romantic piece by the journalist Kitty Cheatham, which begins by returning to a 'very special Wonder Day' in 1862. As 'The young Oxford Don a-rowing peeks here and there for a cool shady spot,' she continues breathlessly, 'the sweet mid-summer things are whispering . . . the threads in the weave are being collected, through the spinning of a fairy tale.' And then, presumably remembering the significance of 4 July for her own readers, she points out that on this 'summer afternoon' seventy years ago, the 'immortal camaraderie' of Carroll's story demonstrated the power of 'Life, Liberty and Pursuit of Happiness'. Exactly how it did this is not explained, but her underlying assumptions are clear enough. Just as the story of *Alice's Adventures in Wonderland* had become a modern myth, so the character of Alice had been adopted as a symbol that brought America's present neatly in line with its past. She was a model of constancy in a rapidly changing world.

What this ignores is how slippery and protean Alice's fictional identity had become by the time her living original arrived in New York. When the Caterpillar in Wonderland asks Alice '"Who are *you*?"' he receives the uncertain reply '"I – I hardly know, sir, just at present – at least I know who I *was* when I got up this morning, but I think I must have been changed several times since then."' Her confusion is understandable; over the course of her adventures she is variously mistaken for a housemaid, a serpent, a volcano, a flower and a monster. It also accurately reflects the changing shape of her stories. Having begun its life as an improvised oral performance in 1862, the first written version of *Alice's Adventures Underground* was presented to Alice Liddell in 1864 as a manuscript that was quirkily illustrated by Carroll himself, the word *Underground* having been tunnelled into to become *Under Ground*. It was then expanded and published the following year as *Alice's Adventures in Wonderland*, with its sequel *Through the Looking-Glass* appearing in 1872, both with illustrations by John Tenniel. But if those were the only complete stories featuring Alice written by Carroll, she would continue to enjoy further adventures of her own, as he repeatedly returned to this character and placed her in slightly different contexts, as if wanting to reassure himself that although her surroundings might have changed she had remained essentially the same. Over the next twenty years, he would publish a facsimile edition of his manuscript, combine both stories for the stage play *Alice in Wonderland*, rewrite the first book for young children as *The Nursery "Alice"*, and even arrange for his most popular characters to appear on merchandise such as stamp-cases and biscuit tins.

Carroll also had to confront the fact that the question 'Who are *you*?'

was one that many other people were keen to answer. W. H. Auden once pointed out that we enjoy imagining new adventures for popular fictional characters like Sherlock Holmes because they do not seem altogether bound to their original stories. They are bigger than their plots, literary escapologists capable of wriggling free from the covers of any book in which we try to contain them. Carroll's Alice is another member of this select group. While Tenniel's illustrations continued to fix her as a young girl with a neat frock and long blonde hair, she could be incorporated into later satires as a Victorian visitor sent to investigate the modern world, like an anthropologist who lives alongside a foreign tribe in order to study its unfamiliar customs; but her ability to survive outside her original stories also lay in her ability to adapt to changes in her environment.

Having begun life as Carroll's 'dream-child', Alice quickly came to populate the daydreams, fantasies and nightmares of many later writers and artists. From the 'golden afternoon' in 1862 to the death of Alice Hargreaves in 1934, and beyond, her fictional adventures never stopped being works in progress. Soon she had been depicted in dozens of sequels and supplements, from serious fictions to slapstick cartoons, in ways that included Alice the suffragette, Alice the wartime code-breaker and Alice the enthusiastic shopper. Rival images to Tenniel's included Willy Pogany's monochrome drawings for his 1929 edition, featuring an Alice with a plaid skirt and pageboy haircut; in the year following Alice Hargreaves's visit to America, Pogany's bobbysoxer would be joined by D. R. Sexton's pouting teenage Alice, who seemed to have wandered into a children's story by mistake, and the even more sophisticated figure who appeared in J. Morton Sale's edition, another Alice considerably closer to seventeen than seven, who boasted an elaborate evening dress and the suspicion of a bust. Meanwhile, Wonderland and Looking-Glass Land spawned a whole galaxy of fictional worlds that included Blunderland, Plunderland, Numberland and dozens more. Even the original Wonderland was colonized by other writers. Taking their cue from Carroll's Alice, who opens the door to her Wonderland in the same way as a reader might open up a new book, revealing a parallel universe to the one we usually live in, these writers busied themselves extending the concept of 'wonderland' until it included everything from the hidden marvels revealed by the microscope to the invisible realm of ghosts.

Yet while Alice has continued to grow larger or smaller in cultural terms according to how close we feel to her, how much space she takes up in our heads, her author has remained strangely elusive. On the cover of the Beatles album *Sergeant Pepper's Lonely Hearts Club Band* he appears at the end of a row of faces, sandwiched between Marlene Dietrich and T. E. Lawrence, in the faded greys of an old photograph that make him look eerily like a ghost. In one sense it is a thoughtless use of his image, given how self-effacing he was, how reluctant to reveal his personality to the world. But in another sense it is an oddly appropriate tribute to a writer who was in many ways the Invisible Man of Victorian culture, detectable chiefly by the movements going on all around him.

'Ah, did you once see Shelley plain?' Carroll's contemporary Robert Browning wrote in his poem 'Memorabilia', reporting an encounter with someone who claimed to have met Shelley before the poet's death in 1822. As Adam Kirsch points out, 'the line is famous because nobody ever has'; so tied together are Shelley's messy private life and his poetry that practically every line he wrote is thickened with hidden layers of anecdote and autobiography. Of course, the same might be said of many other writers, and not just in relation to the messy distractions of sex or politics. It is almost impossible to see any writer plain, because if they are serious about writing their real life tends to take place out of public view, as they sound out words in their heads or juggle them on the page. But even in this context Carroll is unusually good at squirming out of the biographer's grasp. No doubt some of this can be attributed to the fact that parts of his life have been edited out of the official record, most notoriously by whichever member of his family decided to censor a handful of pages in his diary. There are also parts that have fallen through the cracks of history, such as four whole volumes of his diary that have been lost since his death. Yet Carroll's slipperiness also reveals something important about the kind of man he was. Paradoxically, the more that has been written about him, the more elusive he has become.

Physically he presented a lopsided appearance to the world – one of his eyes drooped, and one shoulder was slightly higher than the other – and in other ways too he sometimes seemed to be less a consistent personality than two strangers who merely happened to share the same skin. He was both Lewis Carroll, an imaginative writer who wandered through life with a head full of stories, and the Revd Charles Dodgson, a plodding mathematician for whom the only truly interesting relationships were to be found in algebra. In public, he upheld the doctrines of the established Church; in private, he devoured books about the supernatural. As a friend to hundreds of children, he filled his cupboards in Christ Church with enough toys and gadgets to stock a small toyshop; left alone in his rooms, he busied himself writing letters of complaint about the size of his hassock or how his potatoes were cooked. Socially he could be gregarious, warm and witty; he could also be shy, cold and prickly. To some he was a holy innocent; to others his behaviour justified James Joyce's later characterization of him as 'Lewd's carol'. In his lifetime, he was a frequent target of gossip; since his death, he has continued to attract myths in the same way that an old wardrobe attracts moths. Queen Victoria enjoyed *Alice's Adventures in Wonderland* so much she asked for a copy of the author's next book, and later received a beautifully wrapped package containing *An Elementary Treatise on Determinants: With Their Application to Simultaneous Linear Equations and Algebraical Geometry*. Alice's experiences in Wonderland reflect her creator's experiments with psychedelic drugs. Carroll was Jack the Ripper. None of these stories is true, but so thick is the atmosphere of suspicion that hangs over his reputation, merely pointing this out is rarely enough; deny something often enough, and people may start to wonder what you are hiding.

In his diary, Carroll liked to celebrate notable days by marking them with 'a white stone', a mental paperweight that separated out important memories and prevented them from being lost in the general drift of past events. For example, a day in June 1856 that he had spent photographing Alice and the other Liddell children, 'plentifully interspersed with swinging, backgammon, etc.', was marked 'most specially with a white stone', and three months later he did the same to commemorate his first meeting with Tennyson. The usual explanation for this practice points out similar formulas in classical authors: Pliny, for example, describes the Thracians' habit of putting a white pebble in one urn on happy days, and a black one in a different urn on unhappy days, which allowed them to calculate their overall levels of satisfaction. It is tempting to think that Carroll had such ancient practices in mind when he totted up each day's events, turning his life into one huge sum. That certainly reflects one side of his personality: the fixed principles and steady routines by which he regulated each day, together with a pouncing eye for detail that he acknowledged as his 'super-fastidiousness'. Even when describing something as simple as going for a walk, those who knew him best found themselves reaching for words such as 'always' and 'never'. 'His favourite form of exercise was always walking,' recalled his niece Violet Dodgson, while Margaret Mayhew remembered him striding along poker-straight with his head held aloft, 'never wearing a "dog-collar", but always a very low turn-down collar with a white tie, his top-hat well at the back of his head – reminding me of Tenniel's drawing of the Mad Hatter'.

Yet almost nothing in Carroll's life is capable of being interpreted in just a single way; the more closely the supposed facts of his biography are examined, the more each one starts to divide into a squabbling Tweedledum and Tweedledee. Even his 'white stone' is ambiguous. In addition to being a classical commonplace, the same phrase is found in the Bible, which Carroll knew with the kind of intimacy he tended to reserve for books rather than people, where it indicates absolution from sin: 'To him that overcometh will I give to eat of the hidden manna, and will give him a white stone, and in the stone a new name written' (Revelation 2: 17). The idea of renewal held a particular appeal for Carroll, who spent most of his life being caught up in the rhythms of the academic year, and tended to be far better at carrying on with things than starting them afresh. That is probably why so much of his writing reveals what the critic Elizabeth Sewell has characterized as a 'strong sense of unfinished business'.

'There is a sadness in coming to the *end* of anything in Life,' he noted in his diary on the day he finally retired from his Mathematical Lectureship

at Christ Church, before reaching for a traditional form of religious con-
solation with the thought that 'Man's instincts cling to the Life that will
never end.' Such was his aversion to endings that usually he put them off
for as long as possible. 'I do dislike saying "good-bye" to any person or
thing one has any liking for,' he explained to one child-friend, and while
still an undergraduate he found a way of avoiding it altogether by ending
a long letter to his sister Elizabeth with '(to be continued)'. He preferred
incomplete paintings to those that had been sealed with varnish, enjoyed
impossible riddles such as the Hatter's '"Why is a raven like a writing-
desk?"', and spent much of his time dreaming up schemes he would never
see through, such as a simplified form of money-order and an early form
of Scrabble. Often, when he appeared to have finished something, he
attempted to revise it or add to it in some way: typically, after he completed his first year as Curator (i.e. Steward) of the Common Room at
Christ Church, he published in quick succession *Twelve Months in a
Curatorship*, then a *Supplement to Twelve Months in a Curatorship*, and finally
a one-page *Postscript to Supplement*.

Beginning with his undergraduate mock-epic *The Ligniad* (a one-joke
spoof that ends with a crossed-out 'Finis'), and continuing up to the publication of his final collection *Three Sunsets and Other Poems*, it was in his
poetry and fiction that Carroll's attraction to unfinished business achieved
its most lasting form. He especially enjoyed playing with his readers'
expectations. Sometimes this was achieved by breaking off lines too early,
as with the famous cry '"It's a Boo—"' at the end of a stanza in *The Hunting
of the Snark*, which is followed by an ominous blank space. However,
nowhere is Carroll's commitment to what one of his child-friends called
his 'never-ending, never-failing stories' clearer than in the *Alice* books. The
idea stretches from Alice biting her tongue so as not to offend the Mock
Turtle ('"I've often seen them at dinn—"'), to a poem recited by Humpty
Dumpty that manages to end simultaneously on a perfect rhyme and a
narrative cliffhanger: '"*And when I found the door was shut,* | *I tried to turn
the handle, but—*".' It is a joke made all the funnier by Humpty Dumpty's
own inevitable ending, which interrupts Alice's thought process with a
perfectly timed piece of comic slapstick:

'Of all the unsatisfactory—' (she repeated this aloud, as it was a great comfort to have such a long word to say) 'of all the unsatisfactory people I *ever* met—' She never finished the sentence, for at this moment a heavy crash shook the forest from end to end.

Together the *Alice* books form the imaginative centre of a whole career of unfinished business. Not only does *Through the Looking-Glass* work as a sequel to *Alice's Adventures in Wonderland*, like the first two volumes of an incomplete three-decker novel, but the final chapter of the second story, which is framed as a question ('Which Dreamed It?'), also ends with a question ('Which do *you* think it was?'), and is then followed by an additional poem and an unanswerable question: 'Life, what is it but a dream?'

It is appropriate that the *Alice* books are so full of questions, because these are stories that switch from the straightforwardly transparent to the puzzlingly opaque with the ease of a spinning coin. Sometimes this provokes critics into ambitious feats of exegesis. In the bestselling critical edition *The Annotated Alice*, even a seemingly innocuous remark such as the White Rabbit's '"She'll have me executed, as sure as ferrets are ferrets"' produces a marginal gloss that stretches over two pages, as the editor Martin Gardner moves from Victorian slang ('the word was colloquially applied in England to thieving money-lenders') to modern pet ownership ('Owning a ferret in New York City, which is said to have ten thousand ferrets, is a health code violation') to the founding in 1995 of '*Modern Ferret*, a glossy magazine devoted to praise of ferrets'. Yet no matter how closely the individual elements of the *Alice* books are analysed, the stories as a whole refuse to be explained away. This is not just because they are full of ideas that lurk just out of reach, only occasionally breaking the surface of the text, but also because so much of what attracts new readers – such as Carroll's tone, which makes us feel simultaneously that we are being taken into his confidence and eavesdropping on a private joke – depends upon a relationship that has disappeared from view.

The precise nature of the triangular relationship between Carroll, the real Alice and the fictional Alice has always been notoriously hard to pin down.

As with a blob of mercury, applying any sustained pressure to what we think we know has only made it scatter further. The published facts about how Carroll first met Alice Liddell, how their friendship developed, and why it was abandoned, are not only few in number but capable of being rearranged into many different patterns. Each one generates further questions. Was Carroll in love with her? Were the *Alice* books merely written so that she could read about herself, or were they intended to be substitutes for her, allowing Carroll to create a 'dream-child' who would never age or reject him?

The childhood photographs of Alice Liddell taken by Carroll are equally clouded by ambiguity. An image like *Open Your Mouth and Shut Your Eyes*, taken in July 1860, which shows Ina Liddell teasing Alice with some cherries, while a third sister, Edith, sits demurely a short distance away, contains at least two stories. We know a good deal about the story *in* the photograph: it is a reworking of William Mulready's 1838 painting with the same title, in which a man offers cherries to his sweetheart while being observed by an impassive child, and is based on the popular saying 'Open your mouth, shut your eyes and see what Providence will send you'; another photographer, Oscar Rejlander, had already used it as the basis for a collodion print he exhibited at the Manchester Photographic Society in 1856. It is also a playful modern take on the Greek myth of Tantalus, who was doomed to spend eternity trying to seize fruit that would forever elude his grasp, reminding us that in this frozen image Alice will always be reaching for cherries that will always remain just out of reach. The story *of* the photograph, on the other hand, is one about which we know almost nothing. To some viewers, who would like to think that Carroll was as innocent as a clown, the photograph depicts a joyous scene in which he gathers a surrogate family around himself and encourages them to perform a comic sketch before his lens. To others, for whom Carroll's motives are far murkier, the girls are merely stooges in a more disturbing private drama, flattened and preserved in his album like little white butterflies. (The fact that Carroll kept their arms raised by propping them up on an improvised wooden rest makes them look even more like mounted specimens.) Like many of his photographs, it offers a frustrating mixture of the obvious and evasive. It is both a theatrical tableau presented for our entertainment, and a keyhole for looking into a lost world that is as perfectly constructed and sealed off as the contents of a snow globe. Put another way, it is a wonderland – a scene that might fill us with wonder at its delicate skill, or make us wonder about the reasons for its construction.

The whole relationship between Lewis Carroll and Alice Liddell is capable of producing similar uncertainty in modern readers, and it is not only photographs like *Open Your Mouth and Shut Your Eyes* that ask us to decide whether the surviving traces of their friendship should be viewed as evidence of Carroll's innocence or as something more like a crime scene. The same is true of the *Alice* books. Indeed, there are moments in both stories when Carroll appears to be confronting us with just these questions. In Wonderland's courtroom, the Knave of Hearts is accused of stealing tarts – a crime that in the world of nursery rhymes is as unavoidable as rhyme itself – and the King tries to make sense of the White Rabbit's evidence by muttering selected phrases to himself: '"We know it to be true" . . . "If she should push the matter on" . . . "What would become of you?"' If this is a sly parody of literary critics at work, diligently trying to make sense out of nonsense, it also nervously reflects some of the thoughts that Carroll's Christ Church colleagues might have had about his relationship with the Dean's daughter. *We know it to be true . . . If she should push the matter on . . . What would become of you?* On the other hand, the Queen's conclusion, '"Sentence first – verdict afterwards"', is a glum joke that recognizes how the court of public opinion might treat accusations that are considerably more serious than tart-theft. It is far easier to condemn Carroll than it is to decide exactly what he should be accused of.

Confronted by such a patchy historical record, it is not surprising that later writers have relied on fiction to fill in the gaps. The climax of Melanie Benjamin's 2010 novel *Alice I Have Been* comes when Alice reaches up to Carroll in a train: 'I saw what I wanted and I took it . . . my arm arching gracefully about his neck, pulling his face toward me, his lips so soft, seeking an answer, asking a question –', in a kiss that forces the narrative to stutter to a stop for more than a dozen lines, while Alice fantasizes about 'his lips, lips that moved beneath mine'. Stephanie Bolster offers an alternative version of the scene in her 1998 poem 'Thames':

> The ongoing story has briefly paused.
> Three Liddell girls fidget as Dodgson gazes
> at rushes edging the banks, oaks bending over them.
>
> *Please!* Alice squeezes from her throat and he's back
> in the story: a small doorway, a garden.
> Her mouth opens, each distant lily nodding to her gaze,
>
> but he says she's too tall to get in and her lips clamp shut.

Here a kiss is hinted at but avoided, and instead all we are given is the chaste near-rhyme of 'Dodgson gazes' and 'her gaze'. And once again we are left to wonder.

While Carroll would have hated such fictional inventions, which he would have viewed as little better than gossip with pretensions to grandeur, he might have sympathized with the way each scene comes to a rest in a kind of narrative tableau. This was not only a feature of his photographs; occasionally his stories also found themselves slowing to a halt, as when the King in Wonderland gravely advises Alice to '"Begin at the beginning and go on till you come to the end: then stop"', before going on to himself in an undertone, '"important – unimportant – unimportant – important –" as if he were trying which word sounded best.'

At the same time, Carroll enjoyed experimenting with new ways of capturing life's irresistible onward force. In *Alice's Adventures in Wonderland*, he ensured that Tenniel's illustration of the grinning Cheshire Cat disappearing from view would be printed in exactly the same place as the previous illustration that showed it fully present, so that by turning the page back and forth a reader could make it materialize or dematerialize like a conjuring trick. It is only a small step from this to the dozens of 'moving pictures', such as Walt Disney's popular 1951 cartoon *Alice in Wonderland*, which would later bring the episode to life for a new generation of viewers. By the time of *Through the Looking-Glass*, Carroll had become even more ambitious, signalling Alice's moves across the chessboard with rows of asterisks that blurred where one scene ended and another began, like the mechanism of a magic lantern or a modern film dissolve. Both books reveal Carroll's skill at creating narrative set pieces that could be shuffled into a different order like a pack of cards; both reveal his enthusiasm for assembling the individual fragments of a story into a living whole.

In the following pages I try to do something similar for the story of *Alice* books themselves. The two most important strands in this story are biographical, because behind Carroll's imaginary characters lie the shadowy outlines of two real people, and understanding why these books took on the shape they did cannot be understood without unpicking the strange fleeting friendship between their author and the little girl who became his unwitting muse. The other main strand is more like a complicated plait or tangle, because it involves the unprecedented influence that the fictional Alice had on the wider cultural landscape. We do not usually think of children producing children of their own, but the *Alice* books would prove to be remarkably fertile in creating literary offspring. Most of these works have long since been relegated to the vaults of research libraries, but returning to them reveals more than the efforts made by their authors to adapt Alice for different audiences. They also show how Carroll's stories would permanently alter how readers thought about children both on and off the page.

One model for the powerful but scattered impact of the *Alice* books is suggested by Joseph Campbell's influential 1949 work of comparative mythology *The Hero With a Thousand Faces*. According to Campbell, local variations in the stories of different cultures cannot disguise the fundamental similarity of their plots. Whether the hero is Apollo, the Frog King, Wotan or Luke Skywalker (George Lucas has openly acknowledged the influence of Campbell's book on his *Star Wars* films), his story must always follow the same path: starting with a 'call to adventure', he undergoes a hazardous journey, and eventually proves himself worthy of his calling. In the pages Campbell devotes to the 'Childhood of the Human Hero', he points out that heroes often enjoy a childhood marked by 'wonders' – Heracles strangles a serpent in his cradle; Krishna defeats a murderous goblin by suckling her breasts until she falls down dead – but these are rites of passage rather than ends in themselves; they announce the arrival of a hero who is both a man and a superman. The *Alice* stories represent a different kind of heroism. They offer a triumph of wit over brawn, and playfulness over high seriousness, in which the leading character is not a muscular warrior or a mysterious god but an ordinary little girl, whose original adventures have proven themselves capable of producing endless supplements and offshoots – books, plays, films, toys, tablecloths, advertisements and more – in which she is always slightly different but always recognizably the same. Alice is a heroine with a thousand faces.

In order to discover how this happened, and why it matters, we need to go back to the beginning of the story and look again at how the *Alice* books were written, and why they took on such an unstoppable cultural momentum. It means piecing together scraps of evidence that are to be found in many different locations, from archives to private collections, and deciding how to fill in cracks in the historical record that have opened up over the years. Much of this evidence comes from unpublished sources, because these materials allow us to sidestep the myths that have gathered around Carroll and get much closer to the real world that helped to shape both Alice and *Alice*. It is a world we do not usually associate with the Victorians – one that is noisy, colourful, brimming with energy – and in order to explore it properly, we have to take the fragments that survive, blow the dust off, and restore them to life.

*   *   *   *

*   *   *

*   *   *   *

BEFORE ALICE

'Mathematics becomes very odd when you apply it to people.
One plus one can add up to so many different sums . . .'

MICHAEL FRAYN, *Copenhagen*

One

The idea that anyone else might be interested in his childhood would probably have puzzled Carroll; even he usually avoided the subject, as if nervous about trespassing on holy ground. But if he seldom referred to his early years, that may be because he never really left them behind. Long after he had become an adult, they continued to trail him like a shadow.

Carroll was born on 27 January 1832, in the sleepy, scattered Cheshire parish of Daresbury, the eldest son of a sternly intelligent perpetual curate and his loving but self-effacing wife. His first eleven years would later be recorded chiefly as a happy blank. The biography written by his nephew Stuart Dodgson Collingwood struggles to fill even a handful of pages, and repeatedly resorts to words such as 'uneventful', 'quiet' and 'seclusion', noting with some desperation that 'the passing of a cart was a matter of great interest to the children'. This isolation was chiefly a practical matter, cutting off the Dodgson family from the strong currents of social change that were starting to tug at other lives (1832 was also the year of the first Reform Bill), but it is notable that on one of the rare occasions that Carroll wrote about Daresbury – a name with punning potential he would later exploit – he began by comparing himself to a character in an adventure story. The 'happy spot where I was born', he writes in 'Faces in the Fire' (1860), was 'An island farm – broad seas of corn | Stirred by the wandering breath of morn'. It is a poem that imagines his birth as a kind of shipwreck, as if he was a modern Robinson Crusoe, enviously watching the wind move freely around him as he plotted his escape.

His family's seclusion was probably a blessing in disguise. Whereas in the squalid industrial slums of Manchester, just twenty-five miles away, infant mortality had reached 57 per cent by 1840, Carroll and his ten siblings

– three brothers and seven sisters – would all survive into adulthood. Even by Victorian standards of fertility this was a large family (in the period from the 1830s to the 1870s the average number of children born to middle-class parents was between five and seven), and it was the difficulty of supporting it on a curate's stipend that lay behind the genteel lobbying through which Carroll's father eventually secured a much more valuable living in the small North Yorkshire spa town of Croft-on-Tees. The Dodgsons moved there in 1843, when Carroll (known to his family as 'Charlie') was eleven, and for the next twenty-five years their home would be a rambling Georgian rectory opposite Croft's squat-towered and 'very respectable' Norman church.

It is here that Carroll first made his mark as a writer. On a second-floor window that lit the hallway leading to his bedroom, three workmen had inscribed their names on the outside of the glass, which from their perspective read:

I Young Painted July 23 1836

Plumer an Glazer an Jiner 9th August 1830

Edward Johnson Plumber Darlington 1834

– and as seen from the hallway read:

I Young Painted July 23 1836

Plumer an Glazer an Jiner 9th August 1830

Edward Johnson Plumber Darlington 1834

The strangeness of such reversals, turning everyday words into a form of mysterious code, is something Carroll would later remember when producing the mirror writing of 'Jabberwocky'. However, when in 1878 he signed a letter to one child-friend *Lewis Carroll* he was also retracing a moment from his own childhood, because at some stage he decided to play the workmen's game in reverse. Still visible in the Rectory are the initials 'C.L.D.' (Charles Lutwidge Dodgson) that he etched in fiddly and precise letters on two panes of glass. Seen from the inside, they cast ghostly traces of Carroll's presence on to the trees and sky beyond; seen from the outside, they turned his family into characters in a domestic looking-glass world.

Equally enduring was a collection of objects that he helped to hide under the nursery floorboards, although little is known about when this was done or why these particular items were chosen. Most of the objects have survived, but their secret histories have been lost, so in their current state they are hard to distinguish from the fragile bric-a-brac of any Victorian family. They include a linen handkerchief delicately embroidered with lilac flowers, a child's battered leather shoe, and a hand-stitched glove that may once have been white but is now crusty and liver-spotted with age. Fragments of a clay pipe and crab shell are muddled together with a thimble, a tiny penknife, a crocheting instrument and some pieces from a dolls' china tea set. Other items include a printed cardboard 'S', a geometrical counter for a game and a sample of Carroll's handwriting. Just one or two objects might be dismissed as a household accident, like the missing toy plane in Geoffrey Hill's *Mercian Hymns* (1971), 'two inches of heavy snub silver' that spins through 'a hole in the classroom-floorboards, softly, into the rat-droppings and coins'. However, the fact

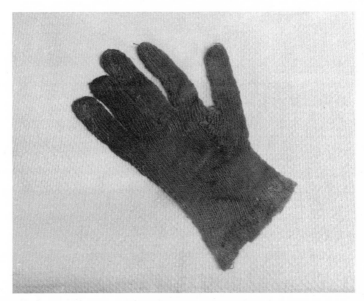

Glove hidden under the floorboards of Carroll's childhood home
in Croft-on-Tees (*c.* 1843)

that the Dodgson family's physical clutter was originally accompanied by a note written by some local builders stating that 'This floor was laid by Mr Martin and Mr Sutton June 19th 1843' suggests that it was a deliberate collection. Possibly it was deposited to mark the family's arrival in their new home: items like children's shoes were still occasionally hidden behind walls or under floorboards as symbols of good luck, rather as horseshoes are hung on walls today, long after a genuine belief in their magical powers had faded to a nagging superstition. Alternatively, it could have been a little museum of domestic life to which everyone contributed, like those that children later in the century would be encouraged to assemble. But whatever the original intention behind this three-dimensional scrapbook, its real importance to Carroll only became clear many years later.

In fiction, scenes such as Esther burying her doll near the start of Dickens's *Bleak House* (1852–53) usually signal a type of symbolic renunciation; Esther puts away her childish things once she learns that childhood is not a fixed period of time but a state of mind she can no longer afford. Carroll, on the other hand, appears to have treated his family's things more like the 'small grey elephant', 'large beetle with a red stomach' and 'finely modelled bull with a *suède* skin' that the children in Kenneth Grahame's collection of stories *Dream Days* (1898) bury in their garden to prove that their love for these old toys 'was not entirely broken . . . one link remained between us and them'. The Dodgson hoard was not discovered until 1950, when the nursery floor was taken up during more building work, but long before that Carroll had shown that he was capable of treating it in a similar way to the children in Grahame's story. It was a private time capsule he could dip into in his writing whenever he wanted to investigate the links between himself and his childhood, allowing him to lift up a loose floorboard in his memory and bring the buried treasures of the past to light.

Even when he was writing about fictional characters, Carroll enjoyed rummaging around in his mind for interesting physical odds and ends. He remained especially fond of objects such as thimbles, which frequently rose to the surface of his writing even when its real subject was something else entirely. Typically, *The Hunting of the Snark* includes an account of the Snark-hunters going forth 'To seek it with thimbles' (Carroll suggested to his illustrator Henry Holiday that he might want to add 'a shower of thimbles' to any accompanying picture), while in 1890 he wrote to Queen Victoria's granddaughter Princess Alice promising her a golden armchair with crimson velvet cushions, 'made so that you can fold it up small, and put it in a thimble, and carry it about in your pocket!' He was equally interested in gloves. Not only did he insist on a particular grey and black cotton style for himself, but he was delighted to notice that 'gloves' has the word 'love' hidden inside it, informing a girl who had sent him 'sacks full of love' that she must have meant a sack full of gloves, and thanking her for the 500 pairs that had just been delivered. He also took pleasure in coming up with fanciful explanations for words such as 'foxglove', telling the young actress Isa Bowman that fairies 'took great pride in their dainty hands', and so 'made themselves gloves out of the flowers', which eventually became known as 'folks' gloves' or foxgloves.

These ideas sometimes sparked off more subtle and sideways connections in Carroll's mind. For example, the fragment of handwriting he hid under the nursery floor was part of an anonymous broadside ballad, which in Carroll's version ran 'And we'll wander through | the wide world | and chase the buffalo.' The ballad was especially popular in the first half of the nineteenth century, the most polished example probably being the one produced by the printer James Catnach in Seven Dials:

> Come all you young fellows that have a mind to range
> Into some foreign country your station for to change
> Into some foreign country away from her to go
> We lay down on the banks of the pleasant Ohio
> We wander thro' the wild woods and chase the Buffalo.

This appears below a clumsy woodcut that shows a clerk being persuaded to leave his job by a sharply dressed friend, who is tipping up his chair in eagerness to be gone. Like many early emigration fantasies, the ballad depicts America as a classical Arcadia that has been relocated to the west and brought up to date, and it is also enticingly close to being a fairy-tale land where 'wild woods' beckon and mysterious shaggy creatures roam. Carroll's misquotation goes even further in this direction: 'wide world' rather than 'wild woods' may simply be a slip of the pen, but in the light of his later works it sounds suspiciously like the preliminary sketch for a literary manifesto – a promise to track down the weird and wonderful no matter how hard it tried to escape.

*

Two

Although Carroll enjoyed playing with ideas, merely chasing them rarely satisfied him. He also needed to tame them. In October 1887, he took Isa Bowman, then aged thirteen, to a matinee performance of the popular Wild West Show put on by 'Buffalo Bill' (Colonel William F. Cody), which included a staged buffalo hunt, and the following year he wrote a mock diary in which he imagined her dreaming of 'a buffalo sitting at the top of every tree, handing her cups of tea'. It is no coincidence that, even in this deliberately silly piece of writing, as soon as Carroll starts to expand on an idea he braces it with a deft internal rhyme; while one side of him is capering across the page, the other side is quietly working as a choreographer behind the scenes. In *Sylvie and Bruno*, similarly, the Mad Gardener describes how 'He thought he saw a Buffalo | Upon the chimney-piece', and once again this 'strange wild song' is provided with enough natty rhythms and rhymes to keep the threat of wildness in check. The same pattern would be repeated with variations throughout Carroll's career. If storytelling was to provide an escape from the real world, it had to be as meticulously planned as a prisoner of war tunnelling under the camp wire. Stories could create an imaginary realm where anything was possible – a place where elephants practised the fife, and rattlesnakes questioned you in Greek – but only if the writer was prepared to subject the potential chaos of his imagination to what Carroll later described as 'the principle of submission to discipline'.

During Carroll's childhood, this meant in effect submission to his father, a moderate High Church Anglican whose conservative nature was revealed by the fact that he had chosen to name his son after himself. The career anticipated for little Charlie could not have been clearer. (Silhouettes cut at the Warrington Exhibition in 1840 reveal that father and son were also physically similar: in both there is the same high forehead, the same slight pout.) Even the Dodgsons were sometimes bored by how respectable they had become: speaking about Carroll in a radio broadcast in 1950, his niece Violet confessed that 'One is supposed to mention forebears, but his were very dull.' Yet Carroll's father also had an unexpectedly mischievous side to his personality. Of the twenty-four books and pamphlets he published, including many sermons and a volume on Tertullian, most were irreproachably solemn, recommending 'steadfastness of purpose' and 'self-denying patience' rather than 'fitful flashes of enthusiasm', and only becoming really animated when describing the 'many aggravations' suffered by 'the poor Clergyman'. The letters he sent to another of his sons, Skeffington Dodgson, are full of advice about the importance of being earnest: 'It is a great pleasure to me to think that you take so earnestly and steadily to your work,' he wrote approvingly while Skeffington was at Oxford, following this up with 'earnest and affectionate wishes' for his birthday. Yet the same writer was capable of producing energetic bursts of nonsense, like the letter he sent to the eight-year-old Carroll in response to a routine shopping list:

As soon as I get to Leeds I shall scream out in the middle of the street, Ironmongers—Ironmongers—Six hundred men will rush out of their shops in a moment—fly, fly, in all directions—ring the bells, call the constables—set the town on fire. I will have a file & a screwdriver, & a ring, & if they are not brought directly, in forty seconds I will leave nothing but one small cat alive in the whole town of Leeds . . . Then what a bawling & a tearing of hair there will be! Pigs & babies, camels & butterflies, rolling in the gutter together—old women rushing up the chimneys & cows after them—ducks hiding themselves in coffee cups, & fat geese trying to squeeze themselves into pencil cases—at last the Mayor of Leeds will be found in a soup plate covered up with custard & stuck full of almonds to make him look like a sponge cake that he may escape the dreadful destruction of the Town . . .

This may be a heavy-handed piece of humour – one critic has likened it to a hippo dancing in a tutu – but it makes a valiant effort to look at the drab workaday world with a comic squint. Whether or not Carroll remembered his father's letter (it seems likely, given that his memory was as sticky as flypaper), he certainly learned from its example. Throughout his career, gleefully sprawling ideas would repeatedly knock up against highly polished literary forms, like a body clanking around in a suit of armour.

This ability to submit to discipline while also playfully testing its limits was a habit that had fixed itself deep in his mind long before he published a word. Until he was twelve years old, Carroll was educated at home, and the notebook kept by his mother between February 1839 and December 1842 unsurprisingly reveals a taste for instructive literature: a list of 'Religious Reading – Private' begins with *The Pilgrim's Progress*, and is followed by pages on 'Religious Reading with Mama' and 'Daily Reading Useful – Private' written up in neat columns. Carroll also owned a linen bag containing fourteen cards on which his mother had assembled a set of biblical texts, under headings such as 'forgiveness' and the motto 'God sees and knows all things.' More unusual was a home-made exercise book labelled 'Skeleton Maps CLD', in which a dutiful collection of geographical facts vied with the thrill of the unknown. One hand-drawn map of the East includes neat national borders and some squiggly rivers; another marks out capital cities like bullseyes. Yet when Carroll came to trace an outline of Europe, despite making an attempt at the fiddly internal divisions of Greece and Turkey, he left large parts of the interior blank. Possibly he just got bored, or ran out of time, but the map hints at his later interest in writing that left room for the reader's imagination to explore.

In *The Hunting of the Snark*, the Bellman celebrates the fact that the Captain's map is 'A perfect and absolute blank', and although this is partly a joke about the patchy state of geographical knowledge at the time, with large parts of the African continent remaining unmapped, and the icy wastes of the Antarctic still being as pure and empty as a fresh sheet of paper, it also reveals Carroll's pleasure in creating imaginary lands that invited readers to fill in their gaps. Some of these were real places that were so far away as to be practically invisible: five years after the publication of *The Hunting of the Snark*, he considered making a new kind of 'star-map', in the form of a three-dimensional pasteboard dome that would be painted blue inside and dotted with white stars, giving the illusion of being wrapped around by a night sky speckled with unknown worlds. However, the more significant imaginary lands for Carroll were those he constructed out of paper and ink in the form of stories. Some of these were as borderless as Wonderland, which appears to stretch indefinitely in all directions; others as strictly ordered as Looking-Glass Land, with its neat chessboard pattern of squares. But in either case, when we explore them in our heads no two readers will imagine exactly the same place; instead we are invited to construct our own mental maps as we move from page to page.

Carroll's ambivalence about 'the principle of submission to discipline' can also be seen in his leisure activities at Croft. Here too he outwardly embraced rules while secretly kicking against their constraints. As the eldest son, it seems that he happily accepted the role of 'family entertainer', as W. H. Auden once described him, inventing games such as those involving a toy railway, made out of a small truck, a barrel and a wheelbarrow, which he used to carry his brothers and sisters between different 'stations' in the Rectory's large walled garden. A suitable soundtrack would have been provided by the Stockton and Darlington line, established in 1825 as one of the world's first passenger-carrying railways, which passed four miles from the Rectory; closer to home, there was a station at Croft that opened in 1845 on the main line to York. But although Carroll enjoyed the physical business of hauling his siblings around – a letter from his mother to his aunt Lucy proudly noted that 'he *tries* & *proves* his strength in the most *persevering* way' – it was not enough to satisfy him. He also wrote out a 'Railway Guide' and a set of 'Railway Rules', in which sensible arrangements for 'refreshments' and 'lost luggage' were mixed up with more violent role-playing fantasies, involving a surgeon who would tend to 'the wounded' and a stationmaster who was allowed to 'put anyone who behaves badly to prison'. Of course, it isn't unusual for children to create games out of their surroundings. Elizabeth Sewell has pointed out that, whether children are playing with water or a set of household objects, the importance of the game is that it allows them to 'gain control' over everyday materials, and its success will largely depend on how strictly everyone follows an agreed set of rules. (Nobody is more outraged by perceived cheating than a child, as parents quickly discover if they fail to tell a favourite story in *exactly* the same way *every time*.) What is different about Carroll's regulations is the suggestion that many other rules might seem equally nonsensical if viewed from a different angle. Trains were a good test case for this idea, because by 1843 they had started to wheeze and grind across the countryside in a way that seemed as impersonal as the ticking of a clock, yet their movements were governed by bureaucratic regulations that had clearly been composed by a group of people sitting behind desks. It did not require any great satirical effort to take the pinched language of a regulation such as Midland Counties Railway Bye-law VIII ('If any Passenger should be found in or upon any of the Carriages, or shall force his way into a carriage, without having previously procured a Ticket, or shall occupy (without permission) a Carriage of a superior Class to that for which he has obtained a Ticket . . . he shall be liable to a fine of Forty Shillings') and turn it into Carroll's Railway Rule III: 'When a passenger has no money and still wants to go by the train, he must stop at whatever station he happens to be at, and make tea for the station master.' Carroll's spoof regulations were a valuable reminder that established ways of thinking can benefit from being rerouted.

The same principle lies behind *La Guida di Bragia*, a scrappy burlesque written by the teenage Carroll for his marionette theatre. The mock-operatic Italian title gestured towards *Bradshaw's Railway Companion*, a book of train timetables that was first sold in 1840 for a shilling and quickly established itself as the railway traveller's bible. In Carroll's *Phantasmagoria* (1869), the ghost tells a story that is 'known as well as Bradshaw's Guide', and a 'Bradshaw' would later become a stock property of Victorian fiction: Phileas Fogg carries one in *Around the World in Eighty Days*, and in Bram Stoker's *Dracula* Harker is surprised to discover the Count studying a copy in his Transylvanian castle. In *La Guida* Carroll's flimsy plot is set in a railway station in which a double-act called Mooney and Spooney – theatrical ancestors of Tweedledum and Tweedledee – somehow secure jobs as stationmaster and clerk, and within minutes everyone and everything is comically jerked out of place. Luggage leaves without its owners, and people leave instead of their luggage. A character called Mrs Muddle, who bears more than a passing resemblance to Sheridan's Mrs Malaprop, gets her tongue in a twist as she worries about the 'steam Indian' exploding. Two lovers swap platitudes such as 'My Sophonisba!' and 'Oh, no! You don't say so!' which together carry a joking echo of James Thomson's notoriously feeble line from his 1730 play *The Tragedy of Sophonisba*: 'O, Sophonisba, Sophonisba, O!' At one point there is even a 'Kaffir' who silently wanders on to the stage and immediately exits, presumably having realized that he is in the wrong play. Finally, George Bradshaw himself arrives as a *deus ex machina*, explaining that in revenge for Mooney and Spooney failing to sing, as the rules of their job required, he has altered the timetable and 'made the world go wrong'. But of course things must go wrong for farce to go right, and the play as a whole depends upon our knowledge that the theatre is a place in which accidents are rehearsed and muddles are planned. Shuffling his puppets around the stage of a toy theatre, Carroll could enjoy the fantasy of losing control even as he was tugging on their wires to make them do his bidding.

Carroll's marionette theatre was just one of the miniature worlds he enjoyed playing with as a boy. The Dodgson family also owned a compact home-made doll's house, containing a single room on each floor decorated with scraps of wallpaper, and a village schoolroom in which a two-dimensional wooden teacher sat at his desk and patiently observed his two-dimensional wooden pupils. These were probably shared toys, but Carroll also made a set of eight tiny tools for his sister Elizabeth in 1846, including a screwdriver, mallet and corkscrew, all of which he packed snugly into a wooden box two inches high. For the rest of his life he sought out equally novel ways of cutting people and objects down to size. The same day he first told the Liddell children the story of Alice, he took them to his rooms to see his 'collection of micro-photographs', while in *Sylvie and Bruno* he introduces a 'Minimifying glass' that can reduce an elephant to the size of a mouse. Unsurprisingly, Carroll's sensitivity to small things was especially sharpened when he wrote to his child-friends. Sometimes he took pains to create letters in minuscule 'fairy-writing', using a fine nib on pieces of 'Lilliputian Stationery', which he posted to selected children to show not how little they meant to him but how much. (One letter to Enid Stevens in 1891 sends her 'ever so much of my love': it is approximately four inches high.) Even an ordinary word such as 'little' could occupy a disproportionate amount of space on the page: *Alice's Adventures in Wonderland* alone contains more than a hundred repetitions of the word – in one paragraph Alice finds a 'little golden key' on a 'little three-legged table' and uses it to unlock a 'little door about fifteen inches high'; Carroll deploys the word as if casting a spell.

Some of the most interesting miniature worlds he created took the form of poems. His first collection was a set of five handwritten booklets stitched together between cardboard covers for his younger brother Wilfred and sister Louisa in 1845, when he was thirteen years old, under the general title of *Useful and Instructive Poetry*. A number of these poems anticipate the *Alice* books: 'A Tale of a Tail', for example, which describes the sad fate of a dog with 'a tail of desperate length', drawn by Carroll straggling limply across the page and then coiling itself up like a whip, is evidently a rehearsal for the 'long and sad tale' of the Dormouse in Wonderland. (One of Carroll's later home-made publications was called *The Comet*, which he promised would have a 'tail of boundless length', suggesting how self-consciously he extended some of his favourite jokes.) There is also 'The Headstrong Man', who stands on a 'lofty wall' until he tumbles down into a crowd of onlookers, like a prototypical Humpty Dumpty. Other poems parody contemporary morality tales for children that divided up the world into neat categories of good and bad, do and don't, as Carroll creates increasingly bizarre comic situations in which the moral of the story – 'Don't get drunk', for instance, or simply 'You mustn't' – is made to seem laughably reductive when compared to the anarchic energy of the stories themselves.

What makes *Useful and Instructive Poetry* especially useful and instructive in terms of Carroll's later literary career is that it contains his only experiments in what would become one of the most popular forms of nonsense writing: limericks. Take the final two examples:

> There was once a young man of Oporta,
> Who daily got shorter and shorter,
> > The reason he said
> > Was the hod on his head,
> Which was filled with the *heaviest* mortar.

> His sister named Lucy O'Finner,
> Grew constantly thinner and thinner;
> > The reason was plain,
> > She slept out in the rain,
> And was never allowed any dinner.

Edward Lear's earliest limericks were published in 1846, a year after Carroll's experiments, so they cannot have been an influence unless Carroll saw them in manuscript, although similar poems had been published before (as Lear acknowledged) in collections such as *The History of Sixteen Wonderful Old Women* (1820) and *Anecdotes and Adventures of Fifteen Gentlemen* (1821). A more significant question is why Carroll was drawn to the form at all. The likeliest answer is that it was another example of what could happen when imaginative freedom encountered formal restraint. Limericks seem to work through irresistible logic, because each one is a small but perfectly shaped world in which everything happens for a reason. Such forms are inevitably appealing to writers, who spend most of their lives trying to make artificial constructions look as natural as the air they breathe, but on closer inspection both stories reveal themselves to be mere parodies of cause and effect. The 'reason' Carroll's young man grows 'shorter' is because he is from a place called 'Oporta'; the 'reason' Lucy grows 'thinner and thinner' is because her surname is 'O'Finner'. What at first sight looks like logic turns out to be nothing more than an accident of language. If the man had been from Galway, he might have got stuck in the hallway; if Lucy had been the Hatter, she would probably have grown fatter and fatter. Put another way, Carroll's limericks show that if poems are a kind of game that depends upon sticking to the rules, a writer's words are not simply counters he can shuffle around on the page like draughts. They are playthings with a life of their own.

Carroll's speech impairment, which he shared to a greater or lesser extent with six other members of his family, may have made writing especially attractive as a form of communication. His term for the problem was 'hesitation', and according to witnesses it manifested itself as an occasional blockage that prevented him from making certain sounds. He would open his mouth and language would simply crack apart. This could be socially awkward (Carroll recalled his 'annoyance' at breaking down 'over a hard "C"' in a shop) but, worse than that, it was unpredictable. When speaking, and especially when reading, he found every sentence a path littered with potential potholes and booby traps, and had to proceed cautiously, testing the ground as he went. Writing was a different matter. The blank page released his tongue: it was an environment where hesitation was just another part of the compositional process, as his pen repeated a word for effect or hovered over the page while searching for the next one. Hesitation could even be incorporated in the finished text. Carroll's early poem 'Rules and Regulations', which formed part of *Useful and Instructive Poetry*, includes the advice 'Learn well your grammar, | And never stammer' and 'Eat bread with butter. | Once more, don't stutter.' This sounds like a mocking echo of his father's voice, but if conversations around the Croft breakfast table were difficult in person, they were far easier to manage on paper. The line endings of his poem could give the illusion of language breaking down while allowing the reader's eye to roll smoothly on, and Carroll could make a joke out of what might have thwarted him in real life.

People who stammer or hesitate sometimes complain that although speaking can feel like wrestling with an unseen opponent, it is made even harder by verbal prompts and other misguided attempts to help: 'I'm going to h – h – h –' 'Harrods? Hand in your keys? Hell?' Carroll's solution as a boy was to surround himself with other people while putting himself firmly in charge. After *Useful and Instructive Poetry*, he produced a series of handwritten family magazines at Croft, and although his brothers and sisters occasionally contributed pieces, their main function appears to have been to serve as Carroll's audience. He was a one-man publishing house: editor, leading author, illustrator, printer, publicist and distributor.

Assembling home-made magazines was a popular leisure activity among middle-class Victorian families. Louisa May Alcott's *Little Women* (1868) contains a fond account of her family compiling *The Pickwick Portfolio*, based on Dickens's novel, and offers a sample of its contents, which included a breathy Venetian romance ('Gondola after gondola swept up to the marble steps, and left its lovely load to swell the brilliant throng . . .'), an announcement of 'the sudden and mysterious disappearance of our cherished friend, Mrs Snowball Pat Paw', and a column of 'Hints' that advises its readers 'A. S. is requested not to whistle in the street' and 'T. T. please don't forget Amy's napkin.' As late as 1891, Leslie Stephen's children, including a nine-year-old Virginia Woolf, were busy putting together the first issues of *The Hyde Park Gate News*, a weekly digest of local gossip, pictures, stories and riddles ('What is the difference between a camera and the whooping-cough? Answer: one makes facsimiles and the other makes sick families') that lasted almost four years.

The ragbag variety of these magazines was matched by Carroll's love of every kind of miscellany, from anthologies to scrapbooks, which would later take on various forms in his fiction, such as the Dormouse's assortment of things beginning with 'M' in *Alice's Adventures in Wonderland* ('"mouse-traps, and the moon, and memory, and muchness . . ."'), or the appearance of the White Knight in *Through the Looking-Glass*, whose determination to be prepared for anything means that he carries around a whole flea market of clutter, including a beehive and a box 'to keep clothes and sandwiches in'. At a grammatical level, the same love of miscellanies would be reflected in Carroll's lifelong addiction to lists, which allowed him to combine control and chaos in teasing and often nonsensical ways; a list establishes order, but always trembles on the edge of disorder, and Carroll continued to enjoy playing with ludicrous juxtapositions such as 'mouse-traps' and 'moon', even if it was a game that was potentially endless.

However, if for some Victorian families such magazines were an open invitation to invent new worlds, like the Glass Town and Angrian sagas developed by the Brontë children, for Carroll they offered an opportunity to take everyday events at Croft and supply them with a set of absurd glosses. Seen through his eyes, a gardening knife looks as if it were 'constructed originally for the rather unusual purpose of murdering crocodiles'; a dead chicken is the subject of a mock-epic poem that ends with a verdict of 'suicide'. Whatever he writes about, in fact, Carroll uses the page like a filter to make the world around him look intriguingly strange.

Several magazines have been lost, including *The Rosebud* (two numbers), *The Star* (around half a dozen numbers), and *The Will-o'-the-Wisp*, which was distinguished by having its pages cut in a triangular shape before it lived up to its name by disappearing, but two survive from Carroll's teenage years. *The Rectory Magazine* (c. 1848), advertised on the title page as a 'Fifth Edition, carefully revised, & improved', reveals the variety of articles Carroll was capable of producing, many of them under assumed initials (V.X., B.B., F.L.W., J.V., F.X., Q.G.), which allowed him to turn himself into a crowd of collaborators when 'the united talents of the Rectory' failed to come up with enough material. A donkey offers ruminative 'Thoughts on Thistles', while a short article on 'Rust' concludes with the illustration of a man who has alarmingly bulbous eyes and is labelled 'Ox-Eyed' – i.e. Oxide, although for a schoolboy with Carroll's classical education, the drawing is also a comically literal version of the Homeric metaphor describing goddesses like Hera as 'ox-eyed'. On several occasions, Charles Dodgson Senior comes in for some good-natured ribbing, including a cartoon of a stern-looking figure in a high collar labelled 'PAPA', and a lengthy fantasy in which a son rebels against his tyrannical father, who is then satisfyingly goaded by remorse 'to the extreme pitch of wretchedness'. There are further examples of interests that would be developed later in the *Alice* books, such as a reference to someone who 'went off in a fluff', an early portmanteau word that squashes together 'flounce' and 'huff', and a story that deals with 'those strange and sudden changes which so frequently occur in dreams', as the victim of a shipwreck fantasizes about drowning: 'Oh! The horrors of that endless falling in dreams, down, down, down he went . . .'

By the time Carroll started to put together *The Rectory Umbrella* (1850–53), he had learned to introduce just as much variety into each article. Sometimes this was limited to small twists and turns of language. He was noticeably addicted to puns, which allowed him to swivel on ordinary words such as 'lay' (the suicidal chicken appears in one of Carroll's 'Lays of Sorrow') and play their different meanings off against each other; as he explained in a later letter, 'We are beings of very mixed motives', and puns were one way of putting this uncertainty into words. The most interesting examples of his love of variety, however, were more like feats of misdirection. Carroll was a good amateur conjuror: his nephew describes how as a boy he would dress up in 'a brown wig and a long white robe', and 'used to cause no little wonder to his audience by his sleight-of-hand'. He grew equally skilled at performing similar tricks in his writing. One of his early cartoons was 'The deceitfull [*sic*] coachman', which shows a passenger asking 'Does this coach go to Charing Cross?' while a smirking coachman touches his cap and replies 'Yes, sir'; on the back of the coach a sign announces its destination as 'Bank'. It was an old joke: in *Sketches by Boz* (1836), Dickens had already made comic capital out of omnibus drivers who snared extra passengers by assuring them they were travelling the right way, and then merrily rattled off somewhere else. In *The Rectory Umbrella*, Carroll turned misdirection into a central feature of his style. For example, when we read the title of a cartoon like *The Age of Innocence*, which according to Carroll's editorial note depicts 'a charming union of youth and innocence', we might anticipate an amateurish homage to Sir Joshua Reynolds, whose 1788 painting with that title shows a young girl sitting on the grass in a scene of pastoral serenity; what we get instead is a hippopotamus daintily reclining under a tree and trying to look bashful. In the first of Carroll's 'Zoological Papers', which deals with the rare species 'Pixies', the swerve comes halfway through a sentence: 'the general expression of their faces is sweetness and good humour', he writes, before solemnly explaining that 'the former quality is probably the reason why foxes are so fond of eating them'. It is a tactic Carroll would continue to use, and might be viewed as a kind of teasing – a tone of voice that invites us to work out how seriously or playfully something is being offered, but without staying still long enough for us to pin it down. Indeed, the most significant joke in these early writings is probably one in a poem about his brother's failed fishing expedition on the local river. 'I'll teach him the meaning of "Tees"!' Carroll writes, and the pun is a compact reminder that living in a large family he was in the perfect environment to learn how to tease and be teased.

For all his joking, with its mixed motives of self-assertion and self-protection, Carroll undoubtedly saw his magazines as important apprentice work. The editorial that opens *The Rectory Magazine* anticipates a day when it will draw praise from 'admiring thousands' as 'one of the staple and essential portions of the literature of England', and Carroll's ironic tone and self-deprecating title ('Reasonings on Rubbish') cannot hide a gleam of genuine ambition. The way he put *The Rectory Magazine* together also offers several clues to his later working methods. Copied out in a neat copperplate hand that was intended to imitate print, the pages were bound together in a battered cover recycled from an old school note-book, with some puncture wounds on one corner, possibly caused by a pair of compasses being jabbed into it, and on the inside a scribbled schoolboy mess of practice autographs, doodles, sums and gossip: 'He said What are you talking for are you Mr Pine's pupil, I said No Mr Cotton's sir – He said very well and wrote down Pine.' But the fact that Carroll chose to hand-stitch the pages of his magazine into this cover, and provide them with a list of contents and detailed index, reveals more than his thrift. It also reveals his more general love of pulling things apart and putting them together again.

This is another familiar part of growing up, because one of the key ways a child learns how the world works is by assembling little models of it, from sandcastles to Lego. The Dodgson family owned at least two 'dissected puzzles', i.e. jigsaw puzzles, one showing scenes from 'The Life of Christ' and the other a startled Mary Magdalene and companion encountering an angel at the tomb. A similar skill is required when children learn to read, as they divide up sentences and words into their constituent parts and then reassemble them into meaningful patterns. However, few children pursue these ideas into adult life with Carroll's restless powers of invention. It can be seen in the care he took over the seating plans for his dinner parties, which allowed him to shuffle guests around until he had arranged them into a satisfying order, a practice that is taken to absurd lengths by the Hatter's tea party in Wonderland. It is also present in many of the games he created. These included 'Mischmasch', which required players to choose a 'nucleus' of letters (e.g. 'emo') and then find words that contained it (e.g. '*lemons*' or '*remove*'), and 'circular billiards', which was to be played on a curved table without pockets, producing endlessly changing geometrical patterns as the balls clacked around on the baize. In writing, the same idea helped to feed his fascination with how words could stick together in more unexpected ways: through rhyme, for example, or verbal coinages such as 'slithy', which Humpty Dumpty tells Alice '"means 'lithe and slimy' . . . there are two meanings packed up into one word"'.

Above all, it helped to shape Carroll's methods of composition. Sometimes he took these to extreme lengths: in one proof of 'The Mouse's Tale', he created the snaking appearance he wanted by cutting out each line and pasting it individually into place, while his later illustrator Harry Furniss reports that he received the manuscript of Carroll's lengthy fantasy novel *Sylvie and Bruno* sliced into horizontal strips of four or five lines, with each tiny segment marked with a code that was supposed to help him assemble them in the right order. When Furniss returned this sack of paper and threatened to go on strike, Carroll had to content himself with compiling another index for the final published version, containing headings such as 'Air, Cotton-wool lighter than, how to obtain', 'Asylums, Lunatic, future use for', 'Bath, Portable, for tourists' and 'Fairies, existence of, possible', which had the effect of retrospectively dividing his finished stories into a set of equally bizarre fragments. It was as if he wanted to turn *Sylvie and Bruno* into a bumper issue of *The Rectory Magazine*, and the thousands of readers he had attracted over the years into a huge extended family.

What links these childhood games and fictional experiments is Carroll's

The following text appears within the image as Carroll's handwritten mouse's tale design:

Nº 1.
A 13

Fury said to
a mouse,
That he
met in
the house,
" Let us
both go
to law :
I will
prosecute
you. (
Come, I 'll
take no
denial :
We must
have a
trial ;
For really
this
morning
I 've
nothing
to do."
Said the
mouse to
the cur,
"Such a
trial,
dear sir,
With no
jury or
judge,
would be
wasting
our breath."
"I 'll be
judge,
I 'll be
jury," said
cunning
old Fury ;
"I 'll try
the whole
cause
and
condemn
you to
death."

Carroll's design for 'The Mouse's Tale'

desire to unpeel some of the layers of cliché and habit that muffle ordinary life. Nothing was off limits to his imaginative prodding and probing, no matter how natural it might appear to other people. For example, the 'Morning Prayer' in a fourteen-page handwritten pamphlet put together by his mother offers thanks to God, 'who hast mercifully preserved me, in health, peace, and safety, to the beginning of another day'; her 'Evening Prayer' is similarly thankful for reaching 'the end of another day'. Yet Carroll remained puzzled by the difficulty of pinning down even apparently straightforward events like these to specific times. In *Useful and Instructive Poetry*, he included a little homily on the importance of 'Punctuality', with an illustration that showed someone staring fixedly at a grandfather clock; he also contributed a piece on 'Difficulties' to *The Rectory Umbrella* that tried to work out whether it would be better to have a clock that had stopped, and so would be right twice a day, or a clock that lost just one minute every day, and would therefore be right once every two years. In an increasingly time-dominated society, which saw the introduction of a standardized clock time in 1847, replacing earlier local variations, and an expansion of the language to include new phrases such as 'behind the times' (1826), 'pass the time of day' (1835), 'not before time' (1837), 'all the time in the world' (1840) and 'time off' (1850), several large questions remained. A poem Carroll read as a boy in *The Parents' Cabinet of Amusement and Instruction* pointed out that, while in Britain 'the pale twinkling stars are bespangling the sky', in China 'the clocks are already at seven' and in New Zealand it is noon. But in that case, Carroll reasoned, if someone travelled around the world in exactly twenty-four hours, arriving everywhere at midnight, at what point would one day become the next? It was a question that in April 1857 led him to publish a letter on 'Where does the day begin?' in the *Illustrated London News*, and it was still puzzling him in 1885, when he wrote down a list of the times in various places around the world when it was midnight in Greenwich. His choice reflected that in 1884 the International Meridian Conference had finally solved this conundrum, by adopting Greenwich Mean Time (GMT) as the standard from which all local variations would be measured, but for Carroll no system was sufficient to explain time's mysteries.

In particular, he remained uncertain over whether objective chronological time could ever be reconciled with the subjective feelings it conjured up. '"If you knew Time as well as I do,"' the Hatter tells Alice, '"you wouldn't talk about wasting *it*. It's *him*,"' and like many of the most absurd situations in Wonderland and Looking-Glass Land, this is only a slightly tweaked version of an idea Carroll treated perfectly seriously elsewhere. One of the girls who knew him in his last years recalled that, when he wanted to meet her at a quarter past six, he would write down the time as '6¼', as if he thought of history as another child who couldn't help ageing by instalments. Earlier he had worried that his friendships might change just as suddenly as one day becoming the next, and asked whether he should keep on file a range of different ways of beginning and ending letters, 'so that as friendships warmed up and cooled down, one might make the necessary changes gently, without inflicting a sudden shock'. And here once again writing provided him with a way to manage his concerns.

48

One of the inventions in *Sylvie and Bruno* is a 'Magic Watch', with a 'reversal peg' that makes time run backwards, so that a family dinner involves adding slices of mutton to the joint, unroasting it, and finally returning it to the butcher. (This is a development of Alice's culinary adventures in Looking-Glass Land, where she is instructed to hand round a cake before cutting it up, and is later introduced to a joint of mutton that responds by standing up and giving her a polite little bow.) But of course the real magic lies in Carroll's story, not in the watch, because like all books it is a time machine that can play around with chronology in any way the author chooses. In narrative, an event that would take a fraction of a second in real time can be drawn out for paragraphs or pages, while experiences that might take years to accumulate can be compressed into a single crisp sentence. Once readers abandon themselves to story time, even nonsense like the Walrus and the Carpenter's song makes a perverse kind of sense, because in fiction if 'The sun was shining on the sea' it is still perfectly possible for the scene to be taking place in 'The middle of the night'. That would be no stranger than the fact that *Alice's Adventures in Wonderland* was published in 1865 and *Through the Looking-Glass* in 1872, yet in the later story Alice tells us that she is '"seven and a half exactly"', suggesting that only a few months have passed between her adventures. The world of stories was a place where the laws of physics were optional, and chronology went on holiday.

*

Three

An anecdote included in Collingwood's *Life and Letters of Lewis Carroll* reveals how Carroll's mixture of curiosity and persistence could work in practice. One day he approached his father with a book of logarithms and asked him, 'Please explain.' When his father told him 'he was much too young to understand anything about such a difficult subject', Carroll's response was simply to repeat himself more insistently: '*But*, please explain!' 'But' was an important word for Carroll; in *The Rectory Magazine*, he included a short piece entitled 'But' that pointed out how many fantasies we could live out were it not for 'the all-potent influence' of the 'little monosyllable' that made them vanish: 'I *would* have every pleasure and convenience that wealth can give, *but* – I can't!' However, such forensic examination of ordinary expressions was unlikely to make him popular at school, where his teachers were more used to asking questions than answering them, and his reports from Richmond School, a religiously orthodox establishment some ten miles away from Croft that he attended from the ages of twelve to fourteen, are tellingly muted. Although a surviving letter to Carroll's father from the headmaster James Tate anticipates a 'bright career' for his son, praising his 'very uncommon share of genius', the same letter also suggests that he should not be encouraged to feel 'his superiority over other boys'. If this indicates that Carroll impressed his teachers without endearing himself to them – and in his praise of Carroll's 'love of precise argument' Tate certainly sounds like someone speaking through gritted teeth – one can only imagine what the 'other boys' thought. Schoolchildren are rarely impressed by genius when it announces itself in their ranks, and a Victorian public school, with its emphasis on discipline and rote learning, was hardly the sort of environment in which it could develop freely. Yet the options for an ambitious middle-class family were limited, and accordingly on 27 January 1846 Carroll entered Rugby School as a boarder. It was his fourteenth birthday, and it may be that his experiences there influenced his later dislike of the date; he greatly preferred the other 364 days of the year that were available for 'unbirthday' celebrations, because the next few years were not especially happy.

In theory, Rugby was a good choice of school for a boy like Carroll. Later in the century, it would be expanded by the architect William Butterfield into a sprawling pile of polychromatic brickwork, featuring spiky turrets and a grand echoing chapel, like a scene from a Gothic novel rewritten by John Ruskin, but in 1846 it was still a comparatively modest educational establishment. Over the previous two decades, largely thanks to the reforming zeal of Thomas Arnold, it had earned a reputation as a place where education and religion were taken equally seriously. The current headmaster, Archibald Tait, had taken over after Arnold died in 1842. Although he was a rather remote figure, who was reluctant to punish his pupils (one boy who escaped and was later found riding on a circus elephant received only a stern reprimand), and undoubtedly lacked his famous predecessor's charisma – a modern history of the school discusses his eight-year tenure in a chapter entitled 'A Parenthesis' – he had continued Arnold's reforms. Mathematics, history and modern languages were taught alongside the standard works of classical literature, and the more creative pupils were encouraged to experiment in their own writing. The month after Carroll arrived, he would have seen February's issue of *The Rugby Miscellany*, a 32-page magazine written by the older pupils, which opened with an editorial urging 'the necessity of intellectual exertion' and continued with imitations of Tennyson, a rather shrill critical essay on Wordsworth ('His faults are, I believe, many and great') and a nostalgia-rich article on 'The Last Year in the Sixth'. However, in the same issue Carroll would also have read 'A Tale Without a Name', a Byronic pastiche that deals with the experiences of a new boy at Rugby, and the events recounted there, especially the 'constant din' of the dormitories, might have made him more uneasy.

Like most Victorian public schools, Rugby's boarding houses encouraged pupils to form tight, self-regulating societies where the older and stronger boys were expected to keep the younger and weaker in line. It was a system that promoted fierce loyalties and passionate male friendships – *The Rugby Miscellany* includes a surprisingly frank poem on 'love's ecstatic dream, | More dear than love of woman' – but the consequences could be brutal, like a Victorian version of *The Lord of the Flies* with sharpened sticks replaced by swishing canes. When the novelist Anthony Trollope looked back on his time at Winchester, he recalled one older boy who made his life a particular misery when he decided that the best way of keeping up house morale would be to thrash Trollope 'as a part of his daily exercise'. He was Trollope's brother. Despite the atmosphere of moral earnestness Arnold had culti-vated, Rugby still had its share of abuses: a boy who arrived at School House in 1849, the year when Carroll left, recalled other pupils 'coming into my study pulling all my books about and preventing my learning by asking me to repeat the most horrid words'; he also endured the annual ceremony of 'Lamb-Singing', in which new boys were forced to stand on a table and perform in front of the rest of the house, before having to drink a jug of 'muddy water crammed with salt', which left his throat feeling 'as if it had been skinned'.

Carroll may not have submitted meekly to such ordeals. At Richmond School he was remembered as 'a boy who knew well how to use his fists', and in one of his letters home from Richmond he described his rough initiation ('they immediately began kicking me and knocking on all sides') before concluding that 'The boys play me no tricks now' – a piece of reassurance that carried a little glint of menace. His earliest surviving letter from Rugby is equally upbeat, or at least dutifully cheer-ful, containing a request for some money to buy a pair of 'warm gloves', and the news that another boy 'unfortunately broke his arm yesterday by falling down'. Academically he was successful, and although his schoolbooks show that he was a conscientious pupil – his 1845 copy of Virgil contains hundreds of neat underlinings and marginal comments – it was in mathematics, where he won five school prizes, that he really shone.

Later in life, Carroll would show off his skill with numbers, publishing an article in 1887 that explained how to find the day of the week for any given date in history, but there is no evidence that he was a mathematical prodigy like the earlier phenomenon of the 'calculating boys': autistic savants like Jedediah Buxton, who could tell you exactly how many words a sermon contained after hearing it just once, despite having no idea what it was about. Even if he could have performed this sort of trick, Carroll would never have contemplated treating either mathematics or religion as material for a parlour game. They were too important for that; both were subjects for thinking with as well as thinking about. One of his father's sermons had pointed out that everyone will have 'an account to render hereafter', and for Carroll the overlap of vocabulary between religion and mathematics revealed a good deal of intellectual common ground. Neither left any room for ambiguity or doubt; both involved what Carroll described in one of his later letters as 'an absolute, self-existent, external, distinction between Right and Wrong'.

If religion helped to make sense of the invisible world, mathematics made sense of what Carroll saw all around him. One of his 'Skeleton Maps' featured a set of tidy dotted lines showing his father's travels around Britain, and it is no coincidence that Carroll tried to find equally soothing patterns in his own life. At Christ Church he ended up spending around half of the year living in a set of quadrangles, and the rest of his time tracing out a series of triangles and parallelograms as he travelled from Oxford to London to Croft and back to Oxford, or from Croft to Ripon (where his father was Examining Chaplain to the Bishop) to London to Oxford and finally back to Croft. His photograph albums would later reveal an equal pleasure in rearranging the world as a series of neat geometrical shapes: squares, rectangles, semicircles and ovals. Mathematics revealed another fixed order underpinning the shifting surfaces of life.

It also generated stories. Some were disguised as academic exercises; one of the textbooks Carroll used at Rugby, an arithmetic primer entitled *The Tutor's Assistant*, included dozens of questions intended to help with basic calculations, which in just a few lines sketched out narrative scenarios that at first glance oddly resemble the openings of parables or fairy tales:

53

A captain and 160 sailors took a prize worth 1360 l. of which the captain had half for his share, and the rest was equally divided among the sailors . . .

A lady's fortune consisted of a cabinet worth 200 l. consisting of 16 drawers, each having two partitions, each of which contained 37 l. and 2 crowns . . .

A young man received 210 l. which was ⅔ of his elder brother's portion . . .

Mathematics also gave Carroll new opportunities to play around with private jokes and examples of magical thinking. He remained addicted to the number forty-two, for example, which long before Douglas Adams selected it as the answer to 'life, the universe, and everything' was making numerous guest appearances in Carroll's stories. Sometimes these were obvious: in the courtroom scene in Wonderland, the King claims that 'Rule Forty-two' is *All persons more than a mile high to leave the court*', and in *The Hunting of the Snark* another Rule Forty-two states that 'No one shall speak to the Man at the Helm', while the Baker has 'forty-two boxes, all carefully packed | With his name painted clearly on each.' At times these appearances were more covert: there are forty-two illustrations in *Alice's Adventures in Wonderland*, for example, and the trial title pages Carroll's publisher Macmillan printed for him reveal that he originally wanted forty-two illustrations for *Through the Looking-Glass*. Meaningless in itself, but packed with private significance, it was a number that offered further tantalizing glimpses of a hidden structure at the heart of things.

What Carroll was also forced to recognize at school, however, is that not every difficulty could be resolved as neatly as a mathematical problem. Whereas his brother Wilfred was a 'keen sportsman' who 'achieved distinction as an oarsman' and was 'one of the best shots of his day', the kind of sports Carroll enjoyed, such as croquet, involved calculating angles and vectors rather than smashing into other boys, and these were not likely to make him popular at the school that had invented the modern game of rugby football. Violet Dodgson is probably right to claim that her uncle 'worked hard and avoided games as far as possible'. What he couldn't avoid was the ritual humiliation of being the sort of boy who ends up being picked last for a football team, or is told to field on the cricket boundary so that he can be kept away from the ball. Evidence that he was thought of as something other than a sporting idol comes from another school textbook, this time a copy of Xenophon he acquired in November 1846, in which he wrote his name and another hand added 'is a muff', before repeating the insult at the top of the page: 'Dodgson is a muff.' The word's general meaning of 'A foolish, stupid, feeble, or incompetent person' was sharpened in school contexts to mean the sort of boy who was clumsy or inept at sports (a 'muff' also referred to a dropped catch at cricket), and it could be deployed in either an affectionate or a more hostile manner. In Thomas Hughes's 1857 novel *Tom Brown's School Days*, written in celebration of his time at Rugby under Arnold, Bill the porter is fondly chaffed as an 'old muff,' while the delicate new boy Arthur is openly laughed at as a 'young muff'. In fiction, of course, young muffs like Arthur were usually protected by stout-hearted heroes like Tom Brown, who saves him from the bullies and then follows Arthur's saintly example by saying his prayers every night beside his dormitory bed. The reality was usually far less reassuring. Another delicate new boy, this time a real one, left a full diary of the months he spent at Rugby before his early death, and it makes unhappy reading. Entering the school on 28 August 1846, seven months after Carroll, John Lang Bickersteth was not only frail and good at mathematics, but also remarkably pious – one of his diary entries reads 'A man buried today – a warning to me' – and he suffered accordingly. Sad and friendless from the start, he was accused of being 'mean and stingy' for not buying any pictures for his study, and was teased mercilessly by the other boys. During one especially bleak evening, he had a dog repeatedly set on him. By mid-September, his diary had collapsed into exclamations such as 'O God, sustain me!' and by the end of the following January he had died at home from a fever.

There is no evidence that Carroll suffered as badly as this, but as an adult his references to Rugby were few and cool in tone, stating only that no 'earthly considerations would induce me to go through my three years again', and 'the hardships of the day would have been comparative trifles to bear' if only he had been 'secure from annoyance at night'. There was no shortage of possible 'annoyances' in a shared dormitory. Collingwood notes that the older pupils would sometimes remove the blankets of the younger ones, leaving them to shiver through the night, while blankets also featured in a popular form of torture that involved tossing the smaller boys up in the air and letting them fall to the ground. (In *Tom Brown's School Days* this is a favourite pastime of Flashman, the school's chief bully, who also enjoys roasting boys in front of the fire like chestnuts.) However, the text Carroll probably had in mind is *Paradise Lost*, which describes Adam and Eve 'asleep secure of [i.e. safe from] harm' before Satan tempts them and they fall. Did Carroll experience something similar? Rugby's dormitories were certainly known as places where sexual activity took place; a history of the school published in 1856 included an oblique reference to 'petty perversions', which could mean anything from masturbation to full-blown affairs. For some boys, sexual knowledge could be just as traumatic as actual sexual activity: the chapter on 'Dormitory Life' in F. W. Farrar's popular schoolboy tale *Eric; or, Little by Little* (1858) describes an evening of fun that starts with a game of leap-frog, but quickly descends to 'indecent talk', leaving one boy, who urges his friends to stop, feeling 'as if I was trampling on a slimy poisonous adder'. In case the metaphor is not sufficiently clear, Farrar explains that another boy listens in on the smutty conversations and becomes 'a "god, knowing good and evil"' – another Adam who falls because of the temptations of a snake-like creature.

Whatever Carroll overheard or witnessed at Rugby, it appears to have confirmed his sense that innocence was a special preserve of childhood that was constantly in danger of being breached. Once that occurred it was gone for ever: childhood was a paradise with gates that all too easily swung shut and locked behind you. Only in a story like *Alice's Adventures in Wonderland* could they be reopened a crack, as Alice glimpses 'bright flowers' and 'cool fountains' at the end of a dark passage, and then shrinks even smaller to enter 'the loveliest garden you ever saw'.

*

Four

Any hope that Carroll might have been able to prolong his childhood in more conventional ways was crushed within a few months of his departure from Rugby. In May 1850 he matriculated as a member of Christ Church, his father's old college at Oxford, which he finally entered in January 1851 after waiting several months for rooms to become available. Within two days he was on his way back to Croft: his mother had died of an unspecified 'inflammation of the brain', possibly a stroke or meningitis, at the age of forty-seven. The long-term effects of this death on Carroll are hard to judge, although it has been noted how rarely mothers feature in his later writing, usually being replaced by figures like the anonymous older sister who appears at the beginning and end of *Alice's Adventures in Wonderland*, or bullying harridans like the Queen of Hearts. In the shorter term, he proved himself to be impressively resilient, or at least good at pretending; within six weeks of his return to Oxford, he sent a chatty letter back home describing his new life as an undergraduate, which included 'a very sad incident, namely my missing morning chapel' after oversleeping. Perhaps he would have benefited from the 'Alarum bedstead, causing a person to arise at any given hour' shown later that year at the Great Exhibition, which, according to a popular shilling guide, 'by some curious machinery' ejected the sleeper if he did not 'leave his bed immediately on the alarum ringing'. The inventor was Robert Watson Savage, of 15 St James's Square in London, rather than (as is often claimed) the Oxford furniture dealer Theophilus Carter, who would later be offered as a possible model for the Hatter, but the desire to link this sort of invention with Wonderland is understandable. Nobody was more likely than Carroll to appreciate such an inspired mixture of craziness and craftsmanship.

When he attended the Exhibition in July, two months after its official opening, his eye was immediately drawn to some of the 'ingenious pieces of mechanism' on display, including a tree full of 'birds chirping and hopping from branch to branch exactly like life', with another bird depicted 'trying to eat a beetle' in 'uncomfortable little jerks, as if it was choking'. The whole exhibition, he declared, was 'a sort of fairyland'. That was a common reaction to Joseph Paxton's Crystal Palace. Designed as a sturdy iron skeleton beneath a shimmering glass skin, the building had been slotted together so quickly that some observers enjoyed pretending that magic rather than engineering had been responsible. Thackeray's poem on the opening ceremony was typical in drawing on the language of fairy tales, transforming several thousand tons of building work into an airy bubble of fantasy:

> As though 'twere by a wizard's rod
> A blazing arch of lucid glass
> Leaps like a fountain from the grass
> To meet the sun.

Equally appealing to Carroll was the extraordinary variety of objects on display. Even the entrance to the building left him lost for words: 'As far as you can look in any direction you see nothing but pillars hung about with shawls, carpets, etc., with long avenues of statues, fountains, canopies, etc., etc., etc.' Better still, as far as Carroll was concerned, was the fact that the Exhibition organizers had taken a potentially bewildering 'etc., etc., etc.' of objects and arranged them into neat classes (the 'Alarum bedstead' appeared in the official catalogue under 'Hardware, Class 22'), so that when he explored a little further the visual assault of the entrance hall turned out to be part of a coherent design: 'The different compartments on the ground floor are divided by shawls, carpets, etc., and you look down into one after another as you go.' If the Great Exhibition was a modern fairyland, it was also the world's largest filing cabinet.

Victorian Oxford might have produced similarly mixed impressions. Visually it was a jumble of styles, where buildings of every kind jostled for attention: proudly thrusting Gothic spires; elegantly repeating neoclassical facades; creaking timber-framed shops. That made it a much easier city to experience than to write about, which may be why those who tried often ended up relying on a kind of literary bricolage, from the comic juxtapositions of Keats ('The mouldering arch, | Shaded o'er by a larch, | Stands next door to Wilson the Hosier') to the busy verbal compounds of Hopkins, for whom the 'Towery city' of Oxford was 'Cuckoo-echoing, bell-swarmèd, lark-charmèd, rook-racked, river-rounded'. But Oxford was a mixture of the old and the new in other ways besides its architecture. By the time Carroll arrived in 1851, a railway station had been constructed on the outskirts of the city, after years of wrangling with the university authorities, which meant that sleepy and traditional Oxford was finally connected to the busy modern world. On the other hand, just a short walk up the High Street, Martin Routh continued to shuffle around Magdalen College after more than fifty years as President, having originally been elected as a Fellow over a decade before the French Revolution, and still insisted on wearing the buckled shoes and wig that had fallen out of fashion decades earlier. When he finally died in 1854, his wig was taken by a colleague, the botanist Charles Daubeny, and petrified in a mineral spring, which was in many ways a fitting tribute to a man who had spent the last years of his life being revered as a living fossil. Nor was he the only relic of old Oxford that had somehow survived into the Victorian age. Many of the University's ancient traditions remained as incongruous and immovable as a gargoyle. Undergraduates were still required to wear academic caps and gowns, and were punished if they failed to attend chapel services or return to their colleges before the gates closed at night. Corporal punishment had only recently been abolished, to the dismay of some old hands in the colleges, and Carroll's matriculation ceremony, during which he was officially admitted as an undergraduate of the University, required him to swear in Latin that he would abide by statutes that included the promise 'not to encourage the growth of curls' and 'to abstain from that absurd and assuming practice of walking publicly in boots'.

The popular perception was that Oxford's students were equally set in their ways. *Hints to Freshmen*, a publication that promised to help 'convert the chrysalis into the butterfly', divided new undergraduates into several distinct 'species', and listed them like a naturalist's field guide: 'the Man who Hunts', 'the Man who Rows' and so on. The period's novelists were similarly quick to distil college life into a familiar set of situations. Carroll owned a copy of *The Adventures of Mr Verdant Green*, which sold more than 100,000 copies within twenty years of its first publication in 1853, and it is crammed with comic examples of the social conventions that the innocent freshman Verdant Green has to learn at 'Brazenface College' (a fictitious version of Oxford's Brasenose College), ranging from why he should hand over a bottle of brandy to his bedmaker (for her 'spazzums') to the perils of making a speech in front of his new friends while staggeringly drunk:

> 'Genelum anladies *(cheers)*, – I meangenelum. *("That's about the ticket, old feller!")* Customd syam plic speakn, I – I – *(hear, hear)* – feel bliged drinkmyel. I'm fresman, genelum, and prow title *(loud cheers)* . . .'

As a result of Green's 'wine' (i.e. drinks party) he misses chapel the next morning, after waking up with a hangover that leaves his head pounding and his hands trembling 'like a weak old man's'. Given how cautious Carroll was when it came to drink – he enjoyed an occasional glass of sherry, but nobody ever reported seeing him drunk – it is unlikely that he ever needed the same excuse, but he would quickly have learned how often this situation was repeated in Oxford, as different undergraduates made the same mistakes, and the rich comedy this could produce.

Christ Church was a promising environment for such thoughts, because even by Oxford's standards it was noticeably out of step with the times. Carroll's second surviving letter home is written in faux medieval English – 'Verily I doe send greeting untoe thee, and wish thee all hail for thy byrthe-day' – which hardly suggests he thought he had joined a dynamic modern institution, and his surroundings would have given this conclusion plenty of support. Although the period's guidebooks praised Christ Church as a 'princely establishment' with buildings of 'uncommon grandeur', its stonework was crumbling, its plumbing was chaotic, and the long-serving Dean Gaisford, fondly nicknamed the 'Old Bear', stubbornly resisted any renovations or reforms. Tom Tower's great bell still rang 101 times at 9.05 p.m. every evening, stubbornly sticking to 'Oxford Time' long after the rest of the country had changed its clocks to a national standard. Undergraduates were still permitted to keep dogs for hunting – Carroll's first Oxford letter recounts a noisy fight between six of them outside his window – and the sons of noblemen, who wore special caps with gold tassels and dined at High Table, were still treated with a fawning deference even if they merely dabbled in learning as a gentlemanly pastime. While this sort of class segregation was starting to grate in Oxford as a whole, Christ Church continued to be thought of as a place where social style trumped intellectual substance. In *Tom Brown at Oxford* (1861), the spoilt Viscount Philippine arranges for a boxing match to take place in his 'magnificently furnished' rooms in Christ Church, and during the bout it is revealed that he has bet £5 and a pony that one of the participants – a 'servitor', or college servant, who received free tuition in return for waiting on the tables of wealthier undergraduates – will be knocked down by the professional boxer he has engaged for the evening. Probably his moral carelessness and 'sulky' demeanour are supposed to reflect more general attitudes.

Some of Christ Church's real inhabitants might have been cut from *Tom Brown at Oxford* as too implausible for fiction. Chief among them was the geologist William Buckland, a celebrated 'zoophagist' who believed that it was his duty as a member of the human race, to whom God had given dominion over 'every creeping thing that creepeth upon the earth' (Genesis 8: 17), to munch his way through the entire animal kingdom. Mole and bluebottle were especially nasty, he observed, and his lodgings in the north-west corner of Tom Quad were famous as a zoological junk shop where cages of snakes competed for space with fossils and crocodile skulls, and a visitor who once heard a soft crunching sound coming from under the table was told that it was probably a jackal eating some of the guinea pigs. Buckland continued to amuse Carroll long after his death in 1856: many unlikely creatures in *Alice's Adventures in Wonderland* are at risk of being killed or eaten, and in one letter he teased a child-friend by telling her that he had been visited by three cats, to whom he offered rat-tail jelly and buttered mice (possibly a memory of one of Buckland's tastier meals, which was crispy mice in batter), and only drew a blank when they asked for boiled pelican. But although Christ Church was tolerant of its eccentrics, some of its other procedures were at best entrenched and at worst astonishingly corrupt. When the future tenth Earl of Wemyss came up for an interview with Gaisford in 1837, prior to being admitted as an undergraduate, the only question he recalled being asked was 'How is your father?'

Another famous Oxford type was 'the Man who Reads' – the sort of undergraduate who quickly realizes that the best way to fit into university life is to sit in a library and use its books as camouflage. Carroll's correspondence from Christ Church, listing the writers he intended to study, and shyly referring to a new friend 'who has been here once or twice to tea, and we have been out walking together', marked him out firmly as a member of this undergraduate species. Although the college's sporting hearties occasionally took exception to their presence – in 1830 the fanatically industrious future Prime Minister William Gladstone was beaten up in his rooms at Christ Church by 'a party of men' – for the most part they were left alone with their books. Sometimes these offered encouraging models to follow. *Christ Church Days*, a novel published in 1867 by the reforming clergyman Frederick Arnold, who was born in the same year as Carroll, uses the experiences of its hero to underline the importance of a steady accumulation of knowledge, informing its readers that 'A university career is a race in which the tortoise has a very good chance of winning something good.' That appears to have been the sort of advice Carroll took to heart.

By the end of 1852, he had achieved a Second Class in Classical Moderations and a First Class in Mathematics, together with a nomination to a Studentship (i.e. Fellowship) in recognition of his 'good intellect' and 'steady quiet conduct'. This came with a small but guaranteed income, and permission to reside in college rooms for the rest of his life, so long as he remained unmarried and proceeded to holy orders. In the end, he managed to achieve a compromise between the demands of his Studentship and his own doubts about whether he was properly suited to full ordination. His reasons for not wanting to become a priest were never fully articulated, although anxiety about having to preach regularly may have played a significant part, as may the difficulty of reconciling his new-found social freedoms with the Church's official policy of discouraging activities such as attending the theatre. In 1861, he was ordained Deacon, which was usually a step on the way to becoming a priest, and although the rules of the college stated that he should take full orders within four years of taking his MA degree, he hesitated on the threshold. He would end up staying there for another thirty-seven years. On 21 October 1862, the Dean of Christ Church threatened to lay the matter before the other college authorities, but by the following day he had experienced a change of heart, and informed Carroll that he would 'do nothing more about it'. Carroll was free to decide for himself whether to follow his father in becoming a priest, or step away from the Church (and Christ Church) altogether. He did neither. Instead he chose to remain at Oxford in an ambiguous role as neither layman nor priest, a sort of ecclesiastical Mock Turtle.

Further evidence of Carroll's hard work survives in the form of three essays he read aloud in Hall to the other undergraduates. Two of these are rather dull arguments from the on-the-one-hand-but-on-the-other school of debating, which focus on the dangers of seeking fame and the difficulty of finding 'unmixed happiness' in life. Only the third example, on the subject of beauty, genuinely fires Carroll's imagination, as he launches into a long catalogue of where beauty is to be found: 'in scenery, in trees, lakes, and mountains, in the vastness of the ocean, in the splendour of Sunrise, and in the rich glow of Sunset, in the broad daylight, and in the majesty of Night, in animals, & last, highest, & grandest of all, in the divine form & features of Man'. By the time he has explained that 'this perception of Beauty in natural objects' is bound up with 'love and admiration for the object in whom this Beauty is perceived', it is clear where his real interest lies: in beautiful people rather than pretty sunsets, 'the object in whom' rather than the object in which.

Carroll's aesthetic sense could be overwhelming: Violet Dodgson recalled that he was 'intensely susceptible to beauty in any form', and once broke down completely while reading her a poem. Such sensitivity would not have been of any great help in his final set of Classical examinations, known as 'Greats', which he passed (Third Class) at the end of Easter Term 1854, and even less so in the final Mathematics papers which he sat in October that year. However, when the results of these examinations were announced, Carroll discovered that he had achieved the highest First among his group of friends, which more or less guaranteed him an academic career for as long as he wanted. 'I feel very like a child with a new toy,' he told his sister Mary, before adding a self-deprecating comic twist: 'I daresay I shall be tired of it soon, and wish to be Pope of Rome next.'

Anyone who saw Carroll entering or exiting Christ Church underneath the bulky stonework of Tom Tower at this time might have been left with mixed impressions. In early photographs he looks like a cross between a military chaplain and a London dandy. His clothes were fastidiously neat,

Carroll's self-portrait (2 June 1857)

featuring crisp white collars and shiny boots, but were also elegant and fashionably cut. His hair fell in glossy chestnut curls around a pale clean-shaven face, but from a razor-sharp parting. He was of average height, around 5'9", but appeared distinctly taller thanks to his upright posture and rake-thin frame. Equally mixed were two assessments of his personality made at around this time. The first was a hastily scribbled 'Character of C L Dodgson' written by Edward Hamilton, an Edinburgh phrenologist who examined Carroll's head in 1852, and from its bumps and depressions somehow deduced that he had 'a strong love of friends', 'much circumspection', 'lofty generous sentiments', 'much good taste for order & dress & elegance' and, as the first characteristic he thought worth recording, 'a strong love of children'. It was, he concluded, 'upon the whole a good Head'. The second was an analysis of Carroll's clear and almost childishly round handwriting undertaken by Minnie Anderson, a family friend he would later photograph, who decided that he had 'a good deal of imitation – would make a good actor – diffident – rather shy in general society – comes out in the home circle – rather obstinate – very clever – a great deal of concentration – very affectionate – a great deal of wit and humour'. Thus far it is little more than a summary of the person she already knew. Her conclusion, however, was more forward-looking: 'imagination – fond of reading poetry – *may* perhaps compose –'.

*

Five

hether or not Carroll would continue to 'compose' was an open question as he contemplated life after his degree. In 1854, he had contributed a poem ('The Lady of the Ladle') and a story ('Wilhelm von Schmitz') to the *Whitby Gazette*, while he was spending two months in the seaside town with a summer reading party; in 1855, four further pieces by him appeared in the new, and as it turned out short-lived, penny periodical the *Comic Times*, which had been founded as a direct rival to *Punch*. None of these would have raised more than a weak smile at the time, and they are largely dead on the page now, with the exception of the parody 'She's All My Fancy Painted Him', which would later reappear in a revised form as the poem read out by the White Rabbit in *Alice's Adventures in Wonderland*. The staff of the defunct *Comic Times* then reassembled to produce a new shilling magazine, *The Train*, which began publication in January 1856. Privately Carroll thought the opening number 'only average in talent, and an intense imitation of Dickens throughout', but anyone who came across his later contributions might have wondered whether he was offering anything very different. As for his gloomy forecast that 'I don't think it has *any* chance of surviving the year', some readers might have drawn the same conclusion from his own fledgling literary career.

Five of his pieces are poems, including a long-winded parody of Tennyson's 'The Two Voices' entitled 'The Three Voices' (November 1856) and two creaky pieces of narrative verse, 'The Path of Roses' (May 1856) and 'The Sailor's Wife' (May 1857), which are so tightly packed with melodramatic flourishes – the 'large hot tears' of a 'pale Lady', the 'agonized embrace' of a mother clutching her baby, and so on – the writing scarcely has room to breathe. More interesting is 'Novelty and

Romancement', a short story in which a young man with poetic leanings notices a rusty sign outside a shop offering 'Romancement' for sale. Giddy with excitement, he approaches the dealer, who is a little bemused by his request but happy to sell him some stock; only when the young man looks more closely the next day does he realize that what he is purchasing is not romancement but roman cement. It is a bad joke wrapped up in a good story, and it brings together many of the tricks Carroll had previously rehearsed in his family magazines, such as narrative misdirection and the need for readers to discover new sources of wonder in a boringly utilitarian world. It also reveals his sheer pleasure in disassembling and reassembling language, as he introduces compounds such as 'brandy-and-water', 'public-house', 'good-natured' and 'life-cherished', which together reflect the hero's belief that something as simple as a hyphen might be enough to stick together the pieces of a daydream.

Carroll's most significant contribution to *The Train* was also his first, 'Solitude', which appeared in the March 1856 issue. It opened with a set of variations on traditional love poetry:

> I love the stillness of the wood:
> I love the music of the rill:
> I love to couch in pensive mood
> Upon some silent hill.

It is unlikely that anyone would claim these lines heralded the arrival of a major new literary talent. Like many inexperienced writers, early on Carroll often confused strong feelings with forceful writing, and when that happened his poems usually collapsed into sentimental mush. In the case of 'Solitude', his writing is also thinly unoriginal, adopting a patchwork of phrases from Wordsworth's poetry and filtering them through the stock Romantic situation of a speaker who wants to escape from the noise and annoyance of real life. Yet it is precisely this lack of originality that allows Carroll to hint at an alternative solution, because even when his speaker is explaining how thankful he is that no footstep 'Breaks in to mar the holy peace | Of this great solitude', he is keeping company with earlier poets. ('Holy peace' is one of the noisiest phrases in literature: it can be found rattling around in the work of poets from Dryden to Elizabeth Barrett Browning.) In effect, he produces two different poems in one. The first poet, who is the spokesman for Carroll's deep and abiding shyness, tells us how much he longs to be alone; meanwhile, the second poet, who speaks on behalf of Carroll's lively social self, reminds us that anyone who follows in the footsteps of his predecessors can be alone without feeling lonely. It is not until the final stanzas that a third voice reveals itself:

> Ye golden hours of Life's young spring,
>   Of innocence, of love and truth!
> Bright, beyond all imagining,
>   Thou fairy-dream of youth!
>
> I'd give all wealth that years hath piled,
>   The slow result of Life's decay,
> To be once more a little child
>   For one bright sunny day.

However unusual it might be for a twenty-four-year-old to indulge in this sort of daydream, at first glance it seems modest enough: a wish to return to childhood for a fleeting period of sunshine before the clouds of adulthood gather. Yet as soon as an event is recorded in writing there is nothing to prevent it from being drawn out and returned to: in a story, 'once more' can become a refrain, and 'golden hours' are potentially endless. That is one important discovery Carroll made in 'Solitude'. The other was his literary pseudonym. Although his earlier published poems and stories had appeared anonymously or under assumed initials – in the *Whitby Gazette* he was again 'B.B.' – the editor of the *Comic Times*, Edmund Yates, asked him to come up with an alternative. When 'Dares', the first syllable of his birthplace, was rejected, he sent Yates a list of alternatives:

Edgar Cuthwellis
Edgar U. C. Westhall
Louis Carroll
Lewis Carroll

All of these were elaborately disguised variations on his first two names, including a couple of anagrams, but the final option was the simplest and sharpest: a mirror image of 'Charles Lutwidge' that had been translated into schoolboy Latin (Charles → Carolus → Carroll; Lutwidge → Ludovicus → Lewis), and on 1 March 1856 he recorded in his diary '*Lewis Carroll* was chosen.'

Looking around him at Christ Church, Carroll might have wondered what kind of life he was going to lead as 'Charles Dodgson' when he wasn't moonlighting as his fictional alter ego. In October 1855, he continued his steady ascent up the college's internal hierarchy by taking up a new appointment as a Mathematical Lecturer, and on his return to Croft at Christmas he reflected on 'the most eventful year of my life'. Having begun with 'no definite plans or expectations', he had ended with a salary of more than £300 a year, and a course of teaching and study marked out 'for at least some years to come'. His final summary was brisk: 'Great mercies, great failings, time lost, talents misapplied – such has been the past year.'

In choosing to pursue an academic career, Carroll was opting for a way of life that, in addition to its other perks, would offer him the luxury of time to devote to his own writing. (The distinguished Oxford historian Keith Thomas is reported to have said that academic life has three things to recommend it: July, August and September.) He was also following in the footsteps of his father, who had written to his old college friend Edward Pusey in 1849 to support Carroll's original admission to Christ Church. Pusey in his reply had been scrupulously careful not to promise any favours, although his conclusion, 'I can only say that I shall have *very great* pleasure, if circumstances permit me to recommend your son', certainly left room for doubt. It was just one example of a widespread suspicion that Christ Church had developed a habit of rewarding the best-connected rather than the most highly qualified candidates at every level of academic life. This suspicion was increased when Dean Gaisford refused to answer any of the questions put to him by the Royal Commission into Oxford University established in 1850, so it was no surprise when, upon Gaisford's death at the start of June 1855, the new Dean (a crown appointment, and therefore effectively the gift of the Liberal Prime Minister Lord Palmerston) was announced as the forty-four-year-old lexicographer Henry George Liddell.

He was a distinguished classicist, who had been a Student of Christ Church before marrying the socially ambitious Lorina in 1846; he had then spent nine years as headmaster of Westminster School, which was where Carroll's father had been educated, and had assembled an impressive list of publications, including a celebrated *Greek–English Lexicon* he co-authored with Robert Scott. More recently, and perhaps more significantly, he had served as a member of the Oxford University Commission, missing only one of the eighty-seven meetings, and had helped to compile the report that led to the University Reform Act of 1854. Put another way, he was an academic insider returning to Oxford from the outside, and his appointment received a predictably mixed response. Inside the House of Commons there were cheers; inside 'the House', as Christ Church was referred to by those in the know, the announcement met with considerably less enthusiasm. His election 'does not seem to have given much satisfaction in the college', Carroll observed neutrally, while some undergraduates greeted him more explosively by fastening a small barrel of gunpowder to the handle of his front door. However, over the next thirty-six years of his Deanship, Liddell instigated a 'peaceful revolution' that included everything from the organization of Christ Church's finances to the quality of its drains, and in pushing forward his agenda of reforms it is not hard to see why he carried the majority of doubters with him.

Dean Liddell was a formidable presence: tall and sternly authoritarian, he had a hawk-like profile surrounded by a dandelion cloud of white hair, and an intellect powerful enough to crush any chippy colleagues. He also had artistic leanings – some of his surviving sketches on pink blotting paper show unusual skill, especially when one considers that they were probably doodled while chairing college meetings – and, unlike Christ Church's other dons, he had a family. For several months after his appointment, the Deanery was noisy with hammering and sawing, as he supervised the alterations designed to make it suitable for his wife and children Harry, Lorina (known as Ina), Alice and Edith, including the installation of oak panelling and construction of a grand new staircase and gallery. In February 1856, the family moved into their new home.

Carroll's construction of himself at this time was an equally daunting project. At some point, probably in 1853, he began to write a diary, which he continued to keep for the rest of his life, periodically adding a new volume to the growing set of well-thumbed notebooks with green cardboard covers and reinforced spines. By the end of his life he had compiled a total of thirteen volumes, four of which would later be lost or suppressed by his family; of those that did survive, a few pages had been removed by someone nervous of what they contained. The earliest volume spans the period January to September 1855, and the first entry reveals the general approach Carroll took to his task:

Jan: 1 (M).   The year begins at Ripon – tried a little Mathematics unsuccessfully – sketched a design for illumination in the title-page of M.C.'s [his sister Mary Charlotte's] book of Sacred Poetry. Handbells in the evening, a tedious performance.

It is hardly gripping stuff, although even handbells would be more exciting than some of Carroll's later entries. The overriding impression they give is of a man who sought to avoid intimacy even when he had only himself for company; usually they read less like a personal confession than a voiceover by a sympathetic actor. To be fair to Carroll, his diaries are no more tedious than those written by some of his contemporaries; the first month of the diary composed between 1886 and 1900 by Thomas Vere Bayne, a friend from Daresbury who became one of Carroll's colleagues at Christ Church, includes such eye-drooping entries as 'More shopping. Very warm' (2 January) and 'Thoroughly wet day' (4 January). Yet even in this context Carroll's diaries are a triumph of self-avoidance. Occasionally the mask slips, and he bursts out with an anguished prayer such as 'Oh God, for Christ's sake, help me to do thy will, to deny myself, to watch and pray!' or 'Tomorrow is Sunday: would God it might be to me the beginning of a better and holier life!' Yet although these might seem strangely out of keeping with his tone elsewhere, they are in fact bullet-like revelations of the purpose served by his diaries as a whole. The daily discipline of writing did more than record what had happened in Carroll's life. It gradually built up a model of how he wanted to live – the sort of existence in which order and routine would conquer unruly contingency.

A key challenge in Carroll's first years as a lecturer at Christ Church was how to reconcile this desire for a settled life with his large number of interests. The early diaries record a period of rapid zigzagging. He read widely, particularly enjoying Patmore's *The Angel in the House* and Tennyon's *Maud*, went on punishingly long walks, socialized with a small but loyal group of friends, and made regular visits to London, often ending up in the picture rooms of the Royal Academy or in one of the many theatres he frequented. He also continued to write light pieces for the comic press, while simultaneously working on a more serious academic treatment of Euclid.

Meanwhile, the number of his pupils, and therefore the long hours he spent teaching logic and mathematics, continued to increase. It seems he was not a great success as a teacher – 'dull as ditchwater' was one summary; 'dry and perfunctory' another – and that is not very surprising. His uncompromising attitude was never likely to be appreciated by undergraduates who were still treated (and often behaved) like overgrown schoolboys, while his speech impairment was especially vulnerable to their sniggering derision. An undergraduate named Fred Sim recalled that Carroll once asked him, 'Sim, what are you laughing at?' to which his reply was 'I'm afraid we were laughing at *you*, Sir!' In January 1856, he summoned sixty of them to a meeting, of whom only twenty-three bothered to show up. However, even if some of Christ Church's undergraduates viewed his lessons as an unwelcome distraction from the serious business of hunting and getting drunk, at least they were usually polite. Younger children were a different matter. After a happy experience teaching the boys in Croft's Sunday School in July 1855, which he liked 'very much', in January 1856 Carroll accepted a part-time engagement tutoring a group of eight boys at St Aldate's School near Christ Church. Initially he enjoyed their high spirits, but it wasn't long before his diaries gloomily recorded that they had become 'noisy and inattentive' and 'unmanageable'. Within a month he had abandoned the experiment, having decided that 'the good done does not seem worth the time and trouble'. Clearly real children were not always as well behaved as the puppets in his toy school.

More reassuring was his skill at organizing all these new activities: in addition to his diary, in January 1856 he contemplated 'beginning a sort of day-book for entering *everything* in', together with another 'private one', with the aim of eventually forming 'special books' (whatever they were), and the following month he devised a 'system of reading' in history and classics, starting with Thucydides 'right through'. 'Thoroughness must be the rule of all this reading,' he sternly reminded himself. It was certainly an important rule of his writing: not only did he regularly update his diary with clarifications and cross-references, but in January 1861 he began a 'Register of Letters Received and Sent', with a number assigned to each piece of correspondence, together with a brief summary of its contents, which by the time of his death had reached 98,721 entries in twenty-four volumes.

Although Carroll seems to have made a determined effort to grow up in the years after graduation, assuming new responsibilities and developing a more serious attitude to life, some of his other activities at the time reveal how easy it was to slip back into old habits. During the Easter vacation at Croft in 1855, while he was busy reading Edward Burton's *Lectures on Church History*, working on complicated equations and learning Italian ('I intend reading Italian, French, and German at Oxford,' he urged himself in his diary), he was again playing with his marionette theatre, putting on a production of *King John*, and contemplated writing a Christmas book, 'Practical hints for constructing Marionettes and a theatre', which 'might be followed by several plays for representation by Marionettes or by children'. The idea that people could take the place of puppets, just as puppets could imitate the actions of people, continued to intrigue him: back in

Oxford, he complained that the characters of the popular Irish novelist Marmion Savage were 'imperfect puppets', and the 'machinery' of his writing was 'thrust on the notice rather than concealed', presumably in contrast to his own skill in contolling the wires of his toy theatre.

That summer at Croft, Carroll returned to another of his favourite childhood activities, starting a new magazine called *Mischmasch* in a handsome notebook with marbled covers and thick cream paper. This time he largely dispensed with the fiction that it was a family production. Alongside the comic squibs and in-jokes, including a cartoon of one of his brothers wearing skintight clothing and a flapping cape that made him resemble a Victorian superhero, an increasing number of pages were taken up with Carroll's published articles and reviews, which he proudly snipped out and pasted into place. It was a transitional work, hovering between a personal scrapbook and a professional miscellany, as can be seen in the double-column design for a handwritten version of Carroll's story 'Wilhelm von Schmitz', which was intended to make *Mischmasch* look as much like a printed magazine as possible. Yet he was not always as confident about his literary future as the comic verve of this writing might suggest.

In *The Rectory Magazine*, an episode in his rambling romance 'Sidney Hamilton' had ended with one character sharply telling another that '"you'd better not waste your sweetness on the desert air"', followed by a swift exit and Carroll's promise that the story was '(to be continued)'. The allusion to Gray's 'Elegy Written in a Country Churchyard', where we are reminded that 'Full many a flower is born to blush unseen, | And waste its sweetness on the desert air', carried a warning that not everyone was given the opportunity to make their voice heard, just as the fact that someone had a voice did not necessarily mean they had anything worth saying. In March 1857, this was still niggling away at Carroll, as he contributed a sonnet to his sister Mary's album that began 'full many a flower'. Gray's poem is one of the great works about frustrated potential, because it describes unfulfilled ambitions within a structure that perfectly achieves the writer's own aims, and choosing the demanding form of a sonnet indicates that Carroll wanted to set himself the same challenge.

"And a pretty dance you are leading him now!"
  In anger answered she,
"But a bantam's cap is a different thing
  'To the cap that there I see!"

"Oh what bait's that upon your hook,
  'Dear brother, tell to me?"
"It is my younger brother," he cried,
  "Oh woe and dole is me!

'I's mighty wicked, that I is!
  'Or how could such things be?
'Farewell, farewell sweet sister,
  'I'm going o'er the sea."

"And when will you come back again,
  'My brother, tell to me?"
"When chub is good for human food,
  'And that will never be!".

She turned herself right round about,
  And her heart brake into three,
Said, "One of the two will be wet through and through,
  'And t'other'll be late for his tea!"

Croft. 1853.

Carroll's family magazine *Mischmasch* (1855–62)

The final item in *Mischmasch*, a poem about a stout man and his sleek love rival entitled 'Bloggs' Woe', is dated November 1862, and is followed by dozens of blank pages. But if that suggests Carroll eventually grew bored with his family magazines, it was not because he had lost interest in storytelling and illustration. (November 1862 was also the month when he started his manuscript of *Alice's Adventures Under Ground*.) It was because by then these impulses had combined in a new creative outlet: photography.

*

Six

In summer 1852, Carroll visited the London home of his uncle Skeffington Lutwidge, a barrister and member of the Lunacy Commission, which had been established in 1845 to oversee the running of asylums and welfare of the mentally ill. There Carroll played with new gadgets and 'oddities' that included 'a lathe, telescope stand, crest stamp . . . a beautiful little pocket instrument for measuring distances on a map, refrigerator, etc., etc.' Observing 'live animalcula in his large microscope' gave him particular pleasure, with the 'conveniently transparent' skin of these tiny creatures allowing him to see 'all kinds of organs jumping about like a complicated piece of machinery'. Three years later, Uncle Skeffington had a new toy to play with, a camera, which was used in the summer of 1855 to take photographs in and around Croft, and by then Carroll had also been introduced to the 'dark art' by his Christ Church friend Reginald Southey (nephew of the former poet laureate Robert Southey), whose small crisp image of Broad Walk, taken from his window in March 1855, Carroll considered 'about the best amateur attempt that I have seen'. Soon he too had been bitten by the shutterbug. Exactly a year later, in March 1856, Southey escorted him to Ottewill & Co. on the Caledonian Road, one of London's finest camera-makers, and there he paid the large sum of £15 – more than the annual salary of most household servants – for a brand-new photographic kit.

Photography was both a fashionable pastime in the mid-1850s and a form of technology that was as surprising as anything seen before. At the 1851 Great Exhibition it had been treated largely as a novelty, with sample pictures grouped together in the Fine Arts court under Class 30, 'Sculpture, Models and Plastic Arts, Mosaics, Enamels, Etc.', but the announcement there of the collodion wet-plate method quickly changed all that. In

January 1853 the Photographic Society of London was inaugurated at the Society of Arts, and thereafter held annual exhibitions of its members' work; by 1860, five years after the last remaining patent on the wet-plate method was successfully challenged, the number of provincial societies had risen to thirty-two. Technical handbooks proliferated, advertisements for cameras and associated paraphernalia crowded the columns of newspapers, and professional studios competed with enthusiastic amateurs to produce portraits for those curious to know what they looked like when sliced out of time and preserved in the strange perpetual twilight of a photograph.

For a newcomer like Carroll, photography was an exciting but exacting hobby. To produce a single print required the knowledge of a chemist, the eye of an artist and the patience of a saint. Later in the century, when Kodak introduced a camera pre-loaded with film that could be sent away for development, the company's slogan was 'You press the button, we do the rest.' It was, their advertisements promised, 'The only camera that anyone can use without instructions'. The list of 'Directions and Instructions' that came with Carroll's photographic chemicals, by contrast, which he kept in a heavy wooden box full of special compartments and glass bottles, ran to fifty-four tightly printed lines. Such precision accurately reflected the fiddly nature of the wet-plate process, which rewarded skill and experience but ruthlessly punished any mistakes. First the photographer had to prepare the glass plate by polishing it to a high sheen, before applying a thin layer of the gummy chemical substance collodion, and dipping it in a bath of silver nitrate solution. Once the plate had been carefully inserted into the camera, the lens cap had to be removed for exactly the right length of time, which varied according to the strength of the chemicals and the quality of the light, and finally the exposed plate had to be taken away and developed immediately in a darkroom, by gently washing it with more chemicals, heating it and fixing it with a layer of varnish. Only when it was completely dry could a sheet of freshly prepared paper be applied to make a print. Too much or too little light and the photograph would be ruined. A speck of dirt or fingerprint on the glass? Ruined. A fidgety sitter? Another blurred ruin. No wonder the word Carroll returns to when describing his early experiments is 'failure'.

An absolutist when it came to his own conduct (after one minor academic disappointment in 1855, he recorded 'how many similar failures there have been in my life already'), Carroll had chosen a pastime that was measured in equally uncompromising terms. It left little room for creative accidents; like religion or mathematics, it was a matter of all or nothing. Photography also gave a new focus to many of his more private preoccupations. It widened his social horizons: in the following years, he would often call on new acquaintances with an album of photographs he had taken, allowing them to browse through his work before deciding whether or not to allow him to photograph them and – importantly – their children. Between 1856 and 1880, Carroll took approximately 3,000 photographs, about a third of which survive today, and although they spanned a wide range of subjects, including buildings and skeletons alongside friends, self-portraits and family groups, more than 50 per cent of his total recorded output were photographs of children, mostly young girls. That simple fact goes to the heart of why he found photography such an arresting pastime. It is not just that his camera allowed him to cut up the world into fragments and put it back together again in a new order, bringing out the hidden beauty in objects usually thought to be ugly or commonplace. It also offered a new way of grappling with the power of time.

In his 1887 article '"Alice" on the Stage', Carroll observed that whereas most adults are haunted by memory and desire, and so tend to 'look before and after, and sigh for what is not', a child can say 'I am all happy *now!*' and mean it. Photography brought these perspectives together. On the one hand, Carroll's early photographs of Christ Church's crumbling cathedral demonstrated that the camera added an extra layer of pathos to whatever it fixed in its sights, reminding viewers that time's relentless creep could only be halted by artificial means. More optimistically, a photograph could take a fleeting moment of happiness and fix it like a fly in amber. To someone who suspected that such moments were largely the preserve of childhood, this meant that a photographed child could never escape from the bubble of happiness he had created. A photograph reduced the world to more manageable proportions; it allowed a little child to stay little for ever.

These games of scale could be played with many subjects besides children. Anyone who possessed a camera could transform a giant into a dwarf, or perch the Alps on their sideboard; even Ruskin, who grew increasingly suspicious of photography's ambition to be taken seriously as an art form, was thrilled to discover the daguerreotypes of Venice that allowed him to pick up miniature versions of the Grand Canal and St Mark's Square and drop them into his pocket. But children were especially closely linked to the history of photography. As a young art it was often depicted as a child: in 1856, the year when Carroll bought his first camera, the pioneering photographer Oscar Rejlander exhibited his allegorical study *Infant Photography*, in which the hand of an artist is seen taking a new brush from the chubby grasp of a baby. Other early photographers were similarly drawn to children as subjects – during Carroll's visit to the Photographic Society in January 1856, he was especially impressed by a depiction of the princes in the Tower – perhaps because the photographic process depended on the prepared plate being perfectly clean and unblemished, making it in many eyes the ideal home for a child. In fact, children were notoriously hard to photograph, finding exposure times of a minute or more a particular challenge, and Carroll had to be resourceful in finding ways to prevent his subjects from dissolving into a fidgety blur. 'You don't seem to know how to *fix* a restless child,' he told the artist Gertrude Thomson in 1893. '*I* wedge her into the *corner* of a room, if standing, or into the angle of a sofa, if lying down.' One of his photographs of the Liddell girls shows how this pragmatic approach could produce unexpectedly beautiful results: placed in a triangular formation on a large sofa, the girls' dark heads are brought together at the centre of the frame, while their matching dresses extend in different directions, like three delicate petals of a single giant flower. But the intimacy of this photograph is hardly surprising when one considers how well Carroll had got to know the Liddell family by the time it was taken in 1858. For during the early years of his new hobby, the subjects who returned most frequently to

(l to r) Edith, Lorina and Alice Liddell (summer 1858)

stand, or sit, or sprawl in a relaxed tangle of limbs before his lens in Oxford were not his colleagues or friends. They were Alice and her sisters.

He probably first saw them through the window of Christ Church's library. From February 1855 he occasionally worked here as a sub-librarian, and from his office on the top floor there was an excellent view into the Deanery garden, where the children played. The first he met was Harry, then aged eight, whom he encountered by the river a few weeks after the Liddell family had moved into the renovated Deanery in February 1856; by the beginning of March they had become friends. 'He is certainly the handsomest boy I ever saw,' Carroll told his diary, and before long he had introduced himself into Harry's life by taking him on boating expeditions and offering to coach him at mathematics. The friendship was not an unqualified success: Harry was at best a workmanlike student, and he was unpromisingly keen on sport. (In one of the few photographs Carroll took of him, he presents a large cricket bat to the camera with something like reproach.) The Liddell girls were more interesting, especially after Harry left Oxford to attend boarding school. On 8 March, Carroll 'took the opportunity of making friends with little Lorina Liddell', the eldest daughter, at a musical party in the Deanery. Shortly before his new photographic apparatus arrived, again he knocked on the door of the Deanery, this time accompanied by Southey and his camera, hoping to take a photograph of the cathedral from the garden. And there he met Alice.

'The three little girls were in the garden most of the time,' Carroll recorded in his diary, and although they were not in the mood to be photographed 'we became excellent friends'. It was a day he marked 'with a white stone'. Possibly this was because one of the most famous classical sources for Carroll's diary marker, a complex elegy by Catullus, is partly addressed to 'Allius', but in any case there were plenty of other things about Alice that Carroll would have found attractive. She was born on 4 May 1852, a year which happened to fall exactly halfway between the first recorded uses of 'nonsense poetry' (1851) and the adjective 'no-nonsense' (1853), and if the close conjunction of those phrases neatly sums up a much larger struggle in the Victorian imagination, between a sensible but rather straitened approach to life and a much zanier alternative, it also hints at the mixture of qualities in Carroll's potential new friend. Alice was undeniably pretty, with dark elfin features, chestnut hair that was, unusually for the period, cut in a neat bob, and fashionable clothes chosen by her mother that made her look rather like a well-dressed doll. But as a child she also seems to have had a more tomboyish side to her character. In a photograph taken in 1858, which was supposed to act as a complement and visual corrective to Carroll's more famous photograph of Alice as *The Beggar Maid*, she is wearing her best outfit, a pale knee-length dress featuring tiny polka dots and complicated ruffled sleeves, but what draws the viewer's attention is an angry-looking bruise on her right shin and the fact that her socks are falling down. In her earliest writings, similarly, she is artlessly keen to show off. The handwriting in her letters is a neat copperplate, and the album of family crests she cut out from letters sent to her parents is assembled with meticulous care. Yet in Carroll's early photographs of her she seems to be smiling at some private joke, as if quietly amused at the fact that his camera, which revealed exactly what he had seen through the viewfinder, would never capture what was going on inside her head.

It has been suggested that Carroll may have seen a reflection of himself in the little girls whose company he sought. Boys from the higher social classes were dressed like their sisters for the first few years of childhood, in a form of sexless cotton smock, so it is certainly possible that seeing the Liddell girls in a large walled garden cast Carroll's mind back to Croft. Here was the perfect opportunity 'To be once more a little child' and a ready-made family to play with: 'three little sisters', as he would later refer to them in *Alice's Adventures in Wonderland*, punning on the fact that the 'Liddell' girls were also little girls. The question was why Alice rather than her sisters snared his storytelling attention; or indeed why he didn't choose a girl like Alice Murdoch, also born in 1852, one of the daughters of a civil servant he had met at a London party in June 1856, who was the subject of an awestruck quatrain he composed shortly afterwards, full of leaping exclamation marks ('O child! . . . on thy head the glory of the moon is shed | Like a celestial benison!'), which he later carefully inscribed opposite a photograph of her sitting on a chair with an expression of obedient wistfulness. Clearly Alice Liddell's personality was a significant attraction, as was her proximity in Christ Church, which made her friendship convenient as well as genuinely enticing. But another and much simpler reason may have been her name.

Some years later Carroll invented the word game Doublets, in which players were supposed to turn one word into another, making the dead live (DEAD, lead, lend, lent, lint, line, LIVE) or mice rats (MICE, mite, mate, mats, RATS). Transforming ALICE LIDDELL into LEWIS CARROLL, or performing the same trick the other way round, is impossible without falling into gobbledygook, although meeting someone whose name had the same shape may still have appealed to a writer who only a few weeks earlier had published 'Solitude'. But even without that sort of manipulation, the name Alice Pleasance Liddell was steeped in storytelling.

'Pleasance' means pleasure or charm, and it had featured in *The Passionate Pilgrim*, an anthology sometimes ascribed to Shakespeare, in lines that would later drift free from their original context and become a general maxim: 'Youth is full of pleasance, age is full of care.' 'Alice' was even more significant. In the first place, Carroll's recent parody 'She's All My Fancy Painted Him' had been based on William Mee's 'Alice Gray', a poem about unrequited love that begins 'She's all my fancy painted her, she's lovely, she's divine, | But her heart it is another's, she never can be mine.' More relevant still was Charles Lamb's essay 'Dream-Children: A Reverie', later reprinted in his *Essays of Elia* (Carroll owned the 1853 edition), which begins with the narrator describing a happy family scene in which his children, including a girl named Alice, cluster around him to hear a story. As he tells them how he courted their mother, another Alice, the features of his wife and daughter start to merge before fading away, and he wakes up 'quietly seated in my bachelor armchair, where I had fallen asleep'. The children are merely dreams of what might have been. It is a subtle exploration of the wishes we hang on to even, or perhaps especially, when they are impossible to achieve, and a section is quoted by the biographer Derek Hudson to support his view that 'a man who loved children as much as Dodgson did must, at some time, have thought of the unborn children who might have been his'. That is certainly possible. However, when Carroll came to use the phrase 'might have been' in 'Faces in the Fire', a poem first published in *All the Year Round* in 1860, it was in the context of a speaker who pores obsessively over his past, recalling the 'true love' whose 'little childish form' grew into that of a 'grave and gentle maid'. And in his memory childhood is where she remains most intensely alive, with her 'red lips' forever pouting for a kiss and her 'dark hair' forever 'tossing in the storm', frozen in time like one of the lovers on Keats's Grecian Urn. 'Ay, changeless through the changing scene,' he concludes, a ghostly whisper haunts him with 'The dark refrain of "might have been"'. That suggests more complicated fantasies than merely wanting to be a parent.

In Lamb's essay, 'Alice' and her brother slowly melt away, until nothing is left but their disembodied mouths, mournfully telling him, 'We are nothing; less than nothing, and dreams.' They are like a pair of Cheshire Cats who have lost their grins. But Carroll knew that there were other ways in which a girl could be made to disappear: in 1853 he had witnessed a conjuring performance in Oxford that included an early version of 'The

Lady Vanishes', in which the magician's assistant was placed on a table and covered in an item resembling a shower curtain, followed by a minute of 'swellings and writhings' that looked suspiciously like 'someone getting down through a hole in the table'. Clearly the magician was not a slick performer, but the length of Carroll's account indicates his interest in a trick that usually ended with the lady reappearing. It was another echo of his own determined efforts to ensure that nothing should ever be gone for good. It was also a perfect illustration of the way of thinking that would eventually produce *Alice's Adventures in Wonderland* and *Through the Looking-Glass*, in which all the individual fragments of his childhood and early adult life – thimbles, theatre, gloves, lessons, poems, puzzles, pictures, miscellanies and more – would be shaken together and transformed.

*   *   *   *

     *   *   *

*   *   *   *

ALICE

'When I used to read fairy tales, I fancied that kind of thing
never happened, and now here I am in the middle of one!
There ought to be a book written about me . . .'

<small>Lewis Carroll</small>, *Alice's Adventures in Wonderland*

Seven

Carroll had plenty of other distractions in the year he first met Alice Liddell. In January, he read a memoir of Charles Mathews, the actor who had achieved fame in the 1820s and 1830s with a series of one-man shows at Covent Garden and the Adelphi Theatre, in which he transformed himself into different characters with slick costume changes and a few twists of his rubbery features. Carroll ended the year by entertaining a group of eighty children at Croft School with a magic-lantern performance, during which he sang six songs and 'employed seven different voices', including Mooney and Spooney from *La Guida di Bragia*, while projecting a series of slides. (The tricks available to a skilled projectionist included making the figures on his slides dissolve, or change size, or transform into each other, although the whole enterprise was fraught with risk – one draught and these characters could be snuffed out like a candle; it was another set of ideas Carroll carefully stored away.) He was equally keen to try out different voices in his writing. In March, he met Edmund Yates, editor of *The Train*, and mentioned 'various subjects I thought of writing on: (1) Nursery Songs, (2) Cipher, (3) Paradoxes, (4) Betting'. If that shows the range of Carroll's literary interests in 1856, he was enjoying an equally scattershot social life. At various times in March he could be found watching the Oxford–Cambridge Boat Race from a steamer on the Thames, poking around in the smoky ruins of Covent Garden Theatre after a disastrous fire, enjoying a performance by soprano Jenny Lind in the *Messiah*, inspecting Roger Fenton's battlefield photographs from the Crimean War and reading *Hints for Emergencies* after watching a friend suffer a fit.

Carroll also found himself spending an increasing amount of time with the Liddell children. A river trip on 5 June featured ginger beer and lemonade, and 'wild spirits' from Harry and Ina; starting on 5 November, he devoted several days to photographing in the Deanery, and an hour in the schoolroom 'making them paper boats etc.' Four days later, another attempted visit ended when Mrs Liddell offered 'a hint that I have intruded on the premises long enough'. Within a few weeks Carroll no longer needed to worry about his presence being unwelcome. On 22 December, Dean Liddell, who had been suffering from serious ill health, left Oxford with his wife to spend the winter in Madeira. Their children remained behind, and for the next few months Carroll was a regular visitor to the Deanery, still trying to improve Harry's mathematical skills, and taking him and Ina on walks accompanied by their governess Miss Prickett. Keeping an eye on the Liddell children was for Carroll a happy coincidence of duty and pleasure; it was also a habit he found hard to break. On 17 May, reporting that 'to my great surprise' his attentions were being 'construed by some men' as a covert way of courting Miss Prickett, he resolved not to take 'any public notice of the children in future'. His resolution lasted exactly ten days. On 27 May, he arranged another photography session, and took Harry to watch some rowing, 'but I did not like staying long, as some of the men there were very undesirable acquaintances for him'. The same month produced his first mention of 'little Alice', when he reported that he had gone to the Deanery to give her a birthday present 'and stayed to tea'.

If she had studied him closely during this tea party, Alice might have seen Carroll checking his watch, because he continued to worry about wasting time. 'I am getting into habits of unpunctuality, and must try to make a fresh start,' he urged himself in 1856; the following year he lamented 'so much lost time', and drew up a tight schedule of topics he would learn off by heart ('Poetry, Elements of Mathematical Subjects, Proofs of formula, ditto . . .') to make up for 'a great deal of waste time'. Occasionally Carroll could poke fun at himself – 'Began a poem on "Nothing",' he noted in November 1856, 'but I have not made much of it yet' – but he was usually more rueful and fretful than this. In February 1858, two years after his last attempt to goad himself into action, he decided on another 'regular plan of reading', embracing mathematics, history, science, divinity, Old Testament history, Greek, Latin and 'miscellaneous Prose and Poetry', and a week later he embarked upon an additional 'system (which I hope to continue) of Scripture reading before chapel'. *Which I hope to continue*: it is a parenthesis packed with anxiety.

One pastime that allowed Carroll to place all this nervous activity on hold was photography. While the fiddly technical side of his hobby required quick and decisive movements, as he swirled his vials of chemicals or gingerly manipulated his glass plates, actually taking a photograph was largely a matter of silence and stillness. After arranging his sitter in a suitable pose, he had to remove the lens cap and watch as the seconds ticked by, until he calculated that he had captured a sharp enough image on the glass: it was a little oasis of calm in the middle of a busy period of action. It was also a process that was potentially ripe for comedy. In his short story 'A Photographer's Day Out' (1860), Carroll noted how easily a photograph could be sabotaged; although the story's romantic hero trains his camera on a picturesque pastoral scene, he fails to prevent real life from continuing while he waits for it to settle into a fixed image, and as a result his photograph ends up showing a large fuzzy spider (a farmer who has carried on walking) and a monster with three heads (a cow that has failed to pose properly). Previously, in his more famous poem 'Hiawatha's Photographing' (1857), a parody of Longfellow's relentlessly catchy 'Song of Hiawatha', Carroll had pointed out that the opposite problem could be equally awkward. Confronted by family members who chatter or squirm before his camera, the harassed photographer produces one failure after another; finally he groups the family together, 'And, as happy chance would have it | Did at last obtain a picture | Where the faces all succeeded: | Each came out a perfect likeness.' Inevitably everyone hates it. Carroll's satire was primarily directed against middle-class sitters who wanted an idealized rather than an accurate image of themselves – a common topic of debate in the early days of photography, when the claim that it told the truth came up against the desire to cast life in a more flattering light. 'Photography' literally means 'writing with light', because when the photographer succeeded in capturing an image, in theory it was the sun that did all the work. However, starting with the first commercially published book of photographs, Henry Fox Talbot's *The Pencil of Nature* (1844–46), with its carefully composed scenes of haystacks and fruit bowls, it soon became clear that nature's writing might benefit from being edited. This was not how the world appeared to an untrained eye; it was how it would appear if an artist were in charge.

Carroll enjoyed tackling this idea with comedy, but his satire was an inside job, because nobody was better at taking photographs that gave the illusion of spontaneity only after every element had been arranged like the pieces in a living jigsaw puzzle. Indeed, it would probably be wrong to say that Carroll enjoyed merely *taking* photographs; he much preferred *making* them, with careful lighting, discriminating use of costumes and props, and artful direction of his subjects. If that makes his approach sound theatrical, the comparison is a fair one. One of the most popular conventions of Victorian theatre was the 'point', reserved for moments of high drama, when an actor moved centre stage and froze in an attitude that expressed the character's emotional state: flared nostrils to demonstrate pride, a twirled moustache to signify cackling villainy, and so on. Less intensely melodramatic, but equally conventional, was the 'tableau', which concluded longer stretches of theatrical action by gathering together the play's major characters and expressing their relationships in spatial terms. Photography extended this idea indefinitely; each portrait was a little piece of domestic theatre that allowed the subject to hold a pose for ever.

Carroll's photographs of the Liddell sisters show some of the variations he played on this theme. One depicts them playing ukuleles in identical lace dresses, like a troupe of gypsy entertainers silently caught in mid-performance; another, taken in the Deanery garden in 1860, places Alice on a see-saw while Ina, in a matching dress and hat, stands to one side and gazes off into the distance. In both photographs, it is noticeable that Alice is the only girl who looks directly at the camera, as if daring it to single her out as the leading actress in the scene. The same pattern is repeated in another 1860 photograph of Alice and Ina, this time wearing oriental costumes under a large paper parasol: again it is Alice who peeks out from under her coolie hat and stares mischievously into the lens, while Ina leans on her chair and concentrates on looking soulful.

Fine art provided Carroll with another set of models to follow. His ambitions were clear from the way he signed some of his prints 'From the Artist', as they were from his construction of albums in which photographs were placed alongside copies of other artworks. (His first album, which contains a selection of his early photographs including some of Alice Murdoch and various family members, also features a print of an androgynous Ariel that Carroll trimmed into a neat semicircle and gummed into place opposite a song from *The Tempest*.) These ambitions were probably sharpened by his recognition that, when it came to painting or drawing, his skill would never reach the level of his enthusiasm. According to Collingwood, Ruskin's later advice to Carroll was that 'he had not enough talent to make it worth his while to devote much time to sketching', and judging from the surviving evidence, such as an awkward 1862 watercolour of the Liddell sisters sitting beside a river, this may have been curt but it was not wholly unkind. Carroll was cheerfully resigned to his lack of talent; when the artist E. Gertrude Thomson complimented him on his discernment as an art critic, he told her that he owed it to the fact that 'I can't draw in the least myself . . . One approaches a subject in such a delightfully open and unbiased manner if you are entirely ignorant of it!' Photography offered a satisfying alternative. From early on, Carroll was interested in photographs that had been touched up by painters, declaring them to be 'exquisite – equal to the best enamel', and he later sent some of his own favourite works to be coloured by hand, including two portraits of Alice and some of his child nudes, a process that made their skin tones look simultaneously more realistic and more artistic.

These overlaps between painting and photography drew attention to alternative ways of telling the same story. In April 1858, Carroll was given a copy of Henry Peach Robinson's 'exquisite' photograph *Juliet with the Poison Bottle*, an imitation 'taken from the life' of Charles Robert Leslie's painting *Juliet*. Both works depicted the young heroine of Shakespeare's *Romeo and Juliet* staring intently at a small glass bottle, and both froze the play's action at the moment when she is deciding whether or not to take the drug Friar Laurence promises will put her into a deathlike coma for 'two and forty hours' (a surprisingly precise number that would have held a particular appeal for Carroll) before she awakes 'as from a pleasant sleep'. Both works also caught the story at a narrative crossroads. This is one of many moments in the play when it could have a happy ending, as its characters hope, or an unhappy ending, as Shakespeare requires. Eventually death triumphs, as it must in a tragedy, but the sense of frustrated narrative potential is something Carroll would later remember when giving the fictional Alice a small glass bottle marked 'DRINK ME'. Sensibly, she decides to see whether or not it is marked 'poison', and eventually awakes from a pleasant sleep with no unpleasant after-effects. Nonetheless, the detail reveals Carroll's interest in stories that could take an unexpected turn.

This was especially important when it came to stories that already existed in several versions. Although the outcome of a fairy tale is rarely in doubt (Cinderella will always go to the ball, and Beauty will always fall in love with the Beast), as anyone who has attended a modern pantomime will know, it is far harder to predict how this conclusion will be reached. In his early photographs, Carroll enjoyed teasing viewers with a similar type of uncertainty, playing on the fact that the camera could seize on a particular moment in a story but could not reveal what happened before or after it. He also enjoyed the uncanny effects created by placing real people in fictional situations. In August 1857, he photographed Tennyson's niece Agnes Weld as Little Red Riding-Hood, and perfectly captured the fairy tale's slippery encounter of purity and danger. Wearing a dark cape over a white dress, and clutching a dainty wicker basket, Agnes is posed against an ivy-covered wall as a substitute for the fairy-tale forest. It was a popular subject at the time: in 1858, Henry Peach Robinson completed his four-photograph sequence 'The Story of Little Red Riding-Hood', and G. F. Watts produced an oil painting on the theme in 1864 that showed a young blonde girl swaddled in red like a warning flag; Carroll himself returned to the story in 1862, photographing the six-year-old Constance Ellison as an even littler Red Riding-Hood. What distinguishes his earlier photograph is its carefully staged ambiguity. In

January 1858, in preparation for the Photographic Society's fifth annual exhibition, where he had decided to display this portrait alongside three other works, he wrote accompanying verses that began 'Into the wood – the dark, dark wood – | Forth went the happy Child', and ended with her emerging from the wood into a 'sudden blaze' of noon: 'Nor trembles she, nor turns, nor stays, | Although the Wolf be near.' The photograph is far less reassuring. It is not just that Agnes Weld's expression could be read as genuinely terrified or just grimly resigned, making her a more interesting character than the serenely untroubled figure of Carroll's poem. She also has to peer down to meet the gaze of the camera, which is at roughly the same height as a wolf, so we must look at her through its hungry eyes. It is like a permanent stand-off between vulnerability and threat in which we have to work out whose side we are on.

Carroll's photographs of Alice Liddell are even harder to read. The statistics show that she shared most sittings with at least one of her sisters, although Carroll took slightly more photographs of her (twenty) than he did of Ina (sixteen), and far more than he did of Edith, who generally looked sulky and bored no matter how he posed her. Alice certainly seems to have been the only sister who found the experience exciting; not the chore of sitting still, perhaps, but she later recalled that being allowed into Carroll's darkroom was 'thrilling'. It was 'so mysterious', she wrote, 'we felt that any adventures might happen there'; watching Carroll gently rocking his glass negatives back and forth in a chemical bath, in particular, gave her the sensation of 'assisting at some secret rite usually reserved for grown-ups!'

Evidence of their growing closeness can be seen in several portraits. In May or June 1860, Carroll photographed her wearing a wreath of flowers as *Queen of the May*, the first non-celebrity portrait in an album that opens with figures such as Tennyson and the Crown Prince of Denmark, and in July she was back in the Deanery garden sitting by a potted fern. 'Miss Alice Liddell', Carroll recorded in his album in pencil, before going over the inscription with a less formal 'Alice Liddell' in ink. Both photographs drew on established cultural conventions. *Queen of the May* echoed Tennyson's 1833 poem 'The May Queen', in which a speaker named Alice boasts that 'There's Margaret and Mary, there's Kate and Caroline: | But none so fair as little Alice in all the land they say, | So I'm to be Queen o' the May, mother, I'm to be Queen o' the May.' The pot plant borrowed from the popular language of flowers, in which a fern signified 'Fascination', and it may also have been a joking allusion to the idea common among Victorian educationalists that children shared many characteristics with plants: naturally beautiful and wild, it took time and effort in a nursery to train them in the right direction. Both photographs posed an interesting technical challenge for Carroll, who was conscious of the trouble foliage caused when trying to capture delicate detail and shading ('green represents an obstacle to the photographer which has never been perfectly overcome', he reported that year in an unsigned exhibition review), but the still more puzzling challenge they pose to a viewer is the characteristic half-smile playing across Alice's lips. It is the sort of thing that reminds us we are looking at a real girl as well as Carroll's idea of a girl – one who was perfectly capable of generating her own meaning without being squashed into an allegorical framework.

Another uncrowned queen had featured in Carroll's celebrated photograph of *The Beggar Maid*, taken in the summer of 1858, which depicted a barefoot Alice wearing a tattered white dress, with her right hand cupped for money. Ragged children had long been popular subjects for sentimental paintings, although most artists tried to avoid dealing with the sort of genuine street waifs who might smell or steal the family silver. A more sensible approach, according to the artist Dorothy Tennant, was to equip oneself with a 'good supply of rags . . . carefully fumigated, camphored, and peppered', and with these 'you can then dress up your too respectable ragamuffin till he looks as disreputable as you can wish'. If no clean rags were available, she advised, the best way to find a suitable child was to give an ordinary boy sixpence to find 'a boy more ragged than himself', and to repeat the process until the right degree of picturesque poverty was reached: 'You can in this way get down to a very fine specimen.' Carroll was equally picky when it came to finding suitable models. In June 1857, he posed Alice modestly holding up her hands for charity while dressed in artfully torn clothing, but he was much less keen on real paupers; three

Alice Liddell as *The Beggar Maid* (summer 1858)

months later, while he was in Edinburgh, he became aware of several 'bare-footed children' in rags 'like ordinary English beggars', and was relieved when he moved further north and noticed 'many clean, well-dressed, and pretty children with feet and legs bare to the knee'. However, in choosing Alice to model as a beggar again in 1858 he was aiming not for social realism but for storytelling. This time the story he had in mind was 'King Cophetua and the Beggar Maid', a fable about a monarch whose aversion to women is overcome by a ragged girl he sees out of his palace window; inevitably they marry and live happily ever after. It was much admired by the Pre-Raphaelites (Edward Burne-Jones produced a large painting on the subject in 1884), who perhaps saw in it echoes of their own sexual habits, and also by Tennyson, who viewed it as a celebration of love's power to transcend social barriers. The specific poem Carroll probably had in mind was Tennyson's 'The Beggar Maid' (1842), which begins:

> Her arms across her breast she laid;
>   She was more fair than words can say:
> Bare-footed came the beggar maid
>   Before the king Cophetua.

The arms of Carroll's Alice are not laid across her breast; instead one hand rests on her hip, in a gesture that could be viewed as either childishly unselfconscious or deliberately provocative, and as a result her dress has slipped slightly off her left shoulder to reveal a nipple. To some viewers she is merely asking for charity; to others, aware that Carroll would have seen equally ragged child prostitutes on London's streets, she is offering something in return. What allows both sets of viewers to feel sure they are right is her expression, which manages to be simultaneously innocent and knowing, and both are supported by Carroll's decision again to lower his camera so that it is looking directly into her eyes. If her face is 'more fair than words can say', it is hard for us to decide what it means for us to be brought down to her level. Does it encourage us to share her innocence, or make us feel a sudden pang of guilt? In effect, *The Beggar Maid* works like one of those trick Victorian pictures, such as a charging horse that upon closer inspection turns out to be made of writhing female bodies, or a scene of happily playing children that is composed in the shape of a skull, by offering us two images in one.

Another complicating factor is the photograph of Alice dressed in her best clothes, which Carroll took on the same day and in exactly the same spot in the Deanery garden. Viewed next to each other, these images resemble two stages in a story, like the 'before' and 'after' pictures that in the 1870s would feature on cards produced by Thomas Barnardo to publicize his homes for destitute children, showing the miraculous transformation of grimy urchins ('Once a Little Vagrant') into cheerful and well-scrubbed members of society ('Now a Little Workman'). Alice's transformation is every bit as impressive, switching from beggar maid to queen in the blink of an eye. But of course the same photographs could be placed in a different order, and when this is done the genre of Carroll's two-stage narrative changes. If one version is a romance that shows a rapid rise from poverty to wealth, the alternative is a tragedy that shows an equally abrupt fall from respectability to the gutter. Put another way, although Alice probably enjoyed this photographic session as a dressing-up game, in which she could act out Tennyson's story of a beggar who is rewarded with love and riches for her 'dark hair' and 'angel grace', once Carroll sat down with the results he would have realized that, without using *Sylvie and Bruno*'s time-reversing 'Magic Watch', he had produced a pair of rival stories. One was a celebration of the transforming power of love. The other was a warning about how badly some romantic entanglements could go wrong.

*

Eight

I f photography reworked old stories it could also rehearse them. In spring 1860, Carroll photographed Alice feigning sleep while lying on a blanket in the Deanery garden. It was a popular pose for child subjects, making it easier for them to be captured without distracting blurs, and it added an extra layer of pathos to the scene by making it impossible to tell merely by looking at the child whether she was asleep or dead. Sleep was often understood by the Victorians to be a rehearsal for death, just as waking could be seen as a type of resurrection, and later in the century there was a macabre fashion for photographs of children on their deathbeds, which were kept by grieving families as a modern form of memento mori. Alice's baby brother James had died of scarlet fever in 1853, shortly before his third birthday, and had later been the subject of a painting kept in a shrine-like gilt travelling case, which showed him in a lace-edged nightgown apparently slumbering on his pillow, so the adult Liddells were clearly aware of these artistic conventions. A more cheerful model for Alice's pose, however, was

Alice Liddell asleep (spring 1860)

the traditional fairy tale of the Sleeping Beauty. This was an appropriate choice for a photograph, given the camera's seemingly magical power to cast people into a state of suspended animation; unsurprisingly, it was also a popular subject for *tableaux vivants* ('living pictures'), the Victorian parlour game in which participants told a story or recreated a famous painting through one or more carefully staged poses. In December 1860, the Liddell family hosted one of these social events in honour of a visit by Queen Victoria, whose son Albert, the Prince of Wales, had matriculated as a Christ Church undergraduate the previous year. Carroll was unimpressed by the Queen, waspishly telling his family that he was 'shocked' to discover 'how short, not to say dumpy, and (with all loyalty be it spoken), how *plain* she is', but he was delighted by the tableaux. 'One of the prettiest was Tennyson's *The Sleeping Princess*, acted entirely by the children,' he wrote, concluding that 'It would make a beautiful photograph.'

The poem he was remembering was in fact Tennyson's 'The Day-Dream' (1842), which contains a long description of the enchanted palace where Sleeping Beauty waits to be released from her spell. It was a good choice of subject, because part of the fun of a *tableau vivant* came from trying to hold a pose without sneezing or dissolving into giggles, and Tennyson's poem showed how this could also be achieved in writing. The longer 'The Day-Dream' continues with nothing happening, the more its stanzas start to look like coiled springs, where verbs and nouns push in different directions, and every line-ending quivers with frustrated potential. Only after the enchanted Princess is revived with a kiss does Tennyson's poem release its pent-up energy:

> A touch, a kiss! the charm was snapt.
>   There rose a noise of striking clocks,
> And feet that ran, and doors that clapt,
>   And barking dogs, and crowing cocks;
> A fuller light illumined all,
>   A breeze through all the garden swept,
> A sudden hubbub shook the hall,
>   And sixty feet the fountain leapt.

From 'There rose' to 'leapt' a single sentence extends across the page, like someone stretching after a long sleep. The figures in a photograph, by contrast, could never break out of their holding pattern, and this was an aspect of his hobby that particularly intrigued Carroll.

The first child outside his family to receive a letter that has survived was Kathleen Tidy, to whom he sent a penknife on her '72nd birthday' (actually her tenth) in 1861. Three years earlier, he had photographed her sitting up a tree, like a human version of the Cheshire Cat, and already Carroll's nervousness about her age was starting to show. The lines on her tartan skirt might look like neatened-up versions of the thin branches that criss-cross her body – indeed the whole composition is like a visual pun on her surname – but these branches stretch out far beyond the frame of the image. The implication is that although children may start out small, like seeds or saplings, they always grow larger. (Alice's experience in Wonderland, when she eats too much of the Caterpillar's mushroom and develops 'an immense length of neck' that rises 'like a stalk out of a sea of green leaves that lay far below her', is merely a speeded-up parody of this process.) But a photograph could control these events; it could take the idea of arrested development – a phrase that was first used in 1859 in relation to theories of evolution – and make it a cause for celebration.

The appeal of photography to Carroll may have been increased by those moments in his life when silence and stillness were beyond his control, as he opened his mouth to speak and discovered that his tongue had fixed itself into an equally static pose. The previous April he had sought help from Dr James Hunt, whose father had pioneered a form of therapy based on vocal exercises. This was greatly preferable to some of the alternative treatments available at the time, such as surgically removing part of the tongue or supporting it with a golden fork, although Hunt had his own quirks: his series of 'Hints to Stammerers' in 1861 recommended avoiding 'sexual excesses' and 'hot slops', and advocated regular boxing sessions for anyone who wanted to practise being 'calm and steady under excitement'. If Carroll had read Hunt's earlier book on stammering, however, he might have been encouraged by the testimonials it contained, including one from Charles Kingsley and another from a 'young clergyman' who had received treatment and become 'an eloquent divine'. Carroll might also have been drawn to some of the wilder reaches of this new science; the index to Hunt's manual on voice production included 'Dog, speaking' and 'Insects, Sounds of' alongside the more expected 'Articulation, Training of the Organs of'. 'I like Dr. Hunt's system very much,' Carroll told his sister Mary, and the following Easter he returned to Hunt's clinic near Hastings for more treatment. This time he was less impressed, and advised a friend against sending her daughter to Hunt, although apparently this was on the grounds of his class rather than his professional competence. 'I think him so little of a gentleman,' he told her, 'that it might be disagreeable for a lady to be in the house.'

One Hastings resident who made a more favourable impression on him was the writer George MacDonald. On a personal level they had much in common: both were religiously devout but fascinated by the occult, equally passionate about education (in MacDonald's 1864 novel *The Portent*, romance blossoms in the schoolroom for a character named Lady Alice), and willing to suspend the usual conventions of adult life when there was an opportunity for play. After the MacDonalds moved to London in 1859, Carroll was a regular visitor to Tudor Lodge, a skinny Victorian Gothic house tacked on to the end of a Georgian terrace in Camden, where his host enjoyed staging mock battles with toy soldiers in his study. Soon Carroll became an honorary uncle to their eleven children: MacDonald's son Greville recalled the 'annual treat' in which 'Uncle Dodgson' would take them on rides in the three-ton iron diving bell that was housed at the London Polytechnic, or to the Coliseum in Albany Street for performances that featured 'storms by land and sea on a wonderful stage', followed by bath buns and ginger beer. Greville's own father was not always so approachable: not only did MacDonald have 'a slight smack of the schoolmaster' in his writing, as one reviewer observed, he was also a strict disciplinarian at home and 'not averse to beating his children, especially boys, when occasion demanded'. His importance to Carroll, however, lay in his commitment to childhood in general rather than the specific welfare of his own children.

Some of MacDonald's stories lingered in Carroll's mind with particular tenacity. His 1858 fantasy novel *Phantastes*, for example, included 'a large white rabbit', a down-at-heel knight, talking mice and a magic mirror, while his 1862 tale 'Cross Purposes' followed the adventures of a girl named Alice who lives 'on the borders of Fairy-land', and after being shrunk to the size of a fairy ends up sinking into a magical pool: 'Down and down she went . . .' But although MacDonald's stories drifted much closer to allegory than anything in the *Alice* books – in *Alice's Adventures in Wonderland*, a golden key is simply a way of getting into Wonderland; in MacDonald's 'The Golden Key' (1867), in which another child journeys underground, it is the key to life itself – what joined the two authors was a conviction that stories were a way of addressing the childlike of any age. 'Oh to be a child again,' the narrator of *Phantastes* exclaims as he drifts in and out of his dreams, 'innocent, fearless, without shame or desire!' The aim of a story like this one, or like *The Light Princess* (1864), in which the heroine is deprived of gravity and spends her time bouncing around giggling delightedly to herself, was not just to create a new world in writing. Like Carroll's family magazines, their aim was to recreate the world around us by making us look at it in a different way – to be 'like a child', as the narrator explains in *Phantastes*, 'who, being in a chronic state of wonder, is surprised at nothing'.

*

Nine

Carroll's childhood reading had been far less exciting than this. In addition to the steady diet of religious books that was recorded in his reading diary, he had been allowed to work his way through a handful of fictional works. Some of these barely qualified as fiction at all, such as *Frank and his Father*, a set of Socratic dialogues intended to make biblical interpretation 'the subject of familiar and affectionate conversation between parents and their children'. Several of the other books Carroll read were written in the same style as the 'nice little stories' that Alice later tries to use as a guide to how one should behave in Wonderland, featuring 'children who had got burnt, and eaten up by wild beasts, and other unpleasant things, all because they would not remember the simple rules their friends had taught them: such as, that a red-hot poker will burn you if you hold it too long; and that, if you cut your finger *very* deeply with a knife, it usually bleeds'. These included Maria Edgeworth's *Early Lessons*, first published in 1801, in which little Frank learns about the dangers of hot wax, using a hammer, eating poisonous berries and so on, in a fictional universe that works rather like the public information films produced in Britain after the Second World War, where almost every object appears to be lying in wait for an unwary child, and every situation ripples with hidden menace. More realistic, and also more sadistic in tone, was Mary Sherwood's bestselling *History of the Fairchild Family*, in which a loving father takes his offspring to see a criminal rotting on the gallows as a warning to them not to quarrel, and a naughty girl who enjoys playing with candles is horribly burned to death. The title of this chapter is not 'Beware of Fire' but 'Fatal Effects of Disobedience to Parents'. Just in case young Charlie Dodgson was unsure of the recommended alternative, the first volume concludes with a triumphant deathbed scene in which a young boy, who is convinced he is 'rotten all through' like a diseased apple, informs his friends that 'I am not long for this world', and shortly afterwards expires, though not before reassuring them that as a result of his unwavering religious faith 'I am happy.' His name is Charles.

Published between 1818 and 1847, the three volumes of *The Fairchild Family* remained in print for over a century, even if successive editions pruned away their more bloodthirsty elements. They were still well enough known in the twentieth century for the Conservative MP Lord Frederick Spencer Hamilton, who had been forced to read them in the 1860s, to have attended a dinner party 'at which every one of the guests had to enact one of the characters of the book'. However, while some of Sherwood's details of gibbets and roasted flesh had a certain ghoulish fascination, it is highly unlikely that the books were as popular with children as they were with the adults who purchased them for the nursery. This was a common pattern. With a handful of exceptions, mostly in the form of fairy tales and nonsense verse, stories *for* children were usually tangled up with stories *about* children – not the characters who inhabited their pages, who were clearly adults in disguise, but all the young people at whom these books were targeted. Even when Victorian writers did not subscribe to the theological view that children were inherently wicked – 'Naterally wicious,' as Mr Wopsle observes with gloomy relish in Dickens's *Great Expectations* – it was still broadly accepted that the primary task of a children's book was to guide manners and improve morals; if it also entertained its readers, that was merely a dusting of sugar on the pill.

Two books that Carroll bought for the Liddell children show how some writers were starting to move away from these assumptions. At Christmas in 1856, in addition to giving Harry a mechanical tortoise, Carroll handed Ina a copy of *Mr Rutherford's Children*, a novel by 'Elizabeth Wetherell' (the American author Susan Warner) that had been published the previous year. Following a preface which explains that this was one of the books collected by 'Miss Alice' at the local parsonage, the story begins unpromisingly: the first time we meet the

two main characters, orphan sisters Sybil and Chryssa, one is teaching the other the Lord's Prayer, and shortly afterwards both vow to
learn a verse of the Bible every day. So far it is a routine example of
children's fiction that was morally improving but imaginatively back-
ward, and it may be that Ina did not read any further. However, if she
persevered, she would have discovered that as the story develops it
acquires an unexpectedly subtle edge. At one point a local boy shoots
off a toy cannon for fun, and although the girls are frightened, there
are no other consequences – he does not blast off his fingers, or accidentally hit a baby lamb, as he would almost certainly have done in
the fictional world of the Fairchilds. The story is equally interested
in seeing life from a child's point of view. Not only are we allowed to
spy on the sisters when they escape from adult supervision, as they
try to bleed one of their wax dolls by stabbing her arm with a pin and
gathering her stuffing in a wooden pail, we are also shown what the
world looks like through their eyes. One result is that even common
domestic objects acquire an unexpected sheen of poetry: the 'green
wire fender' that Chryssa notices is 'studded with brass knobs, like
the turrets on a battlement', or the bird's nest that resembles 'a
rough-looking little tea-cup'. This style is not consistently applied, as
it is in other contemporary works that try to imagine the world from
a child's point of view – such as the opening chapters of *Jane Eyre* or
David Copperfield – and the writing regularly slips back into finger-
wagging territory, as the children are told that flowers are '"as pure
as all Christians will be"', or are severely reminded by the local minister that, as they have two eyes and two ears but only one mouth,
they should '"see a great deal, and hear a great deal, and say very
little"'. Nonetheless, *Mr Rutherford's Children* offered a few glimpses
of what might be possible for a writer who took children seriously
and treated them sympathetically.

Catherine Sinclair's *Holiday House* (1839), a Christmas present from
Carroll to the Liddell sisters in 1861, removed the usual moral shackles
almost entirely. Carroll added an acrostic to the inside cover that placed
the girls' names in order of seniority:

Little maidens, when you look
On this little story-book,
Reading with attentive eye
Its enticing history,
Never think that hours of play
Are your only **HOLIDAY**,
And that in a **HOUSE** of joy
Lessons serve but to annoy:
If in any **HOUSE** you find
Children of a gentle mind,
Each the others pleasing ever –
Each the others vexing never –
Daily work and pastime daily
In their order taking gaily –
Then be very sure that they
Have a life of **HOLIDAY**.

This is far more crudely moralistic than anything in the novel itself. Just as Carroll's poem gives the illusion of emerging naturally from the names of the Liddell girls, so the events of *Holiday House* appear to spring out of real children's experiences. The plot features a series of minor domestic disasters, including a fire and a set of smashed china, but each time one of the children does something reckless they are punished merely by being left to feel stupid and embarrassed. There are no charred corpses and no lofty lectures; the adults' principal reaction to their children's pranks and pratfalls is good-natured laughter. While that might tax a reader's credulity, the children's own thought processes are often incisively described. At a tea party where there is nothing to eat or drink, they dream up alternative foodstuffs for themselves ('"would you like a roasted fly? ... or a slice of buttered wall?"'), and later on, when they need to draw water out of a well, one of the girls volunteers her thimble. There is even an attempt to capture what goes through the mind of a girl as she tumbles down a hill: 'Down she went! down! down! whether she would or not, screaming and sliding on a long slippery bank, till she reached the very edge of a dangerous precipice, which appeared higher than the side of a room.'

If this is more obviously threatening than the fictional Alice's fall down a rabbit-hole ('Down, down, down. Would the fall *never* come to an end?'), it is also infinitely more exciting than anything Alice Liddell would have been allowed to experience outside the world of books. Carroll's gift was probably chosen because the Liddells were about to have a holiday house of their own: a spectacularly ugly neo-Gothic folly named Penmorfa that Dean Liddell had designed on the coast of Llandudno in North Wales. The house was completed in 1862, and for nine years this was where the family spent its summers, but even armed with buckets and spades (one of Alice's surviving childhood letters refers to a 'frolic on the sand hills with Harry') it is hard to imagine the Liddell children being allowed to run riot in the same way as Sinclair's characters. Alice was an imaginative child, who enjoyed acting, having earlier played the fairy in an 1859 family production of *Cinderella*, and had a keen eye for the absurd, telling her grandparents that the lead tip of Tom Tower made it look 'as if it had an old black cap on his head', but her approved leisure activities would have been restricted to playing with her 'doll with wax legs and armes' [*sic*] and riding her pony Tommy, rather than setting fire to things or rolling down hills. She was also encouraged to read – there is a delicate pencil sketch of her from this period by the painter Ann Mary Newton in which her eyes are lowered on a book – but most of the works deemed suitable for young ladies of her class still bristled with instruction, usually offered in the hope that, as the prolific novelist Charlotte Yonge explained, 'children of gentle birth [will] learn . . . they hardly know how' through the example of 'their story books'. If she came across her own name in a book it was most likely to be that of a character like the Alice in Elizabeth Sewell's *Laneton Parsonage* (1846–48), who misbehaves and, after suffering a fever, is finally brought to recognize the error of her ways. Compared to that sort of tiresome moralizing, *Holiday House* offered a genuinely 'enticing' alternative.

Such books served adult as well as child needs, because by the early 1860s the question asked by the Red Queen in *Through the Looking-Glass*,

'"What do you suppose is the use of a child without any meaning?"', had already wormed its way deeply into the Victorian mind. Even if they were kept in the nursery rather than being sent out to earn a living, children had serious work to do in terms of the cultural meanings they were expected to support. Many of these were diluted versions of Romantic ideas that writers like Wordsworth and Blake had previously celebrated. Alongside the older evangelical view of children as little slivers of sin, they were now seen as holy innocents untainted by the dirty compromises of adult life; they were beacons of hope that lit up the moral fog around them. Even more optimistically, spending time with them allowed adults to feel that their own souls could be washed clean of the blots and scuff marks of experience, because if children were good for anything it was showing adults how to be good.

Naturally, none of this had much to do with the actual experiences of children, who were rarely taken in by such cloudy sentiment, and very unlikely to have the sort of blissfully untroubled lives that adults enjoyed dreaming up. Even a broadly happy childhood could include jarring events that continued to send out shock waves deep into adult life. Mary Howitt recalled being terrified by a boy telling her that the sound a grasshopper made was in fact a bloodhound dragging its chain around, while Thomas De Quincey noted in his autobiography *Suspiria de Profundis* that when he looked at clouds through a church window as a boy, he saw 'visions of beds with white lawny curtains; and in the beds lay sick children, dying children, that were tossing in anguish, and weeping clamorously for death'. The myth was far too powerful to be damaged by inconvenient examples from real life, however, and it was eagerly supported by many novelists, who filled their pages with minor child characters whose main function was to encourage adult readers to weep generous tears of self-pity.

Girlish boys were especially attractive angel-substitutes: alongside fig-ures such as Lucy Manette's little boy in *A Tale of Two Cities*, who dies with his golden hair neatly arranged in a halo on his pillow, we might recall that Arthur in *Tom Brown's School Days* is 'a slight pale boy, with large blue eyes and light fair hair', and is usually depicted in the novel's original illustrations looking modestly downwards under his clustering curls. (Carroll also liked boys with long hair: he declared that Hallam and Lionel Tennyson, aged five and three, whose fair hair tumbled down to their shoulders, were 'the most beautiful boys of their age I ever saw'.) Real girls were even better, however, and in novels from *Silas Marner* to *Little Dorrit*, the figure of a pure daughter or daughter-substitute who redeems the gruff hero through her selfless love became one of the mainstays of Victorian fiction. The same language infiltrated real human relationships. Lady Pleasance Smith wrote to her niece Mrs Liddell shortly before the family arrived in Oxford, to tell her that the three-year-old Alice 'looks like one of Raphael's Holy Family' who had 'strayed out of the picture'. The time she spent with Alice, which included feeding her grapes, led her to the conclusion that 'So attractive is innocence and beauty that we feel indeed that "of such is the Kingdom of heaven."'

Victorian Oxford was a place that took such ideas seriously. Edgar Jepson, who was a student at Balliol College in the 1880s, recalled the existence of 'a cult of little girls, the little daughters of dons and residents: men used to have them to tea and take them on the river and write verses to them'. His choice of 'cult' was interesting, because this word could refer equally to 'a collective obsession with or intense admiration for a particular person, thing or idea' (*OED* sense 3), or a small group of people whose beliefs and practices are 'regarded by others as strange or sinister' (*OED* sense 2b), but here he was probably thinking of individuals other than Carroll. One of Jepson's friends, the poet Ernest Dowson, who originated the phrase 'gone with the wind', and later wrote an article entitled 'The Cult of the Child', became so accustomed to the ritual adoration of little girls that after leaving Oxford he became hopelessly entangled with 'Missie, a pretty child of twelve or thirteen', who was the daughter of a Polish restaurant owner in Soho. 'I think that Dowson fell in love with her while she was still a child,' Jepson wrote levelly, and although Missie rejected Dowson's marriage proposal, their tortured relationship 'lasted until she became the lost love of his dreams'. That was a loyally romantic version of events. Dowson himself was refreshingly more direct, telling one friend that it was a pity 'the world isn't composed entirely of little girls from 6 to 12' and another that 'I think it possible for the feminine nature to be reasonably candid and simple, up to the age of eight or nine. Afterwards – phugh!'

Even by Oxford's standards, Carroll was unusually keen on the myth of a redemptive child. When Isa Bowman asked him if children didn't sometimes bore him, he replied that 'They are three-fourths of my life', and if that was not strictly true in terms of the statistics – he also had many adult friends, and almost half of his photographs were of subjects other than children – it is a fair assessment of the intensity and range of his child-related activities. Most of the artworks he singled out for special comment at exhibitions featured children: in 1864, the year when he was working most intensively on *Alice's Adventures in Wonderland*, these included Sophie Anderson's *Rosy Morn*, a painting that featured a girl lying in bed with her nightdress slipping off her left shoulder in the same style as *The Beggar Maid* (Carroll later called on Anderson to 'see if there were any little pictures' of the model), and Millais's *My Second Sermon*, a follow-up to his earlier painting *My First Sermon*, which this time showed the same girl, modelled by Millais's daughter Effie, fast asleep in a church pew. Equally winsome children were among the most popular subjects of the sculptor Alexander Munro, who allowed Carroll to take photographs of the work in his studios after their first meeting in 1858, and whose preference for white stone meant that cherubic figures like *The Sisters* (1857), a sentimental composition of two girls entwined in each other's arms, looked especially pure and clean when placed in the grubby adult world.

Carroll explored similar themes in his poem 'Stolen Waters', which he finished on 9 May 1862, less than two months before his famous river expedition with the Liddell girls, and which aches with nostalgia for the kind of childhood that can only ever exist in writing. It begins as a curious mixture of Keats's 'La Belle Dame Sans Merci' and Christina Rossetti's 'Goblin Market', a poem Carroll finished reading that month, as the speaker, 'Sir Knight', tastes the juice from magical fruit offered to him by an apparently beautiful woman; only after kissing her does he realize that she is a hag with a face that is 'withered, old, and gray'. What restores him to happiness is hearing a song about an 'angel-child', with golden hair that 'ripples free and wild', who sits in a garden and sings with the 'simple joy of being':

> And if I smile, it is that now
>   I see the promise of the years –
> The garland waiting for my brow,
>   That must be won with tears,
> With pain – with death – I care not how.

Like much of Carroll's writing, this is admirably clear on one level and oddly obscure on another. The surface meaning is that the speaker, having been seduced by adult experience, now realizes that he lives in a world of corruption, and can be redeemed only if he accepts the singer's advice to 'Be as a child', which will allow him to 'pass rejoicing through the gate of death | In garment undefiled'. (Like many of his contemporaries, Carroll took seriously the biblical injunction that 'Except ye be converted, and become as little children, ye shall not enter into the kingdom of heaven.') But the private significance of a garland of flowers as the gift waiting for him is one that only those who had seen his photograph of Alice as 'Queen of the May' would have understood. Viewed through the lens of this poem, Carroll's photograph becomes more than a window on the past; it is also a snatched glimpse of a possible future, depicting a paradise that has been lost but might yet be regained.

This is one context in which the prayers punctuating Carroll's diary should be understood. On 12 June 1865, as he awaited the publication of *Alice's Adventures in Wonderland*, he prayed 'on my knees' for God 'to give me a new heart'; a few weeks later he received a trial page from the printers, and again he prayed for help 'to begin a life of more regular habits'. It is tempting to view this desire to slough off his old self, like a snake shedding its skin, as a covert confession of impure thoughts if not impure deeds. But rather than seeing his child-friends as the cause of these feelings, it is more likely that Carroll saw them as the solution. 'It is very healthy and helpful to one's own spiritual life: and humbling too, to come into contact with souls so much purer, and nearer to God, than one feels

Carroll's portrait of himself with the MacDonald family (July 1863)

oneself to be,' he later claimed, and although boys could have this tonic effect if they were as beautiful as Tennyson's sons, they were rarely equal to 'the sweet-relief of girl-society'. Put simply, Carroll tended to view the company of girls as a little heaven on earth, and when they were absent in person he could create a comparable effect through his photograph albums: in March 1863, he began compiling a list of more girls 'photographed or to be photographed' which eventually ran to 107 names, including fives Alices, five Beatrices, six Constances and fourteen Marys.

Appropriately, in a period that saw the publication of Darwin's *On the Origin of Species* (1859), whenever possible Carroll tried to adapt to his environment. Kate Terry Gielgud, the mother of actor John Gielgud, recalled that although she was a shy child, she enjoyed her time with Carroll because 'he would talk with us (not *to* us)'. Carroll prepared carefully for these meetings: one of the books in his library was Sarah Tytler's *Papers for Thoughtful Girls* (1862), a conduct manual that gave advice on how to behave during different kinds of social encounter. He also did his best to fit in physically. One of his sweetest and strangest photographs, which he took in Hampstead in July 1863, shows him at the heart of the MacDonald family. Kneeling nearest to the camera, Mrs MacDonald is almost two feet higher than her son and three daughters, who are arranged in a neat arrow formation beside her. Lying at the tip of the arrow, his head just a few inches above the children around him, is a young man wearing a dark suit and a faint smile. Carroll looks perfectly at home.

The Victorian celebration of childhood was especially vulnerable to mockery when it took place in an artificial fictional environment. Fortunately, the best Victorian writers were capable of seeing through their own illusions. Even a novel like *The Old Curiosity Shop*, in which Dickens tried to highlight the 'innocent face and pure intentions' of his heroine Little Nell by surrounding her with 'grotesque and wild' companions, manages to put its own sentimental excesses into perspective. Drawn to mouldering churchyards as if by gravity, at one stage Nell is clasped in the arms of a tearful little boy who has heard that '"you will be an angel, before the birds sing again"', and she is then brought to the edge of a dark grave by an old man who leaves her 'looking thoughtfully into the vault'. On the next page, however, the narrative switches its attention to Dick Swiveller, a chirpy London clerk who prepares for a meeting of his literary club the Glorious Apollos by carefully pinning a length of black crêpe to his hat, pulling it down over one eye 'to increase the mournfulness of the effect', and soliloquizing that '"Twas ever thus – from childhood's hour I've ever seen my fondest hopes decay, I never loved a tree or flower but 'twas the first to fade away."' Nell's actual death is handled even less securely: although Dickens devotes several paragraphs of lachrymose prose to her corpse, firmly telling us 'So shall we know the angels in their majesty, after death', when her story is retold to some children at the end of the novel, they begin by crying but then laugh and are 'again quite merry'.

Carroll sometimes had equally ambivalent reactions to the myth of the perfect child. In 1880, he was asked to contribute to a volume intended to celebrate the birth of a colleague's daughter, and responded with an impeccably pious poem: 'What hand may wreathe thy natal crown, | O tiny tender Spirit-blossom, | That out of Heaven hast fluttered down | Into this Earth's cold bosom?' This goes on for another six verses in equally lifeless vein, but what saves Carroll from ridicule is the knowledge that in an earlier letter to the girl's father he had suggested an alternative that began 'Oh pudgy podgy pup! | Why *did* they wake you up? | Those crude nocturnal yells | Are *not* like silver bells', and continued by comparing a crying baby to the 'execrable noise' of mating cats. In 1862, Carroll decided to deploy the same double perspective in a new story where, as Dickens had earlier attempted to do with Little Nell, he would take the figure of a little girl and surround her with 'grotesque and wild' companions. This time the results would be remarkably different.

*

Ten

Carroll's diary entry for 4 July 1862 was typically sparse. He had spent the morning taking photographs of a mother and daughter introduced to him by a friend; 'Then they went off to the Museum', he reported, 'and Duckworth and I made an expedition *up* the river to Godstow with the three Liddells: we had tea on the bank there, and did not reach Ch. Ch. again till quarter past eight.' The true significance of the day was only recognized ten months later, when he added an extra note opposite his original entry: 'On which occasion I told them the fairy-tale of "Alice's Adventures Under Ground," which I undertook to write out for Alice.' It is interesting that he did not think the outing worthy of special remark at the time; it was not a 'white stone' day. Only in retrospect did he buff it up into a polished narrative in which perfect summer weather formed the perfect backdrop to a perfect story. Eventually two of the other participants, Robinson Duckworth and Alice Hargreaves, wrote about the afternoon in a similar way, although there are no independent witnesses to what happened on 4 July, and therefore no certain way of disentangling fact from fiction. But despite these caveats, reconstructing the events of that day still tells us a good deal about why Carroll ended up writing the kind of story he did.

Carroll's highlighting of '*up* the river' indicated that this was something of a new departure. He had already taken the Liddell sisters on several earlier boating expeditions, including one on 17 June when they had been caught in a thunderstorm and forced to dry off in a local cottage, but these usually involved rowing downriver, past Christ Church Meadow and on towards the grand Palladian villa and gardens at Nuneham Park. On 4 July, he decided to row upriver to Godstow, a hamlet about two and a half miles north-west of Oxford, where they could picnic on the riverbank and visit the picturesque ruins of Godstow Abbey. This was not as straightforward a journey as it might sound, because the Thames around Oxford is not a straightforward river. In Cambridge, punts and rowing boats idle along the River Cam between banks that are flanked by colleges and their neatly groomed lawns, but there is never any doubt over where they are going. Looked at on a map, the Cam is a smooth blue arc that bisects the city with a clear sense of purpose. The Thames is far more unruly – a watery tangle of tributaries and runnels and backwaters, some of which are broad stretches of water with views across open ground to the city's spires, and others that can unexpectedly narrow to a trickle and disappear.

Retracing Carroll's boat trip today is like a journey back in time. They probably hired a suitable vessel from Salter's Boat Yard by Folly Bridge, a short walk from Christ Church. The building they would have known is still there, its cream paint peeling in the sun, although these days the usual way to travel up the Thames is in one of the pleasure craft that putter along through water as green as turtle soup. The first thing that strikes a modern passenger is how fit Carroll and Duckworth must have been. It takes a pleasure boat at least thirty minutes to make the journey, and rowing against the current can take two hours or more. The first part of the journey is visibly hemmed in by modern life: on either side of the river there is a concrete ribbon of embankments and an architectural patch-work of housing developments. However, after passing through Osney Lock, and a tumbledown area of redbrick Victorian buildings, soon the river returns to a landscape that has remained practically unaltered for centuries. Willows bend overhead, as the banks are broken up by rushes and mildewed tree stumps; plump ducks bob up and down; rabbits lollop comically in the undergrowth; occasionally there is the metallic flash of a kingfisher. A few hundred yards beyond Osney Lock the river passes by Port Meadow, a bleakly beautiful expanse of grassland where cattle and horses have grazed for as long as anyone can remember. A few distant church towers peep over the top of the trees, so there is no danger of get-ting lost, but carrying on upriver it is easy to feel geographically and historically dislocated from modern Oxford.

What happened after Carroll reached Godstow was a picnic tea, and as often happened when he was with the Liddell girls, they demanded a story. 'Mr Dodgson told us many, many stories before the famous trip up the river,' Alice Liddell later recalled, and 'many must have perished for ever in his waste-paper basket'. It is unlikely that these stories were all invented on the spot. Given how many fragments from his family magazines later found their way into the *Alice* books, Carroll's method appears to have been to perform a handful of songs or skits he had prepared in advance, and to link them together with dizzying flights of improvisation. The environment on this particular afternoon was especially well suited to his storytelling skills, because as the Liddell girls gathered around him on the riverbank, their own situation already brought together several different strands of narrative. As an escape from the town to the countryside, a boat trip encouraged pastoral reflections; as an excuse to change into a new costume (Carroll favoured white flannels and a straw boater), it was a fairy tale in which old identities could become unfixed and uncertain; as an opportunity for a picnic, where linen was placed on the ground and ants got into the butter, it was a farce in which everything was shaken out of place.

Drawing inspiration from his surroundings, Carroll could have chosen from many different narrative scenarios. He could have anticipated Charles Kingsley's *The Water-Babies*, which would begin its serialization in *Macmillan's Magazine* the following month, by making a fictional Alice frolic underwater with assorted river creatures. Looking further ahead, he could equally have drawn upon the riverbank and its wildlife to create a different kind of underground adventure, as Kenneth Grahame would do in 1908 with the publication of *The Wind in the Willows*. Instead he decided to go deep into the landscape, and also into his own past, by sending Alice 'straight down a rabbit-hole', although he later confessed that at the time he did not have 'the least idea what was to happen afterwards'.

If the first move in the story that would later become *Alice's Adventures Under Ground* was a step in the dark, Carroll did not have to take it alone. By 1862, few literary environments were as crowded as the underground. His most obvious models were the traditional folk tales in which it was the location of Fairyland, a secret world that was usually entered not by falling down a burrow but by braving the damp and dark of a barrow, one of the ancient mounds of earth that pimpled the landscape and housed the bones of the dead. A related source was classical epic: Carroll would have known the journeys to the underworld in Book 11 of the *Odyssey* and Book 6 of the *Aeneid*, and it has been suggested that some details of Wonderland are conscious or unconscious echoes of these works, including the Queen of Hearts, whom Carroll described in 1887 as 'a blind and aimless Fury', and the bedraggled birds who pull themselves out of the Pool of Tears (compare the dead souls waiting on the bank of the Styx whom Virgil compares to a flock of birds). Dante's *Inferno* was another possible influence, producing creatures such as the Hatter and his friends, who are like comic versions of the souls who refused to learn from their mistakes when they were alive, and are therefore doomed to spend eternity stuck in the same punitive loops of behaviour.

Modern science fiction provided Carroll with a more recent set of narratives to play with, because plots in which characters fell to the centre of the earth, or discovered strange new civilizations underground, were increasingly popular in the nineteenth century. Earlier examples had included Ludvig Holberg's utopian satire *Niels Klim's Journey Under the Ground* (an English translation was published in 1845), which begins when the hero's rope gives way and he falls into an abyss, although he still has enough time to take a cake out of his pocket and eat it; and Jacques Casanova's five-volume *Icosameron* (1787), notable chiefly for a creepy plot that features twelve-year-old twins who marry and procreate, and multi-coloured hermaphroditic dwarfs who feed by sucking on each other's breasts. Other stories of the period claimed to be based on genuine research. During Carroll's lifetime there were determined efforts to prove that the earth was hollow, a theory that was held especially strongly by the American author and fantasist John Cleves Symmes, and these debates later influenced several more novels, including Jules Verne's adventure yarn *A Journey to the Centre of the Earth* (1864), and Edward Bulwer-Lytton's *The Coming Race* (1871), an occult fable in which mankind's overlords turn out to be living under our feet.

Each of these works is a good example of how not to write *Alice's Adventures in Wonderland*. Their enquiries into how life could survive underground, which they grapple with earnestly and at length, Carroll either ignores completely or passes over in a phrase. Arguments over whether there was another sun at the earth's core, for example, or whether there were holes in the poles that allowed light into the interior, only enter Wonderland with Alice's glancing reference to it being 'a very fine day'; exactly how the Queen of Hearts grows her roses, or how anyone can see in a place that logically should be as dark as the grave, is quietly ignored. Carroll would later perform a similar sleight-of-hand in *Through the Looking-Glass*, where the presence of the Jabberwock would have reminded his original readers of the gigantic bones that were being uncovered and pieced together at the time by palaeontologists, a process that in the popular imagination was gradually turning the underworld into a land of dinosaurs, a word meaning 'terrible reptile' that was coined by Sir Richard Owen in 1842; yet while Jules Verne's novel extends a battle between two prehistoric sea monsters into an epic narrative set piece, Carroll's story is tucked away inside a poem of fewer than thirty lines.

Even without specific literary or scientific associations, the underworld was a place to which the Victorians increasingly enjoyed making mental excursions. The earth's surface was being reconceived as a skin tightly stretched over the veins of communication and arteries of power that kept modern life moving, and what lay beneath was a place where stories germinated in the dark like mushrooms. Above ground might have been where most people spent their lives, but as John Hollingshead observed in *Underground London*, published in the same year as Carroll's boating trip, it was in a civilization's subways and hiding-places that the imagination could 'run wild' and indulge in a 'passion for dreaming'. The underground was full of secrets and surprises, like the fossils that had forced Victorian geologists radically to increase their estimate of the earth's true age, or the human skeletons that would in the 1920s be found clinging together in a Victorian punt trapped in one of Oxford's hidden streams. At the same time, it was increasingly thought of as a place where the future was being shaped. Recent legislation to protect women and children working in mines had reminded many people that the Industrial Revolution had been built on foundations of coal. Meanwhile, invisible networks of gas mains and drains were starting to thread their way underneath Britain's major towns: in 1865, Carroll saw Ford Madox Brown's 'remarkable' painting *Work*, which depicted a group of navvies digging up a road to lay new sewers, and Dean Liddell's interest in sanitation was famous – one German professor who wanted to speak to him was told that he had 'just gone down the drain' underneath Christ Church Meadow; when he went in search of him, 'a loud voice was heard from below, and soon the majestic head emerged from the lower depths'.

Further afield, there was the Metropolitan Railway, the world's first underground line, which started from Paddington station, the terminus for the Oxford train, and in 1862 was close to completion after years of construction that had left ragged scars across London. The inaugural trip had taken place in May, two months before Carroll took Alice and her sisters upriver, although there would be further problems before the first paying customers could enter the Metropolitan's smoky tunnels in January 1863. (The seventy-eight-year-old Lord Palmerston excused himself from the official opening by explaining that at his age he wanted to remain above ground for as long as possible.) On 4 July, the day when Carroll sent Alice down a rabbit-hole, *The Times* carried a report describing efforts to clean up after a storm had caused the Fleet sewer to burst, flooding the Metropolitan works with evil-smelling sewage, which may have been another factor behind Carroll's interest in the risk of drowning underground.

While there was a growing interest in lives that were usually hidden out of sight, like those of the poor who were forced to live in London's damp cellars ('To feel most at ease,' wrote the journalist Blanchard Jerrold, 'like the mole, they must work their way under the earth's surface'), the same ideas could be adapted to explore the mysterious forces buried deep inside each one of us. Some of these metaphors were left over from Romantic literature. Carroll especially admired Blake's *Songs of Innocence and of Experience* (1794), where a poem like 'The Garden of Love' not only laments that the garden where the speaker used to play is now 'filled with graves', but demonstrates the result in Blake's illuminated design, where the poem is printed directly underneath a yawning grave, and squiggly worms infest the writing like maggots working their way into a corpse. More recent poems like Matthew Arnold's 'The Buried Life' (1852) had used similar metaphors, arguing that the demands of modern life had driven our true selves so far underground we no longer knew where to find them: 'And long we try in vain to speak and act | Our hidden self, and what we say and do | Is eloquent, is well – but 'tis not true!' Other ideas, such as the association between a hidden world and memory or dreams, were more traditional, but they too were starting to take on renewed force with the emergence of modern psychology. Carroll had already shown his interest in such ideas, with the photograph that depicted Alice Liddell asleep implicitly asking us to imagine what she was dreaming about. Now he invited us inside her head to have a look around.

'The whole thing is a dream,' Carroll told the popular dramatist Tom Taylor, 'but *that* I don't want revealed till the end.' *Alice's Adventures Under Ground* provides an early glimpse of these delaying tactics, because at no point are we explicitly told when Alice falls asleep. At the end of the first paragraph, we observe as 'a white rabbit with pink eyes ran close by her'; at the start of the second paragraph, we overhear it saying '"dear, dear! I shall be too late!"' Only much later do we realize that Alice has drifted off in the blank space between paragraphs. It is a good introduction to a story that in its published form would be full of events that occur, or fail to occur, in an equally charged liminal space, from the lack of time 'to wash the things between whiles' that the Hatter laments at his endless tea party, to the 'secret, kept from all the rest | Between yourself and me' that the White Rabbit mysteriously alludes to in the courtroom. It is also a helpful reminder that, as several nineteenth-century dream theorists noted, even extraordinary events seem perfectly ordinary when we are asleep. 'Nothing', Robert Macnish observed in his popular study *The Philosophy of Sleep* (1830), 'however monstrous, incredible, or impossible, seems absurd' in a dream: scenes can switch as suddenly as the turning of a page; time and space can be distorted or fragmented; people from different periods of history can be 'brought together in strange and incongruous confusion'. Moreover, while a good deal of our daily experience 'is apt to resolve itself into a dream' in 'magnified and heightened' forms, he explained, what is happening around us while we sleep can also influence our unconscious thought processes. Macnish's examples included our bedclothes falling off at night, which might make us dream about walking around naked, or our feet slipping over the side of the bed, which might produce nightmares in which we teeter on the edge of a precipice or experience the sensation of falling.

Carroll provides several clues that certain parts of Alice's dream have similar causes. After she is attacked by the pack of cards, she wakes up to find her sister 'gently brushing away some leaves that had fluttered down from the trees on to her face', and in the published version of the story the Mock Turtle's song is later given added poignancy by 'the lowing of the cattle in the distance' that her sister hears, reminding us that mock turtle soup was usually made from a boiled calf's head. Carroll may also have been aware that children were thought especially susceptible to such effects. He owned a copy of *The Literature and Curiosities of Dreams*, an anthology first published in the same year as *Alice's Adventures in Wonderland*, which includes a section on the 'Dreams of Children' that notes the 'agitation resembling delirium' a child may suffer when awakening from a disturbing dream. (An 1851 article in *Household Words* suggested that children may also be 'more liable to dreams', as they are 'more subject to a variety of internal complaints, such as teething, convulsions, derangement of the bowels, &c.') In fact, as several of Carroll's contemporaries pointed out, dreams did not care greatly for the age of the dreamer, because in sleep even the most jaded adult could think like a child again. 'In the revival of young experience, the delicious fullness of childish sensation, the dreamer may be said to enjoy a prolongation of life's golden prime,' explained the influential psychologist James Sully. 'He sees things with the glad dilated eyes of the child artist, and feels once more the masterful spell of earth's beauty.' Dreams were more than an escape from the ordinary demands of consciousness; they were a form of time travel.

Beginning with a rabbit that disappears and then reappears, like a magic trick that has somehow infiltrated real life, Carroll's narrative quickly generates a genuine dream's mixture of vagueness and vividness.

Usually, when we say that someone writes like a dream, it is an empty cliché, implying a style that is effortless or easy on the eye, but writing like a dream is exactly what Carroll attempted to do in this story, by pulling apart the world Alice Liddell knew and reassembling it in a crazily jumbled form. Reading the final version is like dreaming while we are awake. One result of this process is that in Alice's dreamland even characters like a hookah-smoking caterpillar are made to seem as unexceptional as houseflies; another is that Carroll takes ordinary fragments of above-ground life and turns them into something extraordinary.

Several minor characters are lightly disguised versions of Alice Liddell's family and friends. The Duck, Dodo, Lory and Eaglet that the fictional Alice encounters, for example, are walk-on parts for Duckworth, Dodgson, Ina and Edith, the remaining members of the boating party, while lines such as 'really the Lory and I were almost like sisters!' were evidently included as audience-pleasing in-jokes. Similarly, the tedious passage of history that the Mouse reads to them when they are wet, explaining that it is '"the driest thing I know"', is taken from a book the young Liddells were studying at the time, Havilland Chepmell's *Short Course of History* (1862), while Alice's opening address to the Mouse, a tactlessly chosen '"Où est ma chatte?"', is the first sentence in a French primer entitled *La Bagatelle* (1804) that also included lessons on 'The Rabbit', 'The Fall' and 'The little girl who is always crying'. Armed with these early examples, perhaps it is not surprising that critics have sought specific sources for every other detail of Alice's adventures, from William Empson stating that 'The White Rabbit is Mr. Spooner to whom the spoonerisms happened', to the editors of *The Alice Companion* suggesting that the model for the Mock Turtle was probably Carroll's friend Henry Parry Liddon, on the grounds that in Oxford he had been in hot water for his Anglo-Catholic religious views, and he would have been easy to cook with a lid on.

But although such attempted identifications are understandable, they are also impossible, because Alice is not the only character who would find it difficult to answer the Caterpillar's question '"Who are *you?*"' Almost nobody in the story is straightforwardly singular – even the White Rabbit pops up again as a herald – and almost no event happens in only one way. The croquet game is a memory from the Deanery garden that has collapsed into some pages from a naturalist's handbook. The description of Alice and her friends swimming in the Pool of Tears, and emerging 'dripping wet, cross, and uncomfortable', brings together a distorted echo of the earlier boating trip Carroll had taken with the Liddell sisters on 17 June, and stories such as *Der Struwwelpeter*, Heinrich Hoffmann's grotesque cautionary tales, translated into English in 1848, in which two cats mourn a little girl who has been burned to death: 'their tears ran down their cheeks so fast | They made a little pond at last.' The appearance of a mouse represents an even more complicated coil of memories. Seen from one angle, it is a domesticated version of the savage rats that Henry Mayhew's sprawling sociological survey *London Labour and the London Poor* had revealed were living under London's pavements, capable of stripping the flesh from any creature that fell into the sewers (Carroll owned a copy of the 1861–62 edition); seen from another angle, it is a grim private joke about the humane mousetraps Carroll preferred, which allowed him to catch mice and drown them underwater. Trying to pin the passage down to a single source is no more helpful than the kind of analysis offered by the period's dream almanacs, in which 'To dream one makes pies is joy and profit', walnuts signify 'difficulty and trouble', and so on. Ultimately, Alice's adventures offer something much more interesting: the opportunity to explore a world that exists only in the space between our ears.

Much of this world simmers with latent menace. In Carroll's revised version of the story, the first word in the Dormouse's list of 'everything that begins with an M—' is 'mouse-traps', which suggests its awareness of the dangers lurking in Wonderland, but in *Alice's Adventures Under Ground* it is still a surprise to discover how often Alice finds herself being threatened by her own dream. Almost all the creatures she meets are cranky rather than cuddly, from a young crab that talks 'snappishly' to a mouse that 'growls'; even the White Rabbit is pictured in one of Carroll's illustrations confronting Alice in a taut boxer's stance. In addition to the dangers of execution or being 'snuffed out like a candle', at various times Alice risks breaking her neck against a ceiling, being 'trampled' under the feet of a giant puppy, encountering a pigeon that flies into her face 'violently are ferrets! Where _can_ I have dropped them, I wonder?" Alice guessed in a moment that it was looking for the nosegay and the pair of white kid gloves, and she began hunting for them, but they were now nowhere to be seen — everything seemed to have changed since her swim in the pool, and her walk along the river-bank with its fringe of rushes and forget-me-nots, and the glass table and the little door had vanished.

Soon the rabbit noticed Alice, as she stood looking curiously about her; and at once said in a quick angry tone, "why, Mary Ann! what _are_ you doing out here? Go home this moment, and look on my dressing-table for my gloves and nosegay, and fetch them here, as quick as you can run, do you hear?" and Alice was so much frightened that she ran off at once, without

One of Carroll's hand-drawn pages for *Alice's Adventures Under Ground*

beating her with its wings', and having her toes trodden on by the Gryphon and Mock Turtle.

Carroll was fully aware of the risks a child faced if she wandered off in the real world and not merely in her imagination. One of the books he owned was a memoir about Charley Ross, a four-year-old who disappeared in 1874 after a botched kidnapping, and towards the end of his life, after he learned that Isy Watson, a child model he had been drawing at a friend's London studio, had travelled home alone, he fretted that she could have been 'lost, or stolen', noting that in the area where she lived 'she might at any time be inveigled away by some evil-disposed person'. Children might not be safe even if they stayed close to home: in 1857, Carroll recorded in his diary that a seven-year-old girl had been killed by a falling tree while playing in Oxford's Broad Walk. Such was his gloomy relish for such stories that the longer Alice spends underground the more her adventures start to resemble a narrative game of Doublets, in which the aim is to take 'Alice' and ensure that by the end of her story she is 'Alive'. This atmosphere of danger is partly generated by the withholding of so much information. It is intensified by the fact that Alice does not understand everything she encounters – her models of how to behave are repeatedly shown up as hollow shams – and the reader is rarely given any privileged insight into her experiences. This is probably the most disturbing feature of Carroll's story: it is a dream version of the problems encountered by many children in waking life, where adults can be arbitrary and terrifying creatures, and a mother who shouts 'Go to your bed!' may not be experienced very differently to a storybook character who shouts "'Off with her head!'"

What reassures us is that, although at one stage Alice cries out, "'I am so tired of being all alone here!'", throughout her adventures she is never alone. Despite the fact that he never introduces himself to us, and remains hidden in plain sight for long stretches of writing, the story's other most important character is Carroll's narrator. Often he interrupts himself to confide an extra detail (he is very fond of brackets); at other times he teases Alice for her lack of understanding, or sees things through her eyes, or looks on with studied detachment as events unfold. At his most interesting he is capable of generating several perspectives at once. The result is a fly-eyed narrative style that explores the capacious and capricious imagination of a child by inviting us to see things from more than one point of view.

*

Eleven

Vividly remembering his experience of reading Tolkien's fantasy novel *The Hobbit* as a child, Francis Spufford has acknowledged that, once his desire to read outstripped his vocabulary, there were 'holes in the text corresponding to the parts I couldn't understand'. A child who opens up *Alice's Adventures Under Ground* soon comes across similar lacunae – *Longitude, Latitude, nosegay, draggled, usurpation, prattled, languidly, chrysalis, after-time* – although Carroll's flow of plot is usually strong enough to carry them across any gaps of meaning, and if they remain puzzled they can comfort themselves that they are in the same position as Alice herself. But although the holes in a reader's vocabulary can be filled in with a dictionary, there are holes in the historical record that cannot, and the story of how *Alice's Adventures Under Ground* developed from a spoken narrative to a published book is as riddled with uncertainty as a piece of Swiss cheese.

Strictly speaking, an adventure is 'That which happens without design', and although the day after their boat trip Alice pestered Carroll to write down his story, and 'kept going on, going on' until he agreed, he soon encountered problems in trying to recreate what had been largely a piece of improvisation. Although the next day he jotted down some 'headings' on the train to London, it would be several months before he completed the text, and almost two years before all the illustrations were slotted into place. The result was a narrative as episodic in its construction as it was in its final written form.

If Carroll's other commitments were partly responsible for this, so was the amount of time he continued to spend with the Liddell children. On 1 August, he heard 'the Dean's children' sing the popular song 'Beautiful Star', which would later reappear in his story in a playfully muffled form as 'Beautiful Soup'; from 3 August onwards, he referred to them simply as 'the children', and he paid them regular visits, enjoying 'parlour-croquet' on 21 November and three hours of 'games and story-telling' on 4 December. Another factor in Carroll's long gestation of Alice may have been his reluctance to finish it. On 6 August, after he failed to amuse the Liddells with a new word game, he reported that 'I had to go on with my interminable fairy-tale of "Alice's Adventures."' This was probably an expression of impatience, but Carroll would have known that 'interminable' was also used in religious contexts to refer to what was joyfully infinite or boundless: in Milton's Samson Agonistes, the Chorus refers to those who 'would confine th'interminable', where the word is effectively a synonym for God.

In March the following year, he received an invitation from Alice to accompany her to Oxford's illuminations, the fiery decorations that were part of nationwide celebrations to mark the Prince of Wales's wedding. 'We soon lost the others,' he reported happily, and three days later he began a poem 'in which I mean to embody something about Alice (if I can at all please myself by any description of her)', which he eventually published as the acrostic that appears at the end of Through the Looking-Glass. On 4 April, he took the children to see the 'Enchanted Palace of Illusion', performed by the celebrated Viennese conjurer and self-styled 'Greatest Wonder of the Age' Herr Döbler, and later that month there were 'almost continuous' meetings. In May, he gave Alice a copy of Charlotte Yonge's 1847 novel Scenes and Characters as a birthday present, and heard back from George MacDonald, to whom he had sent a draft of his own story, with the recommendation that he should publish it. (The MacDonalds' son Greville, then aged six, 'exclaimed that there ought to be sixty thousand volumes'.) And then, after another boat trip on 25 June, Carroll broke off all significant social contact with the Liddells – or they broke it off with him – for several months.

The next reference in Carroll's diary is a terse 'Met the Liddells' on 16 October, followed by another blank until some theatricals in Christ Church on 5 December, when he reported that 'Mrs. Liddell and the children were there, but I held aloof from them, as I have done all this term.'

Inevitably this is a vacuum into which many different theories have been sucked. The uncertainty over what happened is compounded by the fact that when Carroll's relatives went through his diaries after his death, one of them cut out a page that followed his entry for 27 June: 'Wrote to Mrs. Liddell, urging her ~~either~~ to send the children to be photographed.' Presumably someone was uncomfortable about the suggested alternative, and crossed out 'either' in a clumsy attempt to make the entry look complete. A pencilled note headed 'Cut Pages in Diary' in the Dodgson family archives summarizes the contents of the excised page: 'L.C. learns from Mrs. Liddell that he is supposed to be using the children as a means of paying court to the governess – He is also supposed by some to be courting Ina – .' Carroll cross-referenced his original diary entry with the earlier rumour about Miss Prickett in 1857, which indicates that his avoidance of the Liddells may have been a strategic withdrawal designed to avoid embarrassing them any further: pointing out that he was 'holding aloof' at a theatrical occasion was perhaps a private reminder to himself that he too was playing a role.

Oxford gossip works in powerful and unpredictable ways: while the high walls of a college can look as if they are turning their back on the outside world, they also magnify any stray whispers picked up within. The 1825 journal of Frederic Madden, who had recently matriculated as a student at Magdalen College, is far racier than anything in Carroll's diaries, with their steady stockpiling of data, but it shows how easily social encounters in the University could encourage gossip's characteristic mixture of public shock and private glee:

Walked again in Chr. Ch. meadow with Mr. Young. He told me that he had been in St. John's Gardens, the most beautiful spot in Oxford and had *witnessed* a curious scene about *one o'clock in the day*, namely in a sly corner he surprised one of the very revd. fellows of ――― College *in flagrante delicto* with Miss Brown, eldest daughter of the *Rev. Proctor*!! So much for Oxford morals! He said the man was old enough to be her father, and the girl, a very pretty, fair creature! Oh shame! The old fellow buttoned up his inexpressibles, and set off with his *inamorata* to Trinity gardens, where he probably renewed his games.

In such a small world, even innocent diversions could be interpreted as thrillingly wayward errors of judgement: one of Dean Liddell's blotting paper sketches shows a man, his boater set at a rakish angle, being rowed along by two young women, and it would not have taken an especially nosy colleague to wonder what was on the Dean's mind as he drew it.

There may also have been some uncertainty in the Deanery itself. Looking back on events in 1930, Ina told Alice that the biographer Florence Becker Lennon had asked her why Carroll stopped coming to the Deanery. 'I think she tried to see if Mr. Dodgson ever wanted to marry you!!' Ina wrote, with a double exclamation mark that perhaps indicated how ridiculous the idea was, or alternatively how close Lennon had come to stumbling upon the truth. Her next letter to her sister was equally ambiguous. 'I said his manner became too affectionate to you as you grew older and that mother spoke to him about it,' she explained, 'and that offended him so he ceased coming to visit us again, as one had to find some reason for all intercourse ceasing.' But this could indicate either that 'his manner became too *affectionate* towards you' (i.e. he behaved inappropriately), or 'his manner became too affectionate towards *you*' (i.e. I was jealous of the attention you were getting, or glad that you were attracting it rather than me). Even her final comment that 'Mr. Dodgson used to take you on his knee. I know I did not say that!' is not straightforward. Was she reminding Alice of a childhood secret they had shared, or complaining that Lennon had tried to put words into her mouth?

Some of her contemporaries were more forthright. 'When the Alice of his tale had grown into a lovely girl', according to the daughter of one of Carroll's friends, 'he asked, in old-world fashion, her father's permission to pay his addresses to her', and Dean Liddell 'rebuffed Mr Dodgson's appeal in so offensive a way, that all intercourse between them ceased.' No evidence is given to support this claim, but it is in the nature of gossip to feed on itself when no fresh information is available, so it is not a surprise to find Lord Salisbury writing even more confidently in 1878: 'They say that Dodgson has half gone out of his mind in consequence of having been refused by the real Alice (Liddell). It looks like it.' Nothing Carroll himself said could ever have competed with the anonymous force of 'They say', but it is worth noting that the only other occasion on which he recorded an intention to 'hold aloof' from someone was when he felt that his friendship was not properly valued by a group of girls, who were 'perfectly obliging, so long as what I want exactly suits their inclinations – but will not go an inch further'. Two days after writing this, he sent his love to one of them, 'but I shall still hold aloof from calling at the house'.

Unless he was merely the victim of an unchecked rumour rippling around Oxford, Carroll certainly seems to have said or done something to disturb the Liddells. Alice later recalled that 'my mother tore up all the letters that Mr. Dodgson wrote to me when I was a little girl', which implies a more violent act than simple waste disposal, and one letter she sent to her mother certainly might have raised an eyebrow: 'Mr. Dodgson wrote and asked me (for fun) if I would send him a piece of hair (he did not mean [for me] to send it) so I send [sic] him really a piece and he wrote and told me I was stupid.' Then there was Carroll's birthday gift of *Scenes and Characters*, a story about three girls who are left alone in the care of a governess after their parents travel abroad for their health, and try to turn their village into 'Dreamland'. If that was supposed to evoke happy memories of the time the senior Liddells had spent in Madeira, it was hardly tactful of Carroll to have chosen a novel that contains a whole chapter on 'Village Gossip', let alone one in which the mother dies on page three. Mrs Liddell might have been even more nervous if she had read Carroll's diary entry after his final boat trip with her daughters: 'A pleasant expedition,' he wrote, 'with a *very* pleasant conclusion.' Was this a kiss? And if so, was it a ceremony conducted with the chaste solemnity of the Dodo giving Alice a thimble, or was it just a spontaneous muddle of mouths?

This uncertainty over Carroll's intentions and motives should be viewed in the context of other contemporary relationships. Victorian life was full of equally odd couples. In the absence of a clearly defined period of adolescence, the point at which a girl became a woman was usually thought to be the onset of puberty, although a lack of agreement on where this line should be drawn in legal terms was reflected in the changing age of consent: twelve until 1865, thirteen between 1865 and 1885, and thereafter sixteen. It was not unknown for girls under sixteen to marry, and even less unusual for them to become engaged: the future archbishop E. W. Benson asked the parents of Mary Sedgwick for her hand when he was twenty-four years old and she was twelve, and they married after she turned eighteen; the writer Hall Caine moved in with his future wife Mary when she was thirteen (she became pregnant when she was fourteen) and they married when she was seventeen. Such marriages were not restricted to Britain – the American writer Edgar Allan Poe married his first cousin Virginia Clemm when he was twenty-seven and she was thirteen – and nor were they unheard of in Oxford. Although John Ruskin did not formally propose to Rose La Touche until 1867, when she was eighteen, he first met her when she was 'neither tall nor short for her age . . . Lips perfectly lovely in profile . . . the rest of the features what a fair, well-bred Irish girl's usually are', and he was soon besotted with a girl who wore her hat 'in the sauciest way possible' and corresponded with him in long, affectionate letters she addressed to 'St. Crumpet'. She was nine years old at the time. Ruskin was thirty-nine.

One way of dealing with such potentially awkward relationships was to turn them into a game. Wilkie Collins, who shuttled between his bachelor's apartments and two adult mistresses in a *ménage à trois* that was spread across three households, also enjoyed a flirtatious epistolary relationship with a twelve-year-old girl named Anne or 'Nannie', who in his letters became 'my darling', from whom he looked forward to a 'conjugal embrace'. Today he might receive a visit from the police, but his contemporaries readily acknowledged that playing with such ideas on the page did not commit the writer to acting them out in person. Nor did games like the mock engagement ceremony that Algernon Charles Swinburne underwent with the seven-year-old daughter of his friend Richard Monckton Milnes, which Lady Trevelyan confessed that she found 'affecting', adding that she was 'thankful to hear [he] had a chance of being saved by a virtuous attachment'.

Carroll was drawn to such stories. In March 1856, he read Charlotte Yonge's *Heartsease* (1854), a novel about a feckless army officer who infuriates his aristocratic family by secretly marrying a beautiful sixteen-year-old, and he retained a keen interest in the doomed but creatively inspiring relationship of Dante and Beatrice, the subject of a poem he composed in December 1862. 'Beatrice' is one of Carroll's serious poems, and it rarely rises above mediocrity as he spins out his long, adoring descriptions of Beatrice's 'angel-birth' and 'innocent eyes'. However, if the Liddells recalled the photograph of *Little Red Riding-Hood*, they might have been unsettled by the poem's conclusion, in which Carroll boasts that the 'living child' who stands before him is so pure that 'if a savage heart, | In a mask of human guise, | Were to come on her here apart – | Bound for a dark and a deadly deed, | Hurrying past with pitiless speed – | He would suddenly falter and guiltily start | At the glance of her pure blue eyes.' Their mood is unlikely to have been improved by the existence of another photograph, *The Elopement*, which Carroll had taken on 9 October that

Alice Jane Donkin in *The Elopement* (9 October 1862)

year, depicting another young girl dressed in a cloak climbing out of her bedroom window. This was Alice Jane Donkin, who was romantically linked with Carroll's younger brother Wilfred at the time and was eleven years old when the photograph was taken. The couple finally married in 1871, and although Carroll's photograph shows that he was capable of seeing the funny side of their relationship, it is hard to imagine the Liddells being equally amused by a plot to steal away a young girl named Alice. They might have been even more nervous if they had known of a diary entry Carroll made in 1867, in which he implicitly compared his brother's situation to his own, reporting that he had twice met his uncle Skeffington for dinner in Oxford, 'and on each occasion we had a good deal of conversation about Wilfred, and about A. L. – it is a very anxious subject'.

Even if Mrs Liddell had been prepared to consider a long engagement for Alice, her plans are unlikely to have included a nervous Oxford don. A popular satirical squib of the time joked that it was really she rather than her husband who ran Christ Church: 'I am the Dean, this Mrs Liddell, | She plays the first, I second fiddle.' There was probably more prejudice than truth in this idea, but if Mrs Liddell was sensitive about her own social rise – Thackeray, who had been at Charterhouse with Henry Liddell, snobbishly described her as a '3rd rate provincial lady' who was nonetheless 'rather first rate in the beauty line' – she was no less ambitious for her daughters. Social pressures for a financially advantageous marriage were strong, and at the time Carroll's prospects were weak. If there is an element of chastened hindsight in Caryl Hargreaves's later remark that 'nobody then expected that this shy, almost brilliant tutor in mathematics . . . would in the years to come be known all over the civilized world as the author of the best books of their kind which have ever been written', there is certainly a whiff of condescension in the way Alice herself, in a letter written when she was eighty, noted that *Alice's Adventures in Wonderland* was at the top of a list of children's books: 'How pleased poor C. L. D. would have been.' Seventy years earlier there were sound economic reasons for assuming that Carroll was a 'poor' catch.

There is also the question of Carroll's own sexuality to consider. In July 1857, he had written plainly in his diary that that he saw 'no present 'likelihood' of marriage, but his later references tended to be more satirical, telling anyone who mocked him for being a bachelor that 'I never yet saw the young lady whose company I could endure for a *week* – far less for *life*!' After his death, there were some half-hearted attempts to uncover an adult love-interest, with the actress Ellen Terry, who had been christened Alice Terry, being offered up as the likeliest candidate, although Stuart Dodgson Collingwood's reasons for thinking this were hazy at best: 'When Ellen Terry was just growing up – about 17 – she was lovely beyond description (I have seen a photo of her, which belonged to L. C., at about that age), and it is highly probable that he fell in love with her.' Terry herself offered a more knowing gloss on her friendship with 'dear Mr Dodgson', noting in her memoirs that 'He was as fond of me as he could be of any one over the age of ten', and Carroll's later remarks make it clear that their adult relationship was based more on nostalgia than desire. 'The gush of animal spirits of a light-hearted girl is beyond her now, poor thing!' he wrote in his diary after watching her perform on stage in 1877, while the most erotic remark of his that any biographer has been able to trace is 'I can imagine no more delightful occupation than brushing Ellen Terry's hair!', which makes him sound more like a lady's maid than a lover. (He found hair equally attractive as an artistic subject: one of the finest photographs he took in 1863 was *It Won't Come Smooth*, which depicts George MacDonald's young daughter Irene in her nightdress, clutching a hairbrush and mirror and staring balefully into the camera while her long, dark hair falls frizzily over her shoulders.)

Carroll was slightly less reticent about other members of his family. When his brother Edwin decided to give up missionary work in 1895, Carroll wrote to Lord Salisbury asking for help in finding him employment back in England. 'I don't believe he will ever marry,' Carroll explained, before confiding that 'His power of winning the affection of boys and young men seems to be almost unique', which was a bold statement to make just four months after Oscar Wilde had been sentenced to two years in prison for acts of gross indecency. In fact, although Caryl Hargreaves's gruff conclusion was that 'I don't think Dodgson was ever in love with anyone, that is to say, contemplated marriage, which is what

I think is generally meant in this connection', a number of Carroll's contemporaries thought that his sexual interests, however pale and repressed, were more likely to have been focused on other men. 'His effeminacy was sufficiently obvious,' notes Phyllis Greenacre, 'that some of his less sympathetic students once wrote a parody of his parodies and signed it "Louisa Caroline".' Perhaps they were aware that he sent letters to his child-friends from their 'affectionate little fairy friend, Sylvie', or perhaps they added up his personal habits and drew even more personal conclusions from them: his preference for violet ink; his clean-shaven face and unfashionably long hair in an era that equated manliness with hair on the chin rather than on the collar; his fondness for jokes that verged on the camp ('we are positively *haunted* by 3 women who sell lace . . . If I was in the habit of dressing in lace from head to foot, I couldn't wish for more frequent opportunities of buying it'); his remark in May 1864 that Mrs Liddell's refusal to allow any of her daughters to accompany him on the river thenceforth was 'rather superfluous caution'.

But such examples offer considerably stronger evidence of our own desires than Carroll's, particularly our need to make his sexuality fit into established modern categories, and these cannot be satisfied by anything we know. They also encourage us to assume that Carroll understood his feelings, whether at a conscious or unconscious level, even if he did not act on them. Yet it is just as likely that Carroll's feelings were as much of a mystery to him as they are to us. Even some of the most straightforward facts about his behaviour start to shift and blur the more closely we approach them. For example, in later years he sometimes accompanied teenage girls and adult women, as well as children, to the seaside: does this fact reflect his true sexual preferences, or their recognition that he was as unthreatening as a kitten? His library included such moderately racy books as *The Ways of Women* and *Physical Life of Women*: do these prove that 'he felt a man's normal temptations', as Derek Hudson has claimed, or that he preferred sex when it was between a set of covers rather than under them?

The most probable conclusion is that Carroll's strongest feelings were sentimental rather than sexual, and the only way he could keep them from fading over time was to invest them in something more permanent than people. Whereas real girls grew in unpredictable spurts, and sometimes changed out of all recognition, art was reassuringly constant. Perhaps that is why, a month after Carroll started to avoid the Liddells in public, he arranged to buy Arthur Hughes's 1863 painting *Lady with the Lilacs*. It was an interesting choice: Carroll disliked real flowers once they had been picked, considering them to be little better than perfumed corpses, and in *Through the Looking-Glass* when Alice plucks scented rushes from the riverbank they quickly melt in heaps about her feet. Hughes's painting avoids this situation by depicting a teenage girl who colours slightly as she reaches up to touch some purple lilac blossom on a tree. In the Victorian language of flowers, purple lilac signified first love, and although the girl's expression could be interpreted either as a blush of innocence or a flush of desire, the fact that it is painted means that her emotional tussle will never have to resolve itself. Like Alice Liddell with her cherries in the photograph *Open Your Mouth and Shut Your Eyes*, she is reaching for something that will remain for ever out of reach; the flowers will remain unplucked. Carroll was interested enough in the idea to buy Sophie Anderson's painting *Girl with Lilacs* in 1864, which depicted another girl smelling purple lilac blossom, once again preserving her on the cusp of experience. He was equally keen to capture the pose for his album: returning to Anderson's studio in 1865, he was introduced to the model, who was 'a beautiful child about 12', and planned a photograph 'in the same attitude as the picture'. Just as a photographed lilac could never wither and die ('"You're beginning to fade, you know",' a rose kindly tells Alice in *Through the Looking-Glass*), so Anderson's model could be added to the human anthology – a word derived from the Greek *anthos* (flower) – he maintained in the reliable present tense of his album.

However, whereas a painting or photograph can be taken in at a glance, a piece of writing is more complicated. Usually it works in two ways at once. Because it is fixed on the page, it reflects our desire to arrange events into a pattern that can resist the aimless drift of time. Equally, as this is a pattern that is revealed in the act of reading, it reflects the fact that a poem or story only makes sense over time. Carroll drew on both of these ideas in his writing. In March 1862, a few months before he sent Alice down her rabbit-hole, he finished the poem 'Disillusioned', later retitled 'My Fancy', in which he reflected with comic alarm on the wooing of a young girl. Initially believing her age to be 'perhaps a score', his speaker is disappointed to discover that in fact she has 'At least a dozen more' years under her belt. As a result, she has become a one-woman zoo:

> She has the bear's ethereal grace,
>> The bland hyena's laugh,
> The footstep of the elephant,
>> The neck of the giraffe;
> I love her still, believe me,
>> Though my heart its passion hides;
> 'She's all my fancy painted her,'
>> But oh! *how much besides!*

It would be interesting to know how the Liddells responded to this poem, Carroll's second parody of William Mee's 'Alice Gray', which would soon be echoed in the adventures of another Alice whose body becomes wildly out of proportion in her dreams. However successfully Carroll deflected such ideas into comedy, 'Disillusioned' hardly suggests that Alice Liddell would have been more attractive to him at the end of a long engagement. Yet in a story like *Alice's Adventures Under Ground*, she could be stretched and squashed until she acquired the illusion of independent life, even as his writing was permanently fixing her on the page. Only in this way could Carroll free up the pun that hovers around 'I love her still' in his poem, because by turning her into a piece of writing she would never be more than his fancy painted her. Only by keeping her still could he love her still.

*

Twelve

I n August 1864, while Carroll was holidaying on the Isle of Wight, he became aware of a local 'mystery': every morning he watched as four little children dressed in yellow passed by him on their way to the beach, 'brandishing wooden spades, and making savage noises', but 'from that moment they disappear entirely'. His explanation was that 'they all tumble into a hole somewhere, and continue excavating therein during the day', returning to the surface at night. It may be that he enjoyed inventing this sort of fantasy life for other people because of the direction his own life was taking. On the surface, he continued to develop a respectable academic career, spliced with visits to theatres and galleries, and occasional creative bursts of photography; simultaneously, and more secretly, he was developing his *Alice* story by hollowing it out from the inside and extending it in new directions.

The fictional Alice had also started to lead a double life. She was central to the original version of Carroll's story, *Alice's Adventures Under Ground*, and in 1864 he was still working hard to complete a manuscript of it that he could present to Alice Liddell; alongside this, she was also the main character in a new and expanded version that would eventually be published as *Alice's Adventures in Wonderland*. The story of Alice was one that looked backwards and forwards; it was a commemoration of Carroll's friendship with Alice Liddell, and a sign of his ambition to involve other children as readers. Between 1862 and 1865, these two stories existed side by side, and might have gone on to resemble each other even more closely, like a textual Tweedledum and Tweedledee, had Carroll not decided that before he could publish the revised version he needed professional help.

Carroll's surviving sketches show how much effort he put into the task of illustrating *Alice's Adventures Under Ground*. One shows a real rabbit

Carroll's sketches of Alice and other Wonderland studies

snuffling around and its transformation into a nosegay-flourishing White Rabbit; another shows a soulful Alice bursting out of some vegetation, surrounded by the heads of various monsters and equally horrific humans. Carroll gave her the flowing hair of a young Pre-Raphaelite model, rather than Alice Liddell's tidy bob, and in almost every picture her expression is as dreamily detached from events as the figures in a painting by D. G. Rossetti. This resemblance may have been deliberate: by now Carroll had met Rossetti, in addition to several other artists associated with the Pre-Raphaelite movement, including William Holman Hunt and John Everett Millais, and by purchasing Arthur Hughes's *Lady with the Lilacs* he had revealed a similar taste to theirs for exquisitely languishing female figures. Yet his illustrations for *Alice's Adventures Under Ground* also warned of how easily story and image could detach themselves from each other. For example, trying to picture 'a large blue caterpillar with his arms folded' should be a pleasurable exercise in mental contortion (does he fold *all* his arms?), but it is not much helped by Carroll's illustration, which depicts the caterpillar coiling himself up like an embarrassed snake; similarly, Carroll introduces the Gryphon by stating 'if you don't know what a Gryphon is, look at the picture', but anyone who followed his advice might assume that this mythical creature had the body of a rat and a toucan's beak. Even Carroll's most successful illustration, which depicts Alice inside the White Rabbit's house, where she has grown so large she fills a whole page, squashed against the frame of the picture, shows Carroll's talent pressing up against its limitations, with Alice's head and arms appearing to belong to different bodies.

In the first paragraph of his story, Alice grumbles to herself, "'where is the use of a book . . . without pictures or conversations?'" but as Carroll worked on his manuscript he had to face up to the fact that he was far better at the conversations than the pictures. What he needed was an illustrator who could make pictures form part of a different conversation, where word and image would engage each other in a collaborative dialogue on the page. Accordingly, after agreeing to publish his story with the London firm of Macmillan, with Carroll himself underwriting all the costs, he approached the leading *Punch* cartoonist John Tenniel. A good deal has been written about Carroll's working relationship with Tenniel, little of it flattering to either party, but after agreement was reached in April 1864 for Tenniel to supply a set of illustrations for the expanded version of the story, matters proceeded much as might have been expected from two busy perfectionists – with a good deal of caution and some annoyance on both sides. Carroll found the process especially difficult: after years of having complete freedom to illustrate his own stories, suddenly he had to deal with a collaborator who was unwilling to be treated as a skilled prosthetic hand. Nor was Tenniel merely prickly; he was also painfully slow, and Carroll's original plan to publish in time for Christmas 1864 had to be abandoned after Tenniel, burdened with other commitments, failed to produce enough material on time. However, when the illustrations were finally complete, it was clear that the wait had been worthwhile.

A reader opening a first edition of *Alice's Adventures in Wonderland* in 1865 might have experienced the sensation of being introduced to an old friend. The little girl we now recognize as Alice – long blonde hair, high forehead, little feet, stiff pale dress – had made an early appearance in the frontispiece to a volume of *Punch* published in June 1864, where Tenniel had depicted her placing a garland around the neck of the British lion, while similar figures had already appeared in other cartoons of the period, such as John Leech's *Little Darling* (*Punch*, 27 February 1864), in which a little girl who could be Alice's sister sits in an armchair complaining that '"Mamma wants me to go to a pantomime in the day time, as if I was a mere child!"' Together these examples suggest that Tenniel was expecting his Alice to be seen as a social type rather than an individual. He also surrounded her with other creatures from the pages of *Punch* – he often drew gaping fish dressed as people, for example, and in January 1862 had rehearsed the pose of the Cheshire Cat in a cartoon that depicted Abraham Lincoln as a raccoon sitting up a tree. Coming across these images again in Carroll's story, a contemporary reader would have realized, even before reading a word, that Alice's dream was a set of fragments from her waking life reassembled into a strange new pattern. Visually as well as verbally, Wonderland was a place where ordinary life met its uncanny double.

The result of this collaboration was a type of book that had never been seen before. Everything that Carroll had hinted at in words was translated into a world of images, from the danger around Alice, which Tenniel captured with a cross-hatching technique that made events appear to be emerging from the surrounding darkness, to the theatrical quality of the dialogue, echoed by Tenniel in a set of deliberately stiff postures that made Carroll's characters look as if they were periodically freezing themselves into tableaux. Opening *Alice's Adventures in Wonderland* meant opening oneself up to a newly integrated reading experience: no longer was an illustrated book merely text plus pictures; it was text times pictures.

As Carroll developed his story, adding new episodes such as 'A Mad Tea-Party', extending others (the trial scene was expanded from two pages to two chapters), and inserting extra songs that included '*Twinkle, twinkle little bat!*', '*Beautiful Soup*' and others, it almost doubled in size from a short story of around 18,000 words to a fragmentary novella of more than 35,000 words. Many of these developments reflected self-consciously on the idea of development itself. In 1860, Carroll had probably attended the legendary debate on evolution that took place under the auspices of the British Association for the Advancement of Science in the new University

Museum. He certainly met the participants – he photographed them in an improvised studio with fabric walls in the Christ Church Deanery garden – and even if he did not witness the debate in person he would have heard about the spiky exchange between Bishop Wilberforce and T. H. Huxley, in which Wilberforce asked if Huxley was descended from an ape on his mother's or his father's side, and Huxley replied with a dignified logic that crushed his opponent like a walnut. Carroll was fascinated by evolutionary theory. Following the publication of *On the Origin of Species* in 1859, he bought no fewer than nineteen works by Darwin or his critics, together with five by the pioneering writer on social evolution Herbert Spencer, and although he took such ideas seriously, he was also happy to use them for the purposes of entertainment. In *Sylvie and Bruno*, he introduces a new form of literature known as 'Darwinism reversed', where 'the Murder comes at page fifteen and the Wedding at page forty', and he created a chessboard game in 1878 that he originally called 'Natural Selection', the winner of which would be the survivor of the fittest.

Whether or not Carroll believed every word of Darwin's theories, they were impossible to avoid in the early 1860s; as William Empson has pointed out, Darwinism was in the air like 'a pervading bad smell'. Suddenly the natural world was revealed to be a place of bloody struggle and unexpected trauma. Birdsong was not a simple expression of joy, but a sexual invitation or a warning; flowers were not innocent splashes of colour in the landscape, but participants in an endless turf war. In *Alice's Adventures Under Ground*, such anxieties had occasionally broken the surface of the narrative, like a shark's fin, but had largely been restricted to Carroll's illustrations. In his interpretation of the Pool of Tears, for example, Alice is surrounded by creatures that include a dodo and a monkey, while her own hands look suspiciously claw-like, as if by swimming in this salty pool she is regressing to a more primitive life form. (Carroll was keen to show Alice being crowded out by other creatures: an earlier sketch had shown her paddling around with only the Mouse and some smiling fish for company.) In Carroll's revised version of the story, by contrast, natural conflict is everywhere. Although Alice pursues the White Rabbit because she is 'burning with curiosity' rather than simply hungry, Wonderland is ruled by aggression: almost every creature is at risk of being killed or eaten, and even the 'good-natured' Cheshire Cat has '*very* long claws and a great many teeth'. In fact, although Alice's dream takes place on a river-bank, the Wonderland of her imagination turns out to be much more like the 'entangled bank' in the final paragraph of Darwin's *Origin of Species*, where 'forms most beautiful and most wonderful', including 'various insects flitting about' and 'worms crawling through the damp earth', are engaged in an endless 'Struggle for Life'. As John Bayley has perceptively observed, Alice's story is 'an essay in the art of survival'.

Also propelling Carroll's story forward in revision was a more general principle of transformation. On one of the rare occasions when he explained how he wrote, he stressed that every idea in *Alice's Adventures in Wonderland* and nearly every word of dialogue '*came of itself*', and in the finished text this extends to the way almost everything emerges from what has come before it. In effect, Carroll's story works like the 'Mouse's Tale' in reverse: whereas the Mouse's story gradually fades to nothing as it curves down the page, Alice's dream grows by feeding on itself. A few sentences after accusing herself of being a 'great girl', she sees the White Rabbit in a 'great hurry', and then confesses that she feels 'a little differ-ent', after which she recites 'How doth the little – ' and makes it very different indeed. Puns are literalized: playing-card soldiers throw them-selves 'flat upon their faces'; the jury is 'upset' after Alice knocks them over. Other literary mutations bring together language and plot: shortly after worrying that she will have to live in Mabel's 'poky little house', Alice ends up crammed into the White Rabbit's even pokier little house; the baby she meets becomes a pig, but 'pig' has also emerged from the earlier 'pigeon'. "'Did you say 'pig', or 'fig'?'" asks the Cheshire Cat, whose sen-sitivity to such linguistic metamorphoses is perhaps heightened by the fact that it appears only after the Caterpillar has disappeared. In real life a caterpillar becomes a butterfly; in dreams a caterpillar becomes a cat. Even a sentence such as "'By-the-bye, what became of the baby?'" is a miniature linguistic gestation in which 'By' swells to produce 'baby'.

Alice's discovery that words can be as hard to control as her croquet mallet (a flamingo that keeps twisting itself around to look at her) and ball (a hedgehog that insists on unrolling itself and crawling away) reveals how language can appear to have a life of its own. This is especially tricky for a child who is learning to read, who may experience words as alien creatures that slither or scatter on the page when she tries to pin them down, but it also draws attention to language as a set of living forms that can still surprise us after we have grown up. It is a nice historical coincidence that on 26 April 1878, almost thirteen years after the publication of *Alice's Adventures in Wonderland*, a meeting took place in Dean Liddell's rooms in Christ Church to discuss the appointment of John Murray as editor of what would become known as the *Oxford English Dictionary* – the first dictionary to be based on historical principles, allowing readers to unpeel the layers of meaning sedimented in every word. But it is not a coincidence that the current edition of that dictionary includes almost 200 examples from Carroll, many of which are words and phrases he either invented or gave a new creative twist: *beamish, chortle, frabjous, galumphing, Curiouser and curiouser!, We're all mad here*. Together they remind us that Alice's adventures are a celebration of language – its pleasures, anxieties, rewards, risks – and a witty demonstration of the fact that it is not just our bodies that are always changing. So is what comes out of our mouths.

On Saturday 26 November 1864, Carroll finally sent Alice Liddell the manuscript of *Alice's Adventures Under Ground* as an early Christmas present. His previous 'aloof' stance might have made it awkward to hand it to her in person, although a few months earlier, two days after her twelfth birthday and the same day he sent Macmillan a portion of the first chapter of *Alice's Adventures in Wonderland*, he had met her with Miss Prickett and walked with them beside the river, so clearly relations with the family were now less strained than they might once have been. Alice's response to her gift is not recorded, although the fact that it used to be shown to visitors in the Deanery indicates that it was not hidden away as an embarrassing family secret. The dedication page was written in an elegant Gothic script: 'A Christmas Gift to a Dear Child in Memory of a Summer Day'. If that made the story sound strangely like an elegy, the final page was more optimistic, as Alice's sister imagines how 'this same little Alice' will 'keep, through her riper years, the simple and loving heart of her childhood'. Then Carroll added a final picture of Alice Liddell: first an ink sketch, which made her look more bushy-haired and squint-eyed than either would have liked, and finally a photograph that he pasted over it. Surrounding this photograph, a trimmed version of the portrait showing Alice with a fern, were two decorative flourishes resembling a figure of eight: Alice's age when the photograph was taken, and also the mathematical sign for infinity. It was a subtle way of suggesting that a literary character's age was not bound by chronology; no matter how old Alice Liddell became, the fictional Alice could stay the same age for ever.

If these details indicated Carroll's desire to make *Alice's Adventures Under Ground* a commemorative volume, so did the fact that Alice's dream ends with her sister gently brushing away some leaves from her face. It is a delicate pun – trees and writers both live in their 'leaves' – like the one that comes at the climax of Tennyson's great elegy *In Memoriam* (a poem Carroll knew well enough to have helped compile an index to it in 1862), in which the speaker reads some old letters from his dead friend, and feels his living presence in 'those fallen leaves which kept their green'. The idea that writing produced leaves that would never fade is one that Carroll gratefully embraced in *Alice's Adventures Under Ground*. Not only was his choice of binding for the manuscript a dark green morocco, but on his title page he illuminated the letter 'A' of 'Alice' with delicate blossom and luxuriously spreading tendrils of ivy, a theme he continued with decorative flourishes around his dedication and chapter headings. Alice's adventures may have germinated underground but they would continue to send out new shoots on the surface. The last time Carroll had employed a similar ivy-sprouting Gothic script was for the title page of his family magazine *Mischmasch*. If this parallel privately acknowledged that *Alice's Adventures Under Ground* was another loose bundle of stories and pictures, the straggling vegetation also warned how easily such a narrative could lose its way. Nor were Carroll's methods of composition likely to help. 'Sometimes an idea comes at night, when I have had to get up and strike a light to note it down,' he explained, 'sometimes when out on a lonely winter walk, when I have had to stop, and with half-frozen fingers jot down a few words which should keep the new-born idea from perishing.' What kept his new ideas from perishing, as he tried to develop them into *Alice's Adventures in Wonderland*, was his skill at grafting them on to several successful features of the earlier version.

One of these was his use of comedy. Not all readers find Alice's adventures uproariously funny, but nor does Carroll expect them to, because Wonderland is a place where Alice explores the full range of comedy, from slapstick and puns to more obvious forms of hostility, and because she makes so few jokes herself she is the perfect stooge for characters with a more mischievous sense of fun. Another structuring device is Carroll's use of questions, which serve an important function in a world where almost everyone is willing to talk but very little declares itself. However, what links everything together most fully is the character of Alice herself. Usually literary works ask us to imagine what it would be like to be someone else. Alice engages in this kind of imaginative sympathy after her fall down the rabbit-hole, as she thinks about her friends Ada and Mabel, and tries to work out if she could have been changed for either of them. What she discovers, however, is that she has entered a world in which she has no access to anyone else's thoughts. Nor do we as readers, because every character we encounter in Wonderland is flat – literally so in the case of the Queen of Hearts and her card subjects – meaning that believable psychology is replaced by obscure or absent motivation, and conversations are always on the verge of disintegrating into catchphrases. Alice may hear the Mock Turtle sighing 'as if his heart would break', but the story gives us no evidence to make us believe he has a real heart; like the little royal children who process before Alice 'ornamented with hearts', his character is all on the outside.

Alice, by contrast, is a flesh-and-blood character surrounded by flimsy caricatures: a believable little girl who is by turns generous and snobbish, keen to please and vainly self-obsessed. Even when we are unsure what she is thinking, it is because she has the opacity of a real person rather than a piece of cardboard. Indeed, given how often the major Victorian novelists tried to find a compromise between realism and romance in their work, one way of reading *Alice's Adventures in Wonderland* is as a narrative experiment that investigates what might happen if a character from one kind of novel entered the imaginative world of another. The result is as brilliantly jarring as it would be to see Jane Eyre wandering around Toonland. This adds an extra level of playfulness to the moment Alice declares, '"There ought to be a book written about me . . . And when I grow up, I'll write one."' Because when we reach Carroll's final paragraph, which informs us that the adult Alice will entertain children with 'many a strange tale, perhaps even with the dream of Wonderland', we realize with a jolt of recognition that this is the book we have been reading all along.

*

Thirteen

Ordinary life was considerably harder to control than a story. On 11 May 1865, a fortnight before he received a specimen volume of *Alice's Adventures in Wonderland* from Macmillan, Carroll bumped into Alice Liddell and Miss Prickett in Christ Church. 'Alice seems changed a good deal, and hardly for the better,' he confided to his diary, before adding that she was 'probably going through the usual awkward stage of transition'. Was it more awkward for her or for him? Alice had just turned thirteen, and 'transition' was a common Victorian euphemism for puberty, just as 'awkward' was often applied to teenage girls, as it would later be in Henry James's novel *The Awkward Age* (1899). Alice had certainly changed physically from the pert eight-year-old Carroll had photographed sitting next to a fern. The previous month he had visited the British Institution in London to see William Blake Richmond's painting *The Sisters*, which depicted her looking 'very lovely, but not *quite* natural' as she studied a picture book on Ina's lap, with Edith sitting on the other side ('the best likeness of the three') as a dreamy Pre-Raphaelite version of the sulky figure in Carroll's photographs. It had been painted at Llandudno, where Richmond had spent seven weeks as the Liddells' house guest in summer 1864, and the artist later singled out Alice for her 'pretty face and lovely colouring' to which 'no reproduction can do justice'. But although one critic praised *The Sisters* as 'charming', it is hard to look now at the girls' open and empty expressions without seeing haunting premonitions of Chekhov's play *Three Sisters*, first performed in 1901, in which the central characters are trapped in the provinces and consumed by impossible dreams of escape.

Alice Liddell's life was nowhere near as gloomy as this, but as she grew up she may have been equally conscious of a widening gap between

William Blake Richmond, *The Sisters* (1864)

fantasy and reality. She was still being educated at home, where the Liddell family had expanded to include three more brothers (Albert, Eric and Lionel) and two more sisters (Rhoda and Violet), all of whom lived in the sort of secluded domesticity that the novelist Margaret Oliphant would describe in 1866 as a 'bower of chintz'. If Alice was conscious that the unpredictable excitement of Carroll's childhood stories had been replaced by the genteel routines of Deanery life, her mood may not have been greatly lightened by the first edition of *Alice's Adventures in Wonderland*, specially bound in white vellum, that she received from Carroll in 1865. (Ordinary copies were bound in bright red cloth, which Carroll considered 'the most attractive to childish eyes'.) He had smuggled in two references to the date – when Alice meets the Cheshire Cat we learn that it is May, and at the Mad Tea-Party we are told it is the fourth – which would have worked like a pair of private winks to Alice Liddell: the story takes place on her birthday. However, in arranging for her copy to be delivered on 4 July, Carroll had chosen the anniversary of their boat trip, and therefore the birthday of the fictional Alice who had emerged from his head on that 'golden afternoon'. Fact was morphing into fiction; Alice was becoming 'Alice'. Carroll's new opening poem further detached his character from her real-life inspiration, in recounting how 'three tongues together' had requested a story:

> Anon, to sudden silence won,
> In fancy they pursue
> The dream-child moving through a land
> Of wonders wild and new . . .

Here Alice has become something more than a child who dreams; she is a child who lives in other people's dreams, as hard to pin down as a thought bubble. Her story is no longer that of a single girl, but a legend where the wonders are always 'new' because they can be imagined afresh by each reader.

This attempt to supplement or replace a real girl with an ideal 'dream-child' was hardly in the spirit of Carroll's story, which is far more tough-minded than his woozily romantic poem. Yet it was curiously echoed in the book's early printing history. On 15 July 1865, Carroll visited his publisher to inscribe some presentation copies, but a few days later he received a letter from Tenniel stating that he was 'entirely dissatisfied with the printing of the pictures'. This has puzzled a number of bibliographers, who cannot see much wrong with the handful of surviving copies, but whatever Carroll thought privately he decided to take decisive action. Scrapping the entire print run of 2,000 copies at his own expense (he estimated the total cost to be £600, more than his annual salary, some of which he recouped by shipping defective copies to a publisher in New York), he switched printers from the Clarendon Press to the London firm of Richard Clay, Son & Taylor, which was more experienced in producing illustrated books, and the new first edition was on sale in time for Christmas. Carroll received a sample copy on 9 November, and pronounced it 'very *far* superior to the old'.

While this complicated textual history may have resulted in a book that was slightly crisper in its visual details and, more importantly, kept Tenniel happy in case of any future collaboration, the biggest change Carroll made between his original manuscript version of the story and the first printed edition was to the title. Having decided that *Alice's Adventures Under Ground* sounded too much like a book containing 'instructions about mines', he first considered *Alice's Golden Hour*, and then sent a sheaf of options to the dramatist Tom Taylor:

$$
\text{Alice among the} \left\{ \begin{array}{l} \text{elves} \\ \\ \text{goblins} \end{array} \right. \quad \text{Alice's} \left\{ \begin{array}{l} \text{hour} \\ \text{doings} \\ \text{adventures} \end{array} \right. \quad \text{in} \left\{ \begin{array}{l} \text{elf-land} \\ \\ \text{wonderland} \end{array} \right.
$$

Carroll's preference was for 'Alice's Adventures in Wonderland', because 'I want something sensational', although to move from 'under' to 'wonder' and 'ground' to 'land' was also a natural development of his earlier title. It has since become so well known that it slips off the tongue without any thought, but at the time it was an unusual choice. Alice often 'wonders', but never names the place she enters in her dream, and nor do any of the creatures who live there; it is only her sister, on the final page of the story, who thinks of it as Wonderland.

Perhaps the book she is reading on the riverbank is supposed to be one of the earlier attempts to locate 'Wonderland'. If so, she would have had a small library of examples to choose from. It was an idea firmly rooted in Romanticism. For German writers such as Friedrich Schiller or Joseph Freiherr von Eichendorff, whose poems 'In fernem Wunderland' ('In a Distant Wonderland') and 'Ein Wunderland' ('A Wonderland') were often translated and anthologized in the period, *Wunderland* referred primarily to a place where anything could happen because it existed only in the imagination. The idea also attracted British and American writers. In *Sartor Resartus* (1836), Thomas Carlyle had referred to 'Fantasy' as a 'mystic wonder-land', and the word was frequently applied to those areas of life that could not be explained by reason alone. In John William Jackson's 1864 poem 'My Lady-Love', an angel's voice is heard singing 'A mystic melody from wonder-land'; according to Sarah Helen Whitman, the mind was capable of conjuring up 'The wonder-land of old romance'; and Carlyle himself had been praised for making 'the old dead past a new and beautiful, and living Wonder-land'.

Wonderland's spatial coordinates were hazy. In travel literature, the word was typically used to refer to any foreign country that was full of marvels ('Where other trav'lers, fraught with terror, roam, | Lo! Bruce in Wonder-land is quite at home'), and if directions were offered they tended to be more metaphorical than geographical:

> Rockaby, lullaby, bees on the clover! –
> Crooning so drowsily, crying so low –
> Rockaby, lullaby, dear little rover!
> Down into wonderland –
> Down to the under-land –
> Go, oh go!
> Down into wonderland go!

However, if Carroll had a specific source in mind, it was probably F. T. Palgrave's 'The Age of Innocence', a poem first published in *Idyls and Songs* (1854). It is rarely read today, and has not previously been identified as a literary model for *Alice's Adventures in Wonderland*, but at the time it would have seemed a natural choice. Palgrave was well known in Oxford, where he was a Fellow of Exeter College between 1847 and 1862, later being appointed Professor of Poetry, and his book had already attracted Carroll's attention. In 1857, Carroll noted that among its poems 'chiefly on children' there was a sonnet addressed to Agnes Weld, his future Little Red Riding-Hood, and it was in this diary entry that he decided 'her face is very striking and attractive, and will certainly make a beautiful photograph'.

'The Age of Innocence' is disconcertingly confessional in tone. Opening with a sonnet to the celebrated portrait painter Sir Joshua Reynolds ('thou art alive in children yet'), it develops into a burst of praise for a child named Alice: 'On little Alice late one morn I gazed, | Darling of many hearts, half risen from sleep . . .' What follows is a long description of another girl, whom the speaker eagerly watches as she plays, asking himself, 'What fancy lodges in thy breast?' She clasps his knee and asks for 'A fairy tale', and he agrees in exchange for a kiss ('There's nothing gain'd on earth for nought'), although he confesses that he had tried to read the book earlier and had been unable to 're-awake the spell'. With a child beside him, however, he can unlock the secret magic of the story, and more importantly of his own imagination:

> O sight of joy assured—I see
> The little wonderer at my knee—
> —Is she the Vision robed in light—
> The Fairy Fair—the gracious sight:
> The angel child, that loosed the chain,
> And bade me be a child again?—
> —Look up! look up! those smiles I know:
> Those earnest eyes—'tis so! 'tis so!—
> Thy hands the pictured leaves turn o'er:
> The fairy tale delights once more—
> That wonder-land once more I see—
> Once more I am a child in Thee.

It is hard to read this now without wincing, so raw and clinging is the speaker's need to use his 'little wonderer' as a passport back to his own childhood. The conclusion is even more awkward, as she thanks him with an embrace, and he lingers over the qualities that assure him of her innocence: 'The white soft frock—the sash of blue—| The edging lace—the tiny shoe; | The sock turn'd down—the ancle fine—| The wavy folds— the bosom line.' If those dashes are supposed to represent his gasps of innocent pleasure, they become more strained as the embrace continues: 'The quick warm breath: the heaving breast: | The tender weight against me prest: | The fair fine limbs—the soft—the pure—| All maidenhood in miniature.' A generous interpretation would be that Palgrave is tempting his reader into a similar yearning for lost innocence. By expecting us to shudder at this blazon of teenage physicality, he is reminding us that, whereas his speaker has been restored to a child's joyful unselfconsciousness, we are more likely to find his words tasteless or embarrassing or worse. This is because we have not yet rediscovered 'wonder-land'. Yet asserting your innocence while allowing people to imagine the opposite is a dangerous game. That is something Carroll would discover to his cost in the years to come.

*

Fourteen

Another chapter Carroll added to his story in revision was 'Pig and Pepper', which opens with a Fish-Footman rapping at the Duchess's door and solemnly presenting an oversized invitation from the Queen. It was a self-conscious addition, because the published *Alice's Adventures in Wonderland* was in effect another giant invitation, which began by asking its readers to follow Alice down a rabbit-hole and then encouraged them to view the real world in an equally playful way. Carroll's final paragraphs had shown this idea being put into practice. As Alice's sister thinks distractedly about what she has heard, suddenly the air is filled with the sounds of rattling teacups and splashing water, as 'the strange creatures of her little sister's dream' bring the countryside to life. Wonderland, it turns out, is not a place but a state of mind: in telling her story, Alice has opened up a portal to the undiscovered world that surrounds us every day.

Carroll enjoyed teasing his readers with the idea that Wonderland could not be located on a traditional map. In 1868, he wrote to a child who had misspelt the name of the seaside town Babbacombe as 'Babbicombe', telling her that as no such town existed she must have been reading about it in a fairy tale: 'Why, my dear child, you might just as well say there is such a place as Wonderland!' Some of his friends preferred to believe that the real Wonderland had been hiding on their doorsteps all along. Christina Rossetti, who first met Carroll in 1863, later recalled that with all the exotic animals her brother collected, including owls, kangaroos, wallabies, armadillos, parakeets, peacocks, a raccoon, a Japanese salamander, two laughing jackasses and a toucan he dressed in a cowboy hat, eventually his house and garden at 16 Cheyne Walk in Chelsea also 'became a sort of wonderland'.

Imaginary lands were not Carroll's invention: some of the bizarre creatures Alice encounters could have crossed into Wonderland directly from Jonathan Swift's much earlier satirical fantasy *Gulliver's Travels* (1726), were it not that the fictional countries created by different authors almost never share the same borders. But in creating Wonderland, Carroll had discovered a territory that readers were unusually keen to explore. Around 500 copies of *Alice's Adventures in Wonderland* were sold in the first three weeks after publication, and when reviews started to appear he collected them in a new olive-green scrapbook like a proud father filing his daughter's school reports. Some were only a few sentences long (the story was often included in general surveys of Christmas gift books), and others were dashed off so quickly that Carroll's title was accidentally altered – *Little Alice in Wonderland* in *The Spectator*, and *Alice's Trip to Wonderland* in the *Monthly Packet* – but almost all rippled approvingly with praise. The book was variously characterized as 'an antidote to a fit of the blues', 'a triumph of nonsense', and 'a work of genius' that was 'as tickling as a pantomime'. The only discordant notes were struck by the *Illustrated Times*, which considered it 'too extravagantly absurd to produce more diversion than disappointment and irritation', and *The Athenaeum*, which concluded that 'any child might be more puzzled than enchanted by this stiff, over-wrought story', although Carroll came off lightly compared to the next book in this reviewer's sights, which produced the sour question 'Why should little folks have this sort of trash prepared for them by people who ought to know better?' Other poets and novelists were more unequivocally enthusiastic. D. G. Rossetti claimed that 'The wonderful ballad of Father William and Alice's perverted snatches of school poetry are among the funniest things I had seen for a long while', while Christina told Carroll that 'My Mother and Sister as well as myself made ourselves quite at home yesterday in Wonderland.' Henry Kingsley thought it 'charming', and stayed in bed the morning it arrived until he had 'read every word'. The one glaring omission in every review was the acknowledgement that a real girl had inspired Carroll to write down his story. If anybody outside Oxford knew of Alice Liddell's existence, they were not prepared to reveal it in print. While the fictional Alice was undoubtedly the narrative centre of the book, the real Alice was already becoming a gaping hole at its heart.

It was not long before *Alice's Adventures in Wonderland* started to roam more widely. In September 1866, a further 3,000 copies were printed, and by the start of 1869 Carroll noted that more than this number had been sold in a single six-month period. Soon his book was being enjoyed by an international readership: in January 1867, he received copies of two reviews from newspapers in New York. However, while Alice was starting to explore the world, Carroll was again in danger of becoming stuck in a rut. He continued to be fascinated by new scientific inventions: in January 1867 he visited the computer pioneer Charles Babbage to ask if 'any of his calculating machines are to be had', and two years later he attended a 'very interesting exhibition' of electricity that created luminous effects by being discharged through rarefied gases in glass tubes – an early fore-runner of modern fluorescent lighting and television. He also remained committed to the reform of Christ Church's creaky structures of govern-ance – although a proposal to abolish traditional distinctions between noblemen and gentlemen-commoners he thought *'very bad'* – and he took a leading part in the complicated negotiations that eventually led to the Christ Church (Oxford) Act of 1867, producing an original set of statutes for the college and a new governing body that for the first time included Students alongside the Dean and Canons. Yet such enthusiasm for reform rarely extended to the world at large. Collingwood would later point out that his uncle was 'nothing if not a staunch Conservative', and his phras-ing summed up the absolute certainty of Carroll's political stance. Like mathematics and religion, for Carroll politics was a matter of all or noth-ing, and he was rarely troubled by self-doubt or even by a great deal of thought.

In July 1867 he observed a demonstration in Trafalgar Square, part of the widespread civic unrest associated with the government's attempts to introduce a second Reform Bill, but his comments were hardly sympa-thetic to demands for a greater enfranchisement of the working class. 'The majority of the crowd seemed to be roughs,' he tutted in his diary, and although 'they were orderly enough' they were 'still swarming about' like angry bees long after dark. Two days later, he recorded 'more fighting, window-breaking, etc.', and quickly moved on to record the details of a new set of children he had been photographing. It was a common pattern: any interest he may have had in political arguments was soon diverted in other directions. On one of the rare occasions he mentioned the Crimean War, a diary entry that opened with 'The glorious intelligence arrived of the *Fall of Sebastopol*' lasted for only two sentences before a change of paragraph and a gear-shift of subject: 'Made acquaintance with the eldest of the little Cochranes, a plain queer little child, Constance.' In 1868, his public contributions to the debate surrounding Gladstone's defeat in the general election were limited to a letter sent to *The Standard* 'commenting on a wonderful sentence' in *The Times*, and an anagram on the Liberal MP's full name: 'William Ewart Gladstone: Wilt tear down *all* images?' He later thought up a better one, 'Wild agitator! Means well', and collected others including 'A wild man will go at trees'. In their form as well as in their sentiments, such jokes illustrated Carroll's conservative impulses, because an anagram creates something new, but only by shuffling around elements that already exist. Even when he liked a work of art that was obviously informed by political concerns, Carroll preferred to ignore specific historical allusions. Three months before the Reform Bill riots, he saw Thomas Heaphy's civil war painting *General Fairfax and his Daughter Pursued by the Royalist Trooper*, but a year later the only detail he remembered was 'the fainting child', and when he commissioned Heaphy to produce a replica, the title he eventually chose was *Dreaming of Fairy-Land*.

Carroll's conservatism was equally evident in his private life; here too he had a taste for exploring old ideas in new ways. One subject in particular had become a creative itch he couldn't stop scratching. On 10 April 1866, the day after Tenniel gave his permission for the first inferior printing of the book to be sold in America, Carroll met Alice and Beatrice, two young daughters of the naturalist Charles Wallich, 'the former *very* pretty'; on 14 May, he photographed 'the two Alices', who were Alice Emily and Alice Jane Donkin, respectively the daughter and niece of the Oxford astronomer William Donkin. Perhaps these were just

Carroll's *The Two Alices* featuring Alice Emily Donkin
and Alice Jane Donkin (14 May 1866)

coincidences. Alice was hardly an uncommon name at the time, and it also had royal sanction (Victoria and Albert had named their third child Alice in 1843), making it a popular choice for families who wanted to express their patriotism or were content to drift along on the currents of fashion. Between the birth of Alice Liddell in 1852 and the publication of *Alice's Adventures in Wonderland* in 1865, the name had been chosen by, among others, the parents of the folklorist Alice Gomme (b. 1853), photographer Alice Hughes (b. 1857), educationist Alice Ravenhill (b. 1859), historian Alice Greenwood (b. 1862) and women's suffrage activist Alice Sennett (b. 1862). It was also a familiar name in fiction: in 1865, another Alice had been central to Anthony Trollope's novel *Can You Forgive Her?*, where Alice Vavasor has to decide whether to marry the respectable but spirit-crushingly dull John Grey or her charismatic but flighty cousin George, a choice that focuses Trollope's much larger question of '"What should a woman do with her life?"'

Yet Carroll's activities could not always be explained by coincidence. He also enjoyed playing with the idea that some girls were joined by more mysterious threads of connection. In 1867, for example, two days before he photographed another Alice, he caught sight of a girl during a service at St Mary's church in Oxford. As she reminded him strongly of Edith Jebb, a girl he had tried and failed to photograph in her bed the previous year, he followed her back to her home, a walk of around twenty minutes, justifying his amateur detective work with the thought that 'I should much like to photograph this Second Edition of "Edith".' The parallel of children and books was a traditional one – in Shakespeare's Sonnet 11, the beautiful young man is advised to have children, because 'Thou shouldst print more, not let that copy die' – although Carroll's wording indicates that he may have had a specific modern example in mind: in Emily Brontë's *Wuthering Heights*, a novel he praised as 'extraordinary' when he read it in 1856, Nelly worries that Cathy is the kind of daughter who will turn out to be 'a second edition of the mother'. However, what Carroll was starting to learn from the reception of *Alice's Adventures in Wonderland* was that the relationship between an author and his fictional offspring might depend as much on upbringing as it did on birth. No matter how many new girls named Alice he put before his lens, once they left his studio his relationship with them would remain in a state of permanent arrest. His fictional dream-child, by contrast, was a little girl who could change without getting any older. He had already demonstrated this by withdrawing the inferior first edition and replacing it with a more crisply printed version. Now, as the fictional Alice continued to grow in popularity, he decided that she would require careful nurturing if she were to develop properly.

On 12 November 1865, shortly after receiving a new set of copies, he wrote to Macmillan warning that 'I shall have a few "errata" to send in case more copies are to be struck off.' This letter set the tone for many more over the following years, as he peppered Macmillan with 'a list of corrections' in 1866, 'errata' in 1867 and a further 'correction' in 1868. Like a pushy parent determined to get the best for his daughter, he scrutinized each new printing with a sharp eye and even sharper tongue: the margins were too narrow; the punctuation was 'capable of a good deal of improvement'; a set of proofs was 'very hideous'; a flaw on the printing block for an illustration of Alice had caused 'a very unsightly mark on the side of the nose' that might have been invisible to anyone else but was to him an 'eyesore'. Nothing was too small to fiddle with, because Carroll's revisions revealed more than his perfectionism. They reflected a strong desire to keep his dream-child alive on the page, always changing and always the same.

Unfortunately, she was also developing in ways that threatened to put her beyond his control. The first American reviews included an early example of this trend. The December issue of *Merryman's Monthly* had 'actually reprinted half the book', Carroll noted crossly, 'and copied about a dozen of the pictures!' The January issue then completed what was in effect an unauthorized extra edition, although the lack of a reciprocal copyright agreement between Britain and America until 1891 meant that such acts of literary piracy could not be prevented or punished. However, if such thefts annoyed Carroll, they also intrigued him, because they chimed with his more general interest in identities that became more precarious over time. The moment a child decided she wanted to be treated as an adult, in particular, often left him nervously joking about how to address her, once a previously secure linguistic category had been opened up to a rush of alternatives:

> My dear Polly,
>
> Did you really take my messages for earnest, and are you really offended,
>
> ~~young person~~
> you extraordinary ~~creature~~   ? (Don't you see what difficulties I'm in?
> ~~child~~
> ~~individual~~
>
> Why can't you help me out with a word, like a good – (difficulty again) – member of the Human Species?)

Other kinds of writing offered Carroll tempting opportunities to play with these ideas. In January 1867, he read *The Fountain of Youth*, a Danish fairy tale published by Macmillan that had been reviewed alongside *Alice's Adventures in Wonderland* in *The Scotsman* at the end of 1866 and that carried a full-page advertisement for his book. The story revolves around a gnarled Spanish soldier who follows Columbus to America, 'the distant land of gold and wonder', and there finds a 'fountain of life' in which wounds are healed and withered flowers brought back to perfumed loveliness. After taking a dip in the fountain, he sleeps for several days, and on awakening discovers that he has been restored to his youthful prime, although with predictably unhappy results: his children fail to recognize him, his wife rejects him, and he realizes that although many people dream of housing a young heart in an old body, this trick does not work the other way round. Recoiling in horror after becoming 'a stranger to himself', he is forced to wait for his blooming exterior to catch up with his crabbed insides. A year later, in January 1868, Carroll wrote a poem that included another version of the same idea, this time from a more optimistic perspective, based on the knowledge that his verse could describe time passing while celebrating the power of memory to return to the same scenes again and again. Contained in a letter to 'Hallie', the elder daughter of a family he had visited at Ripon, it commemorates her piano playing, which Carroll assures her 'Will make my spirit roam' whenever he hears the same songs, and ends with another promise:

And now farewell 'Childe Hallie'!
Though I am growing old,
Fond mem'ry still will charm me,
To you I'll ne'er grow cold.

The pun on 'child' and 'Childe' (a young knight like Lord Byron's Childe Harold or Robert Browning's Childe Roland) adds a chivalric gloss to Carroll's compliment, and the ambiguity of the final line encourages the idea that they will remain fond of each other. But what underlines his vow of constancy is the simple fact that it is made in a poem. Just as Carroll promises to keep returning to her playing in his memory, so the poem loops back to the same scene in stanza after stanza like the refrain of an old song.

Although the journey at the heart of *Alice's Adventures in Wonderland* had taken place entirely in Alice's head, it spurred Carroll into thinking about more conventional forms of travel. Some were relatively unambitious, such as an unpublished ballad entitled 'A Day in the Country', dated 1866, in which he described a photographic expedition that ends in another disastrous family portrait: 'never, never was there seen | A thing so hideous, so distressing!' It is probably more impressive as a puzzle than as a poem, because Carroll's real skill lay in the ingenious use he made of the acrostic form, with every line springing out of one of the letters in his code words 'PORTMANTEAU' and 'PHOTOGRAPHY'. The result was a witty set of variations on the idea of an excursion, for no matter how far each line wandered it always ended by returning to the poem's home key. Once again Carroll had shown how closely his creative freedom was bound up with formal control. But at some point in the next few months he seems to have decided that such limited forms of travel were no longer enough to satisfy him, and soon these rather vague ideas had firmed up into a surprising plan: he would go to Russia.

*

Fifteen

In July 1879, Mark Twain, who was probably better known in his lifetime as a travel writer than a novelist, met Carroll at some amateur dramatics hosted by the MacDonald family. Although Carroll was 'pleased and interested' to make his acquaintance, Twain was less impressed. Carroll was 'only interesting to look at', he reported, 'for he was the stillest and shyest full-grown man I ever met', with conversational skills that were limited to occasionally asking a question.

Meetings between writers are invariably disappointing to anyone who assumes they will be as entertaining as a piece of scripted dialogue. When James Joyce encountered Marcel Proust at a Paris dinner party in 1921, two of the world's greatest living novelists found themselves scratching around for conversational openings like a couple on a blind date. According to William Carlos Williams, Joyce confessed that 'I've headaches every day. My eyes are terrible', and Proust replied with his own medical complaints, ending with 'oh, my stomach'; in another version told by Joyce, their conversation mostly revolved around truffles.

In Carroll's case, the literary meetings that failed to happen were sometimes even more disappointing. It appears that he never met Edward Lear, for example, although they had friends such as Tennyson in common. However, one place they did keep bumping into each other was on the page, and critics of both writers have spent many fruitless hours trying to establish whether the number of common features in their work is the result of influence or accident: a 'treacle-well' (Carroll) and 'deep pits of Mulberry Jam' (Lear); 'cats in the coffee and mice in the tea' (Carroll) and the Old Person of Ewell who made his gruel nice by 'insert[ing] some mice' (Lear); 'the Owl and the Panther' (Carroll) and 'the Owl and the Pussy-Cat' (Lear); creatures that are 'something like corkscrews' (Carroll) and 'the Fimble Fowl, with a corkscrew leg' (Lear). Their uses of literary form were also intriguingly aligned. Many of Lear's limericks, in particular, repeatedly open up little windows of escape before slamming them shut again:

> There was an old man who screamed out
> Whenever they knocked him about:
> So they took off his boots, and fed him with fruits,
> And continued to knock him about.

This is funny, in the same way that a clown being repeatedly smacked on the head by a ladder is funny, but the impression that it is unavoidable is largely generated by Lear's chosen form. The Italian word *stanza* literally means a stopping place or a room, but here Lear has transformed it into something more like a prison cell, in which the alarmingly faceless 'they' have confined their victim. The rhymes hint at an alternative outcome, but this is denied by Lear's self-imposed requirement that a limerick should always return to its starting point. So 'screamed out' leads to 'knocked him about', and 'knocked him about' produces 'knock him about', like a miniature version of the idea that violence breeds more violence. But there is no way out.

If Lear's limericks allowed him to channel his fears of stagnation, his longer nonsense poems opened up more liberating alternatives. From the Jumblies to a Daddy Long-Legs, many of the creatures in his poems travel impossible distances and end up in destinations that exist only in the world of books. They go to sea in a sieve, or search for somewhere to play for evermore at battlecock and shuttledore – any place that will give odd couples and eccentric groups the opportunity to live happily ever after. To some extent they are all disguised versions of Lear himself, who spent his adult life wandering across Europe and the Middle East, pen and sketchbook in hand, and when he pictured himself as an animal usually chose a bird – a creature evolved for flight. Rearranged in alphabetical order, the full list of his destinations reads more like the index to an atlas: Albania, Belgium, Corfu, Dardanelles, Egypt, France, Greece, Holland, Italy, Jerusalem . . .

By contrast, until the publication of *Alice's Adventures in Wonderland* Carroll had never ventured further than the Isle of Wight. In 1856 he had composed a fifteen-page speech about the life of Richard Hakluyt, the great Elizabethan travel writer and former Student of Christ Church, to be delivered at a college dinner. That set the tone for the next decade of his life, during which he was usually happier mapping out long journeys in writing than taking them on in person. And then, in the summer of 1867, he agreed to undertake a two-month trip overland to Russia. It would only have been slightly more surprising if he had announced that he was to lead an expedition in search of the source of the Nile.

On 11 July, Carroll received his passport – a letter signed by Lord Stanley, the Secretary of State for Foreign Affairs, requesting unhindered passage for a British subject 'travelling on the Continent' – and heard from his travelling companion Henry Liddon that 'he can go abroad with me, and we have decided on Moscow!' Carroll was 'much taken by the idea', Liddon recorded in his diary, although Carroll acknowledged that their choice of destination was 'Ambitious for one who has never yet left England'. In fact, their plans would have been thought ambitious even by the most experienced of travellers. Although communications inside Russia had improved significantly since the end of the Crimean War, and in 1865 the publisher John Murray had added a revised *Handbook for Travellers in Russia, Poland, and Finland* to his popular range of travel guides, it was a long way from the usual routes selected by Victorian travellers, a series of well-trodden paths that wound their way through countries such as France and Italy with the reassuring predictability of a modern package tour. The growing popularity of these destinations was confirmed in 1865, the same year as the publication of *Alice's Adventures in Wonderland*, with the opening of a new set of offices in Fleet Street by the canny travel entrepreneur Thomas Cook, where customers could buy tickets, guidebooks and a whole set of other 'tourist requisites' such as 'carpet and leather bags, hat-cases, telescopes, and Alpine slippers'. This new breed of Victorian tourist was soon the target of satire, much of it carelessly snobbish in nature, as can be seen in the stories published by George Rose ('Arthur Sketchley') that dealt with his cockney heroine Mrs

Brown embarking on a series of Cook's tours: *Mrs Brown in the Highlands,* *Mrs Brown up the Nile* and others. But there is no book entitled *Mrs Brown in Russia*, and that is because for most travellers it was still impossibly distant. Russia had been the largest blank space on Carroll's childhood map of Europe, a gaping void that spilled over the edge of his page, and as recently as 1864 he had used the country as a synonym for the furthest place anyone could imagine, writing to George MacDonald's daughter Mary that he had directed some of his letters so violently 'they went far beyond the mark – some of them were picked up at the other end of Russia'. Despite a considerable British presence in major cities such as St Petersburg, visiting it still had an air of voyaging into the unknown. George Augustus Sala, who was sent to Russia as a special correspondent for Dickens's journal *Household Words* in 1856, and later published an account of his travels in *A Journey Due North*, pointed out that looking at a map before he left all he could see was 'one vast and delightful region of mysteries, and adventures, and perilous expeditions: a glorious wonder-land'.

Carroll had chosen his travel partner wisely. Not only was Liddon an old friend and fellow Student at Christ Church, who was about to publish a series of Bampton Lectures on the divinity of Christ that would later approach the status of a theological textbook, he was also a man of unimpeachable good sense and integrity. If that makes him sound a little dull, the accusation may not be wholly fair – one contemporary recalled his sense of humour as 'a most refreshing, sparkling, surprising thing' – but he was certainly Carroll's equal in moral probity. If anything, he was even more upright. His favourite hobby as a schoolboy had been preaching, 'robed in a sheet of *The Times*', having already written sermons with titles such as 'The Danger of Procrastination' and 'Preparation for Judgment', and he later boasted that 'I have never been inside a theatre since I took Orders in 1852, and I do not mean to go into one, please God, while I live.' This self-imposed ban extended to other kinds of public performance: while he was an undergraduate, he attended just one debate at the Oxford Union, and pithily summed up his reaction as 'Disgusted'. As a theologian, he had his own reasons for wanting to visit Russia: his trip was one of several missions being undertaken at the time by Anglicans hoping to explore the possibility of a full reunion of the Western and Eastern churches. For Carroll, however, it appears that Russia's primary appeal lay in the fact that it was a literary environment as well as a real place.

He had already seen a play on a Russian theme in July 1865, Tom Taylor's *The Serf, or, Love Levels All*, just one of a number of contemporary melodramas that dealt with the events surrounding Czar Alexander II's emancipation of the serfs in 1861. Carroll would have known that Russia was also a popular subject for fiction, with several novels taking the Crimean War as a suitable backdrop for rousing tales of heroism. In fact, for readers who relied on books and newspapers for their information, Russia was a country made entirely out of words, and the difficulty of acquiring first-hand knowledge of it meant that the line between fact and fiction was repeatedly smudged. Many Russian novels were assumed to be lightly disguised reportage: as late as 1887, Matthew Arnold used his essay on Tolstoy to point out that 'we are not to take *Anna Karénine* [he had read it in French translation] as a work of art; we are to take it as a piece of life'. Meanwhile, books advertised as historical accounts often drifted into much hazier narrative territory. *A Journey Due North*, which opens with Sala's fantasies about Russia as a 'great storehouse of romance', is brought down to earth as soon as he arrives in St Petersburg and confronts the reality of slippery pavements and haggling shopkeepers, but even then he cannot resist framing events in fictional language, as he describes the city as an 'Arabian Nightmare' or coos over a group of children dressed in miniature uniforms as 'living story-books in themselves'. Other contemporary works deliberately exploited this uncertainty. For example, William Kingston's *Fred Markham in Russia; or, The Boy Travellers in the Land of the Czar* (1858) is principally a traditional travelogue hidden inside a half-hearted attempt at an adventure story, but the narrative conventions of fiction for boys (plenty of plot and very little analysis) mean that Kingston's young heroes set off with minimal preparations: five pages into their story they are being advised to pack 'a complete suit of water-proof clothing, including boots and hat', and two pages later they are on board a steamer and puffing out to sea.

Carroll had at least a week to plan for his journey, and his preparations are likely to have been considerably more thorough. In *Through the Looking-Glass*, the Red Queen tries to help Alice by taking a ribbon out of her pocket to measure the ground and 'sticking little pegs in here and there', before giving very precise travel instructions that make no sense at all. Like many of Carroll's best jokes, it is a parody of behaviour he took perfectly seriously elsewhere. Isa Bowman recalled that he was a meticulous traveller, who used to 'map out exactly every minute of the time that we were to take on the way' and always carried two purses, each divided into a number of compartments, so that he could prepare the precise sum required for each transaction in advance, including train fares, porters,

One of Carroll's pocketbooks

newspapers, refreshments and cabs. (He was especially nervous about cabs: the longest conversation he recorded in Russia was his attempt to negotiate the fare for a droshky ride, and he continued to worry about travellers being cheated by drivers in unfamiliar towns.) Another brown leather pocketbook he owned was divided into ten compartments, each neatly labelled, with designated places for everything from '1. Stamps, visiting-cards, &c.' to '10. Telegraph-forms & 6d stamps'. Doubtless his arrangements for a two-month trip abroad were proportionately elaborate. He certainly showed no desire to be carried along by chance: even his passport was kept separately in a black leather wallet with 'REVD. CHARLES L. DODGSON' stamped on it in crisp gilt letters, just in case there was any doubt over where a document made out to 'The Reverend Charles L. Dodgson' belonged.

Carroll also started a new journal, which would eventually swell to more than 130 pages fluently written in two notebooks. These remained unpublished at his death, but the length and detail of his daily reports, together with the sketches he made of local Russian people and a few key words of vocabulary, indicate that he may originally have planned to turn them into a book. This is not surprising when one considers the growing appetite among readers for more unusual travel narratives. With so many tourists now publishing accounts of their journeys, it was widely suspected that the usual destinations had been worked out like the gold in a formerly rich seam; indeed, countries like Italy had been so thoroughly picked over that writers were being forced into ever smaller geographical niches, producing books such as *Three Months Passed in the Mountains East of Rome* and *A Tour Through the Southern Provinces of the Kingdom of Naples*.

The entries in Carroll's journal are typically precise: in Berlin he visits a gallery that contains '1243 pictures', while the train from Königsberg to St Petersburg takes '28½ hours'. They also reveal his scrambling eye for novelty, as he rattles over potholes in strange cities, clambers up bell towers clutching his spyglass, transcribes some 'alarming' fragments of Russian, such as 'zashtsheeshtshayoushtsheekhsya', which he translates as 'of persons defending themselves', samples the local rowanberry liqueur and attends several theatre productions in the local language. His writing certainly crackles with more imaginative energy than Liddon's diary, with its dutiful recording of the churches he has visited and a weary list of his medical complaints; if Liddon was indeed 'a brilliant story-teller', as one contemporary insisted, on the evidence of his diary he tended to switch off this narrative gift when he found himself alone with his thoughts. The best of Carroll's descriptions, by contrast, show a talent for distilling his surroundings into sentences that at their best work like imagist poems, such as his memory of some trees that resembled a line of soldiers 'bending . . . as if under the weight of ghostly knapsacks'. (Liddon: 'Our rooms look out on the Park of Brussels.')

Carroll also found himself viewing Russia through a thick literary lens, particularly when he used his journal to practise turning the bumbling reality of daily travel into slick comic anecdotes. On one occasion, he describes how he has managed to recover Liddon's coat from a Russian-speaking maid by drawing a sketch of it being handed over, after a series of dumb shows had produced nothing more useful than a large clothes-brush and a pillow, and as he tells the story it rapidly becomes a domestic farce being acted out for the amusement of an unseen audience. Another conversation with a German waiter, which revolved around whether Carroll wanted his eggs to be 'boiled' or 'broiled', is presented in the same way, as a dialogue rooted in the sort of misunderstanding that is much funnier in a play than it is in real life. By the time Carroll offers an account of his visit to a 'wonderful' town outside Moscow, where he meets people in 'unheard-of costumes' and has an 'adventure' at sunset watching the call to prayers at a local mosque, it is unclear whether he is simply recording his impressions as they occurred to him, or filtering them through memories of the play he saw that night: *Aladdin and the Wonderful Lamp*.

The idea that British tourists preferred foreign places when they had been made comfortingly familiar was a standard accusation at the time, and although this could be reflected in something as simple as how their eggs were cooked, it was widely suspected that many tourists were only interested in seeing what they had already read about. Guidebooks were a popular target: in 1844, Thackeray pointed out that the success of Murray's *Handbook for Travellers on the Continent* was such that 'Every

English party I saw had this infallible red book in their hands', and by 1865, the historian James Bryce was complaining that tourists in Italy seemed 'to see the sights for no purpose but that of verifying their Murray'. Murray's guidebooks included a good selection of literary quotations alongside advice about choosing hotels and avoiding pickpockets, building on the earlier fashion that had seen thousands of tourists wandering around Europe clutching a copy of Byron's poems, one of Murray's previous publishing successes, in the hope that it would teach them what they should feel about the sight of moonlight falling on the Parthenon, or how they could remain heroically alone in a crowd. (Byron was one of the first writers to use the term 'guide-book', in Canto II of *Don Juan*, so he could hardly be said to have been unaware of this move towards literary tourism.) Not everyone was convinced that writers were suitable people to prepare a traveller for new experiences: Thackeray pointed out that the 'sweet waters' of the Rhine celebrated by Byron in *Childe Harold's Pilgrimage* were actually filthy, and as for his Rhenish 'peasant girls with deep blue eyes', anyone with eyes of their own could see that they were 'brown-faced, flat-nosed, thick-lipped, dirty wenches!' However, in Carroll's case, the red cloth-bound book that he used both as a supplementary guide and as a way of making sense of his own thoughts was not Murray's *Handbook for Travellers in Russia, Poland, and Finland*, but another 1865 publication: *Alice's Adventures in Wonderland*.

On several pages of his journal, Carroll sounds less like a Victorian traveller ticking items off his itinerary than another Alice in a real Wonderland. He plays games with scale: each of the churches he sees out of the train window looks 'very like a cruet stand'; St Petersburg is so huge that 'it is like walking about in a city of giants'. The transformation of their railway carriage seats into 'very comfortable beds' is like 'an elaborate conjuring-trick'. And repeatedly he returns to the 'wonder' of his surroundings: the 'wonder and novelty' of St Petersburg's illuminated shop signs and blue church domes covered in gold stars; the 'wonderful' Hermitage he visits with its many miniature rooms and a door that is 'about 4 feet high', as if waiting for a Russian Alice to enter it; a monk's house where he discovers 'a little tea-party going on' – a scene 'so entirely sudden and unexpected', at least to anyone unfamiliar with the Hatter's Mad Tea-Party, that 'it felt almost like a dream'. By the time of his return to Britain, this sense of imaginative dislocation had firmed up into a distinct narrative style. Crossing the Channel, he spots the lights of Dover slowly broadening in the distance, 'as if the old land were opening its arms to receive its homeward bound children'. Soon 'a glimmering line on the dark water, like a reflection of the Milky Way', is revealed to be the lights of houses on the shore, and 'the faint white line behind them, which looked at first like a mist creeping along the horizon', turns into 'the white cliffs of old England'. (Liddon's diary was less rhapsodic: 'The passage threatened to be both rainy and stormy,' he reported stoically, but in fact 'the sea was so smooth that not a single person was ill'.) That is where Carroll's travel journal ends. But his interest in a different form of travel – the kind that involved being transported by the imagination rather than by ferry or droshky – had taken on a new momentum.

Carroll returned to Oxford in October 1867, and although Russia continued to linger in his mind for a while longer – in 1874 he composed 'A Russian's Day in England', which used the conceit of a foreign visitor's hourly diary to teach the reader how to count up to ten in Russian – from now on his preference was for travel that did not involve the physical inconvenience of leaving home. Over the years this took on various forms: in April 1868 it was the invention of a 'telegraph-cipher' for sending secret messages in code; between 1875 and 1890 he invested considerable sums of money, not very profitably, in steamships; in 1887 he chose a set of new tiles designed by William De Morgan for his sitting-room fireplace in Christ Church, which depicted a large sailing ship surrounded by a set of fantastic creatures including a dodo and a dragon. At times they were scarcely less mobile than Carroll himself.

Some of this reluctance to travel far reflected his changing family circumstances. In June 1868 Carroll's father died, an event he later described as the 'greatest blow' of his life, and he was forced to find his brothers and sisters a new place to live. The house he chose, the Chestnuts, was a substantial slab of neo-Georgian red brick in Guildford, recently built on a hill with clear views across the town and a short walk from the railway station. On 1 September, the rest of the Dodgson family left Croft Rectory for the last time, and within a few weeks they had moved into their new home. Carroll would continue to visit the Chestnuts at regular intervals, and if he showed little inclination to travel any further, that may be because he now thought of himself as the anchor around which others could move more freely. His missionary brother Edwin set sail for Zanzibar in 1879, and then travelled to Tristan da Cunha in 1881, eventually spending eight years there as the island's religious leader and schoolmaster (also its postman, librarian, meteorologist, entertainer and potato-patch digger), but Edwin could do all this with a clear conscience precisely because he did not have similar responsibilities at home.

The other major change in Carroll's living arrangements came at the end of October, when he took up residence in a spacious new set of rooms located in the north-west corner of Tom Quad. It was his fifth home altogether in Christ Church, and it would be his last: for the next thirty years, he had the luxury of a separate dining room, a spare bedroom equipped with a 'japanned sponge bath', and a large cupboard that he converted into a photographic darkroom. Occasionally he bought new furniture and made small improvements, installing asbestos fires and a 'ventilating globe chandelier', or found space in his study for 'nests of pigeon-holes, each neatly labelled', but he never again felt the urge to move. The most obvious reason is that this expensive suite of rooms, which he could now afford thanks to the growing profits from his writing, was among the best Christ Church had to offer. But there is another possible reason: they were the perfect base from which he could set off on a new series of virtual travels. Some of these were achieved through reading – his library included a generous selection of travel books on places from Belgium to New Zealand – although they also had more unusual forms: in 1888, he took Isa Bowman to see a panorama of the 'Falls of Niagara' in Oxford, a previous version of which had been advertised as the only alternative available 'to those who have never been and never intend to be in North America', and which according to Carroll she thought 'very wonderful'. However, after the success of *Alice's Adventures in Wonderland*, the form of travel he enjoyed most was writing, for as he stood at the mahogany writing desk in his study, the small movements of his hand across the page could create a new world and explore it at the same time. To an outsider this might not have seemed particularly adventurous, especially when compared to the globetrotting activities of his contemporaries, but in some ways Carroll's chosen form of travel was even more radical, because it meant leaving himself behind and leading his readers on an expedition into the unknown. And as one of his child-friends later explained, when he told you a story 'You never knew where he would take you next.'

*

Sixteen

C arroll continued to enjoy the idea of his fictional characters exploring new corners of the real world. One way he accelerated their progress was by sending out presentation copies of *Alice's Adventures in Wonderland* as little emissaries of friendship. He had also started to use his book like a weighty calling card, as he had previously done with his photograph albums, allowing him to gain entry into the sort of social circles that would otherwise have been closed off to him. Occasionally he combined his different reputations as an academic, photographer and author to impressive effect: in June 1870 he applied through Liddon to photograph the children of Lord Salisbury, the Chancellor of Oxford and future Prime Minister, and on hearing that he had been successful he confessed that 'I fancy *Wonderland* had a great deal to do with my gracious reception.' This photography session marked the start of a long and courteous friendship; for several years following their first meeting, he was a New Year's guest at Hatfield House, Salisbury's grand family home, where there was usually a large party of children for him to entertain.

Another way he sought to combine writing with friendship was through translation. The first indication that Carroll was considering foreign editions of *Alice's Adventures in Wonderland* came in August 1866, when he wrote to ask Alexander Macmillan what he thought of 'my idea of putting it into French, or German, or both, and trying for a Continental sale'. By April 1867, he had succeeded in finding translators for both languages: the French edition would be rendered by Henri Bué, son of the Oxford linguist Jules Bué, who had published a dry but sensible textbook on translation in 1857 and had given Carroll some private French lessons in 1867; and the German edition by Antonie Zimmermann, an acquaintance of his aunt Caroline. The fact that both translators had been recommended by colleagues or family members is probably significant, as it allowed Carroll to retain a degree of intimacy even after the story had been taken out of his hands. Progress was again slowed by his meticulous supervision – in June 1867, he asked Macmillan for twenty proof copies of the French text to be printed so that he could ask his friends for their 'opinions and suggestions' – but both translations had appeared by the end of 1869: *Alice's Abenteuer im Wunderland* von Lewis Carroll (green cloth) in February, and *Aventures d'Alice Au Pays des Merveilles* par Lewis Carroll (blue cloth) in August. Alice Liddell received specially bound presentation copies of both: the German translation in green morocco and the French one in red morocco, each with her initials picked out in gilt. Whether she tried to read them is not known, but they provided handsome evidence that her story was drifting ever further away from the riverbank.

According to the critic Donald Rackin, the *Alice* books are distinguished by a 'matter-of-fact' tone and a 'limpid prose style simple enough for little children (and hence for easy translation)'. Carroll might have picked over that last claim. It is only non-words such as the Gryphon's 'Hjckrrh!' that are easy to translate; almost every other aspect of a language is notoriously vulnerable to being hijacked and detoured when it is removed from its original home. That is not only because of the notorious difficulty of finding a perfect fit between the meanings of words in two different languages. It is also because of how these words are linked together within each language, like a spider's web that cannot be touched anywhere without the whole structure quivering into life. '"What's the French for fiddle-de-dee?"' the Queen asks Alice in *Through the Looking-Glass*, to which Alice gravely replies, '"Fiddle-de-dee's not English."' But even an expression like 'Fiddle-de-dee', a common nineteenth-century synonym for 'Nonsense', allows a speaker to enjoy hearing a faint outline of 'de' hidden inside 'Fiddle' and 'dee' as a mouth-stretching version of 'de'. The same principle generates larger coincidences in language, which is why the Mouse in Wonderland can tell a 'long and a sad tale', and Alice can look at its appearance and say, '"It *is* a long tail, certainly."' The pun is a linguistic accident no less lucky than any of the other meetings in Wonderland, but to translate it would be like trying to play a game using two sets of rules at once.

There was also the question of parody to consider. On several occasions, Carroll had encouraged readers of *Alice's Adventures in Wonderland* to think they were being given one kind of poem before giving them something different, but for this narrative trick to work they needed to know the English anthology pieces he was parodying. As early as October 1866, Carroll wondered whether 'the book is *untranslatable* into either French or German: the puns and songs being the chief obstacle', and he continued to worry that 'if, as I fear, the originals are not known', his parodies would be 'unintelligible'. One solution would have been to strip out everything that resisted straightforward paraphrase, but in the end he opted for a style of translation that aimed for generously loose equivalents rather than exact linguistic parallels. The results showed that even a familiar story was capable of producing new adventures in language.

Of the different translations he commissioned, Carroll seems to have preferred the German version, writing a preface that lavished praise on Zimmermann for managing to come up with jokes that were 'due solely to the translator's skills' ('allein der Gewandheit der Uebersetzerin'), and changing small features of the text that might have offended the loyal subjects of Kaiser Wilhelm I, with Bill the Lizard becoming Wabbel, thereby relinquishing Carroll's deliciously cheap gag when 'The Rabbit sends in a Little Bill', and 'You are old, Father William' becoming 'Ihr seid alt, Vater Martin'. The French translation was more troublesome, with Carroll approaching the bilingual *Punch* contributor George du Maurier to suggest improvements to the draft produced by Bué *père et fils*, but the published text was possibly even more successful in allowing Alice to explore a new linguistic Wonderland.

Inevitably several more of Carroll's original jokes are lost: whereas the English Alice's tongue twists itself around the question of whether cats eat bats, or bats eat cats, the French opts for sturdy literalism – 'Les chats mangent-ils les chauves-souris?' On the other hand, the French word for a bat, literally a 'bald mouse', brings it much closer to the first creature

Alice meets underground, and this sets the tone for a translation packed with transformations no less hazily dreamlike in French than they are in English. Alice's fall is signalled with 'Tombe, tombe, tombe!', which means 'Falling, falling, falling' but opens up a new crack of danger in the story by recalling that a 'tombe' is also a grave. The bottle Alice drinks from is still marked 'POISON', a word that is the same in both languages, but in the French text it is later reworked into a footman who looks like a huge 'poisson' (fish). When Alice listens to the Mouse's tale, although the pun on 'tail' is lost, the fact that a French mouse is a 'souris' now carries a new comic charge, because it is a creature that always sounds as if it is about to break into a smile ('Je souris' = 'I smile'). Such moments were no less governed by chance than Carroll's original puns or rhymes, but in revealing how Alice's fall into a foreign Wonderland also involved her slipping into the grooves of a different language they made her adventures seem at once deeply familiar and disconcertingly strange.

Translation was just one of the ways Carroll tried to build on the unexpected success of *Alice's Adventures in Wonderland*. In April 1869, he sent an inscribed German translation bound in green morocco to Queen Victoria's youngest daughter Princess Beatrice, no doubt assuming that it would find a good home in a family with such strong Teutonic roots. (Victoria was certainly aware of *Alice's Adventures in Wonderland*: Carroll had sent Princess Beatrice a copy in 1865, and it was soon 'a proven favourite' in the royal nursery. While the Queen was still mourning Prince Albert's death it is reported that she asked a three-year-old girl absorbed in Carroll's book what she was reading, and the girl replied by pointing to the picture of Alice swimming in the Pool of Tears and artlessly wondering, 'Do you think, please, *you* could cry as much as that!') Carroll also considered using the same binding as his first *Alice* book for a collection of poems he published in 1869 as *Phantasmagoria and Other Poems*. This featured a good deal of material that had previously appeared in journals with a modest circulation, including 'Hiawatha's Photographing' and 'Beatrice', as well as the new ghost story that provided the book with its title, but Carroll finally decided that giving this loose collection of material such a familiar appearance might not produce favourable comparisons, and that for the

Carroll's early sketch of the Pool of Tears

sake of publicity having 'Lewis Carroll' on the cover would suffice. Macmillan wanted to go further, asking if he would consider advertising his new book as '*by the author of Alice*', and by way of compromise Carroll proposed the insertion of 'a loose fly-sheet advertisement of *Phantasmagoria* into each copy of *Alice* you send out'. (Macmillan finally got his way in the second edition, which had 'Author of *Alice's Adventures in Wonderland*' on the title page.) Anyone who read Carroll's title poem, the tale of a young ghost mistakenly haunting the wrong house, would quickly have recognized it as a comic-Gothic variation on one of the main ideas underlying his earlier book. It was in effect a shaggy-dog version of popular Victorian magic lantern shows, which depicted thrilling scenes of ghosts and demons appearing to change shape and advance on the audience. A little earlier in the century, 'phantasmagoria' had also been used by Coleridge to describe the power of the imagination to create dreamlike displays of rapidly shifting images, and this was another idea that interested Carroll. In fact, *Alice's Phantasmagoria* could have been a good alternative title for *Alice's Adventures in Wonderland*, were it not for Carroll's desire to hold back the surprise that Wonderland was a dreamscape rather than a real place.

Phantasmagoria sold respectably well, if not spectacularly, but by then

Carroll had decided that if he was going to experiment with such ideas again, there was a much better way of doing it. A second *Alice* book would allow him to return to his most successful depiction of the mind entertaining itself. Creating what would be simultaneously a new story and a renewal of his old story would also be an ideal way to reconcile his innovative and conservative impulses. As early as August 1866, Carroll told Macmillan that he had 'a floating idea of writing a sort of sequel to *Alice*', and Macmillan replied to say that he would be 'curious' to know more. By January 1868, Carroll had started to assemble another mixture of narrative scraps and comic poems, some of which he adapted from much earlier work – the opening of 'Jabberwocky', for example, had first appeared in his family magazine *Mischmasch* in 1855, where it had been handwritten in imitation of an ancient manuscript, under the title 'Stanza of Anglo-Saxon Poetry'. Central to the idea of a sequel would be its physical appearance on the page, and in April 1868 Carroll tried to secure Tenniel as his illustrator for a second time. After several weeks of uncertainty, and a show of reluctance from Tenniel that forced Carroll to make tentative enquiries into a possible replacement (one option he explored was 'Bab', better known as W. S. Gilbert, whose grotesque comic drawings Carroll thought 'full of fun' although lacking 'anything pretty and graceful'), in June 1868 author and illustrator agreed to work together again. At this stage Carroll referred to the project simply as 'the 2nd volume of *Alice*', although he also had a different name for it. Like the producer of a modern movie franchise, having been successful with one story about Alice, he now started to plan '*Alice II*'.

*

Seventeen

One problem with any fictional continuation is that it risks turning into a bloodless imitation of its original; the sequel is rarely the equal. This is not something Carroll shied away from; indeed, he incorporated it into his writing. There is a nasty moment in *Through the Looking-Glass* when Humpty Dumpty asks Alice how old she is, and she tells him, '"Seven years and six months."' '"An uncomfortable sort of age,"' he replies, before going on thoughtfully, '"Now if you'd asked *my* advice, I'd have said 'Leave off at seven'".' Of course, the only way a real girl could do this would be by dying, as Alice Liddell's little brother James had 'left off' at two years and eleven months in 1853 after a bout of scarlet fever. Fictional girls were different. In reply to Alice's indignant remark that '"one ca'n't help growing any older"', Humpty Dumpty grimly points out that *"One* ca'n't, perhaps . . . but *two* can"', and although this piece of jet-black comedy conjures up scenes of children being offered pills and pillows to help them sidestep the ageing process, it is an accurate summary of the relationship between Carroll and his dream-child. Alice could indeed have left off at seven if he had chosen to keep her the same age in this second set of adventures, but an even easier way to ensure she didn't grow any older would have been for him not to write the book at all. Having decided to take up the challenge, how could he please readers who had enjoyed his first story without simply giving them more of the same? His answer was to send his heroine to a place where everything would be multiplied. Alice I would become Alice II by passing through a mirror into Looking-Glass Land.

Magic mirrors were nothing new in fiction. They had long been a stock property of fairy tales, in which they became windows that revealed hidden truths or showed what was happening far away. As recently as

December 1865, *Alice's Adventures in Wonderland* had been reviewed in *The Times* alongside a modern example of the genre, a linked collection of fairy tales by William Gilbert (the father of W. S. Gilbert) that revolved around an enchanted Venetian looking-glass. The idea that a mirror could be used as a gateway to an imaginary elsewhere was also popular in the period. Earlier in the century, London's Coburg Theatre (now the Old Vic) had become famous for its 'looking-glass curtain', constructed from sixty-three huge plates of glass set in an elaborate gilt frame, which reflected finger-smeared images of the audience back at themselves. The idea that a mirror might contain a hidden rival to the real world, like the impressive stage sets that awaited the Coburg's audience when the looking-glass curtain was lifted, had parallels in Victorian fiction. 'All mirrors are magic mirrors,' George MacDonald had written in *Phantastes*, because they turned ordinary objects into a set of mysterious twins that were 'the same and not the same'. A mirror also resembled a story in other ways: both offered the viewer a neatly framed simulacrum of life; both flattened reality into two dimensions while giving the illusion of depth. MacDonald's conclusion had been that our feelings when we contemplate this reflected world closely parallel our experience of opening a book: 'I should like to live in THAT room if only I could get into it.' Another story Carroll knew, Charles Kingsley's *The Water-Babies* (1863), had entertained readers with an aquatic version of the same fantasy, because although the chimney-sweep Tom is astonished when he looks into the 'great mirror' of Ellie's bedroom and sees an 'ugly, black, ragged figure' grimacing back at him, his desire to be clean makes him plunge into a brook where he instantly becomes fresh and new (actually a newt), thereby discovering the clean inner self that had been hiding on the other side all along.

On a more personal level, mirrors reflected Carroll's simple pleasure in reversing the usual direction of life, which ranged from the transparent code of 'mirror writing' to a collection of music boxes on which he played tunes backwards to produce the comic effect of music 'standing on its head' like Father William. His other stories are no less packed with ideas that invite us to pivot them around or flip them over. In *Sylvie and Bruno* alone, in addition to the watch peg that makes time run backwards, we are introduced to a special kind of wool stuffing that makes packages lighter than air, a purse that has its inside on its outside and its outside on its inside, and a reminder that EVIL is simply LIVE the wrong way round. Carroll's photography made these ideas visible. Negatives depicted a world of opposites: left was right and right was left; white was black and black was white. A surviving negative of Alice Liddell as 'Queen of the May' shows the unearthly effects this could produce: while her face and hands are a chemical black, her normally dark hair and eyes glow with a soft white light, as if the photographic process had transformed her wreath of flowers into a kind of halo. Some of Carroll's images even included mirrors, as if playfully drawing attention to the fact that photography gave people a more permanent way of doubling up reality. Here too Carroll was tapping into a popular set of ideas. In 1859, Oliver Wendell Holmes had characterized photography as 'the mirror with a memory', and not only because the earlier daguerreotype process produced images with a faint silvery sheen. The photograph flattened life

Negative of Alice Liddell as 'Queen of the May' (May or June 1860)

into two dimensions, like someone looking in a mirror, while adding an extra dimension of time.

Through the Looking-Glass is similarly framed as a portal into the past. Carroll's first *Alice* book had opened with a poem about the 'golden afternoon' on the river, and ended with a vision of Alice as a grown-up looking back on 'happy summer days'. His new story invited readers to enter and exit via the same scene, but this time he presented the past as more than just a bundle of personal memories. It was a force as impersonal as gravity. The first two lines of his new opening poem establish a tone of lyrical nostalgia: 'Child of the pure unclouded brow | And dreaming eyes of wonder!' As it continues, these fond backward glances multiply to build up a more detailed reconstruction of the golden afternoon, and Carroll starts to link the form of his poem to its subject matter. He recalls 'The rhythm of our rowing' in lines that float along on their own potentially endless metrical pulse; he promises to keep Alice safe in 'childhood's nest of gladness' within a perfectly rhymed stanza that is itself a snug little nest of words. Carroll's new closing poem performs the same trick even more adroitly:

> A boat, beneath a sunny sky
> Lingering onward dreamily
> In an evening of July—
>
> Children three that nestle near,
> Eager eye and willing ear,
> Pleased a simple tale to hear—

At its conclusion, the poem is revealed to be another acrostic: ALICEPLEASANCELIDDELL. And having chosen this name to serve as the poem's skeleton, Carroll proceeds to flesh it out and bring it to life. 'Lingering' is the first of several present participles that make it sound as if the action is still going on ('moving', 'waking', 'Dreaming', 'drifting'), and many lines flirt with closure before extending themselves with a dash, or using a comma to take a breath and carry on.

The narrative of *Through the Looking-Glass* is equally unstable. "'Things flow about so here!'" Alice exclaims as she tries to seize the goods on display in a shop, vainly pursuing 'a large bright thing, that looked sometimes like a doll and sometimes like a work-box', and her observation is a good summary of the story as a whole. Almost everything in Looking-Glass Land is in a state of flux. Knitting needles turn into oars in Alice's hands; rushes live up to their name by melting as rapidly as snow. Some of these transformations follow the pattern of Wonderland, by being comically distorted versions of waking life. So, when the White Queen exclaims, "'My imperial kitten!'" to a pawn, and the White King tells her, "'I turned cold to the very ends of my whiskers!'" we are being gently reminded that before Alice fell asleep she had been playing a game of "'let's pretend'" with her kittens. The dreaming Alice's mind is again revealed to be a jumble of fragments from her waking life, which is why the Sheep cries out "'Feather! Feather!'" when they are in a boat, because this was something Carroll had taught Alice Liddell to do: 'It was a proud day when we could "feather our oars" properly,' she recalled in one memoir of her childhood. This time Alice's mind also includes odds and ends from Carroll's previous story, which makes *Through the Looking-Glass* even more like a literary miscellany that has been put through a shredder. Consequently, although she repeats her earlier cry that she is lonely (Wonderland: "'I am so *very* tired of being all alone here!'"; Looking-Glass Land: "'it is so *very* lonely here!'"), during this second dream she has some familiar faces to keep her company.

The Hatter has become the King's Messenger, and has been thrown into jail for a crime he has yet to commit, which is a logical extension of the Queen of Hearts's urging of "'Sentence first – verdict afterwards!'" during the earlier trial; later he reappears disguised as 'Hatta', 'with a cup of tea in one hand and a piece of bread-and-butter in the other', like a takeaway from the Mad Tea-Party in Wonderland, and is accompanied by 'Haigha' (the Hare). Many of Carroll's earlier narrative devices also return. Language again produces action: Humpty Dumpty is seen 'breaking into a sudden passion' shortly before he is smashed into pieces; the King asks for a ham sandwich and some hay, which are then magically produced from the Messenger's bag, as presumably haddock or hemp would have been if he had asked for those instead. Characters and words are equally fluid: a Goat disappears to be replaced by a Gnat, which involves a shift of just one letter backwards in the alphabet, and later the White Queen's cry of '"much better!"' dissolves into '"Be-e-ehh!"' as she morphs into a Sheep in a shop. And again, Carroll has fun shuffling around the various elements of his story. Oyster shells, corkscrews, fish, hoarse voices, rushes, whiskers: almost everything disappears only to return later in a new setting, as Carroll rearranges the basic ingredients of his story like a huge narrative anagram.

What is new in *Through the Looking-Glass* is Carroll's use of another game that depends on recombining the same pieces into different patterns: chess. His choice may have been partly a reaction to the freewheeling structure of his previous story, which according to *The Examiner* had 'no plot to speak of', because if chess is a game that has an infinite number of possible variations, it has only one successful outcome. A game of chess is always dominated by the strategy needed to bring it to an end; its plot is infinitely various in detail, but inherently teleological in design. This provided a much more purposeful narrative structure than the picaresque wanderings of Wonderland. Chess also had more private memories for Carroll, a keen player who had taken a special travelling set with him to Russia, because after croquet and cards it was one of the games he had taught Alice Liddell. From the start of this story, the fictional Alice reveals her enthusiasm for the game, because after the opening sentence, with its reference to 'the *white* kitten' and 'the black kitten', the next few pages are richly seamed with examples of doubling up and balancing out: 'half talking to herself and half asleep', 'up and down', '"you wicked wicked little thing!!"', 'yards and yards'. As she already sees the world in terms of her favourite game, it is not surprising that when Alice falls asleep she finds herself in a place that is modelled on a gigantic chessboard. Here everything she encounters involves the same mixture of sameness and difference as two sets of chess pieces: not just the White King/Queen and the Red King/ Queen, but Tweedledum and Tweedledee and the name of Humpty Dumpty. Words are repeated even more frequently than they are on the other side of the glass, not for rhetorical effect but because in Looking-Glass Land saying the same thing twice seems to be as unavoidable as having two arms and two legs. Within a couple of pages the White King proffers '"No use, no use!"', '"A little – a little"', '"Certainly – certainly!"', and asks Alice, '"Do you spell 'creature' with a double 'e'?"' Even the body starts to reveal its natural mirroring tendencies, as Alice weeps and 'two large tears came rolling down her cheeks'.

Carroll's creation of a textual world that puts the reader in Alice's shoes extends not only to his words, but also to what lies between them: his punctuation. Usually punctuation is treated as little more than a grammatical convenience, but for Carroll it is crucial to the journey on which he takes his readers. The dashes that feature so strongly in his closing acrostic are the culmination of a pattern that is worked into the whole story, where they represent both a neat piece of internal stitching and moments where the narrative changes gear or swerves in a new direction, such as the conclusion to Chapter 10 where Alice shakes the Red Queen:

> . . . and still, as Alice went on shaking her, she kept on growing shorter – and fatter – and softer – and rounder – and—

CHAPTER XI
Waking

> —and it really *was* a kitten, after all.

Carroll's use of asterisks is even more original. In his later collection of poems *Rhyme? And Reason?* (1883), he would use a line of asterisks to indicate a sudden break in the lives of five women, who are no longer fresh-faced girls, and have become rather desperate spinsters:

> Five dressy girls, of Thirty-one or more:
> So gracious to the shy young men they snubbed so much before!

* * * * * *

Five *passé* girls – Their age? Well, never mind!
We jog along together, like the rest of human kind . . .

In *Alice's Adventures in Wonderland*, similarly, the sudden physical changes Alice undergoes when she eats the cake or drinks from the bottle marked 'POISON' are signalled by three lines of asterisks. *Through the Looking-Glass* extends this principle to the key moments of transition in her dream. Here they mark Alice's moves across the chessboard, but they also invite us to share her reaction to the world around her, as speech dissolves into little starbursts of surprise.

At one point, Carroll reminds us of Alice's previous shrinking and growing in Wonderland, as the train Guard inspects her 'first through a telescope, then through a microscope, and then through an opera-glass', before telling her that she is going the wrong way. If this is a joke about her new fictional environment – where better to look at her through different glasses than in Looking-Glass Land? – it also draws attention to the fact that this time all her most interesting changes will happen on the inside. From the start it is clear that she has matured in the six months between her adventures. Although she still dreams of characters from nursery rhymes, she is less inclined to defer to them, and the narrator spends less time making excuses for her. (There are far fewer bracketed asides to the reader.) Partly this can be explained by the extra mirroring effect that makes adults in the story behave like children, and vice versa, as Carroll cheerfully exploits a new way of turning ordinary relations upside down. But it also reveals a deliberate effort on his part to show Alice, who is the polite but unwitting victim of her unconscious in Wonderland, being much more in control of her second dream. Most of the time she appears to relish her new authority, as she bosses around Tweedledum and Tweedledee, or deals with a bunch of noisy flowers by quietly telling them, '"If you don't hold your tongues, I'll pick you!"' which causes several of the pink daisies to turn white with shock. In fact, there are occasions when she comes close to being the sort of character Carroll had joked about in 1867, when replying to a girl who had written him a fan letter: 'I have a message for you from a friend of mine, Mr. Lewis

Carroll, who is a queer sort of creature, rather too fond of talking non-sense. He told me you had once asked him to write another book like one you had read – I forget the name – I think it was about "malice".'

The climax of *Through the Looking-Glass* comes in Chapter 9, as Alice arrives at the final square on the chessboard and becomes a Queen. Like many of the best moments in the *Alice* books, it quietly smuggles a private allusion into a public frame of reference. The transformation of an ordinary girl into a Queen was a popular subject of Victorian magazines and advice manuals for girls, because it recalled the moment in 1837 when an eighteen-year-old princess was woken in the middle of the night and informed that she was now Queen Victoria, instantly making her the most powerful woman in the world. But turning the fictional Alice into a Queen also recalled the childhood photographs in which Alice Liddell had dressed up as King Cophetua's bride and Queen of the May, and for this reason it is tempting to read *Through the Looking-Glass* as a form of disguised autobiography. The episodes in which Alice tries to cheer up an accident-prone White Knight or (in a chapter Carroll later cut, on Tenniel's advice) a crotchety old wasp, in particular, have a sad comedy that seems strangely out of keeping with the rest of the narrative. It is as if Carroll needed to include a private story within the public one, even if the sight of Alice leaving these bumbling and grumbling figures behind was a way of tapping one of the most common plots in the world. Children grow up. They move on.

Carroll's introductory poem had warned that Alice's new journey might produce some casualties, noting that 'the shadow of a sigh | May tremble through the story', and there is certainly plenty of sighing, a mere shadow of speech, when Alice meets the Gnat. Having begun by speaking in a small voice, he goes on to emit a 'wonderfully small sigh', and finally makes a joke that turns out to be a kind of suicide note: 'Then came another of those melancholy little sighs, and this time the poor Gnat really seemed to have sighed itself away, for, when Alice looked up, there was nothing whatever to be seen on the twig, and, as she was getting quite chilly with sitting still so long, she got up and walked on.' Carroll's inspiration for this moment was probably Shakespeare's *Cymbeline*, which contains a beautiful speech in which Imogen imagines how she would have watched Posthumus sailing away from her:

> I would have broke mine eye-strings; crack'd them, but
> To look upon him, till the diminution
> Of space had pointed him sharp as my needle,
> Nay, follow'd him, till he had melted from
> The smallness of a gnat to air, and then
> Have turn'd mine eye and wept.

But even if Carroll thought of himself as a creature slowly disappearing from Alice Liddell's life, that did not mean she would disappear from his life. His final acrostic develops the idea of 'Still she haunts me, phantom-wise' into a more optimistic conclusion. The next two lines are:

> Alice moving under skies
> Never seen by waking eyes.

From one perspective, this is a straightforward reference to Alice's dream: she moves under skies that have been seen only by people who are asleep. But from another perspective, it reminds us that when Carroll wrote this story he was anticipating that it would continue to be read long after its initial publication. That was how to keep Alice moving. That was how to keep her still.

*

Eighteen

The decision to make 'Alice II' an extension of Alice I was reinforced by Tenniel's illustrations. Alice herself was slightly altered in appearance: Carroll's advice to Tenniel had included 'Don't give Alice so much crinoline', and Tenniel responded by slightly flattening her dress, adding some jazzy striped stockings and, when she becomes Queen Alice, giving her a whole new outfit that included an adult string of pearls. Tenniel's other illustrations continued the theme of *Punch*-with-a-twist he had developed for *Alice's Adventures in Wonderland*. Both Tweedledum and Tweedledee ironically resemble John Bull, that stock figure of bluff English common sense, and Tenniel not only chose the name 'Carpenter' in place of the dactylic alternatives Carroll had obligingly offered (if he had chosen differently, 'The Walrus and the Carpenter' would now be known as 'The Walrus and the Baronet' or 'The Walrus and the Butterfly'), but also added a standard working man's paper cap he had drawn many times before. Other illustrations echoed the dreamy transformations of Carroll's narrative. The scene showing Alice in a railway compartment, in particular, brought together fragments of several half-remembered pictures in a hazy collage. Alice is sitting opposite a man dressed in white paper who closely resembles contemporary caricatures of Disraeli, as if a newspaper cartoon had managed to unfold itself into three rustling dimensions, and Alice's own travelling outfit of a fur muff and feathered pillbox hat matches those in many other Victorian images, including the sleeping child in one of Carroll's favourite paintings by Millais, *My Second Sermon*. It is also intriguingly aligned with Augustus Egg's 1862 painting *The Travelling Companions*, which shows a girl reading in a railway carriage while her identically dressed companion dozes opposite. They are mirror images, and each has chosen a different form of escapism to looking at the view outside, a sunny landscape framed by the carriage window like a huge painting hung just out of reach. Viewed alongside Tenniel's illustration, it is hard to avoid a feeling of déjà vu. Whether Tenniel deliberately imitated Egg's viewpoint, or both artists arrived at the image independently, the result in *Through the Looking-Glass* is another example of the strange being made to look familiar and the familiar becoming strange.

Tenniel and Carroll continued their commitment to creative page design, so that when Alice first passes through the mirror the two illustrations were originally printed back to back on the same page, producing the illusion of her literally passing through the paper, like a fantastical variation on the idea of losing oneself in a book. Unfortunately, the personal relationship of author and illustrator also proved to be more of the same: more delays, more authorial interference, more artistic digging in of heels. Carroll did not receive the first sketches until January 1870, almost eighteen months after Tenniel had agreed to take on the project, and over the next year his diaries and correspondence recorded a further series of setbacks, as he promised to 'make a great effort to get the *Looking-Glass* out by Easter', then noted that it had been 'postponed to midsummer', and finally had to admit that it would not be published until after Christmas.

Given how closely text and illustration were modelled on the first *Alice* book, it might be asked why Carroll hadn't simply sent Alice back to Wonderland, as Dorothy would later return to Oz or the Pevensie children to Narnia. One answer is that Wonderland was starting to get a little crowded. During 1870 there were several indications that it was attracting other writers, and not all of them were there merely to admire the view. In February, Carroll heard that John Crawford Wilson, the author of a thin collection of poems entitled *Elsie; Flights to Fairyland, etc.* (1864) had submitted a contribution to the *Gentleman's Magazine* 'in which he signed himself "Author of *Alice in Wonderland*"'. Although Carroll wrote in to complain, it was an early warning of the number of publications that would later attempt to piggyback on his success, such as *Elsie's Adventures in Fairyland* (1897), in which a girl who is 'fond of taking imaginary journeys' has a series of suspiciously familiar encounters in Tum-Tum Land after she loses consciousness, including one with men who grow butter-cups and geraniums as beards – a jangled memory of the Garden of Live Flowers. Other publishers were even more brazenly opportunistic. In May, Carroll learned that the children's weekly penny paper *Happy Hours* had printed four instalments of what it advertised as 'a slight sketch of the story, and a few quotations', which amounted to twelve pages of Carroll's original text. Macmillan agreed that this was 'undoubted theft', and was unimpressed by the paper's 'lame explanation' that a 'rather inexperi-enced editor' was to blame.

Any author might have bridled at this, but Carroll was particularly keen to protect *Alice* from plagiarism – a term deriving from the Latin *plagiarius*, the meanings of which included someone who kidnapped or seduced another man's child. The threat of legal action was certainly available to Carroll. Under the Copyright Act of 1842, he owned copyright on his works in Britain for forty-two years from first publication – a number that is likely to have caught his attention – or his lifetime plus seven years, whichever was longer, and this legal protection also covered Tenniel's illustrations. Carroll grumbled that 'it won't do to let the law of copyright be infringed', but until he could distract his readers with another story there were other ways of keeping his dream-child close. One was to involve himself in new adaptations, as he did when the composer William Boyd asked for permission to set some songs from *Alice's Adventures in Wonderland* to music; Carroll not only agreed, but added an extra couplet to ''Tis the Voice of the Lobster' ('While the duck and the Dodo, the lizard and cat | Were swimming in milk round the brim of a hat'), thus ensuring that the finished pamphlet was at least nominally a collaboration. His other response was to extend his story in more minor ways, as he did in the December issue of *Aunt Judy's Magazine* with seven 'Puzzles from Wonderland' – a set of poetic riddles that had no connection with Wonderland beyond Carroll's pleasure in creating games of logic, but helpfully reminded other authors of his fictional territorial rights.

What these early copies and supplements indicate is that Alice's ques-tion in both stories – '"who am I?"' – was becoming ever harder to answer. Even Carroll was puzzled. During this period he met a young girl named

Alice Raikes, who recounted how he called her over after he heard her name: "'So you are another Alice. I'm very fond of Alices.'" Later she claimed to have given him the idea for *Through the Looking-Glass*, by answering his question about which hand she was holding an orange in when she looked in a mirror: "'If I was on the other side of the glass, wouldn't the orange still be in my right hand?'" As his first recorded meeting with the Raikes family was not until June 1871, when he was already close to completing the story, either her memory was at fault or he was humouring her, but of more interest was his comment that she was *another* Alice.

It appears that Carroll did not photograph Alice Raikes, although he did take portraits of her younger sisters Edith and Amy, but it was only rarely that he met an Alice without trying to capture the moment for posterity. On 3 September 1869 he photographed Alice Furnivall and 'another Alice . . . who happened to call', while on 13 January 1870 he met a Mr Boothby 'who promised me a photograph of his child Alice'. And then there was Alice Liddell. Still Alice. Following the earlier social hiatus, there had been a handful of meetings Carroll thought worth recording, including a chance encounter at the Royal Academy on 4 July 1865 – the date on which he had arranged for her to receive the special copy of *Alice's Adventures in Wonderland* bound in white vellum – and then, on 25 June 1870, a 'wonderful thing occurred'. Mrs Liddell brought Alice and Ina round to his rooms, followed by a visit to the studio he had rented in nearby Badcock's Yard to be photographed. It was the last photograph he ever took of Alice Liddell, and it was also the worst. Now eighteen years old, she sits in a narrow armchair, exquisitely dressed and elegantly coiffured, looking stiff and awkward, with her hands clasped in her lap and her eyes gazing off into the distance with an expression that seems frankly bored by the whole affair. If Carroll had wanted to add a literary quotation to the image, as he had to photographs in some of his earlier albums, he might have chosen lines from Longfellow's 1841 poem 'Maidenhood':

> Standing, with reluctant feet,
> Where the brook and river meet,
> Womanhood and childhood fleet!

Carroll's final portrait of Alice Liddell (25 June 1870)

Alice is sitting rather than standing, and as her feet are out of shot it is hard to know whether they look as reluctant as the rest of her body, but Carroll's photograph undoubtedly captures some of the emotions this period in life was thought to produce, from a generalized annoyance with the world to a more specific desire to escape, to be elsewhere and live otherwise. Longfellow's lines were widely quoted in Victorian fiction and advice manuals: in 1877, Sarah Doudney borrowed 'The Brook and The River' as the subtitle for her *Stories of Girlhood*, and in 1887 Ellen Louisa Davies produced *Brook and River* for the Society for Promoting Christian Knowledge. Carroll would also have come across the idea in Tennyson's 1855 poem 'The Brook', which grew out of a notebook draft describing 'Philip's farm where brook and river meet', but it is Longfellow's formulation, slightly misquoted, that influenced a later letter in which he admitted that 'About 9 out of 10, I think of my child-friendships get shipwrecked at the critical points "where the stream and river meet".' The same idea may have influenced his decision to make Alice cross from one chessboard square to the next in *Through the Looking-Glass* by jumping over a series of little brooks. Such transitions were much harder to manage in real life. Carroll's final acrostic in his story ends with Alice 'Ever drifting down the stream—| Lingering in the golden gleam—| Life, what is it but a dream?' The poem completes her name but not her journey: ever drifting but never arriving, she is on a stream that will not enter the river of adult experience. What his photograph of Alice Liddell had shown was that real girls were not so lucky. Or perhaps, from her point of view, it had shown that they were not so unlucky.

Carroll marked the start of 1871 with a New Year's resolution: 'O that this New Year may be the beginning of a new life in me.' It was a standard prayer, one of his periodic fresh starts, but in the context of his other plans it had an additional meaning, because the next day he made another entry: 'Finished the MS. of *Through the Looking-Glass*.' It had 'cost me, I think more trouble than the first', he claimed, and again the title caused more trouble than anything in the story itself. Having toyed with eight alternatives, including *Looking-Glass World* and *Behind the Looking-Glass*, which Macmillan printed on a set of trial pages in April 1870, eventually he took up a suggestion made by Henry Liddon and settled on *Through the Looking-Glass*. But even as Carroll was waiting for the finished book to go to press, he continued to wonder how far the Alice in his new story was a fictional creation and how far the textual trace of a real girl.

On 4 May, he wrote a long diary entry that began 'On this day, "Alice's" birthday, I sit down to record the events of the day.' As a 'specimen of my life now', nothing he says is very remarkable – breakfast with a friend, four hours of lecturing, a pastoral visit to a parishioner dying of consumption, a walk, starting to write a new book on Euclid – but that opening sentence retains a strange edge. The 4th of May was indeed Alice Liddell's birthday, but putting her in inverted commas suggests that he now preferred to think of her as a literary character. The same pattern was repeated on 23 November, when he received a request from the publishers of a musical composition entitled 'The Wonderland Quadrille', asking if he would like it to be dedicated to him or to a member of his family. 'I suggested that the dedication should be "To 'Alice'",' he explained, again leaving it unclear whether this was a public gesture or something more unreachably private.

Such questions were made more urgent by Alice's (and *Alice's*) imminent reappearance in print. A week after his ambiguous musical dedication, Carroll sent a letter to his uncle that concluded with a 'happy thought' concerning 'the thousands of children who will I hope be reading "Through the Looking-Glass" before many weeks are over'. When his 'little book' was published in December, these hopes were quickly realized. Reviewers were almost uniformly enthusiastic – *The Athenaeum* characterized it as 'no mere book' but something that had the power to bring happiness to 'countless children of all ages' – and sales were brisk. By the end of January, over 15,000 books had been bought, and many years later Carroll's first readers still recalled their excitement at getting hold of a copy. In her memoir of growing up in the 1870s, Molly Hughes described receiving the story on her birthday: 'I got through the morning somehow, and then buried myself in it all the afternoon, my pleasure enhanced by the knowledge that there was a boring visitor downstairs to whom I ought to be making myself agreeable . . . As I handle the book now I live over again that enchanted afternoon.' However, the future reader to whom Carroll devoted most of his attention was, predictably, the one whom almost none of the others knew about, still living less than a hundred yards away from him in Christ Church.

He had already shown how sensitive he was to Alice Liddell's 'awkward' physical changes, and now his plans for the presentation copy of *Through the Looking-Glass* took this idea a stage further. 'I want to have the presentation-copy of the *Looking-Glass* (I mean the one for Miss A. Liddell) bound with an oval piece of looking-glass let into the cover,' he told Macmillan; 'Will you consult your binder as to whether the thing is practicable?' He included a sketch of what he wanted, and from this it appears that the mirror was to be trimmed into an oval of roughly the same proportions as many of his photographs, like the hand-coloured print of *The Beggar Maid* he presented to the Liddell family, in which she looks out at the viewer from a gilt-edged hole set in a purple velvet display case. The key difference was that the cover of his book was not going to be a mirror with a memory. It was just a mirror. Perhaps he hoped that she would see it as an invitation to jump into the story and renew her youth; or perhaps it was to remind her of how much she had aged. Either way the plan proved impracticable, and Carroll had to be content with a copy bound in plain red morocco. But despite a reference to 'The pleasance of our fairytale' in the opening poem (a late change made in proof), and the final acrostic on ALICEPLEASANCELIDDELL, this time there was no special dedication page inside. What the gift meant was left for her to decide.

*   *   *   *

*   *   *

*   *   *   *

AFTER ALICE

◆

'With a name like yours, you might be any shape, almost . . .'

LEWIS CARROLL, *Through the Looking-Glass*

Nineteen

*

Twenty

C arroll wasn't the only person in Oxford to confuse Alice Liddell with a fictional character. She also took on a minor role in one of the romances that Ruskin later enjoyed playing out in his head. Shortly after delivering his inaugural lecture in 1870 as the first Slade Professor of Fine Art, and developing a friendship that could be traced back to the time when Dean Liddell had first noticed him as a 'very wonderful' and 'very strange' undergraduate at Christ Church in the late 1830s, Ruskin started to give Alice drawing lessons. Although she was not as accomplished as her younger sister Violet, who would go on to produce an oil painting of Alice in 1886 that had the assured touch of a professional artist, some of her surviving work is unusually fine for an amateur. One unfinished ink sketch of a woman on horseback has a solid muscular grace; a pencil drawing of a house in Oxford is elegantly stippled with detail. She certainly had impressive models to copy: Ruskin lent her some of his Turner vignettes, writing to reassure her in 1871, in a letter that was undoubtedly well intentioned but now reads like toe-curling condescension, that she 'must not be frightened' by them, as 'Turner's *method* is as simple as a child's – and you will need no skill to copy his works.' Other letters show that she exercised some personal influence over him, or at least that he took pleasure in pretending that he was putty in her hands. 'I am horribly vexed with myself for having been at the Prince's party (it was all your fault . . .),' he wrote to her, before requesting 'a time when I can come and show you how to do this sky – & other skies'. She was a quick learner – in 1870, Ruskin presented her with Walter Scott's collection of ballads *The Minstrelsy of the Scottish Border* as a prize for one of her sketches. But undoubtedly part of her appeal for Ruskin was that she was not just another star pupil. She also embodied the possibility of life rearranging itself into the more orderly shape of a story.

In his autobiography *Praeterita*, Ruskin recalled an occasion when 'the Planet Saturn had treated me with his usual adversity in the carrying out of a plot with Alice in Wonderland', and as he explains what happened, fact and fiction slowly start to merge. On a cold winter evening, when the Liddell parents were attending a dinner in Blenheim, Alice invited him to the Deanery for tea:

> The night was wild with snow, and no one likely to come round to the Deanery after dark. I think Alice must have sent me a little note, when the eastern coast of Tom Quad was clear. I slipped round from Corpus through Peckwater, shook the snow off my gown, and found an armchair ready for me, and a bright fireside, and a laugh or two, and some pretty music looked out, and tea coming up.

Just as Alice was 'bringing the muffins to perfection', they were interrupted by the unexpected return of her parents; there followed an awkward silence, broken by Mrs Liddell saying, 'How sorry you must be to see us, Mr Ruskin!' to which he replied, 'I never was more so.' The whole incident is 'so like a dream now', he confesses, that he cannot be sure of the details, but what makes his memory especially unreliable is that it is overlaid by several narrative layers. At first he imagines the evening as a melodrama, casting himself as a lover tramping through the snow to a secret assignation; then he switches genres to a sentimental fireside scene; and finally he freezes the action into a dramatic tableau. There is also a specific story through which he is filtering his memories – *Through the Looking-Glass*, which begins with Alice listening to the snow falling softly outside 'as if someone was kissing the window all over', and then follows her through the mirror to a living room where a fire is 'blazing away as brightly as the one she had left behind'. Ruskin goes no further than this, but in recalling Alice as a perfect muffin-toasting hostess he shows how even as an adult she could find her way into other people's dreams.

Art was just one of the skills she had been encouraged to develop. Another was music: Hubert Parry, who had recently arrived at Exeter College, composed three new vocal trios for the Liddell sisters, and there exists a copy in her neat hand of a 'Mignonette' dated 19 April 1879, which when performed would have shown off her skill in languages as well as singing. There was dancing, too: the Mock Turtle's detailed instructions on how to perform a 'Lobster Quadrille', with elaborate moves that include throwing your partner out to sea, was a mischievous parody of the tuition Alice and her sisters had been given by their own dancing master, the success of which had left their grandmother hoping that 'five or six lessons more will make them dance a quadrille'. The stress on performance in all these leisure activities was no accident. The Deanery at Christ Church was an important social hub in Oxford, where Alice's accomplishments publicly confirmed her status as a young woman of culture and refinement. They also helpfully advertised her as a potential bride for a wealthy and well-connected husband. That was certainly the usual outcome of such an expensive private education, even if it was not a personal goal, and for many girls of Alice's age its likelihood was reinforced by whole bookshelves of popular novels. If the question on the lips of 'hundreds and even thousands of women' of Alice's class was 'what shall I do with my life?' according to Frances Power Cobbe in 1863, fiction's usual answer was: 'Get married.' This romance plot could be embellished with delays and detours, allowing the happy ending to be experienced as a victory against the odds, but however sinuous their trajectory very few of these narratives avoided the altar completely. (Carroll had imagined a slightly later destination in the poem that opened *Through the Looking-Glass*, writing of the 'voice of dread' that 'Shall summon to unwelcome bed | A melancholy maiden', because the 'bedtime' that ended a Victorian girl's life as a maiden was the marriage bed, and the summons would come from her new husband as he invitingly patted the mattress.) Marriage for an upper-middle-class girl like Alice was commonly thought to confer a social role and confirm the transition to adulthood, and in fiction the question of whether or not this would prove to be a happy ending was usually left to resonate in the blank space after the final full stop. Only in brilliantly idiosyncratic works such as Dickens's *Our Mutual Friend*, where Mr and Mrs Lammle are last seen walking down the street arm in arm as if 'linked together by concealed handcuffs', was this uncertainty allowed to seep into the story itself, by making the words of the marriage service about having and holding till death us do part sound more like a suicide pact.

In Alice Liddell's case, probably the most important detour came a year after the publication of *Through the Looking-Glass*, in the form of an extended holiday stretching over nearly three months that took her, Ina and Edith through France and Italy without their parents. It was planned with elaborate care, and when they left Oxford on 7 February 1872 the sisters were accompanied by a small entourage of guardians, chaperones, a doctor (a 'tiresome prig', according to Alice) and, of course, a copy of Murray's guidebook. Traditionally, such European tours were a male preserve, although by the mid-nineteenth century female travellers and families were starting to venture abroad in larger numbers, and the guide-books had been updated accordingly. Murray's *Handbook for Travellers in Southern Italy* (1853) now included a note of 'Caution to English Ladies', which warned them not to become too intimate with the local 'gentle-men', while the Revd George Musgrave's recent publication *Cautions for the First Tour on the Annoyances, Shortcomings, Indecencies, and Impositions Incidental to Foreign Travel* (1863) urged ladies to take an 'Inodorous Standard Pail' abroad with them, thus ensuring that they would not have their sight 'blasted' by the 'pencilled obscenities' written in public conveniences, or encounter 'the moustached foreigner . . . with his waistcoat unbuttoned, cigar in mouth, and his hands fumbling at his braces' in the corridor.

The journal Alice Liddell kept on her travels, a soft leather notebook she filled with a firm and neat hand, shows that she was made of sterner stuff than this. In Paris she took in the sight of 'houses pierced thro' & thro' by shells' after the brief but eventful rule of the Paris Commune in 1871, which had left thousands dead after a series of bloody street battles. She also had to deal with the annoyance of being shouted at by 'rather irate' working-class Parisians, after she put a scented handkerchief to her nose in a market where 'The flowers were lovely but the smell of the fish was too horrible.' That last phrase accurately captures the accent of her adult voice: the stink of fish was not just horrible but *too* horrible. Not that she was sympathetic to the idea that political grievances were also lingering in the air: after travelling to Marseilles, she quickly decided that 'most of the men look real ruffians' and 'the women horrid; no wonder it is a red republican place'. (Her suspicions were never fully assuaged; as late as February 1934, just a few months before her death, she responded to some riots in Paris by declaring that 'The French are too excitable.') The next four weeks aboard the private steam yacht *Kathleen* were more refined, and then it was on to Nice, Genoa, Milan (where she saw the 'very pretty' first production of *Aida*, two months after its prem-iere to celebrate the opening of the Suez Canal), Venice, Rome (where she attended an audience with the Pope), Naples (from where the touring party ascended Vesuvius, 'sinking half way up to our knees' in the cinders, amid 'showers of stones and lumps of red hot stuff and puffs of smoke'), Capri, Sorrento and Pompeii. Her responses were not always sophisti-cated – the Arno, she reports, is 'a great big river & runs right thro' Pisa' – but they were undoubtedly consistent. Almost everything she saw was 'lovely': the weather was 'lovely', views were 'lovely', she had a 'lovely day', saw some 'lovely' pictures, had a 'lovely' drive, and even bought 'a lovely little looking glass' in Venice, perhaps with a nod to her fictional past.

While she was busily gathering new experiences – gliding through Venetian canals on a 'delicious' gondola, or suspiciously appraising the 'ring of anxious horrid looking faces' she witnessed gambling in Monaco – she was putting them into perspective in a series of watercolours. These included many craggy outlines of the Italian shore floating on a deep blue sea, and many little fishing boats bobbing about under a bright blue sky; indeed, a whole series of paintings that were refined in technique but never anything other than solidly conventional. Here her artistic views closely reflected her social views, because if this miniature Grand Tour was supposed to be a kind of mobile finishing school, it also gave her plenty of opportunities to polish up the attitudes she had packed and taken abroad with her.

According to Alice Liddell, French ladies were fashionable but silly, waddling around with 'an immense amount of fur on their dresses'. In Marseilles, she looked for suitable holiday reading and, when she failed to find a copy of Macaulay's *Essays*, chose Jane Austen instead. Genoa was shockingly dirty and pockmarked with decay. Madame Patti's singing performance in Naples was too fiddly, with 'cadenzas, trills and turns and all the various little things' that made her sound unmistakably foreign. Indeed, there are times when it seems that the biggest problem with Europe was that it was insufficiently like England. It was all rather different to the intrepid voyaging of her character in the *Alice* books, if sadly reminiscent of the way in which even in those stories the fictional Alice had tried to understand new experiences by relying on half-remembered schoolroom formulas. Perhaps even then Carroll had recognized that the real Alice had a habit of falling back on the familiar when confronted by the unknown. Finally, after a few days spent shopping in Nice, it was back to Oxford, on a day in May that had a particular significance for her: 'Saturday 4th. 20 years old. Home again—.' But in another sense she had never left home.

Meanwhile, Carroll continued to travel in less physically demanding ways. In October 1871, work was completed on a new glass-roofed studio he had been given permission to construct on the roof of his Christ Church rooms, and after the usual hiatus caused by Oxford's gloomy winter, from March 1872 he was busy photographing again. His extra income from the *Alice* books meant that he could now buy himself out of some of his teaching duties, which gave him more time to poke around in imaginary versions of other foreign countries. Here his virtual travelling companion was not named Alice, but she was the daughter of an Alice: Xie Kitchin, born in 1864, whose mother was married to George Kitchin, a former Christ Church Lecturer in Modern History and Classics who had gone on to become headmaster of the preparatory school at Twyford in Hampshire where Harry Liddell had studied, before returning with his family to Oxford in 1868.

Xie (pronounced 'Exy') was short for Alexandra, and her nickname allowed Carroll to make a generous joke, telling Henry Holiday that to obtain excellence in a photograph, '"Take a lens and put Xie before it"'

(Xie lens: excellence). However, any suspicion that he imagined a missing 'S' before her name would have been misplaced, and not just because the word had not yet entered the English language. His treatment of her was far more professional than that. The only part of their relationship that now looks slightly odd is Carroll's understanding of her role as his 'model'. After trying out some of his favourite poses in the earliest photographs – in July 1870 he took her 'dressed in rags' – once he had settled into his new studio he began to dress her far more exotically, allowing them to make imaginary journeys together under the same glass roof. On 19 April 1873, he photographed her alongside her brother Herbert 'in Indian shawls'; on 14 May, it was 'in winter dress (Danish), in red petticoat, and in Greek dress', on 12 June 'with spade and bucket, in bed, and in Greek dress', and on 14 July he 'Took Xie in Chinese dress (2 positions)'. But if her costume changed between photographs, her expression remained

Xie Kitchin in *The Prettiest Doll in the World* (July 1870)

almost identical, attractively open and studiedly neutral. In fact, in her more elaborate attire, she looks less like a real girl than the title he chose for one of the earlier photographs of her from July 1870: *The Prettiest Doll in the World.*

In March 1872, Carroll had actually investigated the possibility of buying a child-sized mannequin for his studio, taking the measurements of a friend's nine-year-old daughter with the aim of getting 'an exact duplicate of Julia in papier-mâché'. Writing to Julia's sister Mary Arnold (later the novelist Mrs Humphry Ward), he started to conjure up fantasies of how it might be used:

> It will be a grand doll for her, and she may dress it in a suit of her own clothes if she likes. It would be fun to take a picture of it so dressed, to be called 'Miss Julia Arnold (duplicate),' and see how many people it would take in.

This is not quite as strange as it might sound. Life-sized mannequins, known as 'lay figures', were standard pieces of equipment in many artists' studios. Ford Madox Brown reported that when he was painting *Pretty Baa-Lambs* in the 1850s, 'I used to take the lay figure out every morning and bring it in at night or if it rained', and it was a common charge that real models could seem equally lifeless when put in the hands of bungling artists; in 1863, Henry Peach Robinson's composite photographs were dismissed by one reviewer as groupings of 'living lay figures'. What distinguishes Carroll's letter is his pleasure in the idea that a child and a doll might be practically interchangeable. This was another imaginative thread that ran through his life. Several of his early photographs had featured dolls being held by girls, including Ina Liddell in 1858, and in the same year he had photographed a Dodgson family doll named Tim, propped up on a chair and staring blankly out at the viewer. If these dolls were merely props, he also enjoyed books that detached dolls from human control and imagined wholly independent lives for them. In 1887, he sent Edith Blakemore a copy of *Jappie-Chappie and How He Loved a Dollie*, written by the widow of a former Christ Church tutor, in which an oriental doll falls in love with the western Dollie, and ends up marrying her after fighting off a monster with his umbrella. Although Edith was now probably 'over 6 feet high', he told her, this was a book for 'when her *second childhood* comes'.

Occasionally, Carroll sought to speed up this process in his own life by pretending to be a doll. This reversed the procedure of his childhood marionette theatre, where he had tried to make his puppets behave like people, but Carroll took the idea of being a doll equally seriously. On Valentine's Day in 1880 he used his new 'Electric Pen' to produce copies of a 'Letter from Mabel', a one-page document supposedly written by one of Beatrice Hatch's dolls that began 'Last Saterday was my birthday', and was signed 'Your loveing Mabel', intended to illustrate common spelling mistakes. The *Alice* books were also involved in these literary games. In *Alice's Adventures in Wonderland*, the scene of Alice in the White Rabbit's cottage is partly an exploration of what might happen if a little girl's dream of living in a doll's house came true, although it soon turns into a nightmare when she grows too big and gets stuck.

A letter Carroll sent in 1873 shows that he continued to associate dolls with stories. He had bought Beatrice Hatch a wax doll she named Alice, which 'had fair hair brushed back from its forehead, as in the pictures of its namesake, and when pinched would emit plaintive cries of "Papa" and "Mamma"', and later that year he wrote to Beatrice explaining that he had just met Alice 'walking very stiffly' outside Christ Church. After giving the doll some matches to eat and 'a cup of nice melted wax to drink', he invited her to sit by the fire, but she refused. 'And then she made me take her quite to the other end of the room, where it was very cold,' Carroll told her owner, 'and then she sat on my knee, and fanned herself with a penwiper, because she said she was afraid the end of her nose was beginning to melt.'

This is a curious reversal of the situation in *Through the Looking-Glass*, where Alice passes through a mirror when it begins 'to melt away, just like a bright silvery mist', and finds herself in a place where a goat's beard also appears 'to melt away' as she touches it, but it offers a revealing sketch of Carroll's thinking about what was happening to Alice outside the world of his stories. A doll is the perfect recipient of a child's love, because whether it is being fed or changed or hugged, its needs are entirely created by the person who will satisfy them. Carroll's fantasy of Alice the doll taking on independent life was a reminder that the same was not true of fictional creations. In his letter she returns to his study, which is where the fictional Alice had been created, and sits on his knee to speak, like a ventriloquist's dummy that has acquired a life of its own. But for all Carroll's powers of comic invention, there is an unmistakable note of wistfulness in his explanation of what she was doing there: 'I think she was trying to find her way back to my rooms.'

*

Twenty-one

R eaders who purchased a copy of *Through the Looking-Glass* in December 1871 would have discovered an extra Christmas present from the author hidden inside: a tiny leaflet addressed 'TO ALL CHILD-READERS | OF "𝔄𝔩𝔦𝔠𝔢'𝔰 𝔄𝔡𝔳𝔢𝔫𝔱𝔲𝔯𝔢𝔰 𝔦𝔫 𝔚𝔬𝔫𝔡𝔢𝔯𝔩𝔞𝔫𝔡."' Anyone who expected an extra set of puzzles or jokes for the holiday season was in for a surprise. 'Dear Children,' it began, 'At Christmas-time a few grave words are not quite out of place, I hope, even at the end of a book of nonsense', and although Carroll continued by expressing the hope that his story had provided 'innocent amusement', he concluded with an earnest homily:

> May God bless you, dear children, and make each Christmas-tide, as it comes round to you, more bright and beautiful than the last – bright with the presence of that unseen Friend, who once on earth blessed little children – and beautiful with memories of a loving life, which has sought and found the truest kind of happiness, the only kind that is really worth the having, the happiness of making others happy too!

Both *Alice* books had carefully avoided religious impropriety: when Carroll was told that the passion flower he wanted to use in 'The Garden of Live Flowers' might be interpreted as a reference to the Passion of Christ, he quickly changed it to a tiger lily. However, neither book had attempted to ballast its jokes with such moral weight. To do so now made it seem as if Carroll was mentally reworking the stories he had written into the kind of stories he perhaps felt he should have written. But although he now had 'a longing to say *something* in a more real character than a mere comic writer', it is not entirely clear to whom he was saying it. As a clergyman, he was permitted to call people of all ages 'my child', and it was commonly thought that Christmas was a time when adults could become like little children again; even Dickens's Scrooge returns to a second childhood at the end of *A Christmas Carol*, happily burbling, "'I'm quite a baby. Never mind. I don't care. I'd rather be a baby.'" 'He is very fatherly; calls you child,' Charlotte Rix reported of Carroll when she was at least seventeen, and if there was a whiff of the pulpit in his Christmas address, it was the first hint of something that would continue to develop in his mind over the following decade: the idea that his readership was a scattered parish in need of pastoral guidance as well as entertainment.

An equally significant part of the Christmas letter was Carroll's claim that writing was a way of making new friends:

> I have a host of young friends already, whose names and faces I know – but I cannot help feeling as if, through 'Alice's Adventures' I had made friends with many other dear children, whose faces I shall never see.

Some of his readers were happy to reciprocate: when the actress Bessie Hatton first met him, he apologized for calling at her home without an introduction, and she replied, "'But you don't require one. I have known and loved your *Alice* since I was six.'" If Carroll couldn't personally meet his readers, he sometimes wondered if they might be able to introduce themselves to him instead. In 1870, three years after he had proposed a new advertisement containing excerpts from letters written by child fans, he considered inserting a message in copies of *Alice* asking each reader to send in a *carte de visite* photograph. Macmillan told him it was an 'awful idea', explaining that he would be overwhelmed with 'cart loads' of *cartes*, and pleading, 'Think of the postmen.'

Carroll was not alone in wanting to do something that might compensate for the anonymity of the literary marketplace. Steadily improving literacy rates and rising sales meant that many Victorian writers feared losing a sense of personal connection with their readers; indeed, in the increasingly commercial world of books, bestselling authors were in danger of being viewed less as real people than as the literary equivalents of figures like Thomas Keating of Keating's Cod Liver Oil or Thomas Beecham of Beecham's Tooth Paste. Their response was to stress that the relationship of author and reader was far more intimate than that of producer and consumer. Books bound people together; to pick one up was the next best thing to taking the author by the hand. 'No one thinks first of Mr. Dickens as a writer,' explained a critic in the *North American Review*. 'He is at once, through his books, a friend.' Wilkie Collins similarly expressed his satisfaction that his characters in *The Woman in White* (1860) 'have made friends for me wherever they have made themselves known'. But nobody took the idea of fiction as an expression of friendship more seriously than Carroll, and that is because for him it was more than just a vague gesture towards social harmony. It reflected where his stories had come from. *Alice's Adventures Under Ground* had originally been told to a tight family circle of three 'young friends'. Now that his readers could be counted in the tens of thousands, the affection and trust that had leaked into his writing could no longer be taken for granted, but the more readers he got to know personally, the more likely it was that the *Alice* books would continue to be enjoyed in the same spirit of cheerful camaraderie. More readers meant more friends, and more friends meant better readers.

In the years immediately after the publication of *Through the Looking-Glass*, Carroll worked hard to increase his readership. He had already approached Macmillan with plans for a cheaper edition of *Alice's Adventures in Wonderland*, arguing that 'the present price puts the book entirely out of the reach of many thousands of children of the middle classes, who might, I think, enjoy it' – with the snobbish caveat '(below that I don't think it would be appreciated)' – and the book was still developing its international reputation, with further translations into Italian in 1872, Dutch in 1874 and Russian in 1879. It was also being 'translated' in ways that went beyond language alone. In 1876, Dick Cotsford published *In Wonderland: Six Duets for the Pianoforte*; the same year, Carroll received a request from a manufacturer in Leeds who was hoping to turn the story into magic-lantern slides, and another from the composer William Boyd seeking permission to give a 'lecture for children' at the Royal Poly-technic. Advertised as 'Alice in Wonderland; or, MORE WONDERS IN WONDERLAND', it occupied the same bill as 'WONDERS OF THE MICROSCOPE, by Mr. J. L. King' and 'Mr. Taylor's WONDERFUL BOY; Clairvoyance and Plate Dancing extraordinary'. Carroll attended two per-formances, in April and June 1876, reporting that much of the lecture 'was done by dissolving views, extracts from the story being read, or sung to Mr. Boyd's music', and the highlight was 'a rather pretty child of about 10' who played Alice. He had previously seen an amateur production of 'The Mad Tea-Party' performed by the Arnold family in December 1874, and had followed the usual legal route to prevent unauthorized professional adaptations by registering his stories as dramas at Stationers' Hall. Unfortunately, that did not prevent pantomimes such as *Alice in Fairyland* from being staged at Eastbourne in 1877 by the 'Elliston Family of Burlesque Entertainers' because, as Carroll later discovered, registering copyright 'only secures the *drama* from being copied, not the book'. Instead, he forced himself to sit through a 'very third-rate performance', grumbling to his diary about the actors' inaudible voices and singing that was 'painfully out of tune'.

Such local annoyances continued to bob to the surface in the wake of his dream-child's progress; indeed, they were among the most visible signs of that progress. This was especially the case when it came to the influence his books were starting to have on other children's stories. In Wonderland, Alice asks the Cheshire Cat, '"Would you tell me, please, which way I ought to go from here?"' and receives the laconic reply, '"That depends a good deal on where you want to get to."' Their conversation was closely echoed in the development of children's fiction. Where Alice had shown the way, other writers followed. Not all took the same narrative path: some started in roughly the same place (a young girl finds herself in a fantasy land) before wandering off in a new direction; others arrived at the same destination (she wakes up and discovers it was all a dream) by a more cir-cuitous route. But in dozens of children's books published after 1871 it was possible to detect the ghostly outlines of Carroll's stories, which faded in and out of each narrative as unpredictably as the Cheshire Cat's grin.

Two examples from 1869 show how wide a range of approaches was possible. 'Ernest', a short story by Edward Knatchbull-Hugessen, the Liberal MP and great-nephew of Jane Austen, was first published in a collection that included a preface admitting to a certain 'family resemblance' between it and 'that admirable child's book' *Alice's Adventures in Wonderland*. The comparison was well chosen, because as 'Ernest' develops, the familial relationship between Carroll and his imitator is revealed to be a matter of rivalry as well as affection. Ernest loses his ball down a well, and when he goes to retrieve it he meets a large cigar-smoking Toad who allows him to pass through a doorway into Toad-land, where he witnesses hundreds of mice frolicking with toadstools at a grand ball – a dreamlike pun on his reason for being there. The narrative is thick with echoes of Carroll's style, and Ernest's conversations with various creatures repeatedly clench themselves into puns. Only when he falls further into the earth's interior does the story move decisively away from Carroll's influence, as Ernest witnesses people being blown around like leaves as a punishment for being 'undecided' in life. After seeing these 'wonderful things', he awakes.

Jean Ingelow's *Mopsa the Fairy* is even more ambivalent about Carroll's example. On one level, it is a straightforward imitation, in which Jack discovers a nest of baby fairies inside a hollow tree, and then travels to Fairyland, not via a beanstalk but carried there by a talking albatross. On another level, it is a sly revision of Carroll's story, because Jack's favourite fairy, the tiny Mopsa, continues to grow steadily rather than in sudden bursts, and when she has been safely guided to her enchanted castle she tells him to go home. Emotionally as well as physically she has outgrown him. The conclusion involves a piece of wordplay as rich as anything in Carroll: having been impulsively kissed by Jack when '"she looked such a little dear"', it turns out that she is actually the Queen of a herd of enchanted deer; but the story as a whole also includes elements that are far more realistic and downbeat. Jack's fear that she will become '"much too big for me to play with"', in particular, together with his tearful sunset parting from her beside the river they had travelled up on their little boat, reads suspiciously like a rejection of the golden afternoon celebrated by Carroll at the start of *Alice's Adventures in Wonderland*. According to

Ingelow, it is not just real girls like Alice Liddell who grow up; the same thing can happen to fictional girls.

Soon Alice had become familiar enough to be recognizable outside Wonderland. In Henry Kingsley's *The Boy in Grey* (1871) she makes a fleeting appearance alongside a crowd of other literary characters, including Robinson Crusoe and Don Quixote, who have escaped from their own stories into a timeless and placeless Fairyland. After the publication of *Through the Looking-Glass*, this steady trickle of imitations soon became a literary flood. Some of these books were cheerfully and openly parasitic. M. C. Pyle's creaky 1869 poem *Minna in Wonder-land* ('Poor little Minna! She knew, I wot, | The grief of a motherless orphan's lot') also features the discovery of a hidden underground realm, while George Hartley's *A Few More Chapters of Alice Through the Looking-Glass* (1875) is more like a collection of rejected narrative offcuts than a genuine sequel. Other imitations ranged equally widely across both *Alice* books. In fact, by the mid-1870s any clear distinction between Carroll's stories had started to dissolve, and 'Wonderland' was frequently assumed to include both fictional territories, forming a Greater Wonderland or Onederland in the public imagination.

Sometimes it is hard to tell whether these parallels reveal an influence or a confluence; that is, whether they were a literary chain reaction Carroll had sparked off, or a set of narrative arrows moving independently towards the same target. The *Alice* books certainly reflected the growing popularity of fairy tales. When Carroll recalled the 'eager faces' of the Liddell sisters in 1862 'hungry for news of fairyland', he was acknowledging an appetite he could not satisfy on his own, just as he confessed that his decision to send Alice down a rabbit-hole was partly 'a desperate attempt to strike out some new line of fairy-lore'. Such stories also reflected a more general trend towards seeing childhood as a separate realm, and expressing this separation by placing fictional children in places that were cut off from the world inhabited by their parents. Yet even in this context Carroll's stories were an unusually popular source for later writers looking for ideas to make their own. Familiarity bred content.

Carroll's plot of a girl transported somewhere familiar yet strange proved especially hard to resist. Mary Dummett Nauman's *Eva's Adventures in Shadow-Land* (1872) and Clare Bradford's *Ethel's Adventures in the Doll Country* (1880) fall into this category. The first contains several direct echoes of Carroll – a violet picked by Eva falls to the ground, 'melting into fragrance', and later she rescues a 'half-drowned mouse' from a pool of water – and it adapts other narrative elements in more original ways: the boy Eva encounters in Shadow-Land, for example, grows larger and smaller not because of what he eats or drinks, but because he is a 'Moon-Prince' whose body mimics the shape-shifting qualities of his home. The second example is more indirectly indebted to *Alice*, as it follows the journey of a spoiled little girl through a land that is a refuge for maltreated toys, including one of Ethel's dolls that her brothers had earlier subjected to a court-martial and hanged from a tree. However, what most obviously distinguishes both stories from their source is a stringent resistance to comedy. Although the Moon-Prince is menaced by a nameless and faceless 'THEY', there is nothing that resembles the snapping wit of a limerick, and Shadow-Land turns out to be populated mostly by important-sounding capital letters: in just one paragraph we meet the 'Valley of Rest', 'the Dawn Fairies', 'the Night and Shadow Elves', 'the verge between Shadow and Dawn' and a stern warning that 'Darkness always swallows up Light.' Ethel's doll-country adventures are even less enticing. Disgusted by the sight of her battered toys, she threatens to whip them as a punishment for trying 'to excite pity', and her spiteful sense of humour is accurately indicated by her reaction on seeing ten black dolls dancing: '"How ugly they are! . . . why can't they scrub themselves white!"'

Even the most tedious stories were vulnerable to the spirit of Wonderland entering them from time to time. A book like Alice Corkran's *Down the Snow Stairs* (1887) is in many respects a standard work of sentimental fiction, in which Kitty tries to save her virtuous brother Johnnie – a 'tiny cripple' with a 'tiny crutch', like a fictional relative of Dickens's Tiny Tim – who is close to death from a fever because of her thoughtless behaviour. Kitty obligingly follows a snowman 'Down – down' a set of snow stairs, and enters Naughty Children Land, where she encounters a host of unappealing infants, some of whom are so wantonly cruel they crush butterflies for fun, and learns to avoid sins such as vanity and sloth. It is in effect a Victorian schoolroom version of *Pilgrim's Progress*, or Bunyan for Beginners, where the unknown world Kitty explores turns out to be her own conscience. Yet, even in this unpromising fictional environment, *Alice* can occasionally be seen glinting mischievously between the lines. As Kitty journeys home along 'the right path' she meets a man standing arm in arm with his ghostly twin; together they embody selfishness, and are pictured as fictional cousins of Tweedledum and Tweedledee. Clearly *Down the Snow Stairs* is on one level intended to be a rewriting of stories that the author thought worryingly lacking in moral earnestness. But even her narrative occasionally slips its tight ethical leash. Shortly after Kitty arrives in Naughty Children Land, she hears a chorus of angry cats yowling as they try to escape the children's grabbing fingers, and soon one of the cats dashes up a tree and glares at her 'with eyes like green lanterns'. When she tries to engage it with '"Pussy, pussy!"' she receives a '"Hi—ss!"' in reply. The illustration, which shows the cat with its back angrily arched on a branch over Kitty's head, announces this as a more realistic version of Alice's encounter with the Cheshire Cat; the door to Wonderland is opened a crack and immediately slammed shut again.

Many of these post-*Alice* productions revealed the problems of all literary imitations: the difficulty in preventing a second-hand idea from sounding belated or second-rate; the danger that developing selected strands of an original story will produce little more than a lopsided caricature. Some were 'parodies' in the neutral sense Samuel Johnson had defined in his *Dictionary* as 'a kind of writing, in which the words of an author or his thoughts are taken, and by a slight change adapted to some new purpose'. Like the version of his 'Fish Riddle' from *Through the Looking-Glass* that Carroll spotted in the series 'Specimens of Celebrated Authors' in *Fun* magazine (30 October 1878), they asked readers to enjoy making connections between old and new versions of the same idea. But the *Alice* books were also vulnerable to more aggressive forms of parody – the kind that set out to bite the hand that fed it.

An influential early example was Juliana Horatia Ewing's 'Amelia and the Dwarfs', first published in *Aunt Judy's Magazine* (February–March

1870), just a few months before another issue featured Carroll's 'Puzzles from Wonderland'. The story revolves around a 'tiresome little girl' whose favourite antics include smashing ornaments and 'pulling at those few, long, sensitive hairs which thin-skinned dogs wear on the upper lip', and at first glance it appears to be a traditional morality tale. Having disappeared underground to live among the goblins, Amelia is forced to spend a period in the fairy-tale equivalent of Purgatory before she can be released back to the surface world. Yet although on the last page we are told that she 'grew up good and gentle, unselfish and considerate for others', we are also reminded that she is 'unusually clever', which raises the suspicion that her good behaviour is strategic rather than spontaneous, like that of a young Becky Sharp in training. Much the same might be said of the author, because Ewing's story is an equally unruly offspring of its source – a version of *Alice* that performs the literary equivalent of smashing ornaments and pulling at sensitive hairs. Ewing may not have been conscious of this herself, and she would certainly not have wanted to upset one of her most valued contributors to *Aunt Judy's*, but her story is far less well mannered than it might initially appear. At one point underground she introduces a dance in which a 'very smutty, and old, and weazened' goblin admires Amelia's neat footwork. '"I think we will be partners for life",' he confesses. '"But I have not fully considered the matter, so this is not to be regarded as a formal proposal."' It is difficult to read this now without seeing a grotesque version of Carroll and Alice Liddell's relationship capering in the margins.

Elsewhere, the *Alice* books were beginning to be viewed not as a target but as a tool, providing satirists with a set of characters and narrative situations that could be applied to many equally nonsensical aspects of modern life. An early sign of this came in *Punch*, where on 20 April 1872 the article '*Punch's* Essence of Parliament' had noted that upon his recent retirement, J. G. Dodson MP had been complimented by both party leaders, and concluded that 'When Mr. Dodson publishes a third volume of the enchanting adventures of Miss Alice, of Wonderland and Looking-glassland, he shall be duly complimented by the Great Leader of all, *Mr. Punch.*' Carroll wrote to Tenniel asking for the error to be corrected, and

Dodson himself pointed out that he had 'no claim' to the honour of 'being the author of *Alice in Wonderland*, etc.' What their protests failed to recognize was that the joke had much less to do with a mock-confusion between Dodson and Dodgson than with a more general desire to connect the *Alice* books with contemporary political debate. It was an understandable aim. Elizabeth Sewell has pointed out that the two fields in which people are most likely to quote from the *Alice* books are politics and the law. Both are closed systems that operate according to a fixed set of rules, and can seem confusing or bizarre to outsiders; both appear to be 'totally insulated against the normal day-by-day experience of the universe as we think we know it'. But although such limitations are unlikely to appeal to many people beyond the professionals who work within them, they were precisely of the kind Carroll found most attractive. Just as he adopted fixed literary forms in order to find ingenious new ways of twisting them out of shape, so he enjoyed taking social systems that presented themselves as perfectly logical, and tugging at any loose threads until they unravelled in his hands.

Carroll's raids on political and legal absurdity in the *Alice* books show how carefully he applied this lesson. Despite his limited interest in party politics, between writing *Alice's Adventures in Wonderland* and *Through the Looking-Glass* he took the opportunity to witness a parliamentary debate at first hand from the public gallery during the second reading of the Reform Bill in April 1867, and reported that with the exception of one 'very amusing' speech and a 'savage onslaught' in reply, the proceedings were 'tame'. He was a much more regular visitor to the local court assizes in Oxford, a habit that began in March 1851, shortly after his arrival as an undergraduate, where he attended cases that in the year *Alice's Adventures in Wonderland* was published included sheep stealing, riot, rape, embezzlement and a woman accused of infanticide who was 'acquitted on the ground of insanity'. Both *Alice* books are full of legal parodies. The case of 'Who Stole the Tarts?', in particular, is one in which proper court proceedings quickly become indistinguishable from the mechanisms of farce. The books are equally sharp on the arbitrary exercise of power by rulers, and the slippery antics of those that help to keep them

PUNCH, OR, THE LONDON CHARIVARI.—October 30, 1880.

ALICE IN BLUNDERLAND.

(With Mr. Punch's profoundest Apologies to " Alice in Wonderland.")

Tenniel's *Punch* cartoon 'Alice in Blunderland' (30 October 1880)

there. In fact, the satirical undercurrents in Carroll's writing were clear enough for later writers to follow his example without having to invent any new methods. They merely had to update his list of targets.

Once again *Punch*'s contributors were among the first to see the benefits of this approach. The issue of 30 October 1880 featured a cartoon by Tenniel that depicted Alice talking to an annoyed Gryphon and a smug 'Mansion House Turtle' wearing a heraldic breastplate, alongside a skit about the erection of the Temple Bar Memorial in the City of London. This featured a rampant bronze griffin on a sculptural column, which Alice observes is braced by a '"cumbersome pile of scaffolding"' in the middle of the road. Her advice is to demolish it: '"I call it stupid; and it is dreadfully in the way."' The title of both text and image was 'Alice in Blunderland'.

This shift from 'wonder' to 'blunder' was a happy example of a word performing what it described. By evoking one thing but replacing it with an off-key alternative, it prepared readers for much larger disappointments, such as the results of bungled town planning. Welcome to ~~Wonder~~ Blunderland: it was the sound of expectations being deflated like a hissing balloon. The word already had some sort of literary pedigree: 'Blunderland' had long been a disparaging term for Ireland, and it was the name Disraeli had chosen for a beautiful but bloodthirsty country in his 1828 satire *The Voyage of Captain Popanilla*. But it is only after the *Alice* books that Blunderland became somewhere that Victorian and later writers decided to explore further. It was a dystopia with edges that had been softened by humour; a version of the world in which ordinary events could be turned upside down to expose the ridiculous underside they usually tried to conceal.

The first major example was *Our Trip to Blunderland* (1877) by 'Jean Jambon' (John MacDonald), which opens with a mock-apology: 'It may be thought that in introducing a certain little lady ALICEnce has been taken. But royal personages are public property.' The story revolves around three little boys who have spent a day reading about 'the strange, funny things [Alice] saw and did when fast asleep'. They beg her to take them to Wonderland, she sings them asleep with a lullaby, and soon they are passing through their drawing-room wall on magical bicycles, like a troupe of acrobats bursting through a paper hoop. However, when they arrive they discover that the pass Alice has signed is not for the province of Wonderland but Blunderland. It is a place full of 'blunders' in the popular sense of 'errors' – the sort of thing Tennyson had castigated in his 1854 poem 'The Charge of the Light Brigade', when he pointed out that over 600 men had been sent to their deaths in the Crimea because 'Some one had blundered.' Many of the blunders in this new story are comic opposites: people eat 'heats' instead of ices, pupils beat their schoolmasters, and so on. Others involve little jabs of satire, either directed at specific objects, such as the contemporary fashion for tight dresses that made women appear to walk with their knees 'tied together with tape', or offered as more general hints that life outside Blunderland could be equally topsy-turvy. However, the most important way in which MacDonald exploits the idea of 'blundering' is through the word's original sense of "To mix up or mingle'. Adopting Carroll's picaresque narrative style allows him to attack everything from quack remedies to Wagner, as his topics pop up on the page like the targets in a fairground shooting range and are pinged flat one after another by well-aimed jokes.

Some later examples in the genre were even more precise in their satirical ambitions. *Clara in Blunderland* (1902) and its sequel *Lost in Blunderland* (1903), both by 'Caroline Lewis' (a collaboration between three authors), deal primarily with the misadventures of the British government in the Second Boer War and later domestic and foreign policy decisions. Conservative Prime Minister Arthur Balfour features as Clara, who is pictured as a grotesque individual with the sagging face of an old man perched on top of a little girl's body, and after a sharp set of political jibes, the conclusion in each book is that joking about political incompetence should only be the first step towards taking it seriously. Together, these satires confirmed that 'Blunderland' had become the literary equivalent of a sign marked 'Kick Me', a label that could be attached to any contemporary foolishness requiring slapstick correction. In the following years there would also be *Alice in Blunderland* (1907), a satire on municipal ownership in which the Dormouse has been appointed Chief of Police because he is 'the soundest sleeper in town' and a 'Champion Tea Drinker', and the more daring *Adolf in Blunderland* (1939), based on a BBC radio play, where a young Adolf Hitler in frilly knickerbockers longs to be 'the biggest man in the world', and encounters creatures such as the Queen of Heartlessness – Heinrich Himmler in a dress that is stiff with swastikas.

The *Alice* books provided these satires with a helpful narrative template. Employing a naïve child's perspective, in particular, allowed them to see stale conventions with fresh eyes, and much of what happens to Alice found parallels in some of parody's standard techniques, which show what is wrong with an idea by making it seem ridiculously tiny or expanding it until it starts to crack under the strain. One result was that when satirists raided Carroll's stories they did not always include a version of Alice herself. If she had proven that she could survive outside Wonderland, with her guest appearances in stories by other authors, Wonderland was starting to prove that it could survive without her dreaming it into existence.

*

Twenty-two

While the *Alice* books were being developed in new directions, the lives of those involved in their creation went on in more predictable ways. In the case of both Carroll and Alice Liddell, this meant having to confront some of the inevitable differences between fictional characters and real people.

In the world outside writing, time's arrow usually travels steadily in just one direction. People in books are different: they do not age unless the writer wants them to; the arrow can be reversed or suspended or made to loop around until it hits its target in the form of a final full stop. But as Carroll had already discovered through his photographic experiments, writing was no longer the only way of suspending its movement, and although Alice never sat for him again after her sullen 1870 portrait, it was not the last time she found herself in front of a camera.

Benjamin Jowett, the Master of Balliol College and Oxford's undisputed king of the backhanded compliment, was once asked what he thought of Alice Liddell's mother, and replied with crushing politeness, 'I have always admired the way Mrs Liddell has preserved her youth.' Perhaps her success was down to healthy living and plenty of beauty sleep (a phrase first recorded in 1857), but if not she was hardly alone in employing other strategies to roll back the years. From the 1850s to the 1870s, the nation was gripped by scandals surrounding Madame Rachel, whose lavish premises at 47a New Bond Street in London had become a magnet for wealthy and gullible society ladies willing to pay the equivalent of thousands of pounds for beauty treatments that included 'Magnetic Rock Dew Water for Removing Wrinkles' and a top-secret 'Face Enamelling' process that promised to make them 'Beautiful For Ever'. This was not an exclusively female phenomenon – at some level Oscar Wilde's Dorian

Gray is a pathological version of the many Victorian men who sought to touch up their thinning hair and squeeze themselves into the latest fashions – but women were certainly the main target of advertisements that claimed it was possible to pass through life untouched by time.

Alice Liddell continued to preserve her youth by other means. While her family was staying in Tennyson's house on the Isle of Wight in the summer of 1872, they became acquainted with the dazzlingly eccentric amateur photographer Julia Margaret Cameron, and whether or not Alice particularly wanted to return to posing for photographs, Cameron was someone who cheerfully assumed that indifference was just modesty in disguise. Almost nobody could say no to her. In addition to capturing visiting celebrities, she would waylay strangers with interesting faces who passed by her house in Freshwater, swathe them in outlandish costumes, and force them into excruciating poses in the chicken coop she had converted into a photographic studio. On one occasion, Robert Browning was discovered motionless, too scared to move, after she had gone to prepare her plates and forgotten about him. Her photographs were either hauntingly picturesque or bordering on the inept, depending on the observer's point of view, with her use of exposure times that ranged from three to seven minutes producing softly lit images that were soulfully blurred around the edges, as if viewed through eyes misted over by emotion.

The photographs she took of Alice in 1872, together with other members of the Liddell family, display a good range of her work. They include two close-ups of Alice's face emerging from a smudge of darkness, three three-quarter-length 'St Agnes' poses in which Alice is wearing a white dress with an unearthly glow created by the long exposure time, and several half-length examples of mythological figures (*Alethea*, *Pomona*, *Ceres*) that frame her with so many leaves and flowers that she looks less like a human being than an exotic pale blossom unexpectedly flowering in a British garden. In April 1873, Alice herself showed Carroll a selection of these images in the Christ Church Deanery, and although he was not usually impressed by Cameron's technical skills, noting in his diary that he 'did *not* admire' the 'large heads taken out of

Julia Margaret Cameron, *Alethea* (1872), featuring Alice Liddell

focus' she had exhibited in 1864, the photographs of Alice set against a
background of foliage may have given him pause. By this time his own
relationship with Alice had been reduced to the stiff politeness of former
friends. Compared to the period in her childhood when she had made
regular guest appearances in his diary, it was his only mention of her for
several years that did not also involve some mention of the *Alice* books,
and even this meeting was something of an accident, as Carroll had
called on the Dean 'on business'. If Carroll was saddened by their grad-
ual separation he did not admit as much to anyone else, and possibly not
even to himself, but Cameron's photographs were a vivid reminder of
how much had changed since Alice had first posed for him against the
Deanery's ivy-covered wall. Putting the photographs side by side made
it look as if the Beggar Maid had grown up not smoothly and gradually
but with a sudden physical lurch.

The idea that a girl's body could change as quickly as it did in
Wonderland continued to trouble Carroll in the years after *Through the
Looking-Glass*. In May 1879, he recorded a strange dream in which he had

taken 'the *child* Polly' (the younger sister of Ellen Terry), 'looking about nine or ten years old', to see 'the *grown-up* Polly act!', which meant that he had imagined her as '*the same person at two different periods of life*'. He decided that this was 'a feature entirely unique, so far as I know, in the literature of dreams'. It was certainly another example of something that had long intrigued him: the possibility that a girl and her adult self might not be two versions of the same person, like a queen and a beggar maid who 'were really the same child', but two different people altogether. This could move him to nervous laughter; he noted that one girl 'has grown out of all recollection', and another has 'grown from a little girl to a gigantic young lady'. It also led to some intriguing uses of 'but' as a grammatical marker of difference: 'Ethel is much grown, but still very pretty', or 'Ethel is getting very tall, but is still a perfect child.' At other times he imagined girls growing so fast even his camera was unable to keep up. Writing to Xie Kitchin in February 1880, he pointed out that it would be another six weeks before she could bring her sister to be photographed. '*She* won't have grown too tall by that time: but I very much fear *you* will,' he told her. '*Please* don't grow any taller, if you can help it, till I've had time to photograph you again. Cartes like this (it always happens if people get too tall) never look really nice, as a general rule.' He added a sketch showing what he meant: a girl with the top of her head missing, sliced off by the edge of a photograph. Of course, Carroll knew perfectly well that there was nothing to stop him keeping larger subjects within a photographic frame, but his aggressive joke played on the idea that Xie might be growing fast enough to suffer the fate Alice is threatened with by the Red Queen: '"Off with her head!"'

Life in Oxford was more certain. Carroll's Christ Church undergraduates continued to treat their work as an intellectual diversion that could be skipped if anything more interesting came along: one languid note he preserved from 1877 states that 'Lord Victor Seymour presents his compliments to Mr. Dodgson, and hopes he will excuse him from attending his lecture tomorrow as he has an engagement', and in March 1875 the term was brought to a premature conclusion when the undergraduates refused to give up their traditional steeplechase. Carroll was far more committed to trying out new ideas. In 1875, these included a letter published in the *Pall Mall Gazette* and an article in the *Fortnightly Review*, both of which argued against vivisection as a practice that was as bad morally for the person who inflicted suffering as it was physically for the animals that endured it. In the *Alice* books he had already described creatures that had thoughts and feelings indistinguishable from those of human beings, and campaigning against vivisection was merely a logical extension of an idea he had first expressed as a young man: 'I think the character of most that I meet with is merely refined animal.' He was also increasingly interested in homeopathy, which led him to try out some dangerous-sounding home remedies: in 1878, he prescribed himself doses of 'aconite and arsenic' to cure a cold, and in 1882 he was advised to apply 'sulphurous acid' to a patch of inflamed skin under one arm.

Alongside these innovations, Carroll took steps to satisfy the more conservative side of his character. Three months after viewing Cameron's portraits of Alice Liddell, he posed Xie for a photograph asleep on a chaise longue, which he entitled *King Cophetua's Bride*, and later that month he took three more of Beatrice Hatch 'in rags'. He continued to single out little girls named Alice for special attention, at times treating them almost like members of a separate species – a type of girlhood that had achieved its finest manifestation in his stories but was still capable of taking on interesting new forms in real life. In March 1873, he met the parents of five daughters and asked them 'to bring their little "Alice" to be photographed' – the inverted commas around 'Alice' tacitly acknowledging her qualifications for being singled out in this way. In April 1876 he sent off acrostics to two more girls named Alice, one of which began by teasing her with the idea that she had been removed from her proper environment: 'Alice dreamed one night that she | Left her home in Wonderland: | In a house called "Number Three | Carleton Road" she seemed to be.' A year later, he met the Hull family at the seaside and 'gave Alice a copy of *Alice*'. Indeed, so often was the same pattern repeated that anyone who saw Frederick Morgan's sentimental painting *Feeding the Rabbits* (c. 1904; also known as *Alice in Wonderland*), which depicted a little girl surrounded by a dozen white rabbits in a bluebell wood, would have been forgiven for concluding that the artist had misunderstood one of the fundamental rules of Wonderland. In Carroll's mind, the White Rabbit was one of a kind in the sense that he could not be replicated. By contrast, Alice was becoming one of a kind in the sense that she seemed capable of generating any number of successors.

It is not just in his own life that Carroll resisted change. He was equally willing to consider the possibility that the *Alice* books could keep his readers young at heart. One acrostic he sent to a child-friend in June 1876 ended with a hopeful glance into the future:

> Perchance, as long years onward haste,
> Laura will weary of the taste
> Of Life's embittered chalice:
> May she, in such a woeful hour,
> Endued with Memory's mystic power,
> Recall the dreams of Alice!

However, the idea that the dreams of childhood could extend into the 'long years' of adulthood was far from straightforward, as can be seen in the importance Carroll placed on logic. One of the reasons he enjoyed logical problems was that they took the messy ambiguities of experience and pared them down to clean lines of reasoning. Logic recalibrated the world into a place where propositions were either true or false; there was no place for propositions such as 'Lewis Carroll loves girls' that might be both true and false. But of course it is only adults who enjoy imitating the simplicity of children. Children are usually too busy being children.

Other attempts to retain a child's perspective were equally vulnerable to scrutiny. Carroll detested 'grown-up' children, especially girls who aped adult fashions such as pinning up their hair rather than allowing it to fall untidily down their backs, but this was not the only way in which his contemporaries understood the phenomenon of the 'grown-up' child. Alongside the miniature adult there lurked the figure of the fraudulent juvenile, a physically mature individual who cunningly used a Romantic vocabulary of natural innocence to avoid his or her proper social responsibilities. As Malcolm Andrews has pointed out, Dickens's novels are full of both types of 'grown-up' child. In addition to characters such as the Artful Dodger in *Oliver Twist*, a boy considerably less than five feet tall who smokes a long clay pipe and wears 'a man's coat, which reached nearly to his heels', and Ruth Pinch in *Martin Chuzzlewit*, 'a premature little woman of thirteen years old, who had already arrived at such a pitch of whalebone and education that she had nothing girlish about her', there is Skimpole in *Bleak House*, a 'well-preserved' man in his late fifties who blithely declares, '"In this family we are all children, and I am the youngest"', as he shamelessly sponges off his friends.

Carroll was aware that confusing the categories of child and adult could be dangerous. He owned a copy of Thomas Guthrie's 1882 novel *Vice Versa* (written under the pseudonym F. Anstey), a Victorian forerunner of Mary Rodgers's 1972 children's story *Freaky Friday*, in which a father and son swap bodies while keeping their own minds, with farcically disastrous results. *Through the Looking-Glass* had included a variation on the idea, introducing Tweedledum and Tweedledee as 'fat little men' who are also 'a couple of great schoolboys'. Carroll also enjoyed telling children the traditional folk tale of 'The Blacksmith and Hobgoblin', in which a goblin promises to 'turn old folks into young ones'; his alchemy works on an old woman, who emerges from the blacksmith's furnace 'alive, and young, and beautiful', but when her husband tries to repeat the trick he is burned to a crisp.

Carroll's efforts to preserve his own youth were less radical. Mostly they involved regular contact with children, who enjoyed spending time with him almost as much as he enjoyed spending it with them. However, he sometimes appeared unsure how to prevent these relationships from toppling over into unwonted and possibly unwanted intimacy. One child-friend, Ethel Arnold, remembered his rooms in Christ Church as 'an El Dorado of delights', with a row of low cupboards in the sitting room that contained 'wondrous treasures' for their entertainment: 'Mechanical bears, dancing dolls, toys and puzzles of every description came from them in endless profusion.' Even as an adult she could not enter these rooms 'without experiencing over again a thrill of delicious anticipation when a cupboard door swings open'. Yet although Carroll enjoyed playing the role of entertainer, there was never any suggestion that he saw the children as his equals. At the heart of these social occasions there was always the desire to educate.

Ellen Terry's son Edward Gordon Craig recalled being bored by one of Carroll's mathematical puzzles, which involved five sheep being taken over a river in a boat two at a time, to be worked out with matches and a matchbox ('I was not amused,' he recalled, 'so I have forgotten how these sheep did their trick'), while a girl faced with 'the fox, and goose, and bag of corn' problem shrieked out, 'I can't do it! I can't do it! Oh, Mamma! Mamma!' and stormed off in tears. When Carroll had longer with a child, he prepared a full programme of instruction. 'We have had a delightful week together,' he recorded in his diary after being accompanied to the seaside by a twelve-year-old girl named Polly in July 1892, 'with a few lessons, in Arithmetic, Geography and Geometry (she learned one Proposition of Euclid!), and, most enjoyable of all, some Bible-readings.' Whether Polly enjoyed this holiday timetable as much as he did he does not say. Meanwhile, any child who failed to treat Carroll with proper respect was swiftly put in her place. When he caught the young Isa Bowman drawing a caricature of him, he 'got up from his seat and turned very red, frightening me very much. Then he took my poor little drawing, and tearing it into small pieces threw it into the fire without a word. Afterwards he came suddenly to me, and saying nothing, caught me up in his arms and kissed me passionately', which suggests that being on the receiving end of Carroll's forgiveness could be just as awkward as his temper. Another girl made the mistake of calling him 'Goosie', at which 'He pulled himself up, and looked at her steadily with an air of grave reproof', until she substituted 'a very subdued "Uncle"' instead.

Most of Carroll's encounters with children were less self-conscious than this, but he seems to have realized that they had started to fall into a pattern that was in danger of becoming stale. The Drury sisters were typical in being overwhelmed by his charm. Although they were initially annoyed when the stranger sharing their train compartment finished the story they had been telling, they were delighted when he took out of his bag three home-made puzzles, followed by 'three little pairs of scissors and paper so that they could cut out patterns', with the promise of 'many other surprises in that wonderful bag'. Later he sent them a first edition of *Alice's Adventures in Wonderland* with an original poem addressed 'To three puzzled little girls from the Author' written on the flyleaf, and this established a friendship that would later lead to a visit to the Chestnuts and many trips to the theatre in London. It soon became a familiar routine: Carroll would strike up a conversation with a family, bring out the games and puzzles he kept in his little black travelling bag, and follow up their meeting by sending the child a signed copy of an *Alice* book. Every encounter was different and every one was the same. In July 1876, he 'made friends with' a twelve-year-old girl and her mother on a railway journey from Oxford, and 'the adventure had the usual ending, of my promising to send the child a copy of *Alice*'; by September, when he reported that he 'lent the wire puzzle (as a beginning of acquaintance) to three rather picturesque children, sisters, about 12, 10, and 8 years old', a suggestion is creeping in of Carroll as an old clown recycling the same props ('the wire puzzle') again and again.

However, Carroll knew that not everyone had the opportunity to grow old, and that despite Humpty Dumpty's advice to '"Leave off at seven"' this was not always a source of comedy. In April 1876, he wrote to a judge who had recently sentenced a seventeen-year-old servant girl to life imprisonment for killing her employer's baby son, pointing out that the question of 'whether she was sane and responsible for her actions' had apparently not been considered. He had also been given two stark reminders that 'young' was a relative rather than an absolute term, having been forced to deal in quick succession with two sudden deaths and one painfully lingering one. First there was his uncle Skeffington, who had helped to construct the 1845 Act for the Regulation of the Care and Treatment of Lunatics, and was murdered in May 1873 during his inspection of Fishertown House Asylum in Salisbury by a patient who hammered a rusty nail into his head while he was leaning over to inspect a ledger. Then there was Alice's sister Edith Liddell, who died of peritonitis in June 1876, just a few weeks before her wedding, after contracting measles. Between

these deaths, there was another that touched Carroll even more closely –
that of his young cousin and godson, Charlie Wilcox, who in 1874 was
suffering from tuberculosis and being cared for by his family. Carroll took
on his share of nursing duties, first at the Chestnuts and then in lodgings
on the Isle of Wight, writing that 'someone sits up every night', but nothing could be done. Charlie died in November.

Long before that, it would have been obvious that Charlie was doomed;
all his family could do was wait for him slowly to cough his life away. It is
not surprising that this preyed on Carroll's mind, and his diary in 1874
is punctuated by regular medical updates on his cousin's progress and
plans for his care. Slightly more surprising is that he seems to have discovered a kind of mournful comedy in the situation. In 1876 he published *The
Hunting of the Snark*, a poem that took the idea of an inevitable end and
turned it into a method of composition. Carroll had dreamed up the last
line while he was out walking one morning after being in Charlie's sickroom, then set himself the task of inventing a story that would postpone
this conclusion for as long as possible. We learn early on that if the Snark
turns out to be a Boojum, the Baker 'will softly and suddenly vanish away
| And never be met with again', but it takes another 340 lines for this to
occur, and in the meantime the reader is entertained with a lot of joyful
nonsense.

Carroll's poem ends with the Baker being cut off before he can complete his final line, which makes his quest an ideal model for any desire that
can never be fully satisfied. This includes the desire for meaning, which is
probably why *The Hunting of the Snark* has attracted explanations as a
magnet attracts iron filings: the Snark has been interpreted variously as
'material wealth', 'social advancement', 'a symbol of the North Pole' and
even (not altogether seriously) 'the Hegelian philosopher's search for the
Absolute'. Carroll's preferred explanation was that his poem was 'an
Allegory for the Pursuit of Happiness', and this also makes sense. It
describes not only the search for perfect happiness, but also the small but
significant pleasures we can enjoy on the way, whether this is the Beaver
quietly 'making lace' or the Bonnet-maker planning 'A novel arrangement
of bows'. Many of these sound like metaphors for writing poems, and *The*

Hunting of the Snark as a whole proves to be equally good at amusing itself while waiting for its own end, with alternating lines of four and three stresses that create the illusion of a story in which everything counts, and patterns of language that make ordinary objects sound as if they are secretly in league with each other ('paper, portfolio, pens'). In fact, whatever meaning a reader discovers in this poem, its real subject is itself. It takes us on a journey and then teases us for assuming that we are getting anywhere other than further inside our own heads.

Given that Carroll's most successful works in this style had been the *Alice* books, the final non-surprise is how often they are echoed in *The Hunting of the Snark*. There is the same pun on 'fit': the poem is 'An Agony in Eight Fits', just as in Wonderland the King of Hearts quotes the line 'before she had this fit', then asks Alice if she ever has fits. The Jubjub and Bandersnatch are taken from 'Jabberwocky', which is also the source for eight more portmanteau words in this new poem, while Carroll later told Beatrice Hatch that 'snark' was another member of the same linguistic family, the result of a collision between 'snail' and 'shark'. Finally, or firstly, he added an acrostic to the front of the book describing how he had met a little girl named Gertrude Chataway at the seaside, and how 'bright memories of that sunlit shore | Yet haunt my dreaming gaze', together with a dedication to her as 'a dear Child: in memory of golden summer hours and whispers of a summer sea'. Sunlight, dreaming, memories, golden hours beside a stretch of water: if this was a personal recollection, it was also a literary reprise. At one stage Carroll even considered a red binding for his poem 'to match *Alice*'. In fact, the closer one gets to this gleefully opaque work ('They sought it with thimbles, they sought it with care . . .'), the more it starts to resemble an attempt to put off another ending – not that of Charlie Wilcox, but of the dream-child who carries a thimble in her pocket, and when she is asked by the Cheshire Cat where she is going replies, '"I don't much care where— . . . so long as I get *somewhere*."'

*

Twenty-three

Carroll originally wanted to publish *The Hunting of the Snark* on 1 April, which would have been appropriate for a poem that routinely offers up ludicrous ideas with a perfectly straight face. Perhaps he worried that such errant nonsense might have a bad influence on young readers, for when his book appeared at the end of March 1876 it included a three-page leaflet entitled 'AN EASTER GREETING TO EVERY CHILD WHO LOVES "𝒜𝓁𝒾𝒸𝑒"' in which he advised them to follow a much more straightforward path in their own lives. Beginning with an appeal to 'fancy, if you can, that you are reading a real letter, from a real friend whom you have seen, and whose voice you can seem to yourself to hear', it continued by reminding them that God enjoyed seeing 'the lambs leaping in the sunlight' and hearing 'the merry voices of the children, as they roll among the hay', just as much as he appreciated kneeling worshippers. Consequently, they had a much happier ending to look forward to than that of the Baker:

> Surely your gladness need not be the less for the thought that you will one day see a brighter dawn than this – when lovelier sights will meet your eyes than any waving trees or rippling waters – when angel-hands shall undraw your curtains, and sweeter tones than ever loving Mother breathed shall wake you to a new and glorious day – and when all the sadness, and the sin, that darkened life on this little earth, shall be forgotten like the dreams of a night that is past!

Here Carroll's dashes do not cut his sentence off, as they do in the case of the Baker's '"Boo——"', but instead draw it out, in a neat demonstration of his belief that heaven will be an endless extension of earthly delights.

It is like watching a horizon that keeps receding as we sail towards it, and by the time we reach the end of the sentence, 'Surely' is revealed to be not the start of a question but a triumphant affirmation of faith. Carroll's earlier paragraphs in the 'Easter Greeting' are less conclusive; they are peppered with questions that seem to be engaging the reader in genuine dialogue, such as 'Are these strange words from a writer of such tales as "Alice"?' and 'is this a strange letter to find in a book of nonsense?' Such rhetorical tactics closely follow the style Carroll adopted when he wrote to individual child-friends, and in his 'Easter Greeting' they serve a similar purpose. They make it seem as if this is indeed a 'real letter' from a 'real friend' who cares what his readers think. They turn his books from a series of flat statements into one side of a conversation.

The 'Easter Greeting' was just one of Carroll's attempts to develop his 'friendship' with the reading public. In 1875, he thought about publishing a new book of puzzles, and among the titles he considered were 'Alice's Puzzle-Book', 'Alice's Book of Odds and Ends', 'Puzzles from Wonderland' and 'Jabberwocky and Other Mysteries, Being the Book That Alice Found in Her Trip Through the Looking-Glass'. Four months after the publication of *The Hunting of the Snark*, in July 1876, he also printed off a circular offering free copies of the *Alice* books to children's hospitals, a charitable exercise that would allow him to entertain new groups of children without having to be there in person.

In some ways his growing reputation was a sign of the times. The word 'celebrity' was first used in its modern sense in the mid-nineteenth century, and alongside older terms such as 'literary lion' it was increasingly being applied to writers. One of the worst side effects of literary fame, as many people were starting to discover, was that readers seemed to think their favourite authors should devote as much time to personal correspondence as they did to their published works. Dickens complained about the number of begging letters he received, which included requests that ranged from the bold (a new donkey) to the bizarre (a cheese), and the same problem also featured in fiction. In *Jo's Boys*, Louisa May Alcott's 1886 sequel to *Little Men*, she recalled her first major literary success with *Little Women*:

Strangers demanded to look at her, question, advise, warn, congratulate, and drive her out of her wits by well-meant but very wearisome attentions. If she declined to open her heart to them, they reproached her; if she refused to endow her pet charities, relieve private wants, or sympathize with every ill and trial known to humanity, she was called hard-hearted, selfish, and haughty; if she found it impossible to answer the piles of letters sent her, she was neglectful of her duty to the admiring public; and if she preferred the privacy of home to the pedestal upon which she was requested to pose, 'the airs of literary people' were freely criticised.

By the end of the 1870s, Carroll was starting to be thought of in a similar category. Despite complaining about being 'bullied' by 'the herd of lion-hunters who seek to drag him out of the privacy he hoped an "anonym" would give him', and resisting the temptation to write for periodicals when it was 'only the *name* they want', an unsympathetic contemporary reported that he had become 'one of the sights of Oxford', and 'strangers, lady strangers especially, begged their lionising friends to point out Mr. Dodgson, and were disappointed when they saw the homely figure and the grave, repellent face'.

Carroll had mixed feelings about fame. He enjoyed it in other people, as his photographic pursuits showed, but rejected it when it was visited upon his own life, perhaps because it was so hard to reconcile with the humility expected of a churchman. Writing in the third person to someone who asked for his autograph in 1887, he explained that he was 'glad that his books give pleasure' but disliked receiving such strong praise because 'it is not wholesome reading'. Over the next few years, his dislike took on various forms. In February 1876 he rejected an invitation to be caricatured by 'Spy' (the artist Leslie Ward) in *Vanity Fair*, as 'nothing would be more unpleasant to me than to have my face known to strangers', although Dean Liddell had been perfectly happy to have his hawk-like profile featured in the previous January's issue. He was equally unhappy when his face was connected to his pseudonym. The only time his child-friend Evelyn Hatch ever saw him lose his temper was when he was asked to meet a woman who had been attracted by his reputation. 'There is one thing I cannot stand,' he told her, 'and that is to be pointed out as: "That's the man who wrote *Alice in Wonderland!*"' Even the clergy were not exempt: when he was introduced to a dean who cheerfully announced to the assembled company that they were in Carroll's presence, there was 'an immense explosion' and a 'pathetic and serious request' that there should be a warning if the man ever tried to call again. He was equally suspicious of other writers. In 1880, he begged not to be included in a literary dictionary, as it would cause him 'deep' and 'lasting' annoyance, and in 1884 the prospect of being included in the *World*'s series 'Celebrities at Home' was similarly refused on the grounds that it was 'extremely distasteful and annoying'.

He was not the only Victorian writer who disliked having the cover of a pseudonym blown. When Thackeray addressed Charlotte Brontë as 'Currer Bell', the name under which she had published *Jane Eyre*, she replied curtly, 'I believe there are books being published by a person named Currer Bell, but the person you address is Miss Brontë – and I see no connection between the two'; on a later occasion, he introduced her at a public lecture as 'Jane Eyre', and she was observed to tremble with rage.

Carroll's obsession with keeping his two identities separate seems especially strange given that by the mid-1870s their association was an open secret. *Punch* was not the only publication that enjoyed dropping broad hints, but having decided that preserving a clear distinction was a matter of principle, no amount of contrary evidence would shift Carroll's position. 'The statement that my name is "perfectly well known" has really *no* significance,' he told Catherine Laing when she applied to add his name(s) to a catalogue of anonymous and pseudonymous books, 'without knowing *how many* know it'. Even when the connection was not explicit it was concealed by the thinnest of disguises: in 1874, an issue of the Oxford satirical magazine the *Shotover Papers* recommended a book by 'a cunning D. C. L. | "Alice in Wonderland"', we know it well.' However, what such publications could not know was the private significance Carroll's pseudonym held for him. When he signed himself 'Lewis Carroll', it was a confirmation of intimacy and a mark of trust. He was perfectly capable of exhibiting the same kind of behaviour in person, but it was only when he retreated to his writing desk that he could reinvent himself as an ideal friend brimming over with generosity and jokes, rather than a greying bachelor with a wire puzzle in his pocket. Lewis Carroll was someone who existed only in a world of words.

One place where these questions were concentrated every summer was the seaside. In 1860, Carroll had written a poem entitled 'A Sea Dirge' that satirized some of the more annoying aspects of seaside holidays, including 'A decided hint of salt in your tea' and 'a fishy taste in the very eggs', and *Alice's Adventures in Wonderland* had listed the evidence of tourist activity one might expect to find on the coast: 'a number of bathing-machines in the sea, some children digging in the sand with wooden spades, then a row of lodging-houses, and behind them a railway station'. Both works were responding to a national trend: set against the much larger population movements during the century that saw millions leaving the countryside to live in cities, there was a growing seasonal swell of holidaymakers heading back to the coast. In 1854 William Powell Frith exhibited his giant painting *Ramsgate Sands (Life at the Seaside)*, which depicted dozens of people squashed together on a small patch of sand, enjoying themselves by paddling in the sea, reading newspapers, picnicking, playing games, snoozing in the sun or sheltering beneath dainty coloured parasols, and the crowded nature of this scene accurately indicates how popular such activities had become.

Such seaside fun was a relatively recent phenomenon. Before the eighteenth century, the coast had chiefly been a place to be avoided; the home of smugglers and the untamed roar of the ocean, it was where civilization fell away into savagery. Two social trends changed that: the consensus among doctors that bathing in seawater was a cure for everything from leprosy to gout, and theories of the sublime that made the sea newly alluring as a place where one could literally immerse oneself in nature. The coast became even more fashionable after Brighton was adopted by some of the more sickly members of the royal family as their unofficial holiday residence, taking the waters being a much more straightforward remedy than that prescribed to the Duke of Gloucester in 1771, who was advised to suckle at 'the breasts of some healthy country women that were sent for from the mountains'. Soon the word 'seaside' had come to mean a destination for health or fun, and by the 1870s whole stretches of sleepy coastline had been transformed into the nation's playground. 'Everyone delights to spend their summer's holiday | Down beside the side of the silvery sea', claimed the Edwardian music-hall song 'Oh I Do Like to Be Beside the Seaside', and if you're an ordinary Smith or Jones or Brown 'At bus'ness up in town', a trip to the seaside is a particular annual treat: 'You save up all the money you can till summer comes around | Then away you go | To a spot you know | Where the cockle shells are found.' The rapid spread of the railways, and the introduction of paid holidays, meant that most of these holidaymakers were clerks and factory workers dipping their toes into a previously exclusive world of leisure. Many features that now seem central to seaside resorts were a response to their tastes, from fish and chips (previously an urban speciality) to the iron piers which stretched out into the sea in ever larger and more elaborate forms, as if each town was poking its tongue out at its neighbours. And where holidaymakers led, entrepreneurs followed: by 1904, Rhyl boasted a ballroom with 2,500 springs under the parquet floor, a waxworks show, table-tennis rooms and an imitation Venice featuring 'real Gondolas propelled by real Italians'.

Carroll's preferred destination was the more genteel resort of Eastbourne, widely advertised as 'a fashionable watering-place' and 'the healthiest town in England', and between 1877 and 1897 he spent every summer in lodgings at 7 Lushington Road, where he had 'a nice little first-floor sitting-room with a balcony, and bedroom adjoining', or his landlady's subsequent home at 2 Bedford Well Road. Here he could work undisturbed, although when he wanted to relax there was a good choice of leisure activities on his doorstep. The pier was completed in 1872, the Devonshire Park complex (which boasted the largest heated salt-water baths in the country) in 1874, and by the mid-1880s there were two theatres, the Royal Hippodrome Theatre (1883) and Devonshire Park Theatre (1884). Croquet was available at the Eastbourne Cricket Ground next to the station, and if Carroll wanted a taste of more garish amusements he could travel along the coast to see attractions at the Brighton Aquarium such as the 'Electric Lady', or the torso resting on a swing known as 'Thauma', which he described as 'a very clever illusion, looking like the upper half of a female, cut off just above the waist'.

A more significant attraction for Carroll was Eastbourne's ever-shifting population. One tourist guide published in 1863 declared it to be a 'youthful town', and this was true of more than just its recent expansion. Many similar publications explicitly targeted families with young children, carrying advertisements for riding schools that had 'Quiet Ponies for Children', or for patent remedies such as Keating's Worm Tablets ('has no effect except on worms'), and the opportunity to meet new girls every year was one that Carroll happily embraced. He was not undiscriminating; indeed, he could be ruthless in dismissing girls who were unsuitable candidates for friendship, either because they were 'common' or because they failed to live up to his ideals in some other way. He disliked hiring models, as in his eyes they tended to be 'plebeian and heavy' with 'thick ankles', and in the case of children he was similarly fussy, telling one friend that 'I'm not omnivorous! – like a pig. I pick and choose . . .'

His first summer in Eastbourne established a lasting pattern. On 2 August 1877, two days after moving into his lodgings, he wrote a long entry in his diary, explaining that it was 'time to record the various beginnings (or pseudo-beginnings) of child friendships here'. They included 'a handsome little brunette, about eleven years old', a 'nice little girl' who was 'pleasant' but 'not very bright', and Dolly, who 'seemed to be on springs, and was dancing incessantly to the music . . . her eyes literally glitter'. It was the 'fascinating' five-year-old Dolly who continued to take up most of Carroll's attention in the next few weeks. On the 6th he left her a present and she ran away from him ('she is a regular little coquette'), on the 11th he sadly noted that she 'will not speak', and on the 14th she finally thanked him for his present, but after being teased by her family she went off in 'a fit of almost hysterical crying'. An 'experimental visit' on the 17th failed when she 'cried the whole time', and on the 20th he heard that a mutual acquaintance had 'finally abandoned the attempt to reconcile Dolly to me'. More optimistically, the same day he noted that 'It seems that I could, if I liked, make friends with a new set of nice children

Carroll's pencil sketch of a seaside child-friend
(18 August 1884)

every day!' Anyone who stumbled across his diary without knowing the context might think it was that of a seaside worker recording a series of holiday romances, although in Carroll's case the most intimate he became with any of the girls was with one who 'came and sat on my knee after an acquaintance of a few minutes'. Instead they were a set of stories in which he could play around with various scenarios without needing to go any further. He could even illustrate them: two surviving sketchbooks show the pencil drawings he made of various girls posing with their buckets and spades, their skirts carefully pinned up to avoid the waves.

Some of Carroll's photographs of children in similar outfits, which feature one girl preparing to make a sandcastle and three more about to go shrimping, were actually taken in Hampstead, which suggests that he viewed the seaside as an idea as much as a real place. It was a pastoral retreat where he could strike up friendships that were always pure and always new. Put another way, it was another version of Wonderland, so we should not be surprised at his pleasure in meeting 'a veritable "Alice"' on the seafront, nor that he found himself echoing the language of his stories when he recorded that in one morning on the beach he had encountered four girls named Marion, May Miller, Millicent and Mabel, like a human version of the Dormouse's list of 'everything that begins with an M—'.

But while the seaside was somewhere Carroll could play out happy fantasies of innocence being restored to its natural setting, it was also a place of great inconstancy. The sea was always remaking itself in new patterns; different families came and went; the friendships he tried to establish often turned out to be as unstable as the sand beneath his feet. Even if the children did not have time to grow up over a few short summer months, they could be alarmingly capricious in their responses to him; as Carroll observed with characteristic understatement, 'there are few things in the world so evanescent as a child's love'. That was one key difference between 'a veritable "Alice"' he might meet strolling along the beach and the original who was preserved in his books. The loyalty of his fictional Alice was as fixed as the writing in a stick of Blackpool rock.

*

Twenty-four

The uncertainty Carroll experienced over his friendships with children did not only reflect their unpredictable behaviour. It also related to language. His preferred term was 'child-friend', which recognized that the hyphen separating 'child' and 'friend' was likely to become a barrier as a girl aged – the great majority of his child-friends were girls – but allowed for the possibility that it could stretch elastically over the years. Often that is precisely what happened, and Carroll enjoyed the incongruity of having 'many "child-friends" (ages ranging from 7 to 27)' or being visited by 'a "child-friend," who came to see me, 2 days ago, with her *fiancé*'. Occasionally, he tried out phrases such as 'girl-friends' or 'young-lady-friends' instead, but without indicating whether he thought of these as alternative names for the same form of friendship or different categories altogether.

His confusion was understandable, because the Romantic idea that childhood was a separate realm was coming under increasing social pressure during the nineteenth century. Some of this was down to the 'grown-up children' who sought to extend its privileges into adulthood or, in the case of many young women, were trapped in a kind of enforced infantilism, assumed to be interested in nothing more challenging than the latest fashions. Living alongside them were the children with full adult economic responsibilities, like the watercress-seller interviewed by Henry Mayhew for *London Labour and the London Poor*, who was dressed in carpet slippers that were too big for her and told him that as she had to save up her wages to buy clothes she had no spare money to waste on sweets: 'it's like a child to care for sugar-sticks, and not like one who's got a living and vittals to earn. I aint a child, and I shan't be a woman till I'm twenty, but I'm past eight, I am.' The picture was complicated still further by the idea that children who had grown up could enjoy their early years again, repeating past pleasures and redeeming past mistakes, by having children of their own.

This sent out unusual shock waves into the period's fiction. Valentine Durrant's novel *His Child Friend* (1886), for example, centres on the relationship between a writer named Arthur and an eleven-year-old girl named Edith he rescues from her mother, a prostitute who dies with 'her child's name on the ashen lips, and a calm smile upon the lovely face'. Arthur's chivalry is heavily stressed, particularly after he develops a fondness for kissing Edith and sitting her on his knee. 'Do you scent indelicacy in this record?' the author asks. 'Then may your shrewdness be forgiven; and our inexpertness that we have handled the idyll so coarsely.' Eventually Arthur marries his young sweetheart, when she has 'barely passed the border-line between seventeen and eighteen'. But although the purity of this event is again stressed, as we are told that her love is the result of 'touching idolism' rather than years of grooming, there is a subplot that features another man, Ernest, who remembers the request made by Edith's mother: 'You will love her . . . as you once loved me?' and finds himself with a growing 'desire to pet and caress her'. Twelve years after Edith and Arthur marry, Ernest returns to claim their daughter, also called Edith, as his own. She too is eleven years old, and although Ernest waives his 'right' to take her away, he promises to visit her often.

His Child Friend coincided with the publication in Germany of the first edition of Richard von Krafft-Ebing's pioneering work *Psychopathia Sexualis* (1886), the twelfth edition of which in 1903 would introduce the term 'paedophilia' (*paedophilia erotica*) to sit alongside some of the other sexual categories Krafft-Ebing was the first to name in print, including 'heterosexual', 'homosexual', 'sadist' and 'masochist'. But although Carroll, conjuring up the traditional bogey figure of a judgemental prude, often wondered what 'Mrs Grundy' would say about him, there is no evidence that he thought his behaviour anything other than wholly innocent. He would certainly have been surprised by the fact that the only appearance of the phrase 'child friend' in the *OED* is from another work published in 1886, where it is used to illustrate the meaning of 'prison-bound'.

His letters in the years after *Through the Looking-Glass* continued to draw on a sacramental language when describing children: their 'innocent unselfconsciousness is very beautiful and gives one a feeling of reverence, as at the presence of something sacred', he told one correspondent, and to another he explained 'how much nearer to God, than our travel-stained souls can ever come, is the soul of a little child'.

If Carroll had been content to admire the girls' souls he would now be a far less controversial figure than he is. What has troubled many modern sensibilities is his decision to capture the 'innocent unselfconsciousness' of children for posterity by photographing them nude. At the time this would not have been seen as very unusual. Many Victorian artists enjoyed sketching and painting nude children, often with the aim of immortalizing their purity before they were tainted by the adult world, and Carroll viewed such images in similarly refined terms. In 1874 he asked Henry Holiday, illustrator of *The Hunting of the Snark*, to draw some 'nude studies' of children for him 'to try to reproduce in photographs from life', and was delighted by the 'quite exquisite' results. Sometimes it was two-way artistic traffic: having written in 1878 to Gertrude Thomson, whom he praised as 'a professional artist, who takes special delight, and is specially skilful in, pictures of naked children', two years later Carroll asked the mother of one of his nude models for permission to send Thomson some of his own photographs, as 'She cannot get, for love or money, in Manchester, such lovely forms of children to draw from, as you have so kindly allowed me (and will, I hope, again allow me) to photograph.' The potential for such requests to appear sad or sleazy was always present, as can be seen in Ruskin's letters to the children's illustrator Kate Greenaway, one of which edges towards asking for a nude drawing through a kind of rhetorical striptease: 'As we've got so far as taking off hats, I trust we may in time get to taking off just a little more – say mittens – and then – perhaps – even shoes! And – (for fairies) even . . . stockings – and then – .' Carroll's attitude was even more complicated. Although nude studies formed a tiny proportion of his total photographic output, and probably no more than 1 per cent even of his child photographs, they account for a disproportionately large amount of his energy in the 1870s. The reasons for this overlap significantly with his desire to keep Alice in the Wonderland he had created for her.

On the one hand, he insisted that anyone who had the potential for dirty thoughts when looking at young girls would find their souls being scrubbed clean, as 'It purifies one even to see such purity.' Hence his dislike of '*partly* clothed figures', which he felt were 'unpleasantly suggestive of impropriety', gaping or half-missing clothing being worse than no clothing at all. On the other hand, he left instructions on how to erase nine numbered glass plate negatives 'by soaking in a solution of soda' after his death, because 'I would not like (for the families' sakes) the possibility of their getting into other hands.' Similarly, when an eight-year-old boy stumbled upon Carroll and Thomson making nude sketches of the boy's sisters in 1893, Carroll was horrified, and insisted that the girls must be in '*full-dress*' next time, as 'the *risk*, for that poor little boy, is too great to be run again'. Just as Alice is taught in Wonderland that the terms of an equation are not always reversible, so that 'I say what I mean' is not the same as 'I mean what I say', Carroll was uneasily aware that a vision of innocence was not always the same as an innocent vision.

Sometimes his artistic ambitions were satisfied with the minimum of fuss. On one visit to his rooms, the daughters of an Oxford colleague overheard him say how much he would like to photograph them nude. 'They promptly hid under the table,' one of their daughters later recalled, 'which had a cloth nearly reaching the ground, and emerged with nothing on, much to the amusement of their father and their host.' It was as if they had managed to rewind the story of Genesis to a point before the Fall when Adam and Eve were 'both naked . . . and were not ashamed'. However, more often the process of securing possible subjects was fraught with uncertainty, and Carroll's worry that his motives might be misinterpreted led him into feats of moral exegesis that were almost comically earnest. In 1876, and again in 1879, he wrote to mothers seeking permission to photograph their daughters, and on each occasion the correspondence turned into an elaborate dance of questions about how far he might go towards 'absolute undress'. In the latter case, this resulted in Carroll making strained accusations about 'not being trusted', after he asked to photograph three sisters 'in bathing-drawers, to make up for my disappointment' if their mother refused to 'concede any nudities at all'. Yet the real paradox of these letters is that the more strongly Carroll insisted on a child's blissful unselfconsciousness, the more self-conscious his own writing became. Girls were variously 'undraped' or 'undressed'; they were in 'primitive costume' or 'Eve's original dress', or their 'favourite dress of "nothing"', followed four days later by 'the same dress as before'. French words were another way of making his intentions sound suitably highbrow: girls were taken *'sans habilement'*, or in memory of the days before they had learned 'to consider dress as *de rigueur'*. If language was the dress of thought, as some Victorian manuals of rhetoric still claimed, Carroll's increasingly elaborate attempts to avoid saying what he meant were the rhetorical equivalent of a hand-tailored suit with a fancy waistcoat.

His nervousness reflected a much wider Victorian uncertainty about the difference between artistic nudity and personal nakedness. Traditionally, nudity in painting and sculpture had been viewed primarily as symbolic, and far less frequently as circumstantial; rather than merely showing what people looked like under their clothes, it represented lust, or sin or, in the case of the infant Christ, an ideal of purity and the possibility of redemption. Versions of this idea were current well into the nineteenth century, as can be seen in the commercially produced Christmas cards Carroll sent to Agnes Hull (aged fifteen) and her sister Jessie (aged eleven) in 1882, which depicted girls on the cusp of puberty frolicking naked in a lily pond – another vision of innocence caught just in time, and another version of the idea that Christmas was a time for becoming like a little child. But this tradition was under threat, partly from a growing feeling that the figures depicted in works of art were hard to distinguish from people who merely happened to have slipped out of their clothes, and partly from attempts by some Victorian artists to blunt this distinction even further. The shock value of a painting such as Manet's *Le Déjeuner sur l'herbe* (1862–63) had come from its depiction of two women who had apparently escaped from a Renaissance painting and joined a modern picnic, where one casually sat unclothed beside two French

JOYOUS AND GRACIOUS BE THY CHRISTMAS DAY!

Postcard sent by Carroll to Jessie Hull (Christmas 1882)

dandies while the other bathed in a diaphanous shift. Viewed in a formal gallery setting, they were artistic nudes; viewed in the context of a picnic, they were merely naked. Photography was also caught up in this confusion, because alongside the imitations of academic art favoured by photographers such as Rejlander, its potential for more realistic depictions of the human body had been enthusiastically adopted by pornographers. By 1871, up to 150,000 indecent images had been seized and destroyed, and photographic journals were full of articles with titles such as 'Alleged Immorality of Photographers' and 'The Morality of the Nude'.

The six surviving examples of Carroll's nude studies, three of which depict the Hatch sisters in various outdoor settings, fall squarely into the category of artistic imitations. In these, the underlying visual conventions are pastoral rather than pornographic; the Hatch sisters, in particular, are depicted as two more Alices, forever 'moving under skies | Never seen by waking eyes', partly because the skies have been painted on, along with the rest of Carroll's chosen backgrounds. In one, Beatrice Hatch perches on a rock beside the sea, in a pose that makes her look like a mermaid who has unexpectedly grown a pair of legs; in another, Evelyn leans against a tree beside a river, or perhaps where a stream and river meet, with a hazy gypsy encampment in the distance. Inevitably, Evelyn's name leads to her being viewed as a little Eve who has returned to Paradise, but both photographs celebrate what Carroll in a Romantic mood liked to call 'children of nature'. The photographs themselves, however, are more obviously the offspring of culture, for in addition to the painted backgrounds, in the final versions Carroll arranged for the application of some rosy flesh tints to each girl's figure. Unfortunately, these make his subjects look as artificial as the plastic starfish in an aquarium; even their blushes have been painted on. Yet Carroll's artistic ambitions reflect a serious attempt to make them into something other than girls who have obligingly removed their clothes. Like *The Beggar Maid*, each of these later photographs combines two images in one. Whereas a modern viewer might see nakedness, Carroll saw nudity; in his eyes, the girls were personifications of freedom and truth, icons of purity in a flawed and fallen world. (Marina Warner has pointed out that truth is often personified as a naked body because it 'has nothing to hide'.) But of course this is not how every viewer will see them, and our difficulty in knowing what they mean is compounded by the fact that in each case Carroll's true motivations remain a troubling blank.

A similar ambiguity plays across Carroll's language in some of the letters he sent to his child-friends. The same year that he photographed Evelyn Hatch, he wrote a series of letters to Agnes Hull, who was then around twelve years old and with whom he had spent a happy period in London and Eastbourne over the summer along with her family. 'My darling Agnes,' begins one letter, before continuing, 'Please don't mind my beginning so. You may begin to *me* just any way you like.' Within a few weeks he had started to address her simply as 'My darling' ('*Weren't* you just surprised at the way I addressed you at the beginning of this letter!' he teased her), and by the end of the year he had adopted a fully formed vocabulary of courtly love: 'My darling, You are very cruel.' Forms of address are always hard to unpick in letters, because they are caught between thoughtless public conventions and more intimate private appeals. They can even encourage a form of flirting, by allowing the private to be smuggled in under the guise of the public, like someone who can only speak their true feelings when they are hiding behind a mask. We simply do not have enough information about Carroll's relationship with Agnes to know how his words were offered or how they were taken. Perhaps it was a game for two players in which both knew the rules. Perhaps Carroll was pushing the boundaries of innocence to discover the point at which either they cracked or he did, rather as he once chose to observe a man's leg being amputated in St Bartholomew's Hospital as a test of his nerve. Or perhaps he was betraying the fact that for him all letters were love letters – not because he had any particular designs on their recipients, but because they revealed how much he was in love with the creative possibilities of language itself.

*

Twenty-five

Compared to the rumours that had earlier swirled around Carroll, Alice Liddell's life in Oxford was a model of decorum. One of the dresses she purchased, a sensible brown taffeta and velvet number with a tiny matching parasol, shows that she was fairly tall for the period – 5'6" according to her passport – and fashionably wasp-waisted. It was a day-dress, to be worn as she performed her daily social round, and based on the evidence of her surviving letters, it seems that her clothes and her activities were similar in style: carefully tailored to her position in society. By now she had started to take on some of her mother's responsibilities. In February 1874, she wrote to the sculptor and painter G. F. Watts to arrange a meeting with him during a family holiday to the Isle of Wight, and on another occasion she was invited by Benjamin Jowett to meet George Eliot, 'a very remarkable and interesting person, even more so in Conversation I think than in her books'. Nobody at the time is likely to have said the same of Alice herself. Far from being encouraged to follow Eliot's example by seeking financial independence and an unconventional romantic life, all the indications are that she continued to prepare for a traditional marriage. And while she was not in the same social category as another fictional Alice, the prostitute Alice Marwood in *Dombey and Son*, who accuses her mother of making '"a sort of property of me"', there was certainly some suspicion in Oxford that she resembled the women of whom Dickens's character is said to be a 'faded likeness' – the daughters of powerful families who were bought and sold on the marriage market.

Between 1872 and 1876, Queen Victoria's youngest son Prince Leopold studied at Christ Church, and as there was plenty of social interaction with the Dean and his family, inevitably tongues started to wag about which of the Liddell daughters might be about to embark on a fairy tale with this genuine Prince Charming. Political pressure on the royal families of Europe to strengthen their alliances through intermarriage made that almost as likely as Leopold marrying a beggar maid, but Carroll was happy to follow the line that Lorina Liddell was manoeuvring her daughters in that direction. In his satirical pamphlet *The Vision of the Three Ts* (1873), he referred to 'the Goldfish' (i.e. Leopold) as 'a species highly thought of, not only by men, but by divers birds, as for instance the Kingfisher', which was one of his less ambitious forms of code, although anyone who knew of his own energetic efforts to secure a photograph of the Prince (who appears to have been glumly resigned to such approaches) might have wondered if the edge of his satire had been sharpened by a guilty conscience.

It seems that Alice enjoyed the Prince's company without expecting it to lead anywhere. In a set of memories she jotted down in 1932, she recalled accidentally giving him a black eye with her oar one day while they were messing about on the river, concluding that 'I was never ordered to be beheaded', which mischievously made his mother sound like another Red Queen, but hardly suggested the pain of a lost love. However, in the eyes of some at Christ Church, the Prince already had a frustrated rival: Carroll. A waspish theatrical sketch written in 1874 by the Christ Church undergraduate John Howe Jenkins, for which he was later sent down, depicted the Liddell daughters scheming to marry for money and power. 'Rosa' boasts that she has 'trapped a noble lord of high degree', 'Psyche' that she has 'trapped a Pr*nce, the youngest of his race; | Of tender flesh [presumably a nasty jab at Leopold's haemophilia], but yet of handsome face', and 'Ecilia', i.e. Alice, that she has 'securely trapped' the MP's son 'Yerbua', i.e. Aubrey Harcourt, the Oxford MP's nephew who was in fact romantically involved with Edith Liddell at the time. In the second act there is a triple wedding, but it is interrupted by 'Kraftsohn', i.e. Dodgson, 'biting his nails', who swears 'By circles, segments, and by radii, | Than yield to these [marriages] I'd liefer far to die.' Unlike the wicked witch who traditionally interrupts fairy-tale marriages, he is swiftly bundled out by a group of college servants, who are told to 'Leave him in Wonderland' but in fact end the sketch by ducking him in Mercury, the pond in the middle of Tom Quad:

> Full fathom five e'en now he lies,
> Of his bones are segments made.
> Those circles are that were his eyes.
> Nothing of him that doth fade
> But doth suffer a sea-change
> Into something queer and strange.
> Goldfish hourly ring his knell.

The imitation of Ariel's song from *The Tempest* refers to the fact that Kraftsohn has been pushed underwater; however, the mathematical language indicates that his proper home would not be Prospero's enchanted isle, or even his own Wonderland, but somewhere more like Flatland, the imaginary universe that would be dreamed up ten years later by Edwin Abbott Abbott, in a novel where all the characters are geometric figures occupying just two dimensions. The strong implication is that Carroll was thought equally insubstantial as a possible suitor.

The contrast between Kraftsohn's impotent speechifying and his muscular punishment was an especially cruel piece of satire, because it reminded Jenkins's readers that if Carroll had been interested in marrying one of the Liddell girls he was hardly the sort of man to fight off rivals. He was much more preoccupied with the dangers of saying too much or too little than with putting his words into action. And this was not only a matter of practical necessity, given that Christ Church still obliged its Students to give up their academic posts if they married, a rule that would not be abolished until 1878. It was also a question of language.

Alongside the published version of Doublets, which Carroll was developing between 1877 and 1879, he also enjoyed playing the same game in private; in 1881, he wrote to the new husband of a former child-friend, 'Do not make *Ella weep*', and when the bewildered man replied that 'he did not know how to do so', Carroll showed him 'in wondrous few changes': ELLA, ells, elms, alms, ales, apes, aped, sped, seed, weed, WEEP. Words could be equally unstable even if they did not change their outward shape. Indeed, the more closely Carroll inspected perfectly ordinary expressions, the more they started to resemble puzzles without solutions. One of Humpty Dumpty's grandest boasts in Looking-Glass Land is that '"When I use a word . . . it means just what I choose it to mean – neither more nor less"', and if we laugh at this it is because we all do something similar. Just as writers build a distinctive style by honing their vocabulary on the edges of private experience, so friends and families tunnel into ordinary words to create enough space for their own branching memories. So 'kitten' means one thing when we read about it in *Through the Looking-Glass*, but something else when it comes from a lover who has adopted it as a term of endearment: the word taps into an intimate shared past within the much larger history of the language.

The danger with this sort of language game, of course, is that it might not fit happily with the usual conventions of speech; the private significance built up behind a word might never be powerful enough to push its public meaning out of the way. Carroll was especially nervous about the 'heads' and 'tails' of letters, because these social conventions had the potential to be drained of meaning, and he dwelt obsessively on how much significance should be read into their various nuances. In October 1882, he was thrown into despair after receiving notes from the young sisters Agnes and Jessie Hull that opened with 'my dear' rather than 'dearest', and were 'affectionate' rather than 'loving'; in his diary he complained that 'The love of children is a fleeting thing!' and when he next wrote to Agnes he signed himself 'Your (whether loved or not) loving, C. L. Dodgson.' Sometimes he treated such anxieties as another game, telling one mother in 1880 that she should send her daughters his love 'if they are not too grand, in their teens, to accept such a message', but the bantering tone could not hide his nervousness that the words he treated as fixed and absolute were slippery when placed in other people's mouths. 'Gaynor's and Amy's "love" I beg to return in kind,' he wrote in 1881 to a girl who had just turned fifteen, 'but slightly increased in quantity (say 10 per cent) and raised in temperature from 60° to 75°', as if the word's meaning could be made to expand or contract according to the speaker's intentions.

Writing for the public was easier; the final line of *Sylvie and Bruno* was an angel's voice whispering (in capital letters) "'IT IS LOVE'", but here it refers to an abstract idea rather than the messy histories of real relationships. Carroll's private letters were far less confident: if heads could become tails with just a few flicks of the pen (HEAD, heal, teal, tell, tall, TAIL), how vulnerable was love?

Actions could be equally ambiguous, particularly when they involved something as inherently uncertain as a kiss. A kiss could mean nothing or everything; it could be an empty social ritual, or the most intimate of confessions. "'In kissing, do you render or receive?'" Cressida asks in Shakespeare's *Troilus and Cressida*, and Patroclus replies, "'Both take and give.'" But of course something can be taken in a spirit very different to how it is given, and for Carroll a kiss was one of the most difficult parts of any relationship to negotiate. If kisses were a way of sealing new

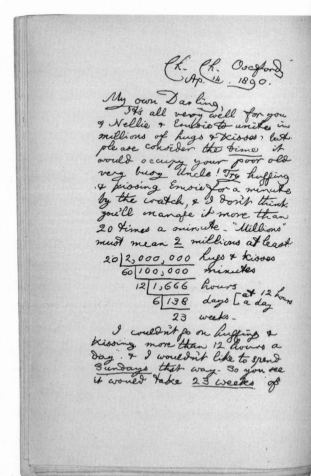

friendships and punctuating old ones, they were also potentially another series of obstacles waiting to trip him up.

Adam Phillips has written that 'kissing resists verbal representation', perhaps because it is impossible to kiss and to speak at the same time, but Carroll had a way around that problem. Writing allowed him to kiss and be kissed at a safe distance. He told one child that 'When I get letters signed "your loving," I always *kiss* the signature', and he thanked another for the lock of hair she had sent him: 'I have kissed it several times – for want of having you to kiss, you know, even hair is better than nothing.' He also enjoyed sending kisses by post, finding a special pleasure in multiplying them ('I send you seven kisses (to last a week)'; 'I send you 1,0000000 kisses'), dividing them ('I send you 4¾ kisses'; 'Please give . . . ½ of a kiss to Nellie, and ½₀₀ of a kiss to Emsie, and ½₀₀₀₀₀₀ of a kiss to yourself'), and making them the basis of even more comically complicated sums:

Letter from Carroll
to Isa Bowman
(14 April 1890)

A letter from his mother sent to him as a boy had told him to give the rest of the family and himself '1,000,000,000 kisses from me', which suggests that the idea may have been rooted in his imagination from early on, and it was often repeated in his poems. When he wrote '"And shall I kiss you, pretty Miss!"' or 'I kissed her dainty finger-tips, | I kissed her on the lily brow, | I kissed her on the false, false lips', placing kisses in a line of verse was another way of making them last much longer than the touch of a real pair of lips.

If kissing on the theatre stage is 'a softened hint at the sexual act', as Freud suggested, Carroll's letters and poems were more like rehearsals for the real thing. To be 'on kissing terms' with a child-friend was something he especially valued, and the kisses themselves were part of a much larger physical ritual. Henry Holiday's daughter remembered that 'When he stayed with us he used to steal on the sly into my little room after supper, and tell me strange impromptu stories as I sat on his knee in my nightie', and when he took the seven-year-old Irene Burch to a performance of *Cinderella*, he noted that 'They let me bring her in without a ticket, to sit on my *knee*: and about once in every half-hour she turned round to give me a kiss.' Most of the girls claimed to enjoy the attention. 'He was so punctilious, so courteous, so considerate, so scrupulous not to embarrass or offend,' his child-friend Ethel Rowell later recalled, 'that he made me feel I counted.' Those feelings seem to have been reflected in Carroll. If his girl-friends counted then so did he, and each kiss was an addition to a total that was potentially as endless as the White Queen's sum in Looking-Glass Land: '"What's one and one and one and one and one and one and one and one and one and one?"'

In trying to work out what Carroll's kisses added up to in his own mind, it is probably significant that he thought '*any* child under 12 is "kissable"', and also that his friendship with Agnes Hull was broken off when 'she felt one of his kisses was sexual'. One interpretation of this would be that kissing his child-friends was a 'softened hint' at other kinds of intimacy both they and he would not permit. The more generous interpretation is that, for Carroll, kissing children was not a prelude to sexual activity but a legitimate alternative to it. Victorian conduct manuals insisted that kissing was not something adults should do in public, because it was too full-fleshed for refined social life. (Language was another matter, and it is probably no coincidence that the Victorians invented so many ways of talking about kissing in disguise, including a 'kiss' in billiards (1836), a 'kiss-me-quick' bonnet (1852) and a 'kiss-curl' (1856).) This is why Carroll so dreaded the moment he would have to greet a girl by shaking her hand or raising his hat: it was proof that she was no longer a girl. To be allowed to kiss her, on the other hand, was tantamount to an admission that she had not yet left the state of childhood; it was like a fairy tale in which the Prince's kiss did not wake Sleeping Beauty but instead confirmed that she was still safely hidden away from the adult world.

Yet the meaning of some kisses could be as hard to grasp as Alice's dream-rushes. For Carroll things came to a head at the beginning of February 1880, when he kissed Henrietta ('Atty') Owen, the daughter of one of his Christ Church colleagues, thinking she was still a child. It turned out that she was seventeen years old. 'I was astonished,' he confessed with faux-ruefulness to his diary, 'but I don't think either of us was much displeased at the mistake having been made!' He wrote a mock-apology to the girl's mother, who was a trained barrister and the niece of the Vice-Chancellor of Oxford University, 'adding that I would kiss her no more', and assumed that would be the end of the matter. It was not. There followed some 'angry correspondence' involving the Kitchins as intermediaries, after Mrs Owen had made it clear that she treated the matter much more seriously than he did. Carroll could hardly be said to have helped his cause: in the same letter that he asked Mrs Kitchin to soothe Mrs Owen's feelings and 'get her to consent to forgive me', he suggested that Beatrice Hatch's mother might agree to share some photographs he had taken the previous summer, in which 'the style of dress' was 'simple and unconventional', i.e. altogether absent. By the end of the month, an uneasy truce had been brokered, but it is unlikely that the chain reaction of gossip stopped there. The consequences for Carroll were twofold. Henceforth he became even more careful to secure consent in advance, writing to the mother of another seventeen-year-old girl in 1895 that although he thought they were 'on "kissing" terms', if it were thought better for him to shake hands with her 'I shall not be *in the least* hurt.' A more serious outcome was that a few months later, on 15 July 1880, Carroll took his last recorded photographs.

There may have been other reasons building up behind this decision – the early mystery of photography had largely gone, now that cheap hand-held cameras could be purchased by the general public, and Carroll's preferred wet-plate process made it 'a very tiring amusement', especially when anything he wanted to record could be 'equally well, or better, done in a professional studio for a few shillings'. But if there was a single tipping-point, it is most likely to have been the Owen affair. In the weeks immediately preceding his decision, Carroll had been devoting plenty of time and money to his photographic work, including the purchase of 'acrobatic' costumes in four sizes, with more pictures of Annie and Frances Henderson (the young daughters of an Oxford colleague) at the end of May 'mostly in their favourite state of "nothing to wear"', and then – a sudden and irrevocable break. 'I fear I am permanently in their black books now,' Carroll wrote of the Owens at the end of July, not only because he had tactlessly offered to photograph another of their daughters, but also because of 'the photos I have done of *other* people's children. Ladies tell me "people" condemn those photographs in strong language: and when I enquire more particularly, find that "people" means "Mrs. Sidney Owen"!' But although Carroll thought this 'sad', it seems that at some point he decided to retreat. Mrs Grundy turned out to be a powerful foe when she was no longer a faceless prude but the implacable and well-connected Mrs Owen.

If real kisses were ambiguous or open to misinterpretation, literary kisses were safer, and in the last two decades of his life Carroll worked hard to give his writing a similar kind of intimacy. The least impressive attempts were books such as *Sylvie and Bruno*, in which he made the characters so tactile and loving they appear to be motivated by a dream of human emotion rather than the real thing. When Sylvie rewards the old Professor 'with a hearty kiss', or later exclaims, '"You dear old thing!"' while 'standing on tiptoe to kiss him', it is about as convincing as a doll that says 'Mama'. The *Alice* books were easier to work with, probably because they had emerged from a genuine intimacy with the Liddell children, and as Carroll continued to develop the stories they were increasingly connected in his imagination with kissing. When he published a facsimile of *Alice's Adventures Under Ground* in 1886, he added a preface in which he explained that 'the best work a man can do is when he works for love's sake only', putting all his powers into a task 'where nothing of reward is hoped for but a little child's whispered thanks, and the airy touch of a little child's pure lips'. The version of *Alice's Adventures in Wonderland* he produced three years later for very young children had an even more syrupy preface, which explained that the story was to be 'read, to be cooed over, to be dogs' eared, to be rumpled, to be kissed', and the same message was repeated in a dedicatory poem:

A Darling's kiss:
Dearest of all the signs that fleet
From lips that lovingly repeat
Again, again, their message sweet!

In the context of the poem, these kisses come from a girl who is 'Full to the brim with childish glee'; they are the silent language of love. Viewed in the context of Carroll's career, however, they come close to describing what he wanted from the *Alice* books. They were not just stories that invited kisses, like the King of Hearts' suggestion that the Cheshire Cat '"may kiss my hand, if it likes"'. They were kisses.

*

Twenty-six

A few months after the Owen affair, Carroll decided to investigate someone else's theories about childhood. On 2 September 1880, a day after he bought a mechanical swimming frog for a new child-friend, he went to hear a 'curious' lecture in Eastbourne by the missionary Lord Radstock on 'training children'. According to Carroll, the lecturer's remarks fell into two categories: they were either 'commonplace' or 'not true'. The idea that encouraging children to be ambitious was 'un-Christian' particularly annoyed Carroll, and he 'escaped at the first opportunity' back to the beach. Here he 'made friends with a family who were banking up with sand the feet and legs of a pretty little girl perched on a sand-castle', and after drawing her he walked further along the beach, where 'a merry little mite, in jersey and bathing drawers, began pelting me with sand: so I drew *her* too'. Evidently training children was much less fun than playing with them.

Meanwhile, the twenty-eight-year-old Alice Liddell, who had enjoyed similar '[frolics] on the sand' as a child, now had more sophisticated ways of amusing herself. In 1878, these included a family holiday to Skye, where the Liddell sisters combined to write a travel diary describing the small triumphs and disasters of their stay, notably their discovery of an *H.M.S. Pinafore* score hidden away in the baronial splendour of Dunvegan Castle, where they were staying as guests of the owners. One of their ink drawings depicts them hammering out a chorus on the piano, with 'WHAT NEVER?', 'NO NEVER', 'WHAT, NEVER?' ballooning out of their mouths, while the rest of the family try to block their ears. Two years later, on 15 September 1880, Alice left Oxford for good. She was getting married.

The groom was Reginald ('Regi') Hargreaves, although anyone who had followed his career closely up to that point might have been forgiven for thinking that she was not marrying an individual but a social type. The Hargreaves family fortune had been made through calico printing in Lancashire, and after the unexpected death of his father in 1863 Reginald's mother had protected him fiercely and spoiled him rotten. At Eton, he was treated to regular Fortnum & Mason hampers, and clothes that included real onyx buttons for his waistcoat at twelve shillings a set (silver buttons he dismissed as 'second-best'), a sealskin waistcoat and a silk umbrella. Just once there was a hint of scandal, when he was 'swished' by his tutor for 'being on intimate terms with a big boy up in the school', but as he grew older his passions were mostly directed towards the wholesome pursuits of a country gentleman: cricket and hunting. By the time he went up to Christ Church in 1872, his main qualities were already clear. He was not stupid, but nor was he offputtingly clever; his degree would eventually take him six years to complete. He believed in God without thinking too much about why. He dabbled in writing without being very good at it; thirty years after his marriage, he won second prize in a competition to come up with a new verse for the National Anthem, with a patriotic entry that began, 'Lands far across the sea, | Empires that are to be, | All homage bring.' He had a relaxed sense of humour, and an interest in the more unusual side of life; when he visited Reading Fair after leaving Eton, he singled out for special mention 'a child five years old which weighed eight stone', and 'a blue horse with no hair on at all'. He was loyal and loving. He was rich. In fact, in common Victorian parlance, he was a most suitable match.

His steady courtship of Alice Liddell was marked out by a series of dance cards. At a New Year ball at Chippenham in 1875 he booked two waltzes each with 'Miss E. Liddell' and 'Miss A. Liddell'. Six months later, at Christ Church's summer ball, again he booked 'A. L.', this time following her initials with a string of exclamation marks and a score of eighteen (Edith scored fifteen). The following year, he danced four times with 'A. L.' at the summer ball, more than anyone else, reserving for her the waltzes 'Sweethearts' and 'Le Premier Baiser' (The First Kiss). Finally, on 13 July 1880, after suffering 'long miseries of uncertainty', he proposed to his 'Darling Alice' and was accepted.

The ceremony that took place in Westminster Abbey on 15 September 1880, conducted by Dean Arthur Stanley, featured all the usual trappings of a grand society wedding. For Alice, these included a gold wedding ring engraved with the motto 'Each for the other and both for God', and an elaborate dress of silver brocade, white satin and old lace. Prince Leopold sent an affectionate letter with his 'warmest & most heartfelt wishes for your future happiness' and a pearl horseshoe brooch, while other gifts on the lengthy wedding list included a pair of diamond earrings, a hunting whip, a set of Byron's works, a gold sugar bowl and spoon, and a silver looking-glass. If Carroll was invited to the wedding he did not attend. The newly married couple went on to spend the first part of their honeymoon at Sedgwick Park, a secluded estate in Sussex where Alice picked mushrooms and Reginald blazed away at the local wildlife. The second part was deferred to the start of February 1881, when they took a leisurely eight-week journey by train through France and Spain. A more adventurous alternative would have been easy enough to arrange. If they had wanted to, they could even have boasted of travelling to 'Wonderland', which by now had become a way of referring to unfamiliar real places as well as their invented counterparts. In 1881, a second edition of *The Natural Wonders of New Zealand (The Wonderland of the Pacific)* was published, while *The Eastern Wonderland* would appear the following year. Sometimes the influence of *Alice* was more subtly pervasive: three years earlier, the English travel writer Annie Brassey had drawn on Carroll's example when describing an eleven-month voyage in the ship *Sunbeam*: she encountered a series of strange sights in Japan that included 'horses and cows with bells on their tails instead of on their necks', and a carpenter 'reversing the action of his saw and plane'; her conclusion was that 'It looked as if they had originally learned the various processes in "Alice's Looking-glass World" in some former stage of their existence.'

Reginald Hargreaves was a much less ambitious traveller than this. In fact, if his journal is an accurate guide to his feelings, he had some misgivings about almost everywhere beyond Dover. In a brown cloth notebook he bought in Paris, he left space for Alice to add some comic sketches – the pair of them awkwardly sharing an umbrella in the rain;

Alice sitting daintily under a parasol in the melting heat of Seville while he sprawls beside her – but for the most part he used his journal to record his mild annoyance that Europe was so unlike Britain. It was like a reprise of Alice's earlier European tour with the volume turned up. Barcelona's streets were 'mostly very narrow & badly paved', and in Malaga they were 'dirty and smelly', while the cathedral was 'hideous'. Seville's equivalent of Bond Street was 'dirty & inferior', and the city's entertainments did not greatly amuse him, featuring 'fireworks of the most feeble description'. A similar accusation might be levelled against his own writing; he tends to respond to complex new experiences with blunt single adjectives – sugar cane is 'nasty'; the Alhambra in Granada 'disappointing' – or hides behind guidebook descriptions like a shield: Cordoba's mosque was 'most curious – for further particulars see Murray'. Tangier made him especially nervous: 'I sh[ld] fancy it looks just the same as it did one or ten thousand years ago,' he reported, 'no European dress no vehicles, no roofs except flat ones to the houses & a mixture of Moors Jews & niggers in the streets some sitting in all sorts of queer attitudes' – a description that gradually loses its grammatical bearings as the writer becomes more unnerved by the scene. Less than a week later he and Alice were back at home, 'happy in the certainty of getting fresh butter for breakfast', and with one final burst of patriotism – 'England with all thy faults I love thee still!' – the journal ends.

In her letters Alice had been more curious, more open to new experiences: in one she describes a long mule journey from Tarragona to Montserrat as 'a confusion of sunniness, jolting roads, mules, bells, Spanish saddles and glorious scenery all jostling each other in my brain!' and a pursuit by some local urchins that ended with one being pitched headlong into an ilex bush, so that 'nothing was seen of him but two feet sticking out soles upwards'. If anything, she was keen for more excitement than circumstances allowed, noting with disappointment that on their journey across to France the Channel was 'smooth to tameness'. That might suggest she and Reginald were an ill-matched couple, but the letters they exchanged six weeks after their return to England tell a different story. He recalls 'that night at the opera when I won you' and celebrates

Cuffnells

'the beginning of all my happiness'; in her reply, she shyly confesses that 'half of myself is gone again, the joyous happy half, dear, that you bring back to me with your love and care for me'. By then they were settled in Cuffnells: a substantial Georgian country house, owned by the Hargreaves family since 1856 but shut up since the death of Reginald's mother in 1872, which was set in 168 acres of parkland on the edge of Lyndhurst in the New Forest.

If Alice's life had been rewritten as a Victorian novel, this is where the final chapter would end: with the heroine snug and happy in her grand new home, as servants bustle below stairs and sheep graze outside the sash windows. Alice had similar thoughts herself. But the story she had in mind was not an adult romance; it was a children's book. A week before her wedding she had visited Cuffnells for the first time, and the next day she wrote to 'Dearest Regi' with her hopes for the future:

> I did not say very much to you yesterday, I think, but can you guess a little bit how enchanted I was? I hope it will be a real fairyland to us both as long as we are both permitted to enjoy it, dear; 'Wonderland' come true to 'Alice', at last!

*

Twenty-seven

'Reader, I married him': the final chapter of *Jane Eyre* opens with a sentence that is good news for the happy couple but bad news for readers. Now that the final segment of plot has been slotted into place, and Jane Eyre has become Jane Rochester, there is little left for us to do beyond admire the finished design. There are a few loose ends to tie up, such as the discovery that Mr Rochester eventually makes a partial recovery from his blindness, but less than a thousand words after Jane describes her marriage as 'supremely blest – blest beyond what language can express', the novel fades into a contented silence. After hitting such a high note of happiness there is really nowhere else for it to go. Indeed, as Jane describes how they are 'ever together', and live in 'perfect concord', Brontë makes their marriage sound less like a developing relationship than an indefinitely extended wedding photograph.

This is a common pattern in Victorian fiction. As Henry James pointed out in his essay 'The Art of Fiction' (1884), for many of his contemporaries the ending of a good novel was like the 'course of dessert and ices' that rounded off a good dinner – the main aim was to avoid disagreeable aftertastes. While real relationships could unravel over the years, fiction offered an illusion of happy permanence; the final full stop was like a button marked 'Pause' that kept a story's characters safe from change. Such stories captured a dream that was strongly identified with the emerging middle class, in which love conquered all and afterwards there was enough money left jingling in one's pocket to enjoy its triumph in perfect serenity. That is why, George Orwell tartly observed, so many Victorian novels conclude with the hero retiring to a place in the country, where 'nothing ever happens' except the regular arrival of new babies. 'The ideal to be striven after,' he explained 'appears to be something like this: a hundred thousand pounds, a quaint old house with plenty of ivy on it, a sweetly womanly wife, a horde of children, and no work.' There are parties and games to enjoy, and maybe some light recreational farming, but otherwise the spirit in which these novels end is 'a sort of radiant idleness'.

Alice's new life as Mrs Hargreaves closely followed this fictional model. A brimming bank account, a quiet country estate, a husband whose hobbies were limited to the traditional pursuits of a country squire – her marriage could have been cut and pasted from the final chapter of any popular Victorian romance. But if the next fifty years were largely radiant and idle, they were trailed by some busy shadows from the past.

Cuffnells may have been a 'Wonderland', but it was also a challenge. Everything was constructed on a grand scale. The sales particulars in 1855 had boasted of its twelve principal bedrooms, six WCs, a drawing room 42 feet long with 'enriched cornices' and 'Patent Ventilators', and a 'splendid lofty conservatory' protecting a copse of ornamental trees. Since then, the Hargreaves family had lavished even more money on the estate. The drawing room now featured an elaborate peacock frieze created by an Italian artist, one of the bedrooms had gold doorknobs, a gilded four-poster bed and a plaque announcing that George III had slept there, and outside the main house lay a wooded area known as the 'Wilderness', stocked with exotic trees and shrubs. Running such an estate was a labour-intensive business, especially if none of the labour was your own; in the 1881 census, the main house alone contained eight servants, including a butler and a footman, all but two of whom were younger than their employers. Trying to maintain authority over such a busy household as a newly married twenty-eight-year-old was always likely to be difficult, and at some point Alice decided to adopt a more impressive social persona. If Cuffnells was a sequel to Christ Church, she was not prepared to be merely 'Mrs Reginald Hargreaves', the name printed on the cards she now carried in a monogrammed ivory case. To the servants she was 'Lady Hargreaves' – a title she clung on to tenaciously despite having no right to it. 'Lady Hargreaves' was not quite 'Queen Alice' or 'Queen Cophetua', but it undoubtedly confirmed the love of social distinction Carroll had observed and mock-celebrated when she was a girl.

The local area already had literary associations. In 1847, it had featured as the setting for Frederick Marryat's popular novel *The Children of the New Forest*, in which a group of aristocratic children (including an Alice and an Edith) have to adapt to a new life in the woods during the Civil War, and from 1883 the neighbouring houses included Annesley, the country retreat of the writer Mary Elizabeth Braddon, who was best known for her sensation novel *Lady Audley's Secret* (1862), in which the heroine is a bigamous arsonist who pushes her first husband down a well. Cuffnells was to be the setting for a very different kind of story. Residents of Lyndhurst used to speak of the time before the First World War when tourist stagecoaches clattered through the village's streets, with a guide perched on the back blowing a post-horn and pointing out places of local interest, including 'the home of the original Alice in Wonderland'. However, if any of Alice Hargreaves's servants entertained the fantasy that she was still the character in the stories, they were in for a nasty shock. For Carroll, the underground may have been a place of comic chaos, but in Cuffnells, life below stairs was a model of good order. In the kitchen that Alice enters in Wonderland, the cook throws 'a shower of saucepans, plates, and dishes'; in Cuffnells, one of the kitchen maid's jobs was to keep a row of copper pots and pans gleaming, and when another maid accidentally smashed a vase while dusting, she was icily informed that all breakages would be paid for. Indeed, while most of the staff loyally praised their mistress as a kind if rather aloof employer, some of their recollections make her sound more like a quietly spoken version of the Red Queen. On another occasion, she came downstairs to discover that the main shutters had not yet been opened, and when she learned that it was because the housemaid was suffering from painful chilblains she sent another servant to the village to buy some ointment. The cost, which amounted to an entire week's pay, was carefully deducted from the housemaid's wages.

Our knowledge about Alice's day-to-day life at Cuffnells, or at the Hargreaveses' equally grand London residence 3 Stratford Place – a house whose scale is indicated by the fact that it is now occupied by the Tanzania High Commission – is not greatly helped by her diaries. The earliest to survive is from 1884, and like all her later diaries its contents are laconically patchy: 'Rode in afternoon'; 'R played at Eton made 31'; 'Papa and Mama arrived in London'; 'Lunched at Gawdy Hall'; 'Cold.' A more rounded sense of Lyndhurst's social world can be found in the diaries of Maria Hibbert, who until her marriage in May 1883 lived at nearby Foxlease, another elegant Georgian house set in several acres of private grounds. It would be hard to claim that the owners of Foxlease enjoyed a particularly rich life except in terms of their financial position; most days involved nothing more demanding than tennis, tea parties, dances, visitors and shopping. The new Mr and Mrs Hargreaves had entered into a life that was equally privileged. They exercised their duties to the local community generously: in August 1884, they put on a Grand Bazaar to raise money for local schools, with attractions that included a regimental band and 'General Gordon's celebrated collection of Chinese trophies, dresses, flags, &c.', and in subsequent years they would also host cricket matches, concerts, flower shows and meetings of the local hunt. But there was never any suggestion that they were attempting to foster a spirit of democracy. Cuffnells was a private paradise that welcomed visitors, but only allowed them to stay if they took a job below stairs.

Whether or not this counted as 'Wonderland' probably depends upon how wonder is defined. It is certainly possible to view the self-styled Lady Hargreaves as someone whose parallel existence on the page was more exciting than anything available to her at Cuffnells. If she shared this opinion she would have been in good company. It was a common fear of Victorian critics and moralists that readers might end up preferring the glamour of fiction to the uncertainty of their own lives; indeed, such anxieties lie at the heart of some of the period's greatest novels. Flaubert's *Madame Bovary*, for example, which began serialization just a few months after Carroll first met Alice in 1856, depicts the frustrations of a woman whose imagination has been so stimulated by stories that she can no longer bear her marriage to a dull provincial doctor. Seen through her fiction-hungry eyes, her life is like the bad first draft of a novel, and she tries to rewrite it in a more exciting genre by having two adulterous affairs and finally poisoning herself. Neither strategy works: both lovers leave her, and as a result of taking arsenic she ends up vomiting blood and writhing on her deathbed; even the romance of suicide eludes her.

But although one of Alice's watercolours, dated 14 September 1883, depicts a large house hunched behind a spiked metal gate, there is no evidence that she thought of herself as another Emma Bovary, or that she was disappointed by her Hampshire 'Wonderland'. Reginald was often away from home, visiting friends in other grand country residences, but her surviving letters to him are uncomplicatedly loving. They buzz with family news, thank him for the latest salmon or partridge he has sent home, and ask about his sporting successes with more than dutiful curiosity. On their eleventh wedding anniversary, she wrote to her 'Dearest' that 'I love you still with as tender a love as the day you took me "for better for worse"', and signed herself 'Yr loving Alice'. If Cuffnells was a cage, albeit one with a butler and a peacock frieze, she seems to have been perfectly happy to spend the rest of her life polishing the bars.

Back in the equally grand surroundings of Christ Church, Carroll was no less comfortably settled. He looked older now – in a miniature painted by E. Gertrude Thomson he has greying hair and a shading of stubble – but he continued to live in the same college rooms, still topped by his now defunct photography studio, and he remained an object of fascination to

Miniature of Carroll by E. Gertrude Thomson

the outside world. In 1890, he was infuriated by the appearance of his 'beautiful suite of rooms', described as 'a veritable children's paradise', in an article about Oxford written for *Harper's Magazine* by his old (and soon to be former) friend Ethel Arnold. Although he was not explicitly named, her decision to identify 'Lewis Carroll' as a mathematician and provide his exact location in Christ Church was scarcely preserving his anonymity. The fact that she included him after pointing out that the dons who lived in college rooms were largely 'confirmed old bachelors, who tend naturally to become more and more crusty as their contact with the outer world diminishes', was also not exactly a masterpiece of tact.

For several years, Carroll had been removing unwanted distractions to concentrate on his writing. In October 1881 he resigned his Mathematical Lectureship, which the financial success of the *Alice* books now made possible, and embarked upon an ambitious range of new literary projects. Between 1881 and 1884, these included a collection of reprinted medical texts entitled *On Catching Cold*, a set of words to accompany a piece of music ('Dreamland') that had supposedly been composed by someone in their sleep, two circulars about an expurgated edition of Shakespeare that would be suitable for children, a sixpenny pamphlet that described a fair but fiendishly complicated method for awarding prizes at lawn tennis tournaments, and another pamphlet explaining the benefits of proportional representation. 'I have a bewildering number of "irons in the fire",' he wrote to Alice Cooper, the headmistress of Edgbaston High School for Girls, in November 1883, and this versatility seems to have been an additional source of pleasure, as he switched from subject to subject as if playing leapfrog with himself.

Such a busy schedule was not exceptional for Carroll, because even by Victorian standards he was something of a fundamentalist when it came to the gospel of work. In February 1882, a friend named Walter Watson who came to stay with him at Christ Church recorded Carroll's 'daily routine':

7 a.m.: cold shower
8 a.m.: chapel service
8.30 a.m.: correspondence

278

9 a.m.: breakfast

9.30 a.m.–12: work

12–1 p.m.: post letters and walk to the Common Room to read newspapers

1–3 p.m.: more work

3–5 p.m.: a long walk

5–6.30 p.m.: more work

7 p.m.: dinner at High Table

9 p.m.: tea and work until bed.

Of course, the desire for a fixed routine is hardly unusual. In his book *Daily Rituals*, Mason Currey has claimed that sticking to a regular timetable can foster 'a well-worn groove for one's mental energies' and help stave off 'the tyranny of moods'. It was also a popular topic among Carroll's contemporaries. 'Be regular and orderly in your life like a Bourgeois,' Flaubert recommended, 'so that you may be violent and original in your work.' Trollope paid an old groom £5 a year to wake him at five thirty every morning, and forced himself to write 250 words every fifteen minutes until he had produced his daily ration. Dickens was equally methodical, going to his study at nine in the morning and staying there with only a short break for lunch until he released himself at 2 p.m. for a long, vigorous walk. But in Carroll's case, such a routine seems to have served a need other than the practical one of ensuring that he turned out enough words each day. Like his determination to shave in cold water with a blunt razor, or a strictly controlled diet which meant that at lunchtime he ate little more than a biscuit, it was a necessary form of self-discipline. Even the occasional late night caused him some disquiet. Having sat up until 3 a.m. one night in 1882, the next day he forced himself to stand at his desk from 9 a.m. to 5 p.m. doing his accounts; 'Must try for more regular habits,' he urged himself. Today he might be diagnosed with a mild form of obsessive–compulsive disorder, and even at the time his behaviour struck some of his colleagues as odd. It was as if only by making his life as predictable as a piece of mathematics could he come close to solving the problem of himself.

Many of the puzzles he created, such as mazes and logical conundrums, involved taking something straightforward and inventing extra difficulties for himself. Plotting a route from A to B would be disrupted by a thick tangle of detours and dead ends; taking geese across a river would be complicated by the presence of a fox or an extra rule about the size of the boat. The more barriers he threw in his way, the more pleasure he gained from working out how to climb over them or sneak around them. And as he grew older, increasingly he took a similar attitude to his own life. Yet despite the huge number and range of his publications he was still not busy enough to satisfy himself, and accordingly, in December 1882, he agreed to serve a term of office as Curator of the Common Room at Christ Church, with overall responsibility for the food, wine, furnishings and other creature comforts of the Senior Common Room. It was a role he would happily and fussily occupy for the next nine years.

In some ways he was an ideal choice. Nobody had more exacting standards than Carroll, even if his numerous letters on small matters of college procedure were sometimes hard to distinguish from the more general complaint that he could not do everything himself. The Steward of Christ Church later recalled a partial list of Carroll's grumbles:

> Occasional letters go out from the Lodge *unstamped*, much to the annoyance of their recipients. How much milk is Mr Dodgson supposed to receive each morning and at what price? There is a 'dangerous effluvium caused by some defect of drainage' which makes the New Common Room 'quite uninhabitable.' The gas supply is inadequate to a new asbestos grate which Mr Dodgson wishes to install. He requires an electric bell-push in each of his two bedrooms. Please tell the kitchens to send him *no more smoked ham* . . . And so on; and so on . . .

Carroll set about his new work as Curator with a steely determination: everything was to be done *properly*. Improvements were made to the size and condition of the wine cellar, and the consumption of each vintage was carefully monitored. The Senior Common Room was made more comfortable by the introduction of what he called 'Airs, Glares, and

Chairs', or extra ventilation, better lighting and new armchairs. And around and within everything else there was a blizzard of extra paperwork to sift and file: cellar books, ledgers, bills, wine tasting notes, letters to tradesmen, updated lists of members and, characteristically, a new complaints book. Agendas for meetings were printed and circulated; notices were pinned up with timely precision; anyone who borrowed a magazine without authorization was crisply requested to return it. He also continued to insist on high standards being upheld elsewhere in Christ Church. In April 1887, the long-suffering Steward received another letter, this time containing a long list of complaints about the college's food, which was said to range from the unappetizing ('Beefsteak too tough to eat') to the inedible: undercooked onions and pastry that tasted more like 'pasteboard'. Reading through this list, one is reminded of Henry Kissinger's witty observation that university politics are vicious precisely because the stakes are so small, even if the problem here was that the beefsteaks were too tough. Indeed, by the time Carroll reaches the cooking of vegetables – 'Cauliflowers are *always* sent with no part soft enough to eat except the tops of the flowers' – he sounds less like a senior academic than a small child stamping his foot.

Comparing the ways that Alice Hargreaves and Carroll ran their respective establishments, there is no doubt which of them managed their task with more adult seriousness. Whereas her letters are stiff-backed with propriety, in Carroll's curatorial paperwork there are still occasional glimpses of the man who created the *Alice* books. In one notice, posted in February 1890 and addressed 'To all lovers of Orange Marmalade', he offered jars of his brother's preserve for sale, an advertisement that would have been hard to read at the time without remembering how Alice takes a jar labelled 'ORANGE MARMALADE' from one of the shelves as she falls down the rabbit-hole and discovers, 'to her great disappointment', that it is empty. It was a good example of what Carroll referred to in 1887 as memory's 'odd corners and shelves', which could easily be restocked with new material but also contained items that were 'dusty from neglect' and waiting to be rediscovered. Another series of notices, posted in 1884, announced that 'Five o'clock Tea' would be made available in the Common

Room. On 22 January, there was a list of prices for 'Cup of tea or cocoa' and 'Bread and butter &c'; two days later an amended notice explained that only 'plain bread and butter' and not cake would be supplied; the following week there was a third notice, again advertising tea or cocoa with 'bread-and-butter'. Carroll's arrangements make the Hatter's tea party seem positively straightforward by comparison. In fact, the more of his curatorial paperwork one examines, such as the alphabetical index to Common Room resolutions he laboriously wrote out in his distinctive purple ink ('Clock – 8', 'Charities, subscriptions to – 10', 'Canons, made Hon. Members – 20', 'Challenge Cup – 22', 'Cup, Challenge – 22' . . .), the more it appears that Alice Hargreaves was not the only person living in her own private Wonderland. In Carroll's reorganization of Christ Church's Common Room into a place that ran as smoothly as a railway engine on a set of tracks, he had succeeded in creating a different kind of Wonderland around himself.

*

Twenty-eight

As potential locations for Wonderland, Cuffnells and Christ Church were equally good, because by the early 1880s Carroll's fictional world was being thought of as not one place but many. 'Wonderland' had become a loose synonym for ideas that ranged from the special preserve of childhood to the unpredictable workings of the imagination, and some writers tried to follow Carroll's lead by combining its various definitions into a single all-embracing vision. In September 1881, the American illustrated magazine *St Nicholas* printed a short poem, 'Alice in Wonderland', that describes how 'Sweet Alice' discovers 'a fine baby-brother' in Wonderland, while an 1885 poem entitled 'Wonderland', written by 'One Who Loves "Alice"' (Mary Manners), eagerly anticipated the day when 'Another Alice', the author's daughter, would encounter Carroll's stories with the same 'dazzled eyes' that Mary herself once possessed. It is an intriguing counterpoint to the main article on the same page, which pointed out how important it was 'to train up children to habits of industry, application, and perseverance'; clearly not everyone had been dazzled by Wonderland. Elsewhere, there were more subtle attempts to blur the distinctions between Wonderland's various meanings. George Dunlop Leslie's 1879 painting *Alice in Wonderland* depicted a mother reading a story with Carroll's distinctive red cover to her daughter (Leslie's own daughter was called Alice), who stared out blankly at the viewer, wearing a blue dress that is nowhere specified in Carroll's stories but would soon come to seem as inevitable as the fact that she meets a white rabbit rather than a brown one. Her expression is hard to read. She could be making her way through the story in her head, or enjoying the licence it has given her mind to roam more generally, or becoming conscious of the fact that childhood is a haven as fragile

George Dunlop Leslie, *Alice in Wonderland* (1879)

as the flowers in her lap. Curled up on the sofa, she looks less like a little girl than a human question mark.

The merging of the *Alice* books in the popular imagination encouraged the idea that they were a jumble of memorable characters and situations in which other writers could rummage for useful narrative details. In addition to satires and parodies, these later works included a number of anthologies, although their connections to the *Alice* books were sometimes stretched so thin as to be practically invisible. *Tales and Stories from Wonderland* (1894) was a miscellany of traditional folk tales and fairy tales that 'convey most useful moral lessons', while *Little One's Own Wonderland* (1893) simply gathered together the issues of a monthly sixpenny children's magazine. Carroll also continued to exercise his influence in more direct ways. A story such as Charles Carryl's *Davy and the Goblin; or What Followed Reading 'Alice's Adventures in Wonderland'* (1885) both reveals and revels in its source, as it describes how a boy who has just read Carroll's book but 'doesn't believe in fairies' is taken on a 'Believing Voyage' in a boat made from a grandfather clock with sponge cakes for cushions. (It is possible that Carryl's debt was even more personal; according to Humphrey Carpenter, he was moved to write children's books 'because of the similarity of his surname to "Carroll."') The previous year saw the publication of *Alice's Wonderland Birthday Book*, produced with

Carroll's permission, which was a diary featuring a different quotation from his works opposite a blank space for each day.

In addition to these imitators and compilers there were more unusual attempts to explore Wonderland's imaginative reach, and here the idea of a blank space took on a powerful new force. If Carroll thought of Wonderland as a place of dreams, it soon started to be associated with another kind of invisible world – the ordinary one that surrounds us every day, full of wonders we have simply failed to notice. Instead of laughing at a fictional character who tries out different lenses, as the train guard does in *Through the Looking-Glass*, books such as *Nature's Wonderland* (1915) and *Wonderland; or Curiosities of Nature and Art* (1897) reminded readers that they could achieve many of the same results by a sharper use of their own eyes. This is why Constance Foot introduces a garden of talking flowers into her introductory guide *Insect Wonderland* (1910). Her intention is not to pun on different kinds of 'beds', or parody the florid language of Tennyson's *Maud*, as it is in *Through the Looking-Glass*, but to teach her readers about the life cycle of the butterfly. Like several similar books of popular science, *Insect Wonderland* carefully redirected Carroll's most extravagant nonsense back on to the paths of sense.

Even fairy tales were not immune to this search for a more rational Wonderland. One of the stories contained in John Ingold's collection *Glimpses from Wonderland* (1900) deals with a seventeen-year-old girl named Alice who views life through a filter of fiction, and in particular the 'fairy stories' that 'made everything possible'. When a very short man arrives in her village she is convinced that he is an enchanted dwarf, and because he generously gives her family some diamonds, she speculates that she will be forced to marry him in return. Only in the last few pages, when he arranges for her to wed the young man she had set her heart on, does she realize that the story she has been writing in her head is very different to the one she has been living out. The dwarf is not enchanted, and his diamonds have been created through a new chemical process rather than a mysterious spell. In fact, she turns out to be a minor character in a fable about the modern entrepreneurial spirit, rather than the heroine of a fairy tale. The only magic in the air is the metaphorical kind produced by love.

Set against this spirit of rational enquiry were vigorous efforts to persuade readers that some questions still needed the answers only religion could provide. And here Wonderland presented itself as a neutral territory where science and religion could stake out their differences. In their 1884 tract *The Wonderland of Evolution*, for example, Albert and George Gresswell begin by animating a speck of primeval matter as 'Protoplasma', a fairy who explains how she created life through her 'mystic sway', and end by rejecting pure chance as a satisfactory explanation for life on earth, preferring to believe that any process of evolutionary development must imply 'a personal Being who set it in motion'. The Revd John Isabell's *Wonderland Wonders* (1897) also sets itself the task of restoring religious equilibrium to scientific debates:

> A well-known book is entitled *Alice in Wonderland*. But why ALICE in Wonderland? Why not Bridget, and Cinderella, and Dinah, and all the rest of the alphabet? It costs nothing to go. It needs no railway train to reach it, or ticket of admission when it is reached . . . Wonderland is only another name for the world we live in.

Although Isabell continues by pointing out some truly extraordinary real creatures, such as the fish that 'hold little lamps over their open mouths and snap up the foolish creatures which come to stare at the light', which he sees as no less remarkable than talking oysters, he is in no doubt about the proper response to such a 'rum world': it is 'wonder and admiration at the mighty power and wisdom of GOD'.

Finally, if Wonderland provided a way of thinking about ordinary but disregarded parts of life, it also allowed readers to consider another hidden dimension – the one that was supposedly inhabited by ghosts. Victorian spiritualists had long claimed that we were surrounded by drifting crowds of the dead, who occasionally seeped in through chinks in the curtain separating the visible and invisible worlds. The most popular ways for spirits to make contact with the living were said to include moving furniture, speaking through a medium, presenting body parts as solidified manifestations of the mysterious substance known as ectoplasm, and slowly spelling out their messages through raps on a table. And although sceptics frequently demonstrated how easy it was to reproduce these 'proofs' through trickery and suggestion, the possibility that the air around us might be thick with ghosts was irresistible to many people at a time when scientists were busy proving that it also hummed with invisible forces such as electromagnetism and radio waves. It meant that even when we were alone we were not alone.

Carroll's early responses to these ideas had largely been comic. The young ghost that featured in his poem 'Phantasmagoria' was intended to generate laughs rather than thrills or chills, and *Through the Looking-Glass* had adopted a similar attitude. Although it opens with a reference to spirit-writing, as Alice guides the pencil of the terrified Red King to make it write '"all manner of things that I don't intend"', and ends with strange manifestations around a table that crashes on to the floor, like an out-of-control séance, both scenes are jokes rather than genuine explorations of the paranormal. During the 1880s, however, Carroll's interest grew more serious. In August 1881, he met someone from India 'who told me strange tales of Indian magic, pigeons put into bottles, thread drawn out of any part of the chest or arm of the performer, and a fulfilled curse on three men, that all should die violent deaths in six years' – a set of stories that moves steadily from stage conjuring to real magic with no apparent increase in his levels of scepticism. By December 1882, he was emphatically telling a friend that 'trickery will *not* do as a complete explanation of all the phenomena of table-rapping, thought-reading, etc.', and although 'I see no need as yet for believing that *disembodied* spirits have anything to do with it', he was 'more and more convinced' that there might be 'a natural force, allied to electricity and nerve-force, by which brain can act on brain'. This conclusion came as a result of reading the first report of the Society for Psychical Research, of which Carroll had been a founding member in 1882, along with many other prominent Victorian writers, including Tennyson, Ruskin and Leslie Stephen, and a whole gentlemen's club of MPs and JPs. From hypnotism to somnambulism, nothing was off limits to the SPR's investigators, and from the beginning its constitution stressed that 'membership does not imply any particular view of the phenomena under discussion'. They were self-appointed pioneers in the exploration of a new world.

Even if he did not take a prominent role in the Society's activities, Carroll remained committed to its aims. At his death, the books in his library included dozens of titles such as *The Wonders of the Invisible World*, *The History of Apparitions*, *The Phantom World*, *Confessions of a Medium*, *The Book of Werewolves*, *The Vampire* and *Nature and the Supernatural*, alongside the more expected works on religion. This may seem surprising, but Carroll was far from alone in thinking of the invisible world as complementary rather than antagonistic to Christianity. Although the established Church officially warned against spiritualism, in accordance with its long-standing objections to conjuring up spirits of any kind, many practising clergymen continued in office while actively looking for signs of the after-life in their spare time. A number were among spiritualism's fiercest advocates, most famously Stainton Moses, the author of a book entitled *Spirit Teachings* that has been called the 'Bible of British Spiritualism', who eventually claimed to have been visited by more than eighty spirits, including those of St John the Baptist, Plato, Beethoven, Benjamin Franklin and Napoleon III. Meanwhile, the ranks of the SPR continued to swell with vicars, deans and canons, and even a sprinkling of bishops, two of whom served as vice-presidents during the 1880s.

In Carroll's case, the idea that the known world was interwoven with an as yet unknown one was also a natural development of his literary interests. Many of his early poems had used lines of print as probes that reached into the blankness of their surroundings, and in Wonderland he had created a fictional environment in which more always seems to be going on than meets the eye. He was also intrigued by the idea that children were much closer to the invisible world than adults. Many of the mediums who attracted the greatest public attention were teenage girls, beginning with the Fox sisters in upstate New York in 1848, and although there may have been good sociological reasons for this, given that being a medium brought ordinary girls the sort of attention and social power they were unlikely to enjoy otherwise, it was commonly assumed that children were naturally better at such work. Compared to adults their senses were thought to be fresher and purer, capable of picking up subtle vibrations in the ether like delicate tuning rods. This overlapped neatly with Carroll's conviction that children were already somewhat unearthly creatures, a nursery of cherubs cast adrift in the adult world. In December 1885, writing to thank Mary Manners for her poem 'Wonderland', he explained that hearing a child speak came a close second to 'what conversing with an angel *might* be', and when his final collection *Three Sunsets and Other Poems* was published in 1898, it included a set of illustrations by E. Gertrude Thomson that purported to show naked fairies doing adorable fairy-like things like sheltering under mushrooms, but who were distinguishable from ordinary girls only by their tiny size. Even though angels and fairies were once thought to be very different orders of being, one muscular and Christian and the other mischievous and pagan, for Carroll they were equally valid models for children. All three were alluring but ultimately elusive figures. Sometimes he wondered if a child might act as a medium in a more practical sense; praising the affectionate nature of one of his child-friends in October 1885, he asked himself whether some of her 'positive electricity' might have been passed on to him. However, for the most part he acknowledged that the otherworldly state of childhood was one to which he only occasionally had access.

In the preface Carroll added to *Sylvie and Bruno Concluded* in 1893, he pointed out that his story was a thought experiment, in which he imagined what might happen if we were surrounded not by ghosts but by fairies, who lived in another dimension that humans could reach only through a trance-like state of consciousness. (Trances were how popular Victorian mediums such as D. D. Home claimed to enter the world of spirits.) It was an intriguing development of the original premise behind the *Alice* books, as it implied that some imaginary lands were not altogether imaginary. They were always there, present but unseen, waiting only for a receptive state of mind to reveal themselves. Other writers made this connection even more explicit. Usually, describing the invisible world was like trying to grab handfuls of smoke, but as the spiritualist craze continued into the 1880s and 1890s, many of its practitioners found solace in Carroll's stories. One explained how she had received signed letters from her 'dear friend in spirit-land', although the ghost himself had a different name for his new home. '"I am in wonderland!"' he told her. '"It does not seem possible that a channel has opened up to me, by which I can communicate with those I have left behind. And yet such is the fact!"' Another spiritualist scoffed that the idea of separate selves being produced by the unconscious, rather than each of those selves having an independent existence that could be tapped into by a sensitive medium, led to the question 'have we glided . . . into Alice's Wonderland, and are we perchance listening to the hatter, the Duchess, and the White Knight?' A third compared modern medicine to traditional miracles, and concluded that 'like the song in *Alice in Wonderland*', what was significant 'may not be really "the name of the thing", but only "what the thing is called"'. Even the possibility of telepathy, which had so intrigued Carroll in the first report of the SPR, was likened to 'only one more wonder in a veritable wonderland'. Such debates were full of nervous disagreement, but what linked them was the language of Carroll's stories, which still retained an edge of strangeness despite having become comfortingly familiar over the previous twenty or thirty years. The *Alice* books allowed wonder to be described without its being explained away.

*

Twenty-nine

In December 1883, Carroll unexpectedly bumped into the real Alice. It was their first meeting since her marriage, and it set off a train of associations that would take on a powerful momentum over the next few years. Writing to Mrs Liddell to request her daughter's address, he confessed that seeing and speaking with Alice again had stirred many 'ancient memories' back into life, and he now wanted to write to 'one, without whose infant patronage I might possibly never have written at all'. Four days later, he sent a signed copy of *Rhyme? And Reason?* to 'Mrs Hargreaves, with sincere regards and many pleasant memories of bygone hours in Wonderland', accompanied by a letter recalling 'the long dreamy summer afternoons of ancient times'.

Both the personal meeting and the literary follow-up echoed a painting Carroll had seen earlier that year at the Royal Academy, Thomas Faed's *They Had Been Boys Together*, which depicted a sleek lawyer trying to make out the name on a card presented to him by a shabby former playmate. Writing to a woman who sometimes referred to herself as Lady Hargreaves had the potential to be equally awkward. However, if she wanted evidence that Carroll's 'pleasant memories' were still helping to shape his writing, she only had to open the book he sent her. Among the few previously unpublished poems was a set of 'Four Riddles', one of which Carroll had written after seeing Marion Terry perform in W. S. Gilbert's comedy *Pygmalion and Galatea* on 10 March 1877. The second stanza provides a set of clues to help readers work out which part of the word Gala*tea* is being described, with references to singing kettles and 'golden fancies', but it ends on a rueful personal note: 'For Youth and Pleasance will not stay, | And ye are withered, worn, and gray. | Ah, well-a-day!' If this was another version of the idea that 'Youth is full of pleasance, age is full of care', why did Carroll write 'Pleasance' rather than 'pleasance'? It seems that the story of *Pygmalion and Galatea*, which depicts the comic consequences of bringing an artistic figure to life, had snagged on something in his memory. Once again his mind had turned back to the ageing process and the inevitable betrayals it brought in its wake.

By now, the physical appearance of his fictional Alice had become so widely known that it was no surprise when another painting entitled *Alice in Wonderland* was exhibited at the Royal Academy in June 1884, depicting another girl in a blue pinafore dress. But of course this Alice was not his Alice; she was just one of the growing army of pretenders trying to wrestle his dream-child from his control. Within a year he had decided to fight back, by restoring his original conception of the character and introducing her afresh to his readers. Accordingly, in March 1885 he wrote again to Alice Hargreaves, this time to ask if he could borrow the manuscript of *Alice's Adventures Under Ground* and have it reproduced in facsimile. Although his memory might be failing, he told her, 'my mental picture is as vivid as ever, of one who was, through so many years, my ideal child-friend. I have had scores of child-friends since your time: but they have been quite a different thing.' If he was hoping to charm his former favourite, it seems that he was only partially successful. A letter to Alice from her father, telling her that 'I think you cannot refuse Mr Dodgson, although he has sold 120,000 copies', indicates that she agreed to lend Carroll the manuscript only under certain grudging conditions. The most significant of these was that she wanted her photograph to be removed from the final page, presumably on the grounds of modesty or propriety. Carroll was happy to agree ('My own wishes would be distinctly *against* reproducing the photograph'), and beyond his desire to smooth over any potential awkwardness, it is not hard to see why. Publishing his manuscript without a physical trace of Alice's seven-year-old self confirmed her status as his 'ideal child-friend'. There was no need to admit that she had outgrown the miniature world he had created for her.

Less than three months later, Carroll met Charlotte Rix, a schoolgirl he had been corresponding with for several weeks, and on their journey to Harry Furniss's studio he told her about the mother of another girl who, when she introduced the subject of *Alice's Adventures in Wonderland*, told him, "'Ah have you heard about the author of that book? He's gone *mad!*'" Such rumours were not uncommon, possibly because some readers had started to confuse Carroll with his stories. Both *Alice* books had cheerfully exploited the porous boundary between sanity and insanity ("'we're all mad here,'" the Cheshire Cat reassures Alice), and it was easy to pretend they were confessional when so little was known about their creator. However, as Carroll planned the facsimile publication of *Alice's Adventures Under Ground*, he found himself being drawn back to some of the other borderlands he had spent much of his life patrolling: not only the line between youth and age, which could be viewed either as a continuum or a sharp division, but the equally uncertain line between innocence and guilt.

A fortnight before Carroll's outing with Charlotte Rix, he had 'borrowed' the ten-year-old Phoebe Carlo (who would be the first actress to play Alice the following year in the official stage adaptation of *Alice in Wonderland*) and gone to view Holman Hunt's 'extraordinary' painting *Triumph of the Innocents*, which depicted the Virgin Mary and baby Jesus being surrounded by a dimpled and haloed crowd of the young children sacrificed by King Herod. The following day, he saw a 'very good' picture of Eve as a naked figure consumed by shame after her first bite of the

Anna Lea Merritt, *Eve in the Garden of Eden* (1885)

forbidden apple, burying her face in a thick curtain of copper hair, and shortly afterwards he was introduced to an artist who gave him 'some charming photos of his own doing, "nude" studies of his children'. Such activities provided yet more support for his claim in 1883 that he was 'an inveterate child-fancier'. But although that made his hobby sound as harmless as breeding pigeons, the idea that his motives were wholly pure was becoming ever harder to sustain in public.

By 1885, the popular Victorian assumption that children were as sweet and sexless as jelly babies was under attack from several different quarters. Only a few years earlier, in 1868, Dickens had been able to publish his novella *A Holiday Romance* without having to worry unduly about it being misunderstood. Part II of his story, 'From the Pen of Miss Alice Rainbird (Aged Seven)', who has already 'married' Robin Redforth (aged nine) in a corner cupboard using a ring bought from a toyshop, describes how a king and queen 'had nineteen children, and were always having more'. The joke is that to her, sexual reproduction is a mystery as dark as every other aspect of adult life, which is why she gravely informs us that the king is daily obliged to go 'to the office', where 'he wrote and wrote and wrote, till it was time to go home again', as if the workplace was nothing more than a schoolroom for grown-ups. Clearly Dickens expects us to find all this charming. As an imitation of adult conventions that have been stripped of their usual meaning, it is supposed to be as delightful as watching monkeys dressed up in little uniforms, or listening to parrots squawk out swear words.

Within a few years such innocent jollity would come to seem either foolish or suspect. Already some psychologists had drawn attention to the secret sexual lives of children. In 1860, James Crichton Browne had published an essay in which he suggested that children as young as three could display signs of sexual awareness, and in 1867 Henry Maudsley contended that the abnormal behaviour exhibited by some subjects, such as a young girl who 'practised lewd movements against furniture', were pathological variations of perfectly normal states. Even William Acton's popular 1857 work *The Functions and Disorders of the Reproductive Organs*, which opened with the firm declaration that 'In a state of health, no sexual ideas should ever enter a child's mind', went on to observe how often this ideal state was breached by the child's own wandering fingers. His conviction that the sort of boy most vulnerable to self-abuse was not a hearty athlete but 'your puny exotic, whose intellectual education has been fostered at the expense of his physical development', might have struck a particular chord with Carroll. But while there is no evidence that Carroll read this book, he did own a copy of Acton's 1857 *Prostitution Considered in its Moral, Social, and Sanitary Aspects*, and this is an area of social life that further complicated the myth of childhood innocence.

Carroll was fully aware that sexual awareness was sometimes forced on children. In July 1878 he had attended the trial of two bargemen charged with the rape of a fourteen-year-old girl, in which the 'chief difficulty was as to her "consent" or not', the case having been brought after the legal age of consent had been raised to thirteen. Three days later, he attended a theatrical production of *Oliver Twist*, which ends with the murder of the teenage prostitute Nancy; Carroll thought it 'too real and ghastly', so he was under no illusions about the possible fate of girls who had been tricked or coerced into early sexual activity. His knowledge of such matters was surprisingly wide: not only did he own a copy of Felicia Skene's campaigning novel *Hidden Depths* (1866), which included graphic descriptions of the brothels in Oxford (thinly disguised as 'Greyburgh'), but his aunt Henrietta had until her death in 1872 been the head of a society for 'the restoration of fallen women'.

In July 1885, while Carroll continued to correspond with Alice Hargreaves about the facsimile reproduction of *Alice's Adventures Under Ground*, these matters came to a head with the *Pall Mall Gazette*'s publication of four sensationalist pieces of investigative journalism under the heading 'The Maiden Tribute of Modern Babylon'. According to the *Gazette*'s editor W. T. Stead, every year hundreds of girls who were not as socially privileged as Carroll's Alice ended up in a very different kind of underworld: a concealed network of brothels and locked rooms that stretched out across London, where young virgins were 'served up as dainty morsels to minister to the passions of the rich'. Officially most of the 'lost souls' wandering through this 'London Inferno' were not under the age of consent, but Stead's purpose in uncovering what he described as 'The sale and purchase and violation of children' was to point out that this was a meaningless term if a girl was too young or naïve to know what she was consenting to, and the law in its current state was therefore tantamount to a rapist's charter. If any of the *Gazette*'s readers preferred to think of this as a minor social problem, Stead's investigation aimed to shock them out of their complacency, because rather than rely on lists of anonymous statistics he allowed those involved to speak for themselves. One brothel-keeper informed him that he could 'undertake to deliver half a dozen girls, ages varying from ten to thirteen, within a week or ten days'. Others he met included a 'repairer of damaged virgins' and another brothel-keeper who assured him that as 'the walls are thick' and there was 'a double carpet on the floor', any girl he chose 'may scream blue murder, but not a sound will be heard'.

When Carroll picked up his copy of the *Gazette*, his eye may have been especially caught by the 'adventures' (Stead's choice of word) of Alice B., who was locked in a bedroom for more than two months, and 'compelled to receive the visits of her first seducer' until the door was opened for the chimney sweep, whereupon she 'fled for her life'. His readers may also have detected some awkwardly angled connections with Carroll's own stories. It is not just that the girls Stead met were trapped in what he referred to as London's 'underground', but in exploring their appalling treatment he drew on similar narrative conventions. Judith R. Walkowitz has noted that Stead's lurid prose style borrowed from several popular Victorian genres, including melodrama, pornography, fantasy and 'the Gothic fairy tale', and it is the last of these that informs the most shocking episode in his series, which appeared in the first instalment under the urgent headline 'A CHILD OF THIRTEEN BOUGHT FOR £5'. Having procured a young girl named Eliza Armstrong, and paid off her mother, a man had arranged for her to be taken to lodgings over a butcher's shop in Poland Street, less than a quarter of a mile from Oxford Circus. Here she was sedated with chloroform supplied by a midwife 'to dull the pain':

A few moments later the door opened, and the purchaser entered the bedroom. He closed and locked the door. There was a brief silence. And then there rose a wild and piteous cry – not a loud shriek, but a helpless, startled scream like the bleat of a frightened lamb. And the child's voice was heard crying, in accents of terror, 'There's a man in the room! Take me home; oh, take me home!'

*   *   *   *   *

And then all once more was still.

Later it transpired that this powerful set piece was actually a journalistic set-up: the shadowy man was Stead himself, and Eliza was later safely returned to the care of the Salvation Army. The line of asterisks signalled what was unrepresentable not because it was too shocking for words, or because the writer wanted to pretend that there was a tear in the manuscript and a piece of the story missing, as had been the case when Gothic novelists used the same typographical device, but because nothing else had happened. However, Stead was clearly leading his readers to imagine something much worse than a lucky escape; the asterisks also hinted at a transformation from one popular Victorian social type (the virginal child) to another (the fallen woman). And while this was not a direct allusion to the events of *Alice's Adventures in Wonderland*, where lines of asterisks had been used to represent Alice's sudden physical changes, it would have been hard for a reader familiar with Carroll's story not to have had an uncomfortable feeling of déjà vu. Here was a dream that had become a nightmare, an 'inverted fairy tale' where the heroine did not triumph over her surroundings, or wake up and abandon the inventions of her unconscious, but instead carried on with her descent into the underground.

Having spent four weeks leading the 'Secret Commission' that had investigated these abuses, dictating the results to 'relays of shorthand writers, marching up and down his office with an icepack on his head', Stead could not have asked for a stronger or quicker public response. On 14 August 1885, just over a month after he threatened to release the names of 'noble and Royal' patrons of the brothels he had investigated, Parliament rushed through a Criminal Law Amendment Act, which raised the age of consent from thirteen to sixteen and made it much easier to prosecute those involved in the sex trade. (A last-minute amendment tabled by the Liberal MP Henry Labouchère also criminalized acts of 'gross indecency' between consenting male adults, a piece of legislation that would remain in force until 1967.) On 22 August, a 250,000-strong demonstration took place in Hyde Park to demand the enforcement of this new law, featuring wagonloads of young virgins clad in white who held aloft banners that declared 'Innocents will they be slaughtered', 'Protection of Young Girls', 'Sir Pity Us' and 'Men, War on Vice', in addition to expressions of outrage such as 'Shame, Shame Horror'. There were also fictional consequences – that autumn, R. L. Stevenson, whose friend W. E. Henley had been excitedly forwarding him the 'Maiden Tribute' articles, sat down to write *Strange Case of Dr Jekyll and Mr Hyde* (1886), in which the darker side of London, full of sexual uncertainty and sudden spasms of violence, drifted in from the margins to become the central focus of his story.

Carroll's response to the scandal was far more muted. A day after the first instalment appeared in the *Pall Mall Gazette*, he wrote to the Prime Minister Lord Salisbury to ask whether he thought the publication 'of the most loathsome details of prostitution, is or is not conducive to public morality'. Evidently he did not share the majority view that the correct answer was a resounding 'yes'. He followed this up with a letter to the *St James's Gazette*, signed 'Lewis Carroll' and published in the issue of 22 July under the title 'Whoso Shall Offend One of Those Little Ones', which set out the case for preventing 'impure scandal' from being reported. There was 'a horrible fashion' developing, he warned, which involved 'forcing the most contaminating subjects on the attention even of those who can get nothing from them but the deadliest injury'. Children were particularly vulnerable. 'I plead for our young men and boys,' he urged, 'whose imaginations are being excited by highly-coloured pictures of vice, and whose natural thirst for knowledge is being used for unholy purposes by the seducing whisper "read this, and your eyes shall be opened, and ye shall be as gods, knowing good *and evil!*"' Girls were even more at risk, and Carroll went on to 'plead for our pure maidens, whose souls are being saddened, if not defiled, by the nauseous literature that is thus thrust upon them'.

Carroll was not alone in disliking the idea that children might read the *Pall Mall Gazette* (there were many complaints at the time about boys gleefully 'quoting pungent sentences' in the streets) and thereby stumble upon information that would destroy their innocence. Nor was his parallel with Eden uncommon. One of the less complimentary letters Stead received, which was subsequently published as a penny pamphlet, accused him of behaving 'like the Devil at the ear of Eve' by employing 'the strongest human passion, thirst for knowledge, to recommend the bitter fruit'. Another pamphlet sarcastically applauded his articles as a 'delightful lesson' for children, and concluded that history was repeating itself like a modern version of 'the seduction of the crafty serpent in Eden'. But even viewed in this context, Carroll's response was peculiarly lopsided in focusing exclusively on the effects of Stead's journalism rather than its substance. The fact that he devoted so much attention to the souls of some children, and wholly ignored the damage being done to the bodies of others, was especially unappealing. Nor were his conclusions beyond scrutiny. The idea that the best way to avoid any 'object of sinful desires', according to a sermon he approvingly quoted, was to 'repress even the slightest image, lest it should strengthen and invigorate evil desire' was particularly odd. In effect, his advice was to preserve one's innocence simply by refusing to think about anything that might threaten it.

But that was not always possible, as the Owen affair had demonstrated, and in this atmosphere of moral panic much that Carroll had previously taken for granted was now open to question. Although he no longer photographed children, just four days before he read the first of Stead's articles he had completed four naked sketches of the five-year-old Lilian Henderson, which he enjoyed as a 'new experience in Art'. 'She has a charming little figure,' he explained, 'and was a very patient sitter.' But although he had previously secured permission from her parents, and immediately showed them his 'studies', the 'Maiden Tribute' scandal made such leisure pursuits seem potentially far less innocent than before.

After all, most of the underage girls Stead encountered had been offered for sale by their parents, which added a new layer of ambiguity to a word like 'consent', and some of the language Carroll had previously used about his child-friends was also starting to cloud over with uncertainty. In 1864, he had promised Robinson Duckworth that if he wanted another river trip 'I could procure some Liddells as companions', but he would have been unwise to make the same promise now. If 'a word means what the speaker intends by it, and what the hearer understands by it', as Carroll argued in 1888, there was always a risk that intention and understanding could fail to overlap. A word such as 'procure' could be used perfectly innocently, as it had been by Carroll in 1889 when he told a Christ Church supplier who had sent him a box of exotic fruit that he could not accept free gifts, as his duty was 'to try to procure the *best* goods he can'. Yet that would not necessarily prevent the word from being tainted by association, given recent revelations of how easy it was 'To obtain (a person, usually a woman) as a prostitute or illicit sexual partner for another person' (*OED*, 'procure', sense 3c). In this context, even the most neutral language could take on a new edge of suspicion. Carroll's usual word for the girls whose upbringing shielded them from the nastier aspects of Victorian life was 'nice', but the same word would soon be used in one of the most vicious scenes in the pornographic (and quite possibly fictional) Victorian memoir *My Secret Life* (1888–92): 'I passed a woman leading a little girl dressed like a ballet-girl, and looked at the girl who seemed about ten years old, then at the woman who winked. I stopped, she came up and said, "Is she not a nice little girl? . . . Would you like to see her undressed?" . . . The little girl kept tugging the woman's hand and saying, "Oh! Do come to the fire-works." The author, 'Walter', pays three sovereigns for the girl, and is disappointed to discover that she is not a virgin.

Carroll had also started to question himself. In January 1888 he drew another girl naked, this time a fourteen-year-old model at an artist's studio in Chelsea, and confided to his diary that 'a spectator would have to be really in *search* of evil thought to have any other feeling about her than simply a sense of beauty'. This simultaneously raised the possibility of sexual desire and offloaded it on to someone else, rather as he kept his nude photographs in an envelope marked 'honi soit', an abbreviated version of the traditional phrase 'honi soit qui mal y pense' ('shame on him who thinks evil of it'), which acknowledged the existence of bad thoughts while denying that they had any place in his own mind. Of course, in 1888 a fourteen-year-old was legally under the age of consent, but a definition is not the same thing as an explanation, and Carroll continued to be interested in the point at which a child's body became an adult one. In March 1886, he tried to discover the original version of a poem he had read many years before, which 'contained 3 visions of female beauty – child, young woman, adult woman', all of whom 'appeared in Eve's original dress'. The lines he remembered were a description of the child:

> No fuller curve yet broke the line,
> That, like a downward stream,
> Clothed her from head to foot, . . .
> . . . . one gleam
> Of lily limbs, such forms design
> Young poets, when they dream!

The dots 'don't mean anything unrepresentable', he assured the correspondent he had asked to hunt for the original poem, just that 'the words have escaped my memory'. However, his interest in a piece of writing that translated human development into three jerky snapshots was striking, as was the fact that the section which had stuck in his memory compared the form of a child to the form of a poem – a set of straight lines that did not bulge in unexpected places.

Carroll's return to *Alice's Adventures Under Ground* in 1886 revealed that the same fantasies could also be central to prose. When he published it at the end of the year, he added a preface that included a rapturous burst of praise for 'the awe that falls on one in the presence of a spirit fresh from GOD's hands, on whom no shadow of sin . . . has yet fallen'. It also imagined some of the sick children who had read his stories 'putting up a childish prayer (and oh, how much it needs!) for one who can but dimly hope to stand, some day, not quite out of sight of those pure young faces, before the great white throne'. This might have surprised readers of the *Pall Mall Gazette*, but for Carroll the publication of his original *Alice* story provided a welcome opportunity to wind back the clock to a time when the purity of children and of his own motives were equally secure.

Producing a facsimile edition turned out to be far from straight-forward. First the photographer responsible for preparing a set of zinc printing blocks fell into financial difficulties, then Carroll had to employ a private investigator and take official legal action to retrieve the negatives. As he told Alice Hargreaves in November 1886, 'I have had almost as many Adventures, in getting that unfortunate facsimile finished, *Above* ground, as your namesake had *Under* it!' The reference to her 'namesake' was interesting, because although it is possible he now considered the real Alice and her fictional alter ego as two girls who shared one name, it is just as likely he thought of Alice Hargreaves as a different person to Alice Liddell. This would have chimed with another common Victorian idea. 'What is self?' asked the novelist Edward Bulwer-Lytton. 'A thing that changes every year and every month. The self of last year has no sym-pathy with the self of the one before.' If it was true that individuals changed radically over the course of a life, and the 'awkward stage of transition' Carroll had previously referred to in his diary was not merely puberty but part of an endless process of self-development, then the woman he had met in December 1883 might have no more in common with the child he had befriended in the late 1850s than a butterfly did with a chrysalis. It meant there was a growing gap between the real and fic-tional Alice that very little could bridge. Privately Carroll could do it through memory, but while he was producing the facsimile *Alice* he had been working on a more public way of bringing his dream-child to life while also keeping her reassuringly constant. He would put her in a play.

*

Thirty

While some of his friendships cooled over the years, and others were broken off altogether, there was one relationship in Carroll's life that never wavered in its intensity: his love affair with the theatre. His diaries record his attendance at more than four hundred plays, several of which he saw more than once, and his interest reached much further than being that of a passive member of the audience. Having run a marionette theatre in his childhood, taking on the roles of designer and stage manager as well as acting every part, as an adult he occasionally offered his assistance to professional companies. In May 1884, for example, he made a 'little suggestion' to the actor currently playing the lead role in W. G. Wills's melodrama *Claudian*, at which Carroll was a 'periodical visitant', noting that when the blacksmith was thrown into a roaring torrent, 'not only do we *not* hear any splash, but I *did* hear (the other day) the sound of his feet lighting on the floor'; for a 'little bit of realism' he advised using a barrel of water with a plunger to create a suitable sound effect, which he was confident would 'add much to the thrilling nature of the incident'. His plan to choreograph how audiences left at the end of a play, which he submitted to Covent Garden in January 1865, was far less practical, involving a division of the theatre's three exits according to the alphabet, matching each playgoer's name to the corresponding exit, and arranging the carriages outside 'so that they should drive in, in sets of three, in the proper order'. The following day he 'Heard from Mr. Russell, manager at Covent Garden, thanking me for my suggestion, and promising to consider it', although it is likely that Russell devoted rather more time to writing his polite letter of acknowledgement than he did to puzzling out how to make real people behave like algorithms.

More troublesome for Carroll than practical arrangements for leaving the theatre was the question of whether he should be entering it at all. Twenty years after Henry Liddon had refused to accompany him to any plays in Europe, many in the Church still considered the theatre a corrupt environment, and Carroll collected works that argued both for and against its influence on public morals. He also resolutely policed the line that divided acceptable plays from those that contained less whole-some elements, especially when he compared the naughty jokes in some pantomimes with 'pure and *absolutely* innocent pieces, like *The Mikado*'. Even productions of highbrow literary works sometimes alarmed him. In 1887, he complained to Ellen Terry about a moment in Goethe's *Faust* when she began to undress on stage, and a girl with him asked, 'When is it going to stop?' His advice was to alter the staging, which made Terry '*furious*', and although he later wrote to ask her 'Will you not forgive me?' he could not resist having the last word the following year with an article on 'The Stage and the Spirit of Reverence' in which he appealed to 'the sympathy shown by play-goers for what is pure and good'.

Carroll worried that his own theatrical pleasures might have a human cost. Most of the young actresses he enjoyed watching were talented but poor, drawn to a life in the spotlight like a moth to a flame, and frequently it ended up damaging them. Newspapers were full of gloomy stories about former actresses who had turned to drink or prostitution, and novels were similarly quick to remind their readers how much misery could exist under a thin coating of greasepaint. In May 1885, Carroll had gone to the Egyptian Hall in London to see Marceli Suchorowski's paint-ing *Nana*, a languorous reclining nude based on Emile Zola's novel about a fifteen-year-old actress who dies of smallpox, ending up as 'a heap of pus and blood, a shovelful of putrid flesh'. Carroll's desire to help other actresses avoid such a messy fate took on various forms. In January 1882, he lent his name to a campaign to establish a School for Dramatic Art, an important first step towards what would later become the Royal Academy of Dramatic Art, which he hoped would improve standards of acting in the theatre and thus 'purify and ennoble its aims'. Three years later, he wrote an unpublished essay on theatrical costume, urging producers not to ask actresses to wear skimpy outfits, especially if 'an innocent young person' might see them and 'have sinful feelings roused'. As he had previously explained in a private letter, an actress was especially at risk if she had 'the dangerous gift of beauty'. Even his former child-friends were not immune; of one girl who had become an actress, he wrote that 'I afterwards heard news that grieved me to the heart', and concluded that 'she had better have died, a thousand times better'.

Another feature of the theatre that intrigued Carroll was its ability to redirect the normal flow of time. For theatre took playing with time seriously. On stage, years could pass in minutes, and seconds could expand to fill hours, as the imaginary time of a play's action ebbed and flowed around the real time of its performance, like a jazz musician playing a set of variations on an underlying beat. Theatre's resourcefulness in avoiding the ageing process also appealed to Carroll. Unlike ordinary people, whose lives continued to tick away as steadily as the White Rabbit's watch, some actors and actresses seemed to have an enviable ability to evade time's grasp. In 1857, he visited the Grand Equestrian American Circus at Drury Lane to see 'the little Ella' perform her dazzling horse-riding routine, and reported sadly that although she was 'as active and graceful as ever' she was 'no longer little'. (Actually, Mademoiselle Ella Zoyara was not a she either: his real name was Omar Kingsley, and in 1860 speculation about his gender in the newspapers led some youths in Boston to throw oranges on to the stage, in the belief that a man would catch them between his knees. Zoyara successfully caught one in his skirt, thereby convincing those present that 'there are exceptions even to the anatomical rule of orange receiving'.) Yet there were performers who seemed capable of rejuvenating themselves under the lights. In January 1866 Carroll returned to Drury Lane to see the pantomime *Little King Pippin*, and reported that although Ellen Terry had told him the leading actor Percy Roselle was eighteen or nineteen years old 'he looks about 8'. Of course, this may partly have been a result of stage make-up and the laws of perspective – all actors become little again when viewed from a sufficient distance. There was also the danger that performers who tried too hard to retain their youthful appeal might end up like Ninetta Crummles in Dickens's *Nicholas Nickleby*, an 'infant phenomenon' who has been 'kept up late every night, and put upon an unlimited allowance of gin-and-water from infancy, to prevent her growing tall', and has consequently remained the same age 'for five good years'. But even if an actress became too old for a particular stage role, her character would remain the same age. In June 1869, Carroll met Nina Boucicault, the 'pretty little daughter' (aged two) of the successful playwright and producer Dion Boucicault. She was 'a tempting subject for the camera', Carroll declared, but her later acting career would show that the theatre was equally good at providing the illusion of people who had been frozen in time. Cast as Peter Pan in the original production of J. M. Barrie's play at the Duke of York's Theatre in 1904, she remained in the role for most of the first season, and when she was replaced by her understudy shortly before the run ended on 1 April 1905, the change did nothing to alter the eternal youthfulness of Barrie's character. Peter Pan could remain 'The Boy Who Wouldn't Grow Up' by the simple expedient of periodically replacing the actress who played him.

The popularity of child performers on the Victorian stage was especially significant for Carroll. In two published letters, on 'Children in Theatres' (1887) and 'Stage Children' (1889), he defended the practice of allowing children to act professionally, arguing against a growing tendency to view the theatre as an unsuitable environment for performers under ten years of age, and pointed out that not only were their wages necessary to 'many a poor struggling family', but he had just enjoyed a five-hour outing on Brighton Pier with three child actresses who were 'happy and healthy little girls'. All three were currently appearing in a touring production of *Alice in Wonderland*, and it was through the development of this play that Carroll explored the idea that the theatre need not be a damaging or dangerous place for children. In fact it could be another Wonderland.

In 1867 he had attended the Haymarket Theatre to see the Living Miniatures, a company of twenty-seven children who performed comedies and burlesques. Their success reflected a common Victorian trend, and although some of this was probably down to sound business sense as well as sentimentality (if child actors were cute they were also comparatively cheap), many of these productions were garlanded with critical praise. When a different troupe of juvenile performers tackled a Gilbert and Sullivan operetta in 1880, the *Theatre* reviewer did not believe that 'London has ever seen anything better than the baby *Pinafore*'. Carroll was not blind to the faults of such productions – his lukewarm assessment of *The Children's Pinafore* was that it was 'pretty as a whole' – but when he returned to the Haymarket for a tour behind the scenes his critical faculties quickly melted. In a long diary entry, and a letter to his brother Edwin, he recorded his impressions. At times he sounds positively starstruck, as when he sees one of the girls in the wings hopping around in imitation of the dance being performed on stage, 'out of sight of the audience, and solely for her own amusement'; at other times he peels away some theatrical spangles to reveal what else is usually invisible to the audience, such as a consumptive actress who is 'not so pretty when seen close'. What all these impressions share is Carroll's fascination with the idea that what looked like spontaneous fun on stage was actually arranged 'like a piece of clock-work' behind the scenes. Such a combination of freedom and organization closely echoed his chosen writing style, so it is not surprising that he followed up his 'adventures in Greenland' by sending a copy of *Alice's Adventures in Wonderland* to the company manager Thomas Coe, with 'vague hopes' that 'it may occur to him to turn it into a pantomime'.

Over the next nineteen years, Carroll remained interested in an official theatrical adaptation that could compete with versions such as Kate Freiligrath-Kroeker's *Alice and Other Fairy Plays for Children*, a copy of which she sent him in November 1879. (Her preface thanked Carroll 'for the permission to dramatise his charming story'; in 1882, she issued a second volume entitled *Alice Thro' the Looking-Glass and other Fairy Plays for Children*, again with Carroll's 'kind permission'.) In September 1872, he met an eight-year-old actress named Lydia Howard, the daughter of a widowed dressmaker, who he thought 'would do well to act "Alice" if it should ever be dramatised', and the following month he sent both *Alice* books to the theatre critic Percy Fitzgerald, whose recent study *The Principles of Comedy and Dramatic Effect* had 'much impressed' Carroll, seeking his advice on whether either story 'has sufficient dramatic element to warrant the attempt to exhibit it'. In 1873, it was the turn of the impresario Thomas German Reed to receive a letter from Carroll 'suggesting the idea of producing a drama founded on *Alice* or the *Looking-Glass*', but although Reed contemplated a production featuring 'endless fairy visions of surpassing prettiness' his plans came to nothing. The same thing happened with Arthur Sullivan, of Gilbert and Sullivan fame, who was approached by Carroll in 1877 and replied that the books could probably be turned into 'a delicious little extravaganza' with the right settings, but warned that the cost of hiring him to write songs on which he would not control the copyright would be 'absurdly extravagant'. Next Carroll turned his attention to the opera composer Sir Alexander Campbell Mackenzie, who expressed his interest in collaborating at the end of 1884 or beginning of 1885, but this time it was Carroll who abandoned the idea of writing a libretto, on the grounds that 'I feel quite sure I have not the needful constructive talent.' Even then he continued to have vague plans for a theatrical version: after jotting down fifteen 'literary projects on hand' at the end of March 1885, he added that among his other 'shadowy ideas', including 'a Geometry for boys' and 'a volume of Essays on theological points freely and plainly treated', was 'a drama on *Alice*'.

His determination was understandable. It is not just that by the mid-1880s Alice had become as recognizable as the figures in traditional nursery rhymes. (In the Drury Lane pantomime *Cinderella* in December 1883, she made a guest appearance in the ball scene alongside other famous storybook characters.) In some ways the theatre was her natural home. Near the beginning of *Alice's Adventures in Wonderland*, the White Rabbit drops his glove and fan, a standard plot device in many stage comedies, and in one of Tenniel's early illustrations (reproduced above on page 205) Alice is seen pulling aside the curtain that hides the door to Wonderland, like a nervous actress about to step on to the stage. Much of what she discovers is equally theatrical in nature. Not only do the other characters refuse to engage her in ordinary conversation, preferring to swap stagey lines of dialogue or steal the spotlight for a solo recitation, but in Tenniel's illustrations several creatures, including the Dodo and Caterpillar, appear to have fully formed human hands, as if their bodies were merely elaborate costumes they could remove whenever they shuffled off into the wings. Carroll could also be confident that Victorian audiences would be receptive to an authentic theatrical Wonderland. In December 1875, a few months before George Buckland staged an entertainment at the Polytechnic that was variously billed as *Alice in Wonderland* and *More Wonders in Wonderland*, audiences at the Crystal Palace had been treated to the new pantomime *Jack in Wonderland*. And although Carroll continued to dislike pantomime's reputation for smutty innuendo (in April 1886 he agreed to a request for a pantomime at the Soldiers' Recreation Room in Woolwich to be entitled *Alice in Wonderland*, provided that the piece contained no 'coarseness or vulgarity'), he would have known that many of the scenic effects it shared with other popular plays were perfect for his stories, such as dreamy visions of fairyland that were achieved by the use of subdued lighting and strategically positioned sheets of gauze.

On 28 August 1886, Carroll's slumbering plans finally burst into life when he received a request to adapt the *Alice* books from the young dramatist Henry Savile Clarke. Carroll agreed, again upon one 'condition', which was that the play should contain nothing that might 'pander to the tastes of dirty-minded youths and men in the Gallery', and he added several 'wishes', the most significant of which was that his stories should not be merged in a single production. When Clarke replied to accept most of these requests, offering the compromise of performing each *Alice* book in a separate half of the show, he probably did not anticipate the flurry of additional thoughts Carroll would send him over the next four months. To generate a proper sense of scale, the cast should contain adult actors as well as children. The actress playing Alice should not drop her H's. There was the opportunity for an extra piece of comic business in the Pig and Pepper scene, with some new lines he volunteered to write. The Hatter should '*drawl*, not *hesitate*, with long pauses between the words, as if half-asleep'. The play should be three acts rather than two. Alice should receive extra acting and singing lessons. Some of these 'requests' and 'suggestions' Clarke gladly accepted, and others – such as Carroll's thoughtful offer to act as Alice's personal dresser – he politely declined.

"—— you know you say things are 'much of a muchness';
did you ever see such a thing as a drawing of a muchness?"
ALICE IN WONDERLAND.

ALICE AND THE DORMOUSE.

Phoebe Carlo in *Alice in Wonderland: A Musical Dream-Play*
(Prince of Wales Theatre, 1886–87)

Carroll's most substantial contributions were the casting of Alice and the title of the play. The first of these was straightforward: in October, he suggested the name of Phoebe Carlo, a 'dear little friend' he had twice entertained in Oxford after seeing her perform on stage in 1885, and Clarke was happy to take his recommendation. (Carroll later showed his more ruthless side in a cast-list he sent to Clarke with the heading 'A Dream-Cast (!)', putting an asterisk by the names of 'incompetent' performers he thought should be 'sacrificed'.) His second suggestion was to add 'dream-play' to the subtitle; as the play did not fit easily into any existing dramatic genre, he pointed out, 'for a new *thing* try a new *name*'. Clarke was less enthusiastic, but as often happened when Carroll had set his mind on something, eventually he got his way. A playful dream was now a dream-play – one that could utilize all the resources of theatre to bring Alice's mazy imaginings to life.

At 2.30 p.m. on 23 December 1886, the electric lights dimmed in the new 960-seat Prince of Wales Theatre, and the curtain rose on the first performance of *Alice in Wonderland: A Musical Dream-Play*. The opening scene gave a good flavour of what was to come. The audience found itself in '*A Forest in Autumn. Alice asleep at foot of tree and Fairies dancing around her.*' After a chant of 'Ours be the task to keep watch o'er thy slumbers, | Wake, Alice, wake to the Wonderland dream', the fairy chorus trooped off, and the scene changed to a garden where the Caterpillar was '*discovered smoking on a gigantic mushroom*' as the White Rabbit dashed across the stage. The stage direction '*Scene changes to Wonderland*' was the first of many occasions on which technical trickery was used to disguise the fact that this was a Wonderland constructed chiefly out of pasteboard and glitter.

If Clarke's intention was to impress audiences with his visual flair, he faced serious competition. The 'greatest theatrical treat' Carroll had enjoyed in 1855 was Charles Kean's production of *Henry VIII*, in which he was especially struck by the 'wonderful' staging of Queen Katherine's vision, featuring sunbeams that carried 'a troop of angelic forms, transparent, and carrying palm branches' which they waved over the sleeping queen while 'sweet slow music' played; 'I almost held my breath to watch,' he confessed, 'and I felt as if in a dream all the time it lasted.' The stage effects in some later Victorian productions were even more elaborate. In 1884, Carroll especially enjoyed a scene in the three-act drama *Claudian* that featured a temple being destroyed by an earthquake, and the following year Henry Irving's interpretation of Goethe's *Faust* featured lavish special effects that would not disgrace a modern Hollywood blockbuster. In just one scene, '*A flock of owls flap their solemn wings through the stormy night . . . Mephistopheles, with laughing approval, reclines upon a rock which gives forth flashes of electric light, a pair of apes fondling him . . . Earth and air are enveloped in a burning mass. Then rocks seem to melt like lava. A furnace of molten metal has broken loose . . .*'

Perhaps recognizing that his budget could never compete with such no-expense-spared spectacles, Clarke chose an alternative strategy. Rather than try to surprise his audience, after taking them to Wonderland he gave them exactly what they were expecting. This was to be a communal celebration of Carroll's stories rather than a fresh interpretation of their meaning. The costumes had been copied from Tenniel's illustrations, with whatever small adjustments were necessary to meet the requirements of three dimensions; each soldier wore a contraption like a sandwich board, for example, which gave the illusion of his head and legs sprouting out of a playing card, provided he did not turn sideways too often. Similarly, many children applauded when they saw the Hatter and March Hare enter with their tea table, because they knew exactly what was coming next. The play as a whole was less like a traditional drama than a series of animated pop-up illustrations. However, if it encouraged the audience to anticipate Carroll's jokes and hum along to their favourite songs, it also reminded them of what had been lost in the translation from page to stage. Private thoughts had become public asides ('He's looking for his fan and gloves' or 'He takes me for his housemaid'), which changed Alice from being a confused little girl to a self-aware performer. Characters she had merely stumbled upon in the book now appeared to be meeting her by appointment. And scenes that had previously been left to the reader's imagination were now embodied in ways that were inevitably disappointing, producing impressive stage directions such as 'Enter all the king's horses and all the king's men' that no chorus could possibly live up to. ('I couldn't send all the horses, you know,' the Red King limply explains, 'because they're wanted.') On the other hand, some of Wonderland's crazy logic was perfectly suited to the theatre. The tea party could continue for ever because the theatre was a world of magical replenishment, so that if the Hatter followed another stage direction and '[bit] a piece out of his teacup instead of the bread and butter', it would always be restored in time for the next performance. When the scene shifted to Looking-Glass Land at the start of the second half, Alice could easily 'pretend the glass has got all soft like gauze', as she had in Carroll's original story, because on stage that is exactly what it was made from. Finally, when Alice told the White Queen that her memory only worked one way, and 'I can't remember things before they happen!', anyone with theatrical experience would have known that for an actress this was patently untrue. Remembering things before they happened was precisely how she got through each performance.

Compared to some of the period's big theatrical hits featuring child stars, such as E. L. Blanchard's pantomime *Little Goody Two-Shoes* at the Adelphi in 1876, *Alice in Wonderland* was a modest success, running for more than fifty performances before going on a provincial tour, and later returning to London. Most of the reviewers were charmed by a production they variously described as 'sweet and wholesome' (*Daily News*), 'wholesome and innocent' (*Graphic*), 'exceedingly pretty' (*Times*) and 'a pretty tale, delightfully told' (*Illustrated London News*). The only sour note came from *Punch*, where Tenniel continued to produce his spiky political cartoons, in a notice that strongly advised any fathers or uncles who found themselves in the Prince of Wales Theatre to leave their children and 'retire to their Club' for a smoke, thereby avoiding the 'unsatisfactory' jollity of chess pieces that 'look like bottles of salad mixture' and songs that are 'oh dear, oh dear – utterly lost'. However, there was enough public demand for a revival in 1888 at the Globe Theatre, when Isa Bowman (who had played one of the oyster-ghosts in the original production) took over the leading role, thereby adding an extra theatrical in-joke to lines such as 'I think I must have been changed.' There were also amateur productions of Freiligrath-Kroeker's version: in December 1889, Carroll agreed to attend one at Edgbaston High School for Girls in Birmingham, joshing with the headmistress that he hoped to 'kiss the Alice of the play' but that would be 'an unheard-of liberty, and not to be permitted on any account!'

By the end of the decade, Carroll's attitude to his dream-child had become richly uncertain. He was fully aware of her commercial value, producing lightly revised versions of both stories for the cheaper People's Edition in 1887, which now included his 'Easter Greeting' and 'Christmas Greeting'. He also did what he could to protect his property from unwanted interlopers, encouraging amateur writers and enjoying the free publicity that came from magazines such as *The Jabberwock*, a 'clever little school paper' in Boston that began publication in February 1888, while refusing permission for some of his comic verse to be printed in the 1889 anthology *Humorous Poems of the Century*, on the grounds that none of it had been written by C. L. Dodgson. (The editor included 'Father

William' and 'The Walrus and the Carpenter' regardless.) Yet when he viewed Alice as a thread woven into his own life he could be surprisingly sentimental. In April 1887 he published his essay '"Alice" on the Stage', in which he tried to explain how his original story had come into existence. Although he began by establishing the basic narrative coordinates of every subsequent account (three little maidens, rowing, stories, a golden afternoon), he concluded with the sort of swollen prose his younger self would have been quick to puncture:

> What wert thou, dream-Alice, in thy foster-father's eyes? How shall he picture thee? Loving, first, loving and gentle: loving as a dog (forgive the prosaic simile, but I know no earthly love so pure and perfect), and gentle as a fawn: then courteous – courteous to *all*, high or low, grand or grotesque, King or Caterpillar, even as though she were herself a King's daughter, and her clothing of wrought gold: then trustful, ready to accept the wildest impossibilities with all that utter trust that only dreamers know; and lastly, curious – wildly curious, and with the eager enjoyment of Life that comes only in the happy hours of childhood, when all is new and fair, and when Sin and Sorrow are but names – empty words signifying nothing!

It is clear from this that something has badly corroded Carroll's intelligence. The more urgently he tries to get back in contact with his original storytelling mood, the further away he proves to have drifted. But although this newly sentimental approach to his 'dream-Alice' would have some fairly disastrous effects on his later writing, it was fully in line with the attitude he now took to her real-life model. In November 1888, Carroll met Reginald Hargreaves, 'the husband of "Alice"', and confessed to his diary that 'it was not easy to link in one's mind the new face with the olden memory – the stranger with the once-so-intimately known and loved "Alice" whom I shall always remember best as an entirely fascinating little 7 year-old maiden'. It was more than twenty-eight years since he had photographed her next to a fern that signified 'Fascination', and although she was eight years old when that was taken, in the intervening years she had become fused in his memory with the character he had pictured at the end of *Alice's Adventures Under Ground*. Alice had become 'Alice'. Fascinating, little, seven years old and a maiden – she was none of these things now except in his stories, and that is where he intended to keep her.

*

Thirty-one

'An inventive day' was how Carroll described 24 September 1891. Having long wanted to be able to write in the dark, he 'conceived the idea of having a series of *squares* cut out in card', to be filled by a special alphabet made up of dots and lines. After making a grating of sixteen squares, and experimenting further with his code by working out the different combinations of pen strokes that could be made along the edges and in the corners of each square, he was pleased to report that 'It works well.' He decided to call it the Nyctograph. In a letter to *The Lady* on 29 October, he explained that 'I do not intend to patent it', and anyone 'is welcome to make and sell the article'. It seems not to have occurred to him that most people would probably rather get up and light a candle. For Carroll, however, the simplest solution was rarely the most satisfying one. There are echoes here of the White Knight in *Through the Looking-Glass*, who tells Alice that among his inventions are anklets for horses '"To guard against the bites of sharks"', and a new pudding made out of ingredients such as blotting paper, gunpowder and sealing-wax. The pride he takes in his crackpot ingenuity is only a minor comic exaggeration of Carroll happily explaining how he could avoid losing any stray thoughts by fiddling with his cardboard squares under the bedclothes.

Some of Carroll's other attempts to deal with everyday annoyances were no less complicated. In 1896, he sent his sister-in-law Alice Dodgson a new coffee-pot, and after suggesting that 'it may be useful to tell you how I manage with mine', he went on to outline an eight-stage process that took him more than 250 words to summarize. His preferred way of making tea was even more time-consuming. 'He had got a blacksmith to attach to his own kettle a long handle,' one of his child-friends recalled, 'and with this he always lifted his kettle off the fire, and filled the teapot.' The next stage strayed even further into White Knight territory. 'He was very particular about his tea,' according to Isa Bowman, 'and in order that it should draw properly he would walk about the room swinging the teapot from side to side for exactly ten minutes.' He took just as much pleasure in other people's inventiveness. In 1890 he attended an exhibition of Edison's Phonograph, which for the first time allowed people to hear the ghostly crackle of voices that had been recorded on to wax cylinders, and excitedly declared it 'the new wonder of the day', lamenting only that he would not be alive in fifty years 'to get this wonderful invention in its perfect form'. He was also an ardent collector of less influential mechanical novelties. In the last twenty years of his life he found space in his Christ Church rooms for an orguinette (an early form of pianola) that played music automatically when hole-punched paper was fed into it, a Chromograph for copying documents, Dr Carter Moffat's Ammoniaphone (a flute-like metal contraption through which a chemical solution was inhaled to produce 'a rich, powerful, melodious voice of extraordinary ringing clearness and range'), patented pencil sharpeners and a Whitely Exerciser – an apparatus of adjustable pulleys that claimed to be 'the most simple and practical, and complete device in the world for scientific physical training'; Leopold Bloom owns a model in Joyce's *Ulysses*, where he records that it has increased the size of his biceps by an inch and his thighs by two inches.

Carroll enjoyed applying his mechanical knowhow to other people's inventions, coming up with numerous modifications to help them work more smoothly. He called these alterations 'dodges', as if they came naturally to someone called Dodgson. Typically, in June 1882, two days after trying out a friend's three-wheeled Velociman in Oxford, he sent over 'a plan that has occurred to me for improving the steering', and two days later he advised that the machine should also include some gears, and a lock 'so that it will stand on a hill'. Eventually, Carroll bought a Velociman of his own, thereby following his own advice: 'In youth, try a bicycle, in age, buy a tricycle', but despite his refinements he sadly reported that a trip around North Oxford 'was much more tiring than walking would have been'. In March 1886, he advised Edith Rix that the knack in refilling a 'Little Giant' fountain pen was to put some Vaseline on the thread – 'Then it won't leak, and you won't ink your fingers.' Two years later, he bought a 'Hammond Type-writer', a machine with a distinctive curved design, and within a week he had devised 'a very simple dodge for getting paper past ridges in cylinder' and aligning the right-hand margin. Nor were less exotic objects safe from his busy fingers, revealing instead their potential to become something entirely new when his imagination got to work on them: handkerchiefs that could be transformed into rabbits; sheets of paper that were folded into boats or reassembled into pistols that made an audible crack when fired.

Carroll's love of novelty marked him out firmly as a man of his age. In just ten years, between the original *Alice* boat trip in 1862 and the publication of *Through the Looking-Glass* in 1872, the new products that had been made available to Victorian consumers included the first breakfast cereal, urinal, steam-powered motorcycle, paper clip, vibrator, clothes hanger and can opener. The comparison is not as absurd as it might seem, for writers and inventors were often thought of in the same creative bracket. As Clare Pettitt has observed, 'by the end of the 1830s, analogies between mechanical inventors and literary inventors were commonplace', not just because both put together old materials in new ways, but also because both faced the same struggle to protect their work from being copied without authorization. In Carroll's case, the problems he had already experienced in copyrighting *Alice* for the stage were compounded by the story's obvious commercial potential, and much of the final period of his life was spent puzzling out how to preserve the personal relationship he had celebrated in '"Alice" on the Stage' with the fact that his dream-child now belonged to the public.

Carroll's understanding of 'invention' was twofold: he used the same word to refer both to thinking up a new idea and to turning it into a physical object. Often there was a sizeable gap between these two meanings, and his diary is dotted with 'inventions' that had only a mayfly existence in his mind before he moved on to the next project – a 'new kind of postal order' with perforated corners, for example, or 'a substitute for

The Wonderland Postage-Stamp Case (1890)

gum, for fastening envelopes'. One object that went further than this memorandum stage, and ended up being commercially produced, was 'The Wonderland Postage-Stamp Case' Carroll dreamed up in 1888. The fact that it was based on *Alice's Adventures in Wonderland* was probably not a coincidence. In a diary entry on 29 October, he reported that he had 'Invented a "stamp-case" . . . I hope to get it published', and although Macmillan turned it down on the grounds that 'there is no practical use in the invention', it was eventually issued for a shilling in 1890 by the local Oxford publishers Emberlin and Son.

In some ways it was another version of the special travel purses that Isa Bowman recalled him using, this time targeting the clutter of daily correspondence. The central feature was a piece of stiff folded card in which twelve sewn pockets allowed stamps of different values, from a halfpenny to a shilling, to be stored. On the rear it proudly declared, 'Invented by Lewis Carroll'. What made it more unusual were the two 'Pictorial Surprises' he included: the cover featured a design on one side of Alice holding the baby, and on the other side the Cheshire Cat, but pulling out the inner case revealed two new pictures in which the baby had turned into a pig and the Cat had been caught in mid-fade. It was the simplest of conjuring tricks, but the real point of interest was Carroll's decision to dip into Wonderland for such a mundane object. Several factors are likely to have influenced his choice. The stamp-case brought together two of his main literary interests – transformation and travel – in a single object. It also combined them with another feature he regularly associated with the *Alice* books – friendship – because it was first issued in an envelope with a booklet written by Carroll entitled 'Eight or Nine Wise Words About Letter-Writing', a set of tips on how to write better letters. If these 'Rules' drew upon Carroll's extensive experience as a correspondent, the combined package of stamp-case and booklet was a natural extension of the public letters he had previously addressed to readers of the *Alice* books. Here was another opportunity to combine the exploration of Wonderland with the cultivation of new friends. Most of his advice was practical in nature: '*Write legibly*', for example, or '*don't repeat yourself*'. However, his main reason for making this a *Wonderland* object was suggested by his introduction, in which he pointed out, tongue firmly in cheek, that 'Since I have possessed a "Wonderland Stamp Case", Life has been bright and peaceful, and I have used no other. I believe the Queen's laundress uses no other.' His allusion was to a long-running Victorian advertisement – 'USE ONLY THE GLENFIELD STARCH. THE QUEEN'S LAUNDRESS USES NO OTHER' – and the sudden lurch of his writing into an advertising catchphrase would have reminded his original readers that by now his books had generated several more products in addition to stamp-cases. Wonderland had become a marketplace.

The only specific toy to appear in *Alice's Adventures in Wonderland* had been smuggled in through Carroll's allusion to 'Bob the Bat', a gauze-and-wire flying contraption powered by an elastic band, which once flew out of his Christ Church window, startling a college servant so much that he dropped the glass bowl of salad he was carrying. If the Liddell sisters had been introduced to Bob, they would have especially enjoyed the Hatter's song '*Twinkle, twinkle, little bat!*', because the words '*Up above the world you fly | Like a tea-tray in the sky*' took a toy that could only whirr around for half a minute and gave it the illusion of permanent flight. Commercially produced Wonderland products did something similar for other episodes from Carroll's stories. By the end of the century, key moments from both *Alice* books would feature in jigsaw puzzles, stereoscope slides, nursery ware, card games and many other pieces of merchandise, and although factory-made 'Alice' dolls would later sit alongside the version Carroll had bought for Beatrice Hatch in 1873 (the Hargreaves family owned one made in the 1930s that had blue eyes set in a pink felt face, topped by a long blonde wig), these products were not only aimed at children. Many were made by companies hoping to add a touch of glamour to otherwise hum-drum objects, such as a carved ivory parasol handle featuring Tweedledum and Tweedledee that Carroll sent to Alice Hargreaves in January 1892.

Carroll's stories had started to be used in advertisements, the best of which both borrowed his characters and aped his style, picking up on the fact that his writing was already packed with memorable parodies and nudging them a little further until they became catchy jingles. It did not take any great stretch of the imagination, or even of the dictionary, for the Mock Turtle's song 'Beau—ootiful Soo—oop! | Beau—ootiful Soo—oop!' to become an advertisement for Pears' soap in which Alice observes a mermaid singing 'Beau—ootiful So—oap! | Beau—ootiful So—oap!' on a giant lozenge of the product. Within a few years she would also be involved in selling Sozodont toothpaste, in a booklet that ended with a surprisingly practical 'LAW OF WONDERLAND': 'Clean the teeth before going to bed with a few drops of Liquid Sozodont sprinkled on a wet toothbrush, to prevent mouth acids and germs collecting at night.' A story that had mocked the 'simple rules' laid down in earlier children's books, such as the advice not to drink from bottles marked 'POISON', was now being used to support the far more sophisticated rhetorical tactics adver-tisers used to target consumers.

It was not the first time a popular Victorian book had produced mer-chandising spin-offs. Dickens's extraordinary success with the *Pickwick Papers* in the 1830s had been accompanied by Pickwick chintzes, Fat Boy sweets and Weller corduroys, and on its publication in 1859–60 Wilkie Collins's nerve-jangling sensation novel *The Woman in White* was used to promote cloaks, bonnets, perfumes and toiletries, as well as musical cele-brations such as 'The Woman in White Waltz' and 'The Fosco Gallop'. However, Dickens and Collins had not been in a position to exert any control over what manufacturers made of their works; despite paying careful attention to their publishing contracts, when it came to the commercial borrowing of a detail such as a character's name, they had no legal right to be consulted about where it would end up. In this respect, at least, they were merely onlookers of their own fame. Carroll was different. Despite his continued nervousness at what might happen to his dream-child in other people's hands, he did more than merely observe her entrance into material culture. Occasionally he got involved.

In April 1891 he was approached by Mary Manners, author of the 1885 poem 'Wonderland', on behalf of her brother Charles, a director of the Nottinghamshire firm Barringer, Wallis & Manners ('Tin Plate Decorators, and Manufacturers of Decorated Enamelled Tin Boxes'), which would later become famous as a supplier of containers for everything from gas masks to Quality Street chocolates, to ask if he would allow his name to appear on the lid of a new Christmas tin. She immediately captured his interest by referring to it as 'a children's tin', and although he confessed that he had no idea what this meant, he agreed to consider a sample of the proposed design. He was impressed by the '*permanent* character' of the pictures, printed on a tough enamel coating, which closely followed Tenniel's illustrations for *Through the Looking-Glass* (on which he still held the copyright), and after acknowledging that they possessed 'considerable artistic merit' he gave permission for the tin to be commercially produced.

Whoever chose the images that appeared on the Looking-Glass tin had read the book carefully. Wrapped around the sides were some of the most popular scenes, including Alice meeting the fawn, and the battle between the Red and White Knights, but the most interesting example appeared on the lid: a version of Tenniel's illustration that showed Alice passing through the mirror. The enamelled surface was not as shiny as a real mirror, perhaps, but it did allow users to play out a different version of the scene in their heads. In the book, what finally spurs Alice into pretending that "'there's a way of getting through'" into Looking-Glass Land is the thought that "'I'm sure it's got, oh! such beautiful things in it!'", and when the mirror dissolves into a silver mist she finds herself in a place that does indeed contain a good selection of Carroll's favourite things, from games of chess to offcuts of his family magazines. In effect, the story is an animated version of the sort of collection that as a boy he had placed under the floorboards of Croft Rectory, and he seems to have assumed that other children would treat these tins in the same way. The reality was more mundane: when each one was opened, it was revealed to contain a selection of Jacob's Biscuits, with an Alice-themed advertisement pasted on to the underside of the lid. This annoyed Carroll, who complained to Charles Manners that he would never have approved of the product 'had I foreseen that the intention was to vulgarise the boxes by turning them into advertising mediums', and insisted that from now on every tin sent to one of his friends was 'to go out *empty*'.

Carroll would have been even less impressed if he had known that, by 1922, Kemp's 'Alice in Wonderland Biscuits' would feature consumable versions of his characters. If he worried about vulgarity, he is unlikely to have approved of Kemp's advertisements, in which Alice asks, 'What does K stand for?' and is told that it is 'Krisp' by Tweedledum and 'Krunchy' by Tweedledee, especially as the company promised a free copy of *Alice's Adventures in Wonderland* to the first 10,000 readers who sent in ten coupons from special packets. Then again, some of his child-friends were equally annoyed by his attitude to commercialization, one which he thought of as high-minded but could just as easily have been viewed as high-handed; forty years later, Alice Standen still recalled her 'childlike disappointment' when she and her sisters were sent a batch of tins by Carroll: 'There was one for each of us girls, but I, the youngest, did not at the time share the delight and enthusiasm of the elders . . . The biscuit tins were empty!'

If Carroll disliked the commercial exploitation of his stories, other than in objects such as his stamp-case, the question is why he gave permission for the Looking-Glass tins to be manufactured at all? The answer appears to be that, although Carroll did not receive a royalty on sales, Manners had agreed to send fifty tins as gifts to anyone he chose, and this developed the relationship in his mind between the *Alice* books and friendship. With typical thoroughness he set about taking up the firm's offer, and ended up extending it much further than originally intended.

His initial list on 1 September 1892 contained 120 names and addresses, neatly arranged in alphabetical order, including three for 'Mrs and the Masters Hargreaves', which would have allowed Alice to give one to each of her three young sons Alan (born 1881), Leopold (known as 'Rex', 1883) and Caryl (1887), and after totting up a revised list of names on 13 October he announced that 'the total number is 364!' A few weeks later he asked for another hundred tins. To these letters Manners sent wearily polite replies, until he was eventually forced to suggest that if the firm went ahead with a follow-up 'Alice in Wonderland' tin, he 'would certainly allow you & your friends to have as many as you liked; but I should prefer them to go through you'.

As an expression of friendship, there was something sadly appropriate about Carroll sending out hollow receptacles that were to be filled with secrets and memories, but there was another reason why he enjoyed treating them as something other than hammered sheets of tin. Sending one to Princess Alice, the nine-year-old daughter of Prince Leopold, on 15 August, he told her that 'children use them to keep biscuits in, or sweets, or anything', but his advice was to turn it into a prison for her little brother: 'Whenever Charlie is very naughty, you can just pop him in, and shut the lid! Then he'll be good.' Alice replied with stubborn literal-mindedness that 'Charlie is much too big to get into it', but that was not really the point of Carroll's suggestion. He wanted the tins to be more than just receptacles for miscellaneous small objects (Charlie received one too, and told him that 'I keep all my toy animals in it'). He wanted them to be containers for the imagination.

*

Thirty-two

C arroll's willingness to foster a new *Alice* industry threw into sharp relief the familiar routines of his personal life. Despite the fame he had reluctantly attracted, or perhaps because of it, he continued to keep regular hours at his desk in Christ Church, producing numerous publications on his favourite subjects – logic, mathematics, games and puzzles – in addition to his usual thick sheaves of correspondence. Wherever possible, he punctuated his studies with strenuous timed walks and 'very *restful*' periods spent with children (including another Alice – Alice Mott – to whom he shyly referred in 1892 as 'my new friend'), occasionally interrupting his diary to make long lists of his favourites, like someone planning a party that would never happen: Mabel, Enid, Sydney, Weenie, Vera, Aileen, Gwendolyn, Clare, Eliza, Connie, Gladys, Daisy, Edith, Florence . . .

He also continued to tell stories. Some of these he had already published, such as 'Bruno's Revenge', a fable about a boy-fairy who must learn to help others, which appeared in *Aunt Judy's Magazine* in December 1867. Others, such as 'Prince Uggug' or 'Bruno's Picnic', were narrative fragments he had jotted down in memorandum books and polished to a high sheen by telling them to audiences of children over the years. In 1874, he decided to take these scraps of storytelling and piece them together into a single linked narrative. This time the gap between intention and execution was longer than ever, and it was not until 1889 that he finally published *Sylvie and Bruno*, followed by *Sylvie and Bruno Concluded* in 1893, both illustrated by Harry Furniss. Carroll wanted to present the books as something entirely new. 'I do not know if "Alice in Wonderland" was an original story,' he pointed out in a preface, 'but I do know that, since it came out, something like a dozen story-books have appeared, on identically the same pattern. The path I timidly explored . . . is now a beaten highroad: all the way-side flowers have long ago been trampled into the dust: and it would be courting disaster for me to attempt that style again.' That was bad news for his publishers Macmillan, which had sound commercial reasons for promoting Carroll's latest book as another written in the *Alice* style, and had advertised *Sylvie and Bruno* in March 1890 with the promise that 'This book contains 395 pages – nearly as many as the two "Alice" books put together', which came close to claiming that it was the third in a loose trilogy of titles. Carroll's preface may also have surprised his readers, because the lines that opened *Sylvie and Bruno* were closely modelled on those that ended *Through the Looking-Glass*:

> Is all our Life, then, but a dream
> Seen faintly in the golden gleam
> Athwart Time's dark resistless stream?
> (Sylvie and Bruno)

> Ever drifting down the stream—
> Lingering in the golden gleam—
> Life, what is it but a dream?
> (Through the Looking-Glass)

In Carroll's new acrostic, ISA Bowman had supplanted Alice LiddELL as his official muse, but nothing else had changed; ignoring the seventeen-year gap between *Through the Looking-Glass* and *Sylvie and Bruno*, he had lined up his rhymes as neatly as the patterns on two pieces of wallpaper. What followed was equally reminiscent of the *Alice* books in terms of structure and style. Although Carroll's ambition had been to take his 'odd ideas' and 'fragments of dialogue' and string them together 'upon the thread of a consecutive story', his new two-part book was no less episodic than *Alice's Adventures in Wonderland* and *Through the Looking-Glass* had been, and it was even jerkier in the way it moved from one kind of writing to the next. Fairy-tale enchantment gave way to scenes of mawkish senti-ment; slapstick comedy was muddled together with passages of political commentary and stodgy moral instruction. And whereas the *Alice* books had used dreams and fantasy to explain their unexpected jumps between one idea and the next, in this case Carroll's decision to replace 'a mere unconnected *dream*' with 'a *plot*' left him no such excuse. His new book was in effect an anthology disguised as a novel.

The *Sylvie and Bruno* stories have attracted some influential admirers since their first publication, among them James Joyce and Evelyn Waugh, but they are hard to read now without regretting that Carroll went to such lengths in attempting 'to strike out another new path'. Some regret that he wrote them at all. His aim, he explained in the preface, was to share 'some thoughts that may suit those hours of innocent merriment which are the very life of Childhood', and the capital letter that elevated child-hood to 'Childhood' accurately indicated what was to follow. These were not stories about individual children, but a fable about Childhood that he had pinned on to two young fairies named Bruno and Sylvie, the latter of whom he had decided was 'a sort of embodiment of Purity'. Bringing a character like that to life would have been as much of a challenge as sculpting a cloud, and for the most part Carroll did not try. Instead he chose to replace believable psychology with a shimmering veil of allegory.

There are still some glimpses of the old Carroll at work. Near the start of *Sylvie and Bruno*, there is a descent underground to Elfland, which was one of the alternative names he had originally considered for Wonderland, and in the first paragraph of the sequel he refers to Sylvie and Bruno as 'Dream-Children', as if he was starting to think of them as Alice's fictional siblings. In both books, however, Carroll's jokes and puzzles carry far more moral weight than the equivalent moments in the *Alice* books, because each time the plot advances it also edges closer towards what the preface referred to as 'graver thoughts of human life'. Many incidents give rise to these thoughts, such as the dead mouse that Bruno uses as an impromptu measuring-tape, or a dead hare over which Sylvie weeps hot tears 'as if her heart would break', but whereas in the *Alice* books the threat of death was dissolved in laughter, here it continues to lurk in the background. Some of the writing is distinctly unsubtle. Bruno's innocent perceptions of the world, in particular, are delivered in a style of baby talk that is supposed to persuade us that children see more clearly than jaded adults, but in practice has a rather different effect. At one stage, a gardener lets the children through a door in the garden wall, having told them that, "'It's as much as my place is worth!'" and Bruno 'innocently' enquires, "'How much *are* it wurf?'" Of course, any six-year-old child who did ask an adult such a question would either be thought simple-minded or suspected of having satirical intentions (few words make someone seem less innocent than 'innocently'), but that is not how Carroll expects us to respond. Whether his fictional children are mis-pronouncing 'dandelions' as 'dindledums', or 'bounding over the turf with the fleetness and grace of young antelopes', their antics are put forward as evidence to support Carroll's tentative suggestion at the end of *Sylvie and Bruno* that 'the heavenward gaze of faith' was not wholly dissimilar to a belief in fairies. It too depended upon *'the evidence of things not seen'*.

It is tempting to view *Sylvie and Bruno* and *Sylvie and Bruno Concluded* as *Alice*'s dark twins, flabby rivals to books that were as slim as snakes, but in some respects they were merely extensions of the same line of thought. Having already used Alice in his 'Easter' and 'Christmas Greetings' as a pretext for delivering advice on spiritual matters, his original understanding of her was becoming less significant than what she had come to represent. A feisty and occasionally spiteful explorer of imaginary worlds had become identified in his mind with an even more abstract realm – the possibility of perfect goodness, or, more simply, heaven – and although Carroll thought that young children gravitated naturally towards this place, he was happy to use his writing as a way of supplying directions to everyone else.

Several of the characters he included in *Sylvie and Bruno* could claim to be speaking on his behalf, including the Professor with a fondness for madcap inventions who accompanies the children, and the moralizing Arthur, with whom Carroll admitted he was 'much in sympathy', and whose name was teasingly close to 'Author'. A slightly more unexpected affinity was with the fairy-cum-clown Bruno, but Carroll's expertise in logic depended on similar powers of literal-mindedness to those his character demonstrates. When Bruno is asked if he has enjoyed a good night, he tri-umphantly replies, "'I's had the same night *oo've* had . . . There's only been *one* night since yesterday!'" which makes him sound like an accidental expert in syllogistic reasoning. There may also have been an element of nostalgia at work, because if Sylvie was the sort of child Carroll secretly wanted to be, Bruno was much closer to the one he had actually been. His earliest surviving letter, written when he was around five years old, was to his nurse: 'I love you very much and tend you a kitt from little Charlie . . . I'd like to give you a kitt, but I tan't, betause I'm at Marke. What a long letter I've written. I'm twite tired.' It is unlikely that he was pretending to be a patchy speller at this early age, but the long recoil of his memory certainly leaves open the possibility that he tried to recapture this mood when little Charlie had become the Revd Charles Dodgson, and could no longer tend people kitts without worrying about the possible consequences.

The only problem with Carroll's happy celebration of childhood in these books is that it bore very little relation to what real children were like. The letters written by Alice Hargreaves's middle son, Rex, in the years between *Sylvie and Bruno* and *Sylvie and Bruno Concluded*, are noticeably lacking in similar evidence of piety and purity. Other than a dutiful prayer when he learns that his brother Alan is ill – 'I shall ask GOD to make you well' – his principal sources of amusement involve real or imagined violence, as he stages battles with his toy soldiers ('we pretend they are at war with the French and the[y] fight and the English always win'), plays annoying practical jokes ('Mrs. Lloyd . . . said that she would chop off my head and saw me in half') and later at Eton writes to tell his parents he is 'so glad' to hear that his other brother Caryl has shot his first birds. There is no weeping over dead hares. Little girls were not much better. The first time we meet Sylvie in Carroll's story, she is sitting on her father's lap: 'one of the sweetest and loveliest little maidens it has ever been my lot to see,' sighs the narrator, with 'rosy cheeks and sparkling eyes' and a 'wealth of curly brown hair'. The first time Carroll met the eleven-year-old Nellie de Silva, by contrast, was on the beach in Sandown on 6 September 1876, when she decided that she disliked how the keeper of the bathing-machines was treating his horse, and took her revenge by feeding the man's lunch to it. Subsequently she armed herself with a stick and 'deliberately smashed the glass in all the little peep-holes of the machines she could reach', before Carroll intervened and carried her away. Even if Carroll secretly approved of her actions, it is hard to imagine the horse's owner agreeing that criminal damage was a reasonable way for her to prove her status as an embodiment of purity.

During the 1880s and 1890s, more realistic children were becoming equally visible in fiction, and this made readers far less tolerant of earlier writing that had tried to turn ordinary boys and girls into scale models of adult saints. In an article on 'Children and Modern Literature' published in 1891, the Revd Henry Sutton pointed out that new liberal attitudes to children, which stressed the need to love and understand them rather than beat them into submission, owed 'a good deal to the way in which they have come to the front in literature'. Because of this development, he was suspicious of characters that appeared to be insufficiently lifelike. Many of the children in Dickens's novels, in particular, were in his view as artificial as garden gnomes: Little Nell was 'a charming child' but 'utterly unlike ordinary children', he sadly noted, while Paul Dombey was 'perfectly delicious' but also 'weird and unearthly'. More believable fictional children also reflected the views of experts in the new field of child development, who pointed out that children experienced emotions that were every bit as rich and mysterious as those that beset adults. While this meant that childhood continued to be thought of as a parallel world – an article on Christmas published in 1888 had invited its readers 'to go back to childhood or wonder-land, where we have all been "once upon a time," and ramble a little over enchanted ground' – by the end of the century it was hard to view it simply as an Eden or Arcadia that would eventually be outgrown. Childhood was a time to be wondered about as well as wondered at. In a novella such as Henry James's *The Turn of the Screw* (1898), the inner workings of a child's mind are made to seem as mysterious as an object lost in thick fog. As the governess tries to fathom what her young charges Miles and Flora are thinking, she repeatedly tries out variations of the same word: the 'wonderful' way Miles casts a spell on her; Flora's 'wonderful little face . . . still flushed with sleep' and the way she submits 'wonderfully' to the governess's grip 'without a cry or a sign of fright'; discovering Miles in suspicious circumstances when 'I had wondered – oh, HOW I had wondered! – if he were groping about in his little mind for something plausible' as an excuse. Each time she holds the word up to the light it catches a slightly different set of reflections from its surroundings, and although she tries to assemble these clues into a story that will reveal what the children are keeping from her, the gaps in her understanding remind us that the real secret is not what they know. It is who they are.

The *Alice* books were often enlisted in these debates. In 1895, for example, *Alice's Adventures in Wonderland* made a brief appearance in 'Sawdust and Sin', a chapter in Kenneth Grahame's bestselling collection *The Golden Age*, where once again Carroll's characters proved to be adept at escaping from their own story and populating a child's hidden imaginative world. Although the children in *The Golden Age* are engaged in a ceaseless struggle with the adults around them, who have forgotten what it is like to be young, the narrator reminds us what they are missing when he eavesdrops on his young sister Charlotte 'chattering to herself' as she assembles her dolls for a story. '"Well,"' she begins, '"so the White Rabbit scuttled off down the passage, and Alice hoped he'd come back, 'cos he had a waist-coat on and her flamingo flew up a tree. But we haven't got to that part yet; you must wait a minute, and – where had I got to?"' At that point one of her dolls keels over and Charlotte punishes him with a good spanking. Here too Wonderland turns out to be primarily an attitude adopted by the main character, rather than a physical location. Yet Carroll's story is not the reason for Charlotte's powers of make-believe, any more than *The Swiss Family Robinson* provides a narrative template for her brother's fantasies about 'the push and rustle of great beasts moving unseen' through a jungle of suburban rhododendrons. They merely provide the raw materials on which each child's imagination can get to work.

In 1889, Carroll attempted something similar with the publication of a new book he entitled *The Nursery "Alice"*. As he explained in a letter to Mary Manners, it was 'meant for very young children, consisting of coloured enlargements of 20 of the pictures in *Alice*, with explanations such as one would give in showing them to a little child'. He had first thought up this project in 1881, and by 1885 Tenniel had been engaged to produce coloured versions of some of his illustrations, making this the first English edition of *Alice's Adventures in Wonderland* in which Alice appeared in colour. (In Tenniel's version she wears blue stockings and a big blue bow on a pale

Front cover of *The Nursery "Alice"* (1889)

orange dress.) However, it is probably no coincidence that Carroll started to work on the text just over a month after he met Reginald Hargreaves and recalled his wife as 'an entirely fascinating little 7 year-old maiden'. *The Nursery "Alice"* was another attempt to turn back the clock. Just as the facsimile edition of *Alice's Adventures Under Ground* had been a copy of the story he first told in 1862, so this new version returned to the oral performance he had given on the riverbank, by printing large pictures for a child to look at and a script that encouraged adult readers to bring them to life. (In the first chapter, Carroll explains that the White Rabbit is scared of the Duchess, and helpfully suggests, 'Just shake the book a little, from side to side, and you'll soon see him tremble.') It also matched the events of the story by making Alice both larger and smaller than she had been before. The book was more than two inches wider and taller than the first edition, but Carroll decided to shrink it in every other way, by cutting the poems, streamlining the narrative and simplifying the vocabulary. The result was a story for children who were as young as the real Alice had been when he first met her.

Morton Cohen has noted that the publication history of *The Nursery "Alice"* is 'a tale of enormous tangles', and unpicking them one by one –

Carroll's rejection of the first print run as '*far* too bright and gaudy', his attempt to sell these copies in America, the interim printing of a version in brown ink to send to his friends, his insistence that the first edition should be rebound after discovering that one of the animals on E. Gertrude Thomson's cover design was ⅝ of an inch off centre – is enough to make even a hardened bibliographer wince. The book itself was far more sweet-tempered in tone, although anyone who picked up a copy in 1890 expecting only a simplified version of Carroll's story would have been disappointed. The opening and closing sentences set out to hold Alice in a tight embrace:

> ONCE upon a time, there was a little girl called Alice: and she had a very curious dream.
> Would you like to hear what it was that she dreamed about?

> *

> *Wouldn't* it be a nice thing to have a curious dream, just like Alice?
> The best plan is this. First lie down under a tree, and wait till a White Rabbit runs by, with a watch in his hand: then shut your eyes, and pretend to be dear little Alice.
> Good-bye, Alice dear, good-bye!

Between these passages, Carroll repeatedly swaps one narrative persona for another, adopting in quick succession the voice of a fussy school-master ('*You don't know?* Well, you *are* an ignorant child!'), a nervous foreman ('Oh, work away, my little men! Hurry, hurry!'), a games instruct-or ('Did you ever play at Croquet? There are large wooden balls . . .') and a naturalist ('do you know why it's called a *Fox*-glove?'), but the face underneath all these masks remains the same. It is that of a sentimentalist who keeps confusing the story with his reactions to it, so that in the second chapter we are introduced to 'poor Alice', 'Poor Alice!' and 'poor little Alice', and Carroll's writing is littered with excitable exclamation marks: 'She grew, and she grew, and she grew. Taller than she was before!

Taller than *any* child! Taller than any grown-up person! Taller, and taller, and taller! Just look at the picture, and you'll *see* how tall she got!'

Usually critics have simply ignored *The Nursery "Alice"*, as if averting their eyes from a nasty accident, but the revisions Carroll made to his original story suggest that it was not only Alice who had changed since the 'golden afternoon' of 1862. So had he. There was nothing inherently wrong with using pictures as a guide to telling a story; Carroll did something similar with his fireplace tiles in Christ Church, which he sometimes pretended were a depiction of the events in *The Hunting of the Snark*. His problem with *The Nursery "Alice"* was that turning his original narrative into a commentary wholly altered the kind of story it was. In *Alice's Adventures in Wonderland*, Tenniel's images had worked like a series of theatrical tableaux: every few pages the characters froze at a dramatic moment before breaking out of their poses and carrying on with the story. In this new version, the illustrations were more like the magic lantern slides that a London firm was offering for sale in the same year: they illuminated the story but kept it safely a distance. Carroll's narrator is so busy explaining everything – we know all along that Alice is dreaming – that any tension is lost. Instead of allowing us to experience Wonderland as a surprising jumble of characters and events, he turns himself into a tour guide who explains everything *very* carefully, seeking to avoid any *possibility* of a child misunderstanding him through *liberal use of italics*. Unfortunately this means that we no longer see things through Alice's eyes. Instead of the double perspective Carroll had perfected in his original story, which allowed readers to experience Alice's feelings of alarm while being confident in her remaining safe, in *The Nursery "Alice"* she is merely a character acting out a familiar tale. Perhaps that is why the cover shows her asleep next to what looks suspiciously like a red-covered copy of *Alice's Adventures in Wonderland*, while characters from the story float above her head on a puff of cloud, because what follows is no longer simply Alice's dream. It is her dream of a book.

Carroll's descriptions of Alice were closely paralleled by the attitude he now adopted towards his readers. In a preface he addressed 'to any mother', he celebrated the 'pure fountain of joy that wells up in all child-like hearts', regardless of their actual age, but he was especially interested in 'the illiterate, ungrammatical, dimpled Darlings, that fill your Nursery with merry uproar, and your inmost heart of hearts with a restful gladness!' Only someone who has never had to cope with young children at bedtime would assume that their 'merry uproar' would create feelings of 'restful gladness' in a mother, but evidently Carroll's sense of delight was founded upon the idea of such scenes rather than their reality. A similar thought process appears to have influenced his attitude towards Alice. A fictional character who had originally been based on a real child, and written about in a way that was intended to appeal to her as an individual, had slowly drifted away from this specificity until she had become the sort of child he enjoyed thinking about but found it hard to imagine having thoughts of her own. In fact, comparing *The Nursery "Alice"* with a work like *The Golden Age*, it is hard to escape the conclusion that by this stage in Carroll's life other writers were proving to be rather better at following his early example than he was. While they continued to experiment with fiction that considered how the world looked from a child's perspective, Carroll was regularly confronted by a gap between his ideals and his experience that only his imagination could fill.

In 1891, he spent a happy day playing with Princess Alice and her brother Charles at Hatfield House, following it up with an illustrated edition of William Allingham's poem 'The Fairies', which he inscribed to Alice 'in memory of a certain day when two live fairies did certainly appear to him'. That was a year after he had sent her a copy of *The Nursery "Alice"*, together with a puzzle and the promise that if she managed to solve it he would give her a 'golden arm-chair, that came all the way from Wonderland!' Her recollection of their encounters was rather different, pointing out that when she first met Carroll she was so perplexed by his stammering, she 'suddenly asked in a loud voice "Why does he waggle his mouth like that?" I was hastily removed by the lady-in-waiting.' But if real children sometimes disappointed Carroll, they could always be relied upon when he picked up his pen. In a story, every child could be a delightfully tousled scamp or an awe-inspiring little angel; the blank page was an environment in which they revealed their true purity.

*

335

Thirty-three

In August 1889, Carroll sent Alice Hargreaves a presentation copy of the brown-ink version of *The Nursery "Alice"* in a decorated leather binding. Inside was the polite inscription 'Mrs Hargreaves with kindest regards from the Author'. Seven months later he sent her a copy of the full-colour version, again with a crisp formal acknowledgement: 'Mrs Hargreaves, with the Author's sincere regards'. Sandwiched between these events she gave her eldest son an edition of *Alice's Adventures in Wonderland* to mark his eighth birthday, on 25 October 1889, and this time the inscription was much more familiar: 'Alan from his Mother "Alice in Wonderland"'. It was a signature veined with ambiguity, because the inverted commas around 'Alice in Wonderland' made it uncertain whether she was boasting or making a joke. She was both the child Carroll had packaged up in a story and launched into the world more than twenty years ago, and an adult who now had children of her own. The unanswerable question was which life felt more authentic. Where did Alice stop and 'Alice' begin?

Similar questions clustered around 'Wonderland'. Not just one writer's imaginary universe, by the end of the nineteenth century it had become something more like a cultural multiverse, a loose network of real places and intangible ideas where the line that divided the actual from the possible could be stretched and blurred. Inevitably, deciding where the ordinary world shaded into a more exotic alternative was largely a matter of perception. For the young Ethel Rowell, with whom Carroll travelled to London in June 1896, the bewildering 'complications of luncheon' in a hotel, followed by a matinee performance at the theatre, were enough to make a day that had 'shone in prospect with all the glitter of a new Wonderland' drift closer towards the darker side of Carroll's story: 'as the day progressed it more and more assumed the character of a strange dream, blissful for the most part but holding also certain nightmare elements for one totally inexperienced'.

London's smog and traffic made it unlikely that most people would think of it in purely glittering terms, but the city contained plenty of opportunities to enjoy equally unreal experiences. Carroll never visited music halls, which specialized in the sort of popular entertainment he considered vulgar, but if he had walked with Ethel down the Whitechapel Road, he could have taken her to the newly refurbished Wonderland theatre, which boasted of being 'the most PALATIAL AND POPULAR RESORT IN LONDON!' and on Easter Monday 1896 was offering a packed programme that included performances by Mons. Hayden ('See his Wonderful Performance of swallowing a Watch, which can be Heard Ticking'), Miss Flo Riley ('A most Beautifully and Artistically Tattooed Lady'), the Great Carle's 'Troupe of Performing Pigeons', and a Ladies' Orchestra 'IN FULL UNIFORM'. If he had returned the following month, he could have seen a man with a beard over seven feet long, and the 'Armless Midget Lady', who was 32 inches tall and went through 'a MARVELLOUS PERFORMANCE WITH HER FEET'.

However, if some people enjoyed turning Wonderland into a place where theatre lights twinkled or luxuriantly bearded men

Playbill for the Wonderland theatre (May 1896)

were put on display, others treated it far more seriously. Although 'scarce the wonderland of elf and fay | For all our wooing, may be won today', as the writer and member of the Independent Labour Party Amy Morant lamented in 1898, expressions of solidarity could open up new 'vistas' to explore: 'A Wonderland! Say, shall we wander there?' For social reformers, in other words, Wonderland could be more than an imaginary elsewhere; it could also be a way of thinking differently about the world everyone already knew. Alongside the various *Alice*-based satires that pointed out what was wrong with the current political situation, Wonderland offered a glimpsed alternative: a future where 'though the track be strange, | And other footsteps lie not for our guiding, | The wonder-light shall fail us not who range | Strong-knit in brother-bonds to ply the quest | Without haste or rest | For treasures which the Wonderland is hiding'.

The latest *Alice* imitations were usually less politically ambitious than this. Some preferred to abandon the real world altogether, such as Herbert S. Sweetland's mistily allegorical *Tom's Adventures in Shadowland* (1888), which ends with the hero arriving at a heaven that is approached by a golden staircase flanked by triumphantly singing angels. Other works clustered together in their visual as well as their narrative style. Maggie Browne's *Wanted – A King* (1890), Norley Chester's *Olga's Dream* (1892) and the most successful of the three, G. E. Farrow's *The Wallypug of Why* (1895), all revolve around a girl who dreams up a comically distorted version of her waking life, and all three were illustrated by Harry Furniss, the artist responsible for the illustrations to Carroll's *Sylvie and Bruno* books. In these later commissions he proved himself to be good at turning out a whole gallery of Alice-alikes with long blonde hair and cherubic features.

More interesting was Anna M. Richards's *A New Alice in the Old Wonderland* (1895). A reader who glanced at it quickly might well have confused it with Carroll's original story – it had an almost identical red cover, decorated with a gold roundel, and the illustrations by her daughter impressively matched Tenniel's original artwork – but in this case the author's central motivation was not parody but homage. The main character is Alice Lee, a young American girl who adores the *Alice* books, so that when she falls asleep after nibbling a slice of cake, naturally she dreams of walking around Carroll's Wonderland – a place that is again united with Looking-Glass Land – and meeting the characters. Very little has changed since Carroll's Alice was there, although the White Knight has developed a taste for oriental art objects, in keeping with modern Aesthetic tastes, and Humpty Dumpty has hard-boiled himself to prevent future accidents. Much of the pleasure this new Alice feels comes from a certain patina of familiarity, so that when she spots 'The Hatter, the Dormouse, and the March Hare', even an ordinary word like 'the' receives a special jolt of recognition: she is looking not just at *a* Hatter but *the* Hatter. What makes Richards's book more unusual is her skill in making her readers also feel 'delightfully at home' in familiar surroundings, while simultaneously fleshing out Carroll's story until it becomes much stranger. At one point, Alice peers through a crack in the door and spies the Duchess 'sitting asleep in an arm-chair near the fire', like an old actress resting in the wings. Something similar happens when she peeks inside the Hatter's house, where she sees 'an immense pile of china things on the floor, heaped up in the greatest confusion, all covered with dust and leaves, and most of them broken'. Once again Wonderland appears to have an independent existence outside Alice's head, as if Carroll's dreamscape stretched far beyond the margins of his own story, and only the limitations of print had prevented him from exploring it further.

Carroll was alternately flattered and irritated by the rising flood of *Alice* imitations. He had started to collect popular examples, listing several in his diary on 1 September 1891, and the previous month he sent a copy of *Wanted – A King* to his child-friend Maggie Bowman, with an inscription that played on the resemblance of her name to that of the author:

> Written by Maggie B—
> Bought by me:
> A present for Maggie B—
> Sent by me:
> But *who* can Maggie be?
> Answered by me:
> 'She is she.'

He signed this 'C.L.D.' – an extra rhyme to join with 'me', 'she' and 'Maggie B' / 'be', and thus another joke about how easy it was to confuse an original voice with an echo. It was a private version of the warning he had already offered readers of the *Alice* books. Between 1889 and 1894, various editions of his works included a note headed 'CAUTION TO READERS' which frostily pointed out that Carroll was not the author of a story mistakenly attributed to him in *Aunt Judy's Magazine* in 1881, and also rebutted the mischievous suggestion made in another journal that *Alice's Adventures in Wonderland* (1865) may have been influenced by Tom Hood's children's book *From Nowhere to the North Pole* (1874). If anything the current of influence flowed the other way, as the publication dates proved, but Carroll's defence was a timely reminder that cultural author-ity depended upon more than chronology. Who came first in the history of literature was not nearly as significant as who lasted longest.

Less than four months after Carroll sent off his rhyme about 'She is she', he wrote again to Alice Hargreaves to arrange what would prove to be their final meeting. The version printed in his collected correspond-ence, which was taken from a later article by Caryl Hargreaves, is a straightforward invitation to tea. The actual letter is considerably longer. 'My dear Mrs. Hargreaves', he began, before going on to tell her that he had recently enjoyed visits from her mother and three sisters, but had been conscious of a gap in the social circle, and 'I should not like the 5th lady (with whom my relations have never been what one would call "unfriendly"!) to go away with the thought that I have been *unconscious* of it, & have not tried to remedy it.' His conclusion was a direct echo of the note he had previously made in his 1889 diary, as he explained that he had met Reginald 'not long ago', and ruefully admitted that 'It was hard to realise that he was the *husband* of one I can scarcely picture to myself, even now, as more than 7 years old!' There may have been a quiet private joke in 'picture', given how inescapable Tenniel's images of the fictional Alice had become, but for the real Alice Carroll's phrasing contained an extra overlap of fact and fiction. The final paragraph of *Alice's Adventures in Wonderland* had imagined Alice's sister looking to the future: 'Lastly, she pictured to herself how this same little sister of hers would, in the after-time, be herself a grown woman; and how she would keep, through all her riper years, the simple and loving heart of her childhood: and how she would gather about her other little children, and make *their* eyes bright and eager with many a strange tale, perhaps even with the dream of Wonderland of long ago.' There had been sadly few indications over the past thirty years that Alice Hargreaves had retained her childlike simplicity and sense of wonder. What Carroll probably did not know was that, having passed on a copy of the book to her son two years earlier, she had already taken his advice.

After noting in his diary that it had been a 'wonderful experience' to meet Mrs Liddell and Ina during the previous week, his entry for Wednesday 9 December was far leaner in style: 'As Mrs. Hargreaves, the original "Alice," is now at the Deanery, I invited her also over to tea. She could not do this, but very kindly came over, with Rhoda, for a short time in the afternoon.' It is an account that implies much and explains nothing, but even this is fuller than Alice Hargreaves's pocket diary, which does not mention the occasion at all; under the heading for 9 December 1889, the page is completely blank.

Carroll's letter had expressed a willingness to meet Alice whenever she liked, because 'To a prisoner in his cell, all days are alike.' Whether his tone was supposed to be confessional or self-mocking, the idea that his life at Christ Church had dwindled into a predictable routine was not far from the truth. In the last few years of his life, many of his long-established patterns of behaviour asserted themselves in a final reprise. He remained nervous about children ageing, reassuring the father of one tall girl that he could 'see the child-face still, on top of that mountainous maiden', and another father of a young actress that it was '*very* sad' to learn that she was 4ft 10½ inches high '*without* her shoes', rather than the 4ft 10 inches she had claimed to be '*with* them'. Perhaps her father had knocked an inch off her height 'in order to secure some engagement she was trying for', Carroll gently suggested, and urged him not to be angry at receiving a lecture on honesty from one who longed to help other people 'escape the shame and misery' of the sinfulness he recognized in himself. It seems not to have occurred to him that the father might have

341

queried why Carroll was measuring his daughter at all. Meanwhile, Eastbourne continued to be his favoured location for seasonal 'adventures', where he could host his child-friends and engage in the activities that made him such a refreshing and strange companion: inventing games, enjoying jokes and puns ('sofa, so good'), and completing ambitious feats of mental gymnastics apparently for no other reason than to prove that he could. (In July 1893, he told one correspondent that he had made up some rhymes to learn 'the specific gravities (to 2 decimal places) of the common metals'.) Writing in January 1897 to the headmistress of a girls' boarding school in Eastbourne, Carroll explained that if *The Hunting of the Snark* was 'an Allegory for the Pursuit of Happiness', this interpretation worked especially well in relation to the Snark's 'fondness for bathing-machines', because it suggested that 'the pursuer of happiness, when he has exhausted all other devices, betakes himself, as a last and desperate resource, to some such wretched watering-place as Eastbourne, and hopes to find, in the tedious and depressing society of the daughters of mistresses of boarding-schools, the happiness he has failed to find elsewhere'. Clearly this was a joke, but for a joke to be found funny the listener must detect the seed of something true inside the fantasy whipped up around it, and in Carroll's case the number of times he now mocked himself as 'a lone, lorn creature' or 'a solitary broken-hearted hopeless old bachelor' may have indicated a genuine loneliness underneath the comic froth.

Many of his later letters to children are similarly hard to pin down in their tone. In 1891, he told Mrs Liddell that he gave invitations to 'lady-visitors of *any* age' because 'all romantic sentiment has quite died out of my life', but that did not prevent him from continuing to ape the conventions of love letters when writing to some of his younger visitors, addressing the teenage Enid Stevens as 'My darling', or making 'engagements' with them that would not lead anywhere. It is as if he had recognized that the absence of stage directions in print allowed him to say something and unsay it at the same time; every endearment could be read simultaneously as a confession and as an attempt to pull the reader's leg. Sometimes his behaviour stirred up new flurries of gossip – in 1893, he was forced to write to his sister Mary from Eastbourne, reassuring her that he had the '*full* approval' of his current guest's parents, and that his actions were 'entirely innocent and right, in the sight of God'. Every memoir subsequently written by his guests indicates that he was telling the truth, but Carroll no longer cared greatly what Oxford's gossips said about him. Indeed, he sometimes enjoyed imagining ways of making their tongues wag even faster, as when he commemorated the ten-year-old Maggie Bowman's visit to Oxford in June 1889 with a long comic poem that included the lines:

> They met a Bishop on their way . . .
> A Bishop large as life,
> With loving smile that seemed to say
> 'Will Maggie be my wife?'

> Maggie thought *not*, because, you see,
> She was so *very* young,
> And he was old as old could be . . .
> So Maggie held her tongue.

Once again Carroll edges towards a scandal, hovers on the brink of some ghastly revelation (each '. . .' is like a breath held in anticipation), before slipping back into the style of a versified diary entry. Even when he is doing nothing worse than talk about going for a stroll, he teases the reader by holding his own tongue.

One of the last letters Carroll wrote, just before Christmas 1897, was signed 'Your affectionate old-new friend'. It was a formula that summed up far more than the relationship between a man who now described himself as 'antiquated', and a 'charming' girl he had met for the first time earlier that year. Much of Carroll's life had been spent trying to reconcile his trust in tradition with his love of novelty, which manifested itself in everything from the poems he wrote, in which he made himself at home inside familiar forms before gleefully warping them out of shape, to choosing grand rooms in Christ Church he could cram with exciting modern inventions. The *Alice* books had been his most successful attempt to reconcile these twin drives, and in the last year of his life he was still trying to keep them close through another series of revisions, changing words such as 'can't' and 'won't' to satisfy his new preference for 'ca'n't' and 'wo'n't', correcting small misprints, sprinkling the text with extra commas, *italicizing* key words and so on. These fiddly alterations did nothing to alter the sense of his stories, but the time he spent on them indicates how much they meant to him. They provided even more evidence that his dream-child could continue to change while remaining essentially the same.

It was the traditional side of Carroll that asserted itself most strongly in his final years. More than four decades after his arrival in Oxford, he no longer enjoyed the fact that Christ Church was also old–new, an ancient institution that periodically renewed itself with a fresh intake of undergraduates. Now being surrounded by so many noisy young men merely irritated him, and when he reported their latest escapades in his diary it was not with amused tolerance but frank distaste. In 1890, a rowdy gang dressed up as vicars and nuns to celebrate a mock-Mass with whisky and biscuits; in 1893, a group of dinner-jacketed Christ Church undergraduates, annoyed that they had been refused permission to attend a ball at Blenheim Palace, retaliated by daubing the walls of Tom Quad with slogans such as 'Damn the Dean' and 'Damn the Dons'. For their part, the undergraduates treated Carroll with the sort of respect that is usually reserved for an elderly and not greatly loved relative. One who sat opposite him at his first dinner in Christ Church viewed him with awe as 'the living embodiment of the old Oxford'; unlike the bustling modern city, he observed, Carroll's Oxford was an early-Victorian backwater, 'a haunt of people who played croquet and little girls with short frocks and smoothly brushed hair and quaint formal politeness'. That is why the *Alice* books could never be written now, he concluded, because 'the sleepy afternoon air, the quaint grace and the mock dignity are all the property of an elder and vanishing world'.

Yet the *Alice* books were proving to be far better than their creator at adapting themselves to the modern world. Some good examples of this can be seen in the debates over women's rights that came to prominence in the 1890s. Here Carroll's attitudes were a predictable mixture of the forward-thinking and the reactionary. Between 1886 and 1887, he gave a series of lectures in logic at Lady Margaret Hall, which had been founded in 1878 as Oxford's first women's college, and in 1896 he intervened in Oxford's fierce arguments over whether or not to grant degrees to female students by circulating a paper that proposed the establishment of a women's university. Slightly less progressive were his reasons for wanting to educate women separately, namely his conviction that Oxford's main function was 'to prepare young Men . . . for the business of Life', and that 'an enormous influx of resident Women-Students' could only have a retrograde moral effect. He revealed a similar ambivalence in an earlier letter to the mother of a brilliantly unconventional woman named Edith Rix, who rode a bicycle, cut her hair short and later became a 'computer' (a human calculator) at the Royal Observatory in Greenwich; while he could 'only gasp in surprise' at her decision to tackle differential calculus, which left most male students scratching their heads in puzzlement, he warned her mother that 'Several of my girl-friends have been seriously affected by the modern craze of excessive brain-stimulation.'

In this context, it is probably not surprising that campaigners both for and against women's rights enjoyed using his writings to support their cause. In 1893, for example, Charlotte Smith pointed out that even a relatively enlightened individual such as Walter Besant was capable of producing comments that made women appear to be not just a different sex but another species. His main objection to opening the professions to women, Smith observed wryly, was that this would damage men's job prospects, and women therefore 'ought to get married, and not bother after work', but as this was an argument he would never dream of making in reverse, 'here indeed we have "Alice in Wonderland", a vision of topsy-turvydom'. Elsewhere the same vocabulary, appropriately, could just as easily be turned on its head. In some later 'Anti-Suffrage Notes', published in a journal dedicated to opposing 'the mad purposes of the militant female iconoclast', the anonymous author noted with alarm that women were now tackling every job from policing to engineering, and it was therefore only a matter of time before all men followed the example set by the fictitious mountain tribe of the Fanatistanese, 'the women of which are the farmers, the soldiers, the property owners and the politicians, while the men keep the hearthstones warm and remodel last year's sheepskin kilts – a real topsy-turvy, Alice-in-Wonderland country'. Follow that example, the author chortled, and soon men will hardly be men at all. In the worst case, they might even start weeping and blushing.

Such contrasting opinions would gain extra traction in the coming years, as writers of all political persuasions ransacked the *Alice* books for suitable quotations, and their arguments added a powerful new dimension to the idea of a female protagonist exploring a new world. For although W. H. Auden once pointed out that 'Wonderland and Looking-Glass Land are fun to visit but no places to live in', debates over what the future should look like reflected the fact that Carroll's original Wonderland was not merely a world Alice had dropped into as an unexpected guest. It was one she had brought into existence.

*

Thirty-four

Although Carroll had often written of the need to be prepared for death, a speck on the horizon that was getting closer all the time, his own end was unexpected. In 1896, he confessed to one of his sisters that hearing about the loss of his friends was becoming 'less and less of a shock', but he had long been aware that every moment was potentially his last. One of the central tenets of his religious faith was that he could be summoned to give an account of himself at any time, producing a balance sheet of pluses and minuses that only God's mathematical skill was capable of working out. In his final years he spurred himself on with the thought that he might not have long to put all his plans into effect. 'I am beginning to realise that, if the *books* I am still hoping to write, are to be done *at all*, they must be done *now*,' he told his sister, 'and that I am *meant* thus to utilise the splendid health that I have had, unbroken, for the last year and a half.'

Carroll's health finally broke at the end of 1897. He had returned to the Chestnuts in Guildford, as he did every year, to spend Christmas with his family, where he now continued to work on the second part of his *Symbolic Logic*, but by the start of January he had fallen ill with 'a feverish cold, of the bronchial type'. His worry that it might develop into pneumonia proved to be accurate. Within a week he had been confined to bed, where his breathing worsened and he had to be propped up with pillows. He had suffered from intermittent bronchial trouble for several years, but this time he would not recover. Towards the end he asked one of his sisters to read him a popular Victorian hymn that began:

> My God, my Father, while I stray,
> Far from my home, on life's rough way,

O teach me from my heart to say,
'Thy will be done.'

To another he said that his illness was a great trial of his patience. Soon it was over. 'Take away those pillows,' he said on 13 January, 'I shall need them no more', and at around half past two the following afternoon someone in his room noticed that he had stopped breathing. He was sixty-five years old.

Unsurprisingly, Carroll's relatives discovered that he had left his affairs neatly ordered. A four-page handwritten list of instructions directed that his coffin should be 'quite plain and simple', and that he would prefer 'a small plain head-stone' in Guildford cemetery; a short will appointed his brothers Wilfred and Edwin as joint executors, and divided up his estate equally between his surviving siblings. Edwin was away at the time of Carroll's death, so it was Wilfred's responsibility to write to Alice Hargreaves. The letter he sent on 30 January included a generous tribute to her father, who had died four days after Carroll, and reminded her of happy excursions on the river, 'where so many of [Carroll's] stories grew to maturity'. He also offered to return 'a good many photographs' of her that he had discovered among the 'curiosities and treasures' in his brother's Christ Church rooms, and asked if he could keep one to remember 'the original pilgrim into Wonderland'. Finally, he thanked her for the beautiful wreath she had sent, which 'still lies on his grave in one of the prettiest parts of the cemetery'.

While Alice's wreath marked a solid full stop to her relationship with Carroll, the stories it had generated continued to enjoy a flourishing afterlife. By 1898, more than 150,000 Wonderlands and 100,000 Looking-Glasses were in circulation, and a poll conducted that year in the Pall Mall Gazette on 'What Children Like to Read' revealed that the winner (a verdict 'so natural that it will surprise no normal person') was Alice's Adventures in Wonderland, with Through the Looking-Glass coming a respectable eleventh. That would have pleased Carroll, as would the revelation that The History of Sandford and Merton, an earlier bestseller and one of the earnest moral fables his stories had supplanted, 'scored not a solitary vote'. But probably nothing would have pleased him more than the comment made by the doctor who confirmed his death. Coming back downstairs where the family was gathered, he told them that the years had melted away from Carroll's face: 'How wonderfully young your brother looks!'

*

Thirty-five

On 28 January 1898, Wilfred Dodgson arrived at Christ Church to clear the rooms his brother had lived in for the past thirty years, and on opening the door to Tom 7:6 he quickly realized the size of his task. The scene before him was a cross between an archive and a junk shop. Carroll's colleague Vere Bayne, who put Wilfred up in his spare room, reported in his diary that 'he is appalled at the mass of papers &c', and the infinitely flexible nature of that '&c' reflected the full range of material left behind by a man who had not always found it easy to distinguish between collecting and hoarding. There were scores of green cardboard boxes in which Carroll had kept records of everything, including summaries of his own records – thick drifts of paper he had both created and fought to control. His famous cupboards were still full of toys and mechanical gadgets, now silently gathering dust, and there

Carroll's study at Christ Church

was also the aftermath of his photographic hobby to deal with, such as the studio, long disused but still perched on the roof of Tom Quad, which had to be dismantled and removed. With the college authorities keen to reassign the rooms to a new inhabitant, Wilfred worked with an efficiency that might have impressed Carroll himself. A selection of mementoes such as Arthur Hughes's painting *Lady with the Lilacs*, and private papers such as his journals, were retrieved for the Dodgson family or various close friends, and sacks of other papers were taken away to be burned. Everything else was to be sold locally on 10 and 11 May by the Oxford auction house E. J. Brooks.

Reflecting on this sale in a poem, a fellow Student at Christ Church grumbled that it was wrong to have the 'Poor playthings of the man that's gone' made 'The prey of every greedy hand'. A more fitting end, he suggested, would have been to pile up Carroll's possessions, place his body on top and consign the whole lot to the flames: 'Better by far the Northman's pyre, | That burnt in one sky-soaring fire | The man with all he held most dear.' However, that sort of heroic bonfire was unlikely to find much favour in Oxford, and instead more than 900 lots were wheeled out in Holywell Music Room and sold to the highest bidder, starting with the 18-foot-square Turkish carpet from Carroll's sitting room, and moving on to smaller curios that included a plaster bust of a child, Thomas Heaphy's oil painting *Dreaming of Fairy-Land*, a magnifying glass, a set of chess pieces, 'various photo albums', a human skull, two Whitely Exercisers, a bundle of walking sticks, and 'Fancy costumes for photographic purposes'. Some of the sale prices would make a modern collector weep with envy: a first edition of *Alice's Adventures in Wonderland* with a handwritten poem to 'M.A.B.' (Ellen Terry's daughter) fetched £50, and after 'spirited competition' a first edition of *Through the Looking-Glass* initialled by Carroll was sold for £20. (By comparison, the copy of *Alice's Adventures in Wonderland* marked up by Carroll for *The Nursery "Alice"* was auctioned by Christie's in 1998 for $1.54 million, making it at the time the most expensive children's book ever sold.) After Brooks's commission was deducted, Carroll's possessions fetched a grand total of £902 2s. 3d.

If the contents of Carroll's rooms scattered in all directions, the surviving members of his family exercised a much tighter control over his memory. Carroll had said nothing in public about a biography – appointing an official biographer or trying to frustrate the work of other writers might equally have been interpreted as a sign of pride – and none of his brothers and sisters felt able to take on such a daunting task. Instead, they passed it on to Stuart Dodgson Collingwood, Carroll's nephew and a former Christ Church undergraduate, who had known him well but not too well, and could therefore be trusted to assemble a book without allowing his judgement either to be clouded by sentiment or sharpened by thoughts of revenge. Sitting down to cut and paste his way through the papers that Wilfred Dodgson had saved from the flames, he completed his task with impressive speed. On 22 August 1898, he advertised in *The Times* for copies of any interesting letters sent by Carroll 'and also any reminiscences of him, anecdotes about him, &c.' and the finished biography was in bookshops before Christmas. Drawing on his family's memories and files of unpublished writings, including the early magazines, Collingwood produced a book that was ambitious in scope but modest in tone. Perhaps recognizing that his uncle's sharp wit did not run in the family (Collingwood's one attempt at levity was a reference to tobacco as 'the harmless but unnecessary weed'), he confined himself to stitching together long quotations from Carroll's writings with a brisk chronological narrative. The result was a story in which the main character kept having the last word. Indeed, anyone who had known Carroll might have wondered whether this was really a biography at all; at times it seemed more like an autobiography that had been ghosted from beyond the grave.

Collingwood's *Life and Letters* was published on the cusp of a period that would see a new type of biography starting to compete with the usual Victorian approach, at once weighty and insubstantial, that Gladstone had dismissed as 'a Reticence in three volumes'. Already J. A. Froude had published his unsparing life of Thomas Carlyle, in which he had revealed that the great sage was probably impotent and that he treated his wife with a lofty indifference interspersed by episodes of bruising domestic violence. Within twenty years, this swell of interest in biography that poked around in the most intimate parts of its subject's life would produce gossipy volumes such as *Stories of Authors' Loves* (1904) and the more notorious *Eminent Victorians* (1918), a series of biographical portraits in which Lytton Strachey cheerfully unpicked the legends that individuals such as General Gordon and Florence Nightingale had woven around themselves. Collingwood's book, by contrast, exemplified a more traditional style of biography that followed a subject's funeral with 'the slamming of doors' and 'the scrubbing of marble'. Whereas the real subjects of some later biographies would be the living rather than the dead – *Eminent Victorians* is just as revealing about Strachey as about the individuals whose lives he probes – Collingwood was modestly self-effacing. Allowing Carroll to 'tell his own story as much as possible', for his own linking passages he retreated into a prose style so unmemorable as to be practically anonymous.

Probably Collingwood's boldest choice was his title. Carroll's tombstone had relegated his pseudonym to a bracketed aside: engraved on the plain white marble cross was 'REV^D. CHARLES LUTWIDGE DODGSON. (LEWIS CARROLL.)' Collingwood reversed the relationship; the title page of his biography advertised it as:

THE
LIFE AND LETTERS
OF
LEWIS CARROLL
(REV. C. L. DODGSON)

His uncle had sometimes enjoyed playing on the idea that 'Carroll' and 'Dodgson' were two different people, telling one girl that 'A friend of mine called Mr. Lewis Carroll, tells me he means to send you a book. He is a very dear friend of mine. I have known him all my life – we are the same age and, of course, he was with me in the Gardens yesterday – not a yard off . . . I wonder if you saw him?' The same double identity could also provoke him into more waspish behaviour. One visiting American journalist was flatly told, 'You are not speaking to "Lewis Carroll"', and his publisher or Christ Church colleagues were sometimes asked to write third-person replies to unwanted letters on his behalf. In 1890, he even arranged for a circular to be printed explaining that 'He neither claims nor acknowledges any connection with any pseudonym, or with any book that is not published under his own name', which pushed implication as far as it would go without crumbling into an outright lie.

Yet although many people took him at his word, including the editors of the first *Who's Who*, published in the year of his death, in which separate entries were given to Lewis Carroll and Charles Dodgson, Carroll himself frequently blurred the distinction. He introduced himself to other children as Dodgson and then sent them letters and books signed Carroll; indeed, one letter to a girl in 1875 was signed 'Your affectionate friends, Lewis Carroll and C. L. Dodgson'. Usually he preserved 'Dodgson' for his academic work and 'Carroll' for his popular writings, but even this distinction could be wobbly: *Curiosa Mathematica Part II* (1893) was by 'Charles L. Dodgson'; *Symbolic Logic Part I* (1896) was by 'Lewis Carroll'. Inevitably these twin personalities have been viewed as a more benign version of Jekyll and Hyde, with the same person alternating between jolly children's entertainer and dour don. In fact, most of the time they were more like a double act of comedian and stooge who collaborated in almost everything they wrote. The 'Dodgson' who was known to his colleagues turned out a steady stream of satirical squibs on everything from the temporary housing for the new belfry at Christ Church (he was against it) to the University's plan to allow games of cricket on its Parks (he was against this too), but even his most stubbornly conservative arguments crackled with mischievous wit. The *Alice* books took the same approach from the opposite direction. Here nonsense was not a rejection of sense but a way of encouraging it to give a clearer account of itself, and as a result even the most absurd situations were braced by logic; a figure like Humpty Dumpty, who viewed from one perspective is an Oxford egghead in disguise, is funny principally because he keeps trying to apply the rules of the classroom to an ordinary conversation.

The idea that writers were multiform creatures had become even more popular by the time Collingwood sat down to compile his biography, with many influential literary figures claiming that the person who went to parties and swapped gossip was not the same as the one who wrestled with words on the page. In Henry James's short story 'The Private Life' (1892), when the narrator stumbles upon a famous writer sitting by himself in the dark, immediately after seeing him in conversation somewhere else, he concludes that the only possible explanation is that '"There are two of them"', a bourgeois socialite and a literary genius, who have nothing in common beyond their name and physical appearance. But if Collingwood was sometimes uncertain how to negotiate his uncle's double identity – in five successive pages towards the end of his book, he refers to 'Mr. Dodgson', 'Lewis Carroll', 'Mr. Dodgson', 'Lewis Carroll' and finally 'Mr. Dodgson' again, like someone spinning a coin – he knew which version most people wanted to read about.

Punch's appreciation of Carroll had taken the form of a poem that opened with the triumphant apostrophe 'Lover of children! Fellow-heir with those | Of whom the imperishable kingdom is!', and although the phrase 'Lover of children!' was potentially awkward, Collingwood understood that he would have to explain why it was Carroll rather than one of his contemporaries who had managed to retain the attention of so many young readers. His response was to turn his uncle into something like the patron saint of childhood. *Life and Letters* was dedicated 'TO THE CHILD-FRIENDS OF LEWIS CARROLL', and it ended with seventy pages devoted to their reminiscences. It also hinted that Carroll's attraction to children was a force as powerful and unavoidable as gravity. In the chapter that deals with the writing of *Alice's Adventures in Wonderland*, an anecdote of Carroll telling stories to some open-mouthed children, 'his knee covered with minute toys', is swiftly followed by a holiday in Freshwater where he is seen 'taking great interest in the children who, for him, were the chief attraction of the seaside', and then a scene in which a four-year-old actress climbs on to his lap to tell him how she longs to act the part of 'Miss Mite'. Viewed in this context, the *Alice* books were merely an attempt to fix in print what Carroll had been doing privately for years.

Such anecdotes worked as extra advertisements for the appeal to establish a suitable memorial to Carroll, following the suggestion made by 'a little friend . . . the daughter of one who was in her childhood his little friend also', that the most fitting tribute would be a sponsored cot in his name at the children's hospital in Great Ormond Street. The organizing committee included Alice Hargreaves (who donated £10 10s.) alongside many others who had played important roles in Carroll's life, including Sir John Tenniel, Xie Kitchin, Frederick Macmillan and Beatrice Hatch. Further contributors included George MacDonald (£2 2s.), Jerome K. Jerome (£1 1s.), W. M. Rossetti (£1 10s.), the pupils of several girls' schools, and a few wags who chose to adopt pseudonyms such as Bill the Lizard, the Cheshire Cat, the Slithy Toves and the Mock Turtle. Within two months of the appeal being launched at the end of February 1898, it had raised the £1,000 required – more than the amount generated by the auction of all Carroll's possessions. Perhaps that is why 'there was not such a large attendance as might have been expected' at Holywell Music Room in May. Readers did not need to queue up to purchase a keepsake from his library when they already carried his most important books around inside them.

A few months later, when Collingwood was piecing together his biography, he adopted a similar line of thought. While he was careful to acknowledge the richness of his uncle's life, especially his talent for friendship and his wide social circle, he quickly realized that most people were interested in Carroll chiefly as the man who had written *Alice's Adventures in Wonderland*. Published almost exactly halfway between Carroll's birth in 1832 and his death in 1898, it was the hinge on which his career had turned, and in Collingwood's biography it therefore became both an entrance into his life and a suitable exit from it. A few pages into the first chapter of *Life and Letters*, Carroll's boyhood in Croft-on-Tees is recalled as a period when it seemed that he 'actually lived in that charming "Wonderland" which he afterwards described so vividly', with stories of him peeling rushes to give the pith 'to the poor', and encouraging earthworms to fight 'by supplying them with small pieces of pipe'. At the end of his life, Collingwood affirmed, Carroll had now passed into 'that "Wonderland" which outstrips all our dreams and hopes'. From the mysterious realm of childhood to his religious faith, in Collingwood's view

Wonderland was the soil from which everything else in Carroll's life had sprouted.

Not everyone approved of attempts to gather together private recollections of Carroll into a shared cultural memory, like individual bricks being assembled into a grand public monument. 'I have no *"reminiscences"* whatever of either Lewis Carroll, or in connection with "Alice", to give,' an annoyed Tenniel told a correspondent who had sent him a 'Wonderland' calendar in 1899, adding that 'in plain truth I shrink at the mere mention of "Alice in Wonderland"'. That was a trifle disingenuous, because earlier in the year he had gone back to the same characters for a political cartoon in *Punch* entitled 'Alice in Bumbleland', published in the 8 March issue, which depicted the Conservative MP Arthur Balfour dressed as Alice and peeking out coyly from behind a government bill. Tenniel's refusal placed him in a very small minority. Many dozens of people felt the need to respond to Carroll's death in some way, and how they did so reflected the unusual place he had come to occupy in the public imagination.

Because of the relationship Carroll had built up with his readers over the years, as several journalists pointed out, his death was felt 'almost like a personal loss', yet even to those who knew him best he was practically a stranger. In this respect, he contrasted strongly with other popular writers. When Dickens died in 1870 his grave in Westminster Abbey was left open for two days, and at the end of the first day a thousand people were still waiting to pay their respects. This reflected his public visibility as well as his literary fame, because if everyone felt they knew Dickens from his writing, many people had also seen him performing one of his barnstorming public readings, or glimpsed him briskly walking through London scanning the streets for characters he could pluck from life and insert into his fiction. Carroll, by contrast, had been willing to acknowledge his literary identity only when he was alone, carefully constructing it in his study out of paper and ink, so it was appropriate that the place where mourners congregated most thickly was not beside his grave in Guildford, but on the page.

Alongside the usual letters of condolence received by his family, there were dozens of obituaries published in the British and American press.

Almost all of these were generous, even if one or two speculated that Lewis Carroll (rather than Charles Dodgson) had probably died several years earlier, if plodding stories like *Sylvie and Bruno* were any kind of guide. Yet what was most notable about the obituaries was how often they borrowed from each other, as if engaged in a form of higher gossip, and how keen they were to introduce unexpected snippets of new information: the dodo was entirely his invention; he wrote a book entitled *In a Looking-glass*; and so on. Alice was also put through the news-gathering mangle: she was variously reported to have 'died young', 'long been dead', inspired Carroll to write so that he could 'amuse the weary hours of a sick child', and been brought up in Llandudno. Practically the only thing everyone could agree on was that by now Wonderland was 'so well known' it had taken up a unique place at the heart of English literature.

Carroll's death heralded the start of two different versions of the story of Alice, because while his books were now firmly established in nurseries and living rooms around the world, the main source of information on how they had come to be written remained Collingwood's account. It was a story that would become increasingly familiar as later biographers got to work on Carroll's life, picking up stray barnacles of rumour along the way, but not for another thirty years would Alice Hargreaves become known more widely as the 'real' Alice. In the meantime, she restricted herself to a short paragraph in the *Life and Letters* that explained how *Alice's Adventures Under Ground* had emerged from an appeal made to Carroll one summer afternoon to '"Tell us a story."' Other than that she remained at Cuffnells and kept silent.

There were plenty of new Alices willing to take her place. During Christmas 1898, a revival of Henry Savile Clarke's adaptation of *Alice in Wonderland* was staged at the Opera Comique Theatre in London; soon this included the bonus of a miniature *Theatre News* printed nightly and given away to the audience between acts. The first issue, on 4 February 1899, carried 'A Letter from Alice' written by the twelve-year-old actress playing the lead, in which she confessed, 'I always fancy I am the real Alice.' She was not alone in having such thoughts. The same year also saw the publication of a memoir written by the actress who had performed the role in 1888, and the title page of her book asserted her credentials just as strongly:

THE STORY OF
LEWIS CARROLL

TOLD FOR YOUNG PEOPLE BY
THE REAL ALICE IN WONDERLAND

MISS ISA BOWMAN

Nor was it only those with first-hand acquaintance with Carroll who viewed themselves as the true heirs of his dream-child. For the obituary writer of *The Academy*, this was because Carroll had written about a human type rather than an individual: 'Alice is a matter-of-fact, simple-minded child, and the world is full of Alices, and always will be.' Others were not so sure. Many readers felt that in the *Alice* books Carroll, while speaking to them as a group, also spoke for them as individuals; seeing Wonderland through Alice's eyes was the next best thing to being able to look inside their own heads. Or, as the author of a 1901 article put it, Carroll's success as a children's author was not simply a reward for his 'daring and original' imagination or 'brilliant' wit. He succeeded because everything that happens to Alice his readers could imagine happening to themselves, even if it was the sort of thing that only made sense inside the impossible world of Carroll's stories: 'We are all "Alices" more or less.'

*

Thirty-six

A week after Carroll's death, Henry Liddell's replacement as Dean of Christ Church, the Rt Revd Francis Paget, preached a sermon in which he noted how few authors had written books that had 'travelled as widely, and reached as many minds'. That was partly a matter of geography. If the *Alice* books were stories of imaginary exploration, they had also been adopted by those venturing into equally hostile environments in the real world; in 1901, copies of both books would be included in the small library on board Captain Scott's ship the *Discovery*, allowing his crew to while away the long Antarctic winters with adventures that replaced confinement with escapism, ice with Alice. But Paget's claim also reflected how deeply the *Alice* books had penetrated the wider literary culture. The market for what Carroll had referred to in 1891 as 'books of the *Alice* type' was still expanding, and more writers than ever before were adopting his narrative template of departure–adventure– return. Walter Burges Smith's *Looking for Alice* (1904), for example, centres on a little girl named Harriet who goes in search of her favourite story- book character, having 'often thought how nice it would be if only Alice could come and play with her', but is forced to endure lessons in spelling and grammar before the Red Queen tells her that Alice can only survive if she is kept within the strictly controlled conditions of a book: '"there she is always young and fresh and bright; the same little Alice whom your mother and father knew when they were little children of your own age, when they also started on the journey along the Royal Road to Learning to find Alice and her Wonderland for themselves!"' The story ends with Harriet opening up her copy and stepping inside. But although this is offered as a loving homage, on the understanding that 'Alice's Wonderland [is a good] place for every human child to dwell in for at least a little time', one might wonder how roughly Harriet would have played with Alice if they had met in person. Is she trying to find Alice or to supplant her?

One of Alice's initial fears in Wonderland is that she has been replaced by a doppelgänger, as she thinks over 'all the children she knew that were of the same age as herself, to see if she could have been changed for any of them'. In the years immediately after Carroll's death, this started to look uncannily like a premonition. Now that he was no longer in control of Alice's fate, she could be changed for any number of alternative children. Carroll's own stories continued to be the standard against which all successors would be measured, but alongside his original heroine there was now a growing army of pseudo-Alices that threatened to blur the sharp outlines of a character he had fought tirelessly to protect while he was alive. And together these narrative offshoots and postscripts created the curious phenomenon of a literary figure who was becoming more complex not within a single work, by revealing more of herself with each turn of the page, but by generating extra versions of herself.

This had the potential to create confusion. One of the more unusual criminal cases tried at the Old Bailey in 1896 involved two men who were charged with passing forged banknotes supplied by the Wonderland Co., Buenos Aires, and the line between authentic and fake documents soon became equally shifty in relation to the *Alice* books. A good example is provided by the fate of another popular fictional character: Pinocchio. Having originally been translated into English in 1891, *The Story of a Puppet; or, The Adventures of Pinocchio* first crossed the Atlantic in 1892, at which point the president of its American publisher Cassell embezzled the company's money and fled the country. In 1898, the story reappeared in an edition published by the Boston firm Jordan Marsh, which fraudulently tried to copyright the material, and this time the title page announced it as *Pinocchio's Adventures in Wonderland*. On one level this was simply an advertising gimmick, but for anyone who read the book it might also have served as a warning. While Pinocchio was a puppet struggling to become a real boy, the publisher was pretending that his story had been an imitation all along.

Other new works took up a wide range of stances in relation to the *Alice* books. Some of these, such as the political comedies published by H. H. Munro ('Saki') in the *Westminster Gazette* between 1900 and 1902, followed the example set by earlier satires by assuming a thorough knowledge of Carroll's original text: the March Hare tells Alice that his watch is '"dreadfully behind the times"', and the Hatter casts a gloomy eye on the Boer campaign by singing '"Dwindle, dwindle, little war."' More straightforward was the desire to come up with further adventures, as if trying to make up for the fact that Carroll had only written two *Alice* books rather than a whole shelf of them. John Rae's *New Adventures of "Alice"* (1917) is typical, because his title refers to Carroll's books rather than Alice herself. Dedicated to readers 'who have loved "Alice" and wished there were more', it begins with a young girl named Betsy asking, '"Isn't there another book about Alice, mother?"' before dreaming that she discovers one in her attic. Betsy settles down to read it, and 'In her dream she seemed to change and become dear, quaint little Alice herself, and to be *living* and *acting* in the story, instead of simply reading it.' Nothing she discovers in Wonderland is very unusual – there are nonsense rhymes, a pun-hungry poet who persuades her to grab hold of an arrow as it whizzes past her ear so that he can tell her she has had '"An arrow escape"', and so on – but Rae's decision to replace 'Alice' with 'Betsy' (a straightforward move from A to B) suggested that Carroll's character was now thought to be a role anyone could take on.

Far more successful were adaptations like Winsor McCay's popular comic strip 'Little Nemo in Slumberland', which originally ran in the *New York Herald* between 1905 and 1911, and treated the bare outline of Carroll's plot like an empty box that could be filled with new material. Each episode began with a little boy named Nemo falling asleep, which was the cue for him to travel to strange places and meet even stranger creatures in his dreams. Beginning just five years after Freud published *The Interpretation of Dreams*, Nemo's adventures crackled with dangers that seem just as real to him as Alice's do to her, but were also teasingly symbolic: in just the first couple of strips, he charges across the sky on a huge horse ('her spunk was up') before being thrown off, and is then crushed by a forest of huge mushrooms that collapse on top of him; in the third strip he tries to walk on giant stilts before falling off and almost getting impaled. The unconscious turned out to be another version of Wonderland – a place that gave the impression of being chaotically lawless, while secretly working according to its own rules.

A family resemblance with Carroll's stories was even more obvious in the many other books published between his death and the First World War which added a new twist to the formula 'X in Y Land': *Alice's Adventures in Pictureland* (1900), *Alice in Motorland* (1904), *Alice in Plunderland* (1910), *Alys in Happyland* (1913), *Malice in Kulturland* (1915), in addition to the characters who shared everything with Alice but her name, as they busied themselves exploring Merryland (1901), Emblemland (1902), Monsterland (1902), Fantasma Land (1904), Thunderland (1905), Rainbowland (1911), Justnowland (1912) and, in an unusual concession to realism, Cambridge (1913). Once they had detached themselves from his plots, Carroll's ideas could travel more widely and reach more minds than ever before.

Wonderland also continued to enjoy a multiple identity under its own name. The idea that it was a miscellaneous environment, where very little remained the same for long, encouraged writers who wanted to assemble children's anthologies such as *Days in Wonderland* (1910; in one story there is a brief encounter with Tweedledum and Tweedledee), and comics such as *Wonderful Tales*, the first number of which in 1919 opened with a complete story, 'Dicky in Fairyland and His Wonderful Adventures There', before moving on to a lucky dip of riddles, handy hints ('How to Make a Parachute'), a Grand Colouring Competition, and cartoon strips that ranged from the whimsical ('The Doings of those Darling Ducks') to the jarringly racist ('That Naughty Nigger and his Bunny Bimbo'). More imaginative were a few attempts to show that there might be as many different Wonderlands as there were children to dream them up. Mary Stewart's *The Way to Wonderland* (1920) begins in typical post-*Alice* fashion, as dreaming Billy is invited by some fairies with whirring wings to enter '"Fairy Land, or Wonderland, or whatever you choose to call it"'. Not until the end of the story is the moral spelled out, as Billy and his sister listen to the North Wind telling them that if they can hold on to the sense of beauty and joy they feel at Christmas, "'you have found the way, you can never really lose it – the way to Wonderland!'"

Such stories worked like shadowy alternatives to the usual publications that were bought by readers caught up in the new fashion for literary tourism. Visiting the places associated with popular books had become a thriving hobby in the nineteenth century. Ethel Arnold's article about Carroll's Christ Church rooms in 1890 was just one of many attempts to describe the homes of famous authors; others included William Howitt's *Homes and Haunts of the Most Eminent British Poets* (1847), and the *Idler* series 'Lions in their Dens' or the *World*'s 'Celebrities at Home'. Many readers insisted on making literary pilgrimages of their own, and in her study of the cult that grew up around the Brontë family, Lucasta Miller points out how far some were prepared to go in order to prove their devotion. The American collector Charles Hale, for example, purchased various fragments of wood from Haworth Parsonage, from which he made photograph frames that were glazed with the glass from Charlotte's bedroom window, so that he could look at his pictures 'through the same medium through which Charlotte Brontë saw the dreary landscape before her window'. Nor was he alone in deciding that the best way to understand how a writer's mind worked was to follow in their physical footsteps. By 1895, Haworth was attracting 10,000 summer visitors every year, who could peer at other literary relics gathered together in a newly opened museum above the Yorkshire Penny Bank, before going off to traipse romantically across the moors. Some of the later attempts to exploit this Brontëmania were in much worse taste; Miller gives the example of 'Brontë Natural Spring Water', sold in bottles in the early 1990s with a label that alluded to 'the moorlands which were the playground of the Brontë children', presumably hoping consumers would be unaware that the Parsonage's own water supply was surrounded by a large cemetery that was the perfect breeding ground for typhoid.

Wonderland was more complicated as a site of literary pilgrimage than Brontë country, because although travel writers continued to apply the word to impressive natural landscapes – among the places that were described as genuine wonderlands in books published during the twenty years after Carroll's death were Iceland, several parts of America, India, Mexico and Cornwall – for most people it was not a real place overlaid with literary associations but an idea. That made it impossible to explore while reciting Carroll's best lines, as other tourists could wander across the Yorkshire moors pretending to be Heathcliff or Cathy, but infinitely flexible as a way of adding a sparkle of enchantment to otherwise perfectly ordinary locations. Even the great British seaside was not exempt. Playfully reversing the tourist cliché 'See Naples and die', a magazine advertisement in 1903 offered 'See BLACKPOOL and Live', and under a drawing that purportedly showed 'Blackpool in July – Beautiful Weather', it boasted of the resort's attractions: 'The ideal holiday spot. Every taste gratified. Everything to please everybody. A wonderland by the waves.' With enough determination, Wonderland could be reshaped to fit just about anywhere.

Within a few years, something similar had started to happen to Alice too. While the text of Carroll's stories was now fixed, with minor exceptions such as a 'Little Folks' Edition' of *Alice's Adventures in Wonderland* published in 1903, and a more radically simplified version in 1905 that was 'Retold in Words of One Syllable' (this posed a challenge for important words such as 'Alice' and 'Wonderland'), her appearance was far less stable. In December 1907, *Punch* published a cartoon captioned 'Tenniel's "Alice" Reigns Supreme' that showed the character familiar from the original illustrations sitting on a throne and looking suitably regal, while at her feet clustered various other girls – a scrawny teenager and three figures as blank-faced as dolls – with '"Alice"' written over their heads. The original Alice asks, '"Who are all these funny little people?"' and when the Hatter tells her they are imitators, she responds with the Carrollian catchphrase '"Curiouser and curiouser!"' The cartoon was a loyal defence of Tenniel by the magazine that had employed him for so many years, but it also revealed that his version of Alice was in danger of being usurped. British copyright on *Alice's Adventures in Wonderland* had lapsed earlier that year, and as a result many new editions – at least thirteen in 1907 alone – were rushed into print, to compete with designs that over the previous forty-two years had become as familiar as Carroll's text. In the Christmas

1907 issue of the weekly journal *Black and White*, Arthur Rackham depicted a crowded book party where characters from popular children's books mingled under the mistletoe, and he reserved more than a quarter of his cartoon for Tenniel's figures. Interestingly, however, few of his rivals had sufficient confidence to break with Tenniel's example altogether. When deciding how to depict Carroll's most popular characters they often borrowed details that Tenniel had invented, such as the fact that the Hatter actually wears a hat, and as a result the final illustrations tended to look more like artistic sequels than genuinely original works.

Compared to Tenniel's sharply etched domestic world of chimney pots and boot-scrapers, most of the environments depicted in these new editions were hazily indistinct. The most fully realized landscapes were to be found in Rackham's watercolours, where Wonderland became a muddy-coloured place full of tree stumps that appeared to be twisting and straining, as if trying to uproot themselves from the background and become part of the action. Yet even Rackham's black-and-white illustrations melted away at their edges, reminding us that in Carroll's story each detail of Wonderland exists only at the moment Alice dreams about it. Most of the other illustrators also chose to depict a largely featureless Wonderland, and this provided a helpfully neutral backdrop against which their different versions of Alice could be displayed, although in each case the Tenniel cartoon in *Punch* turned out to be an accurate forecast of how likely they were to displace Queen Alice from her throne. All chose to make her appearance less stagey than in Tenniel's illustrations, but otherwise they struck off in different visual directions. Some decided to keep her as a little girl, or, in the case of the chubby toddler depicted by Bessie Pease, even made her appear younger. At the other extreme, Thomas Maybank turned her into a gangly teenager who could easily pass as an adult in some pictures, so that when she was shown in the middle of the courtroom at the end of the story she looked less like a child than an ineffective teacher being ignored by her pupils.

The most important decision readers had to make in 1907 was not how old they thought Alice was, but whether or not they wanted her to be their contemporary. To buy a traditional edition with Tenniel's illustrations was to choose an Alice whose stiff poses looked especially unnatural in a world where Victorian fashions were slowly being replaced by clothing that was designed to mimic the shape of the body, rather than avoid it through liberal use of whalebone and crinoline. It meant that visually she was no longer a reader's representative in the story. Yet this was not altogether a bad thing. If reading about Alice in her original form was partly an exercise in nostalgia, it also added an extra air of strangeness to her perception of the world. It made Wonderland seem less like a fictional leisure resort than a place that was always just out of reach. Buying an edition like the one illustrated by Charles Robinson, on the other hand, which included eight colour plates and more than a hundred striking black-and-white images strongly influenced by art nouveau design, brought Alice into a world much closer to *The Yellow Book* than to *Punch*. It is true that Robinson's Alice might have looked familiar to anyone who had seen some of Carroll's early photographs of Alice Liddell, because both girls sported a neat chestnut bob rather than long blonde hair, but otherwise his illustrations worked to bring Carroll's story into the twentieth century.

This question of whether Alice was Victorian or modern reflected more than changing attitudes towards a single fictional character. It was also a way of thinking more broadly about what joined or separated the nineteenth and twentieth centuries. Contemporary writers often drew upon the *Alice* books when they wanted to consider how far the modern world had managed to outgrow its past. This was not always a conscious process. In 1919, for example, Sir Arthur Conan Doyle was famously fooled by two young girls into believing that they had photographed a number of fairies two years earlier in the West Yorkshire village of Cottingley. As a devoted spiritualist, he did not need much convincing, and his critical faculties were soon overwhelmed. Excitedly he announced his findings in an article published in the Christmas 1920 issue of *Strand* magazine, following it up with another article in March 1921. His desire to believe that some fragments of the country's past had survived the twin modern ravages of industrialization and war, and that children still had the sensitive eyes required to see these mysterious gauzy creatures, was

'Alice' and the Cottingley fairies (1917)

simply too strong to resist. (The photographs had first been brought to public attention in 1919 at a meeting of the Theosophical Society in Bradford, and the appearance of fairies to young people also matched some central tenets of theosophy, such as the belief that nature was surging with invisible life, and that developing more acute powers of perception was an important stage in humanity's spiritual evolution.) The rest of the story was sadly predictable: Doyle's articles were greeted with a mixture of eager acceptance and scoffing rejection by the *Strand*'s readers, and only many decades later did the hoaxers finally confess that their fairy friends were actually book illustrations they had copied on to cardboard and propped up with hairpins. Largely lost in the controversy was the pseudonym that Doyle chose for the younger girl, who was ten years old when the first photograph was taken, in which she could be seen posing in a wooded glen while four fairies with elaborate butterfly wings frolicked before her eyes. He could have chosen any name in the telephone directory, or even used her real name, Frances, as he did in 1922 when he reworked his articles into the book *The Coming of the Fairies*. Instead he called her Alice. Pictured on a bank of earth, and surrounded by fantasy creatures, she was another Alice in another Wonderland.

*

Thirty-seven

Carroll's Wonderland is a place where nothing is quite what it seems. From the white roses that the Queen's gardeners are frantically painting red, to words that crack open into puns or give way like trapdoors when put under any pressure, almost everything appears to be something else in disguise. By the time Alice reaches Looking-Glass Land, even an apparently straightforward word such as 'meaning' has become hazily uncertain: in a single meeting, Alice and Humpty Dumpty use the word no fewer than twenty-six times in various forms (mean, means, meant, meaning) without ever managing to pin it down. 'Meaning' turns out to be as hard to grasp as the baby that turns into a pig and trots off into the wood.

By the end of the nineteenth century, some readers wondered whether Carroll's heroine was also in disguise, a refreshingly contemporary figure hidden underneath a starched Victorian exterior. An obituary of Carroll in the *Saturday Review* pointed out that she 'moves through her wonder-world with much of the modern spirit, which has now and then to be wholesomely repressed'. The notion that repression of any kind could be wholesome might sound surprising, although it was a standard idea at the time, bound up with a wider celebration of self-sacrifice in public service; hence Tennyson's dedication of *Idylls of the King* to the recently deceased Prince Albert, in which he praised the 'sublime repression of himself' that had distinguished a life 'modest, kindly, all-accomplished, wise'. It might sound even more surprising to anyone who recalls that both of Carroll's stories end with a violent outburst, as Alice's mask of polite interest slips and she unleashes the full force of her temper. However, for many later writers this was yet another reflection of her modern spirit, and as she moved into the twentieth century her stories

369

were used to explore some of the less personal forms of dissent that continued to simmer under the surface of social life.

The most radical literary reworking of the *Alice* books was probably Henry T. Schnittkind's *Alice and the Stork: A Fairy Tale for Workingmen's Children*, published in 1915 by a Boston press that also offered titles such as *The ABC of Socialism*. Adopting the same pro-suffrage line as some earlier commentators, Schnittkind extended it into a full socialist parable. Not only does his Alice grow up over the course of the narrative, ending it as a married woman with a child of her own, but she develops a thoroughly egalitarian viewpoint. Starting as a spoiled brat who believes that some people are poorer than others '"because they're lazy"', a series of fantasy adventures in which she rides on a rainbow and is told about the '"brave people"' who '"want all men to be Comrades"' allows her to develop a fully working heart. Once again, Wonderland is presented as a utopian dream that could be turned into reality if only enough people chose to follow fiction's example.

Other works were more subtle in their political arguments, but equally far-reaching in their ambitions. Several authors continued the trend for new stories that were closely modelled on the *Alice* books, and the best of these followed Carroll by muddling up established literary categories. In an influential study, Humphrey Carpenter has argued that there were two main streams of children's literature that 'divided in about 1860 and never really came together again until the 1950s'. On the one hand there was 'the breezy, optimistic adventure story, set firmly in the real world', such as R. L. Stevenson's *Treasure Island* (1883) or *Kidnapped* (1886); on the other hand there were the fantasy worlds of J. M. Barrie (Neverland), A. A. Milne (the Hundred Acre Wood) and others, which 'posited the existence of Arcadian societies remote from the nature and concerns of the everyday world', while commenting satirically on the conventions of that world. Wonderland and Looking-Glass Land fit neatly into this second category, but what distinguishes them is the fact that their central character has an understanding that remains firmly rooted in the everyday. Much of Carroll's comedy arises from the clash of these perspectives, and several later writers learned from his example.

One of Rudyard Kipling's stories in *Stalky and Co.* (1899) begins with the smart anti-establishment pupil Stalky receiving copies of F. W. Farrar's popular but tooth-grindingly dull schoolboy tales *Eric; or, Little by Little* (1858) and *St Winifred's* (1862) from his aunt, inscribed 'To dearest Artie, on his sixteenth birthday'. Having failed to pawn them, his next response is to read out selected passages to his friends, laughing in 'intimate and unholy' fashion at their ridiculous plots, and then to go hunting. Carroll enters the story when Stalky and his companions shoot a cat, and decide to revenge themselves on a loathed schoolmaster by hiding its rotting corpse inside the roof of his boarding house. The idea tickles them so much they launch into a chorus from 'Jabberwocky': '"Come to my arms, my beamish boy," carolled M'Turk, and they fell into each other's arms dancing. "Oh, frabjous day! Calloo, callay!"' Comparing a dead cat to the slaying of a mythical beast might seem inappropriate, but that is precisely Kipling's point. The crowing of the boys is like a miniature exercise in mock-heroic, as they puncture any pretence that their actions are noble or grand. That may be how the characters in most school stories behave, Kipling observes, but if so it is merely a delusion of sentimental clergymen like Farrar. It is certainly not an accurate reflection of what really motivates boys like Stalky.

A similar alliance of realism and fantasy was central to L. Frank Baum's *The Wonderful Wizard of Oz* (1900), which he began in 1898 while the newspapers were still full of articles about Carroll ('the quaint and clever old clergyman', as Baum later described him, though he also criticized the *Alice* books as 'rambling and incoherent'), and published in the same year as a collection of children's stories he entitled *A New Wonderland*. The 1939 MGM movie, which is where most people now encounter Oz for the first time, deliberately turned it into an updated American version of *Alice*: when Dorothy uses her magical ruby slippers to return to Kansas it transpires that she has dreamed the whole thing up after suffering a knock on the head, and all the major characters are based on people who surround her at home. '"You, and you, and you, and *you* were there,"' she exclaims, as neighbourly versions of the Tin Woodman, Scarecrow and Cowardly Lion cluster round her bed, and an uncostumed Wizard leans in through the window, all smiling good-naturedly as she insists "'it wasn't a dream'''. Nobody believes her. Yet Baum's original story had sided firmly with Dorothy. When the cyclone hits her house in the first chapter, there is a plausible meteorological explanation of how it could carry away such a large structure, and only after many hours of being buffeted along by the wind does she decide to go to sleep. That is, her journey to Oz is presented as a freak natural occurrence rather than a mind-voyage, and within a few pages the ordinary and extraordinary have become practically interchangeable. The existence of winged monkeys is made to seem no odder than the fact that the Emerald City is green only because the Wizard makes everyone there wear tinted spectacles.

However, it is not only through their influence on later children's books that *Alice's Adventures in Wonderland* and *Through the Looking-Glass* established themselves at the heart of much twentieth-century culture. They also provided a way of thinking about what it meant to be modern. This was by no means a straightforward matter. The early decades of the twentieth century are commonly referred to as a period of modernism, but although this has sometimes been presented as a clean break with the past, at the time it was experienced as something more like a mutiple fracture. While some writers undoubtedly agreed with Ezra Pound's announcement that the Victorian era was 'a stuffy alley-way which we can, for the most part, avoid', others were far less sure of their ground, and here the *Alice* books proved to be a helpful resource when deciding whether being modern meant abandoning the past or merely adapting it in more original ways.

Even before Carroll's death, *Alice* was being used as a reference point in arguments about the dangers of growing up too fast. At the start of 'The Prodigies' (1897), one of Willa Cather's early stories, a mother excuses her lateness by explaining that her children "'would not stay in the nursery and poor Elsie has lost her 'Alice in Wonderland' and wails without ceasing because nurse cannot repeat 'The Walrus and the Carpenter'.''' Her husband responds with bluff good humour by telling her, "'I should think everyone about this house could [repeat that poem]''', and confessing that "'I know the fool book like the catechism.''' (That his wife does not is obvious from the fact she has forgotten that 'The Walrus and the Carpenter' is actually from *Through the Looking-Glass*.) His comment offers as much of an insight into his character as his pity for the child singers they see perform later that evening, who are 'pitifully fragile' and seem 'tired out with life', the joy of childhood having been leached from them by their ambitious mother.

By 1901, when G. K. Chesterton published an essay entitled 'A Defence of Nonsense', a familiarity with Carroll's writing was assumed to have implications that stretched further than the psychological health of individuals. Ultimately it was a rare shaft of light in what Chesterton characterized as 'this twilight world of ours'. The literature of nonsense was one of the nineteenth century's greatest triumphs, he argued, because it gave readers a 'fresh, abrupt, and inventive' way of looking at life. Nor was it merely a Victorian relic. Nonsense was 'the literature of the future', he announced, because in teaching us to see a bird as 'a blossom broken loose from its chain of stalk', or a house as 'a gigantesque hat to cover a man from the sun', it released in us 'a sense of wonder' that had been lying dormant since childhood.

Chesterton's essay set the tone for much of what was to follow in the coming years. Roger Fry, who chose to attend Angelica Bell's Wonderland-themed eleventh birthday party in 1929 dressed as the White Knight (Virginia Woolf went as the March Hare, 'and mad at that'), singled out *Alice's Adventures in Wonderland* as one of only two 'jewels' that could be picked out of the 'mud' of Victorian culture, the other being Thackeray's fairy tale *The Rose and the Ring*. Everything else he dismissed as 'mawkish sentimental drivel'. Like the contemporary artists he championed, particularly Cézanne, Fry admired Alice because she saw things as they were, rather than through the filters imposed by those around her. Poets and novelists were equally attracted to the *Alice* books as they tried to refresh forms of expression that were suspected of having gone stale. When Ezra Pound grew bored with discussing *vers libre*, a poetic innovation that rapidly became a cliché tossed around by editors and critics, he chose an example from Carroll to separate himself from the herd: 'I have taken damn small part in the current diarrhoea of muck concerning "vers libre" (*ver* meaning worm and *slibre* meaning oozy and slippery . . . à la Alice in Wonderland),' he wrote in 1917. Borrowing material from the *Alice* books was a popular tactic for anyone who chose to adopt a similarly quizzical stance towards some of the other absurdities of literary life. In 1916, for example, Katherine Mansfield was invited to tea by D. H. Lawrence and his wife Frieda, and found herself in the middle of a violent row over the literary merits of Shelley. She confessed that 'I felt like Alice between the Cook and the Duchess. Saucepans and frying pans hurtled through the air. They ordered each other out of the house – and the atmosphere of HATE between them was so dreadful that I could not stand it; I had to run home. L. came to dinner with us the same evening, but Frieda would not come. He sat down and said: "I'll cut her throat if she comes near this table."' It is unusual for arguments about Shelley to generate this much passion, and Mansfield's choice of parallel reveals how ludicrous she thought the situation was.

Other writers treated the sheer strangeness of Carroll's stories as an invitation to put the whole of modern life into perspective. After Evelyn Waugh reread *Alice's Adventures in Wonderland* as an undergraduate ('It is an excellent book I think,' he told Tom Driberg in 1922), it became one of his standard narrative templates. In *Decline and Fall* (1928), this takes the form of a boarding school stocked with ludicrous characters, and a hero (Paul Pennyfeather) who after his 'fall' at Oxford seems to be as detached from real life as Alice is from the events that surround her. In effect, he is a naïve figure set adrift in a world that has lost its innocence, and on several occasions the parallels between Waugh and Carroll show just how much has changed. Sent to the red-light district of Marseilles, he arrives at a brothel called Chez Alice, and when he ends up in prison a former teacher from the school working there as a chaplain meets a grisly death by being decapitated by a religious maniac. 'Off with his head' indeed. Similarly, *Vile Bodies* (1930) opens with two epigraphs from *Through the Looking-Glass*, and once again the novel features a world that seems no less hallucinatory and chaotic than the one Alice encounters. However, it was not until *Brideshead Revisited* (1945) that the full force of Carroll's impact on Waugh became clear, as his narrator Charles Ryder recalls preparing to attend an undergraduate lunch party, significantly in Christ Church, in

1923. 'I went full of curiosity,' he explains, 'and the faint, unrecognised apprehension that here, at last, I should find that low door in the wall, which others, I knew, had found before me, which opened on an enclosed and enchanted garden.' It is there that he is introduced to a social circle through which he will eventually be taken to Brideshead, the family home of his host Sebastian Flyte, a place that will later be carelessly damaged by the army during the Second World War but in his memory remains perfectly beautiful. The allusion to Alice's first glimpse of Wonderland is therefore entirely appropriate. It works like a little entrance into another enclosed and enchanted world that is now as untouchable as a dream.

The earliest appearances of *Alice* on film revealed even more of the continuities between twentieth-century culture and its Victorian roots. The later history of the Wonderland theatre on the Whitechapel Road is typical. Although moving pictures had been shown there as early as April 1896, in the form of a disappointingly blurry 'Theatrograph', it soon became more famous as the boxing venue where Canadian fighter Tommy Burns defended his world heavyweight title against Newcastle's Jack Palmer on 10 February 1908, before the theatre burned to the ground in 1911. After being rebuilt, it continued to operate occasionally as a film venue, and in 1921 it reopened as the 2,000-seater Rivoli Cinema. If the alteration of a theatre to a cinema seems emblematic, it is not only because film had long since overtaken live drama as the most popular form of public entertainment. By then, Carroll's reinvented Wonderland attracted its biggest audiences on screen. Already three different film adaptations had appeared, in 1903, 1910 and 1915, and although this was not as many as some other literary works (by 1915 there had been six versions of *Jane Eyre* and nine *Dr Jekyll and Mr Hydes*), the cinema was an especially welcoming home for a figure like Alice.

That is not to say these early films were wholly successful. All three suffered from the same underlying problem: whereas a book's illustrations capture selected narrative snapshots and ask readers to fill in the blanks, film leaves very little to the imagination. If every reader's Wonderland is slightly different, every viewer's Wonderland is essentially the same. Inevitably this produces a certain visual thinness in the films themselves.

Alice in Wonderland (dir. Percy Stow and Cecil M. Hepworth, 1903)

In the nine minutes of scratchy action that survive of the 1903 version (dir. Percy Stow and Cecil M. Hepworth), which at 800 feet was then the longest British film yet produced, the appearance of Wonderland alternates between some creaky stage sets and outdoor shots in which cows graze placidly in the distance like unpaid extras. The accidental comedy of this is echoed in the way Carroll's animal characters are dealt with: although the White Rabbit is an actor in a furry suit, the Cheshire Cat is a real ginger tom filmed sitting in a shrubbery and looking miserably resigned to its fate.

The 52-minute 1915 version (dir. W. W. Young) attempted a more sophisticated approach: a title card explained that 'The things we do and things we see shortly before we fall asleep are most apt to influence our dreams', and it was followed by scenes that showed Alice picking up a rabbit and observing a cat up a tree before she settles down to dream of Wonderland. But this drew attention to a different problem, namely the difficulty of distinguishing between conscious and unconscious states on screen. Whereas the literary Alice is a real girl who dreams up imaginary creatures, in a film every character has an equally solid identity before it is flattened into two dimensions; whether it exists in the waking world or in Wonderland, everything has the same black-and-white certainty, the same grainy quality of truth.

What saves these early experiments from failure is the recognition that many aspects of filmmaking being developed at the time were already close to Carroll's more experimental literary techniques. I have previously mentioned some of these, such as his placing of certain illustrations so that when the page was turned one image of the Cheshire Cat was replaced by another showing a shadowy outline of its body and a sharp white grin, which might now remind us that a body which rapidly appears and disappears while giving the illusion of continued life is the very essence of film. However, even more significant was the simple fact that everything in Carroll's Wonderland happens underground. To enter the auditorium of somewhere like the Rivoli Cinema was not only to return to another place that had formerly been known as Wonderland. It was also a hallucinatory modern parallel to Alice's original experiences, allowing viewers to enter a dreamlike state where bizarre situations flickered into life and lit up the surrounding darkness.

*

Thirty-eight

The fictional Alice continued to be associated with more familiar locations. An advertising booklet published in 1914 as *Alice in Holidayland* showed her exploring Yorkshire seaside resorts such as Scarborough and Whitby, with the aim of showing that a real Wonderland was just a short train ride away. Here holidaymakers could imagine local versions of the Walrus and the Carpenter strolling along the beach, or the Hatter and his friends enjoying an endless cream tea – pastoral scenes in which adults could renew their youth and that altered little from one year to the next. Meanwhile, life at Cuffnells went on in a similarly predictable fashion. Evidence of this can be found not only in the Hargreaves family's letters and diaries, but also in an unpublished set of reminiscences written by Ernie Odell, the son of their head groom, who was born in 1897 and lived on the estate until he was eighteen. He seems to have enjoyed an unusually happy childhood, much of it spent scrumping apples or avoiding the local policeman, who had a habit of giving naughty boys 'a boot in the backside', but if such anecdotes strike a modern reader as sepia-tinted that may be because they captured more than his private memories. They were fragments of a whole way of life that would soon exist only in faded photograph albums.

He was especially observant when it came to the hidden inner workings of a country house, explaining that the cooking was done over 'a very large open fire with a spit worked by clockwork on which huge slabs of meat were roasted', and noticing that the perks available to the village postman included cutting as much fresh bread as he wanted from a loaf kept on a special table in the larder, and drawing a daily pint from a cask of ale. At Christmas, a party of mummers would visit and perform two shows in the house, one in the servants' hall and another in the drawing room, 'so that Mr. and Mrs. Hargreaves and any guests they had staying could see it in more comfortable surroundings'. His memories of Alice Hargreaves herself were 'a trifle blurred', he admitted, as 'the demarcation lines between servants and gentry were very strict in these days', but one episode he vividly recalled was 'being told by Alice herself how [her] famous stories came to be written', and re-enacting the afternoon by punting across Cuffnells lake for 'an old-style Dodo and Ducky picnic'. In 1902, she gave him a signed copy of *Alice's Adventures in Wonderland* as a Christmas present.

The following years saw a handful of modern improvements brought to Cuffnells: electricity ('the nasty new-fangled stuff') was finally installed in 1909, and Ernie's father was sent on a six-month course to learn how to maintain a Rolls-Royce, which could later be seen chugging around Lyndhurst with the registration plate R 733, only the fifty-ninth car built by the firm, sometimes with the mistress of the house at the wheel. Otherwise life continued much as it had since 1880. The servants bustled about under Lady Hargreaves's watchful gaze; the annual round of hunts and flower shows punctuated the sleepy routines of village life; every day the farm delivered a fresh pat of butter to the kitchen; every Sunday the family sat in their reserved pew at the local church, with Reginald proudly wearing a carnation he had grown in one of his own greenhouses. And then, in July 1914, during a hot summer that was lit up by violent thunderstorms, everything changed.

Alice and Reginald Hargreaves's eldest son, Alan, had already spent fourteen years in the army. He had followed a traditional career path from Eton to Sandhurst, after which he was posted to South Africa, where he spent a period guarding Boer prisoners and staving off boredom by playing polo and reading *Country Life*. There followed several years of equally placid military service in other outposts of the Empire. In one letter he sent from Malta at the start of 1909, he explained that he had been going 'pretty often to the opera' ('Rigolletto [*sic*] I like best of all') and was planning a hunting trip up the Nile, but 'I don't think that you need be in the least bit afraid of my getting blown up or coming to any harm.' On another occasion, writing from Gibraltar, he told his parents that 'I have left my fur coat

& a good deal of hunting kit at home which might as well be put carefully away & protected from moth under the careful eye of Nanny.' It was in this frame of mind that he crossed the Channel in September 1914 as a Captain in the Rifle Brigade, and began the long march to the front. Two months later he was joined by his younger brother Rex, who had graduated from playing with toy soldiers to being a Captain in the Irish Guards, embarking in November upon a campaign that would eventually take him from Ypres to the Somme. Left behind at Cuffnells, Alice Hargreaves busied herself raising funds for the British Red Cross (she would later be awarded a special commemorative medal 'For War Service'), but otherwise, like thousands of other mothers across the country, she was forced to sit and wait.

The first telegram arrived on 14 October 1914: 'Bullet wound shoulder not dangerous Alan.' In fact he had been shot through the lung, after which he had been forced to spend two hours lying on his back in no-man's-land 'to avoid haemorrhage', while bullets smacked into the wet mud around him. Awarded the DSO for gallantry, and sent home to convalesce, he returned to the front in March 1915, and two months later he led 'C' Company in an assault on the German lines near Fromelles. This time the telegram home was sent by someone else; on Sunday 9 May he had been shot in the stomach and killed. Alice added a note to the 'Memo'

Telegram about Alan Hargreaves being wounded in action

section of her appointments diary: 'Alan was ~~killed~~ hit,' she wrote, as if unable to believe the news herself, before working herself up to acknowledge that he had 'died on Monday about 4 a.m.' A fortnight later, his commanding officer explained that 'He was hit just as he got to the German trench', where he lay all day growing steadily weaker, and although he was carried back to his own lines as soon as it was dark, 'he died next day in hospital'.

More news from the front arrived in September 1916. 'We received telegrams from W[ar] O[ffice] with information of Rex being wounded & subsequent death,' Alice wrote in her diary on Friday the 29th, one of the only entries composed in permanent ink rather than pencil. He had died the previous Monday in an attack on the village of Lesboeufs, just one more statistic in a campaign that by the end of the year would produce over a million casualties. A photograph of his grave was later sent to his parents: a plain wooden cross in a forest of similar crosses poking out of the rutted mud at jagged angles. Yet while their relatives wrote in eulogistic terms about how the brothers were the 'best and the bravest', and had fallen 'in the most glorious death one can imagine, at the head of their men in attack', that was not the whole story. In his detailed campaign record of the Irish Guards, Rudyard Kipling, whose short-sighted son had joined the regiment in 1915 at his urging and died when a shell ripped his face apart at the Battle of Loos, explained how during the assault on Lesboeufs the British artillery had miscalculated their range and started firing on their own troops, who were dug into a potato field to the east of the village. A pigeon was urgently dispatched, but it took up to two hours for the guns to fall silent, and during this period Rex – who was later described by his commanding officer (a fellow Etonian) as 'the coolest officer under fire that I have ever come across' – was mortally wounded. He may have died bravely, but it was almost certainly as a result of 'friendly fire', an expression that was first recorded in 1918.

In this context, it is probably not surprising that the *Alice* books took on a grim new life during the war. A powerful example is R. C. Sherriff's play *Journey's End*, which is set in a British trench during a few days in 1918. For most of the action the *Alice* books stay in the background, like the steady grumbling of the guns; only occasionally do they flare into life to remind the audience that they have been there all along. The night before a planned raid on the German lines, one of the officers takes 'a small leather-bound book from his pocket' and starts to read:

TROTTER: What's the title?

OSBORNE [*showing him the cover*]: Ever read it?

TROTTER [*leaning over and reading the cover*]: *Alice's Adventures in Wonderland* – why, that's a kid's book!

OSBORNE: Yes.

TROTTER: You aren't *reading* it?

OSBORNE: Yes.

TROTTER: What – a *kid's* book.

OSBORNE: Haven't you read it?

TROTTER [*scornfully*]: No!

OSBORNE: You ought to. [*Reads*]

> How doth the little crocodile
> Improve his shining tail,
> And pour the waters of the Nile
> On every golden scale?
>
> How cheerfully he seems to grin
> And neatly spread his claws,
> And welcome little fishes in
> With gently smiling jaws!

TROTTER [*after a moment's thought*]: I don't see no point in that.

OSBORNE [*wearily*]: Exactly. That's just the point.

TROTTER [*looking curiously at* OSBORNE]: You *are* a funny chap!

Initially, Osborne's choice of reading material appears to be straightforward escapism, rather as he proposes that they avoid thinking about the busy worms in their trench by talking about croquet instead. The *Alice* books would fulfil a similar function in the Second World War: in the 1942 film *Mrs Miniver* a mother recites Carroll's line about 'remembering her own child-life and the happy summer days' as her family listens to the muffled thump of bombs falling during an air raid. Yet as *Journey's End* grinds on to its inevitable conclusion, it becomes clear that nobody fighting on the front line really needs to read Carroll's story, because in some ways they are already living through it.

Even though the raid is bound to fail, the men are told to carry it out anyway, since the plan is fixed and the commanding officer 'can't disobey orders'. The outcome is as inevitable as a rhyme like 'claws' and 'jaws': Osborne charges towards the German lines, and is blown to pieces by a hand grenade. It is like a slapstick routine gone wrong, and as the play continues Carroll's plot becomes central to the action. Much of what happens is revealed to be a distorted version of events in the *Alice* books, from the need for the men to have plenty of pepper in their soup ('It's a disinfectant') to the list of objects that Osborne recites ('Of shoes – and ships – and sealing wax – | And cabbages – and kings'), which later comes back in mutilated form when a British soldier searches the pockets of a young German captured on the raid, and discovers 'bit of string . . . little box o' fruit drops; pocket-knife . . . bit o' cedar pencil . . . and a stick o' chocolate'. Any doubt that this is a deliberate strategy on Sherriff's part is removed when a second soldier, the fresh young recruit Raleigh, is wounded by shrapnel in the raid that kills Osborne. Talking together before they go over the top, he reveals that he lives 'just outside Lyndhurst', somewhere Osborne tells him that he likes 'more than any place I know'. The play was written in 1928, just a few months after Alice Hargreaves sold her manuscript of *Alice's Adventures Under Ground*, when she too was revealed to be living just outside Lyndhurst, and the climax of *Journey's End* is like a vicious parody of the story she first heard back in 1862. Raleigh's final whispered line is 'It's – it's so frightfully dark and cold', as he lies dying on Osborne's bed, and within a minute the shelling rises in intensity and '*the timber props of the door cave slowly in, sandbags fall and block the passage to the open air. There is darkness in the dugout.*' It turns out that not all underground adventures have a happy ending.

Literary works published during the First World War did not usually respond to the *Alice* books in such unpleasant detail, but Carroll's stories were often echoed in the magazines produced by different regiments. As early as December 1915, the snaking maze of trenches outside Ypres was being described as 'a sad, enchanted region' in which the unearthly sounds made by bullets and shells turned the air into a clotted soundscape like that in 'Jabberwocky', where slithy toves gyred and mome raths out-grabe. By the final year of the war, the *Alice* books had taken on a wide range of extra meanings. They could be used to illustrate happy dreams of home ('Back to the Wonderland'), the inescapable reality of 'a land | Composed of quantities of mud and very little sand' ('Alas: In Wonderland'), or a crazy version of the supply line that was designed to keep soldiers alive until they could be sent into action ('The Quartermaster in Wonderland'). Pushing slightly harder against military rank, they were also used to satirize ideas from commanding officers such as 'Let's change the shape of hats', a parody of 'The Walrus and the Carpenter' that was published 'With sincere apologies to the authors [*sic*] of "Alice in Wonderland"'. They were even the basis of a pantomime written by two of the team of Whitehall code-breakers known as I.D.25, which was at one stage run by William Milbourne James, the naval commander whose nickname 'Bubbles' reflected the fact that as a boy he had featured in the famous Pears' soap advertisement based on the painting by his grandfather John Everett Millais. Beginning with Alice's fall down a long communications tube under Admiralty Arch, most of her subsequent adventures revolve around a complicated series of jokes aimed at other code-breakers. At one stage, Alice is told that if she were to be turned into code, '"you wouldn't be you any longer, you'd be something else"', where a pun flickers on 'you' and 'U', and when her name is fed into a machine, 'Alice' first becomes 'ASES', and then something more familiar: '"AS is AB and ES is UN. There you are, you see. ABUN. You're a bun."' It is both perfectly reasonable and perfectly unreasonable – the ideal combination for a group of people who understood how to turn ordinary words into coded nonsense, and sought out the key that would restore apparently random strings of letters into meaningful patterns of sense.

Such wartime activities revealed a new potential for danger in the *Alice* books, for it was only now that readers could appreciate the full force of Alice's famous conversation with the Cheshire Cat. When they meet for a second time, it tells her '"we're all mad here"', and answers her doubtful query '"How do you know I'm mad?"' with an argument that loops back upon itself like a lasso: '"You must be . . . or you wouldn't have come here."' Visually, the sloppy mud trenches of the First World War were the direct opposite of Wonderland, a beautiful garden with 'beds of bright flowers' and 'cool fountains', but in other ways they were a natural extension of its crazy logic. Everyone living in a trench was mad. They must be, or they wouldn't be living in a trench.

*

Thirty-nine

Reginald Hargreaves never fully recovered from the deaths of Alan and Rex. In later photographs he looks pale and gaunt, hollowed out by grief, and when news came that he had died in February 1926 it was widely thought to be a merciful release. Alice's younger brother Eric told her that Reginald was 'part of the wreckage' created by the war, another example of the sort of casualty that did not appear on any official lists. In a small blue envelope left to be opened after his death, Reginald thanked his wife for sharing his life over the past thirty-five years: 'God bless and keep you for all your love and care for me. No words of mine can express what you have been to me.' Their remaining son Caryl, who had followed his brothers from Eton into the army before being sent home in 1916, officially inherited Cuffnells but spent most of his time in London, leaving Alice to rattle around in a large house that probably seemed twice the size now she was left to run it alone. A place she had once celebrated as a genuine Wonderland had revealed its potential to make her feel just as isolated as her fictional namesake. 'I am afraid these are rather hard days for you – but cheer up,' Caryl wrote to her in 1929, 'I hope the future will not be as lonely for you as you think.'

Cuffnells fell into a decline after the war, crippled by the social and financial changes that led to dozens of country houses being sold or demolished, and the slow decay of a whole way of life. One of the major difficulties faced by the owners of these properties was finding servants who were willing to work long and unsocial hours for low wages. That was less of a problem at Cuffnells, where people such as the coachman-cum-chauffeur Charles Odell remained loyally in post, but the Hargreaveses' money was proving somewhat harder to hold on to. Falling agricultural rents and rising taxes meant that landowners nationwide were no longer making a sufficient return on their properties, with the value of land slumping from £53 an acre in 1871 to as little as £23 during the worst of the interwar years. The Hargreaveses' income from investments was also severely reduced, Reginald having disposed of considerable assets during his lifetime, meaning that he had left around £26,000 to his family compared to the £40,000 he had inherited. Squeezed between a falling income and rising costs, a widow like Alice Hargreaves had few options open to her. If selling Cuffnells was difficult in a 'glutted and shrinking' market for country houses, continuing to live there was also a challenge. While there is no evidence that she withdrew from the world socially – in 1927 she became the first President of the Lyndhurst branch of the Women's Institute – she did shrink into a smaller space within the house itself. In *Alice's Adventures in Wonderland*, Alice finds herself in a house so small she is forced to stick one arm out of the window and one foot up the chimney, but for Alice Hargreaves the situation was reversed. She now spent more of her time in a compact suite consisting of a drawing room, study, bedroom, bathroom and WC, which was easier to manage and cheaper to heat than the draughty main rooms.

There was still enough money left for her to take a six-week tour of Italy in April–May 1926, accompanied by Caryl, perhaps in an attempt to raise her spirits after the funeral. His unpublished travel diary shows the influence of both his parents: while the handwriting and many of the sentiments strongly resemble his mother's earlier letters from Europe (although his preferred adjective was 'beautiful' rather than 'lovely'), he had room for some of his father's more uncompromising attitudes towards foreign life, pointing out that the harem in Algiers 'seemed small & must have been very stuffy if [the owner] had many wives, as there was no ventilation & only a few windows about 1 ft square'. But although Caryl occasionally complained about being fleeced by unscrupulous hotel-owners, money was otherwise not an interesting enough topic for him to mention. He simply took it for granted that they had enough of it to do whatever they liked, and when he noted that a General Strike had started while they were in Italy, it was only in relation to his fear that it might be difficult for their ship to dock on its return. Even if Cuffnells was proving to be an unsustainable drain on the family's resources, serious economic hardship was still something that only happened to other people.

In this uncertain social and financial climate, the *Alice* books continued to serve as a cultural barometer that revealed how much had changed since their original publication. Inevitably there was some resistance to this idea, especially from those who wanted to believe that modern life was essentially the same as Victorian life, with a handful of new inventions and slightly different clothes. The earlier explorers who had written about distant parts of the British Empire as wonderlands, in particular, found several twentieth-century travellers willing to develop the same line of thought. For these writers, Alice was 'that prime heroine of our nation', as Robert Graves described her in a 1925 poem, punning on the fact that her fictional age of seven was a prime number, but although he went on to praise her willingness 'To learn the rules and moves and perfect them', some of his contemporaries preferred to think of her as a national heroine in a different sense. For them she was a champion of British common sense, who remained rationally detached from the confusion of her surroundings, coolly appraising odd customs and seeing through nonsense. Before the war, this had already manifested itself in works such as Alexander Davis's *The Native Problem in South Africa* (1903), in which the writer congratulated himself on not being taken in by the 'gross imposture and crass stupidity of the witch-doctor and his dupes', which he observed was 'reminiscent of "Alice in Wonderland"'; Mary Gaunt's memoir *Alone in West Africa* (1911) continued the theme with a description of some garden fences in Accra that were either missing or made from curved barrel staves, making the whole scene so unlike what she was used to that 'I fancied myself stepping with Alice in Wonderland'. The same vein of awkward comedy extended as far as Evelyn Waugh's account of his journey to witness the coronation of Haile Selassie in 1930. 'How to recapture, how to retail, the crazy enchantment of those Ethiopian days?' he asked, and concluded that the only way to understand life in the capital Addis Ababa was to think of it as a true Wonderland, because 'it is in *Alice* only that one finds the peculiar flavour of galvanised and translated reality, where animals carry watches in their waistcoat pockets, royalty paces the croquet lawn beside the chief executioner, and litigation ends in a flutter of playing-cards'.

Translators were equally adept at picking up Carroll's stories and carrying them across the invisible barrier that separated the nineteenth and twentieth centuries. Of the many new *Alice* translations made in the post-war period, including the first to appear in Spanish (1922), Irish (1922), Chinese (1922), Hebrew (1923), Hungarian (1924) and Polish (1927), none was as well crafted – or indeed as crafty – as the Russian version completed in 1923 by the young Vladimir Nabokov. *Ania v strane chudes* was commissioned in 1922 by a publisher in Berlin; Nabokov's family were among the tens of thousands of Russian refugees who had settled in the city after fleeing the 1917 Revolution and its bloody aftermath, and Nabokov himself was scraping a living as a tennis coach and translator of construction manuals. His advance was a single US five-dollar bill. Intended to be a textual plaything for émigré children, the translation has been characterized by Nabokov's biographer Brian Boyd as 'a gleeful raid on the toys and tags of a Russian nursery', crammed with puns, word games, nonsense and parodies. 'The kind of Russian family [to which] I belonged,' Nabokov wrote later, 'a kind now extinct – had, among other virtues, a traditional leaning toward the comfortable products of Anglo-Saxon civilisation', such as Pears' soap and English toothpaste. However, his version of Wonderland was far more than an exercise in Anglophile nostalgia. By encouraging his readers to enjoy the full range of Russian culture in miniature, he invited them to make a brief excursion back home, but anyone who read his translation carefully would also have been reminded of what else they had left behind. In the final chapter, 'Ania's Evidence', the Queen does not say '"Sentence first – verdict afterwards!"' as she does in Carroll's original, but '"Execution first – sentence afterwards!"' ('"Sperva kazn', a potom uzh prigovor!"'). Viewed as a piece of nonsense, it develops Carroll's humour by reminding us that a legal sentence cannot be reversed as easily as the clauses in a grammatical sentence: executing someone, and then deciding whether or not they are guilty, is as absurd as undergoing divorce before proposing marriage. Viewed through the lens of contemporary politics, however, the joke is much darker. Condemned even before a judgment has been pronounced, Alice has become the victim of a show trial – the sort of nightmare from which many of Nabokov's fellow Russians were unable to wake up.

The familiarity of Carroll's characters and situations made them equally attractive for authors whose plots depended upon clear distinctions between the known and the unknown. Many writers of the so-called Golden Age of detective fiction were especially good at taking the dangerous situations Carroll had turned into slapstick comedy (falling, drowning, beheading and so on), or deflected into metaphor (there is a 'dead silence' when Alice speaks in the Rabbit's house, and another 'dead silence' in the courtroom), and putting them in the service of new stories. Sometimes this was clearly signalled in a book's title: in 1933 John Dickson Carr published *The Mad Hatter Mystery*, which centred on a newspaper reporter who is killed after investigating a series of bizarre thefts of hats, and in 1941 there appeared Francis Durham Grierson's *The Mad Hatter Murder*, which opens with the death of a millionaire who '"was called the Mad Hatter as a joke by his friends because he'd been a hatter and because he was so fond of that kid's book, 'Alice in Wonderland'"'. Other detective novelists preferred to add an element of humour to their writing by lacing it with *Alice* allusions. Dorothy L. Sayers, for example, whose father was headmaster of Christ Church Choir School in Oxford when she was born in 1893, and whose letters are full of playful quotations from Carroll, often revealed her love of the *Alice* books in her own fiction. In *The Unpleasantness at the Bellona Club* (1928), not only are many of the chapters named after card games – including one, 'Quadrille', which is also the name of the lobster dance in Wonderland – but conversations with Sayers's detective hero Lord Peter Wimsey frequently return to phrases such as 'Curiouser and curiouser', or 'I do like a story to begin at the beginning', as her characters deal out familiar lines like another set of cards. Even the travel book Agatha Christie wrote in 1946, *Come, Tell Me How You Live*, borrows a line from the White Knight's poem in *Through the Looking-Glass* for its title. It then begins with a parody of the same poem, which makes fun of her own professional interest in death, as she imagines talking to an archaeologist while secretly thinking up ways 'To kill a millionaire | And hide the body in a van | Or some large frigidaire' or 'how to thrust some arsenic into tea'.

By the 1920s, the character of Alice was simultaneously Victorian and modern, old and young; she belonged everywhere and nowhere. Even stories that attempted to treat her as timeless ended up depicting her instead as a type of literary time-traveller. When Florence Scott Bernard published *Through the Cloud Mountain* in 1922, describing the further adventures of Jan, the name she gives to the lame boy from Robert Browning's poem 'The Pied Piper of Hamelin', she chose Alice to be his giggling companion. Together they explore the Land of Eternal, where the characters from children's stories are supposed to dwell. "'I'm so thankful that Lewis Carroll created me and that I can live here for ever and ever,'" Alice tells Jan. "'Just think, if he hadn't written me into a book I shouldn't have been here at all. I am so thankful. Carroll! Carroll! It's great fun to roll your tongue over the r's and l's.'" The Land of Eternal is revealed to be a place where the sun rises and sets, but in every other way the clock has stopped: the Hatter still drinks his tea, Humpty Dumpty still regularly falls off his wall, and characters from Robinson Crusoe to Santa Claus continue to repeat the same familiar storylines, as if trapped in an unusually happy hell. Alice tells Jan that she has fallen down the rabbit-hole so often she has become quite used to it. "'I like to take the new people down,'" she explains. "'They all love my adventures and it makes them happy.'" Yet even here some unexpectedly modern elements occasionally loom into view: Jan makes his way to the Land of Eternal on board an airship, and when Alice attends Cinderella's fancy-dress ball she chooses a Shredded Wheat biscuit as her costume, a breakfast cereal that was first made in America in 1893.

Other characters in the *Alice* books were also capable of being updated, but it was Alice who had become the most restless of Carroll's characters in the public mind, repeatedly slipping her original fictional moorings and venturing into new imaginary worlds. Here Walt Disney's career provides an influential example. When he arrived in Los Angeles in August 1923, he was holding a cheap suitcase that contained an equally cheap suit, a sweater, some drawing materials, $40 and a 12½-minute reel of film mixing live action and animation that he called *Alice's Wonderland*. He had previously produced a handful of 'modernized fairy tales' through his Laugh-O-Gram studio in Kansas City, such as *Little Red Riding Hood* and *Puss in Boots*, but he chose *Alice's Wonderland* as his Hollywood calling card. This is probably because, unlike other popular fairy tales, his version of *Alice* did not have a fixed plot with a predetermined conclusion; its contents were as limitless as the scope of his imagination. He was certainly aware of Max and Dave Fleischer's popular cartoon series *Out of the Inkwell*, in which animated characters got into mischief in a live-action world, and in *Alice's Wonderland* he had chosen to reverse their scheme. The film opens with a scene in which 'Little Alice', played by a chirpy ringleted four-year-old named Virginia Davis, who is 'chuck full of curiosity', pays her first visit to a cartoon studio and is shown around by Disney himself. Wherever she looks, large sheets of paper teem with slapstick cartoon life: a jazz band plays while two cats jive, and elsewhere another cat is knocked out by a dog in a boxing match. Later Alice goes to bed and dreams about visiting Cartoonland, where she is welcomed by a grand procession. The rest of the film depicts her getting into various scrapes, until a pack of lions chases her off a jaggedly drawn cliff, like another Nemo in Slumberland, and she wakes up. 'We have just discovered something new and clever in animated cartoons!' Disney boasted to possible film distributors. One of them, the ambitious young New York distributor Margaret Winkler, agreed, and in October she signed him up to produce a whole series of Alice shorts. The next day he and his brother Roy formed Disney Brothers Studios.

Between *Alice's Day at the Sea* in 1924 and *Alice in the Big League* in 1927, the Disney brothers produced a total of fifty-six 'Alice Comedies', and during this period the future direction of their studio became clear. Not only was Virginia Davis replaced by a series of different actresses, but the time Alice spent on screen gradually reduced, as Disney's anthropomorphic cartoon animals took over, particularly a cunning feline named Julius that, perhaps not wholly coincidentally, looked and behaved much like his popular cartoon rival Felix the Cat. It turned out that the jokes in a cartoon were better when human beings weren't getting in the way. An early indication of what was to come had already appeared in *Alice's Wonderland*, where one of the drawings that springs into life is a scrawny mouse. He is more inventive than the Mouse in Carroll's Wonderland who tells a long and sad tale, and certainly more aggressive than the Dormouse who spends his time sleeping in a teapot; his antics include poking a real cat with a sword, and then jabbing at it with his muscular corkscrew of a tail. If he is a direct ancestor of Mickey Mouse, the cartoon rodent whose invention in 1928 would make Disney the most successful animator in the world, *Alice's Wonderland* was also a natural successor to Carroll's Wonderland. In 1926, a book on nonsense poetry suggested that 'The realm of Nonsense is not so much Fairyland as Dreamland, for in Dreamland the two worlds meet and the memories of the day are twisted into many queer and unexpected shapes by the imaginations of the night.' Carroll had already shown how this could produce stories on the page; now Disney invited spectators to enjoy a modern alternative. Watching a cartoon was another way of dreaming while remaining awake.

Alice Hargreaves was ambivalent about her namesake's growing fame. Yet if she remained silent about the story itself, Cuffnells contained a large collection of editions, translations, printed ephemera and miscellaneous objects associated with the *Alice* books, some received as gifts and the rest acquired either by her or Caryl. There were pop-up books, puzzles, wooden toys, a home-made screen covered in large coloured prints of Wonderland characters, a china ornament that depicted a child perched on a mantelpiece and gazing longingly into a mirror, and copies of advertising pamphlets such as *Alice in Fi-co-land* (1919), in which Alice is encouraged to swallow the contents of another bottle marked 'Drink Me' (she declares it to be 'delicious'), and after a regular series of adventures wakes up to discover that she is shaking a bottle of the fruit syrup laxative Ficolax. However, if Alice Hargreaves was interested in the commercial offshoots of Carroll's stories, she was also increasingly aware of the value of her original manuscript of *Alice's Adventures Under Ground*. Although this had been printed in facsimile, it remained a unique document in itself, a work of art in an age of mechanical reproduction, and this made it all the more desirable for collectors. With increasing rates of death duty now being added to the general burden of post-war taxation, such considerations far outweighed any sentimental attachment she may have felt to a fragment of her childhood. In 1928, while Caryl tried to let Cuffnells at a rent of £400 per year, she decided to put it up for auction.

The announcement that the original Alice was to sell the original *Alice* set the news wires humming. Almost immediately the story split in two. In the first place, there was the sale itself, which took place at 1 p.m. on Tuesday 3 April, when 300 spectators squeezed into Sotheby's dark oak auction room in Mayfair. The *Alice* manuscript was to be sold alongside other pieces of literary memorabilia, including Samuel Johnson's final letter and a pair of Byron's duelling pistols, and from Alice Hargreaves a selection of the books she had received from Carroll over the years, together with a 'Wonderland' postage-stamp case. But there was no doubt which item was the star of the show: Lot 319, which alongside Carroll's manuscript included six letters from him about the facsimile edition. 'IT IS HARDLY TOO MUCH TO DESCRIBE THIS LOT AS THE MOST ATTRACTIVE LITERARY MANUSCRIPT EVER OFFERED FOR SALE,' trumpeted the sales catalogue, and the outcome proved this to be more than just auction hype.

After preliminary skirmishes over a first edition of *Alice's Adventures in Wonderland*, attention in the room soon focused on four bidders: the wealthy private collector Dr Rosenbach of Philadelphia, the British Museum represented by the London firm of Quaritch's, and two antiquarian book dealers. Bidding rose swiftly in increments of £100, and after the British Museum dropped out at £12,500, and the last dealer at £15,200, Dr Rosenbach finally secured his prize for £15,400. At the time it was a record for a book sold at auction, beating the £15,100 paid for a First Folio of Shakespeare in December 1919. 'A few hands clap,' reported the *New York Times*. 'Then the crowd starts melting away. Over near the rostrum an old woman, once little Alice, brushes a handkerchief across her eyes. Then she, too, vanishes.' That piece of creative reporting introduced the other part of the story, which was the revelation that Alice herself was still alive. Although Carroll's early biographers had pointed out that Alice

WHAT TO WEAR AT EASTER: By LADY DUFF GORDON IN PAGE 9

DAILY SKETCH

INCORPORATING THE DAILY GRAPHIC

£20,000 FOR **EMPIRE TRAVEL** *ENTER NOW*

No. 5,922. [Registered as a Newspaper.]   WEDNESDAY, APRIL 4, 1928.   ONE PENNY.

"ALICE IN WONDERLAND" AS SHE IS TO-DAY

A page of Lewis Carroll's manuscript of "Alice in Wonderland." Inset: Dr. Rosenbach, the famous Philadelphia collector, who has acquired so many literary treasures.—(*Daily Sketch*.)

A quiet old lady sitting behind the auctioneer opened her eyes in wonder when the manuscript of "Alice in Wonderland" was sold at Sotheby's yesterday for £15,400, the record figure at which Dr. Rosenbach acquired the treasure. She was the original Alice—Mrs. Alice Hargreaves, to whom the author gave the manuscript.

A *Daily Sketch* exclusive photograph, taken yesterday, of Mrs. Alice Pleasance Hargreaves, the original of Alice. Mrs. Hargreaves has not been photographed for many years.

The scene in the crowded saleroom. It was afterwards announced that Dr. Rosenbach would allow the nation to buy the manuscript for the price he had paid for it.—(*Daily Sketch*.)

Sir John Tenniel's drawing of Alice—one of the original illustrations.—(By courtesy of Messrs. Macmillan.)

Alice Hargreaves pictured the day *Alice's Adventures Under Ground* was sold at auction

Liddell was now Alice Hargreaves, to the general public her appearance was as surprising as would have been an announcement that Betty Boop had been spotted dining at the Ritz. The front page of the *Daily Sketch* on 4 April was typical: under the headline '"ALICE IN WONDERLAND" AS SHE IS TO-DAY', there was a large picture of her wearing pearls and a fur coat, with the caption 'Mrs Hargreaves has not been photographed for many years'; underneath this a small picture of Tenniel's Alice holding the 'Drink Me' bottle encouraged readers to consider how she had changed in the intervening period. But although some reporters viewed the financial story as secondary to the human one, that is not how Alice herself saw it, as she carefully marked up her copy of the catalogue. Like most people, she usually took herself for granted; much more exciting was the money she had made, a grand total of £19,191 10s. before commission, and the peace of mind it had brought her. Writing to Caryl on 10 April, she summed up the sale in one word: 'wonderful'.

What happened afterwards was equally significant, because although Dr Rosenbach offered the manuscript to the British Museum for the price he had just paid, they declined, and accordingly he carried it back to the United States on board the ocean liner *Majestic*. Three weeks later he met Eldridge Johnson, founder of the Victor Talking Machine Company, who was unable to resist 'the lure of the little volume' and bought it for £30,000. When it was exhibited at the New York Public Library later that year, more than 23,000 people queued to see it. In 1948 it returned to Britain as a gift presented to the nation 'as an expression of thanks to a noble people who held Hitler at bay for a long period single-handed', but in the 1920s such generosity seemed a long way off. To all intents and purposes Alice appeared to have emigrated.

This movement of the *Alice* manuscript across the Atlantic was just one symptom of a much larger shift in economic and cultural power. The American collector Morris L. Parrish had already wooed Carroll's family into selling various photograph albums and other pieces of Carrolliana, sending his limousine to fetch family members so that he could treat them to the theatre when he was in London, and arranging valuations followed by private sales to avoid the possibility of being outbid at auction. But although such tactics were far from unusual, losing the *Alice* manuscript to a foreign buyer hit a particular nerve in Britain. Even before the auction, *The Times* had carried an article with the heading 'Farewell to Alice?' which pointed out how long she had survived as a literary character: 'We dare not say that she has grown up with us, for she is of the sort that does not grow up except by cake and mushrooms.' Its conclusion was that it was 'a melancholy prospect' that she should end up in America, 'for her Wonderland is a peculiarly English place. Her nonsense is our nonsense, her caterpillar sits upon our native mushrooms . . . No lady in so short a life has done so much, and there is none whose compulsory exile we should more bitterly regret.'

The same patriotic rumblings had reached America; a collection of sharp satirical pieces published that year in the *New York Herald Tribune* by Edward Hope, and subsequently brought together in his book *Alice in the Delighted States*, climaxed with Alice meeting Uncle Sam at a political circus, where she notices that he has 'an enormously fat stomach' and whenever he moves there is 'a chink of gold coins from his bulgy pockets'. This did little to appease British, and more specifically English, readers who still considered Alice to be 'the prime heroine of our nation'. A competition in *The Observer*, announced two days before the auction, had offered a prize of three guineas for a continuation of the Hatter's tea party 'in which the American Eagle turns up as a fifth guest', stressing that 'The conversation must be courteous, and the question of the American Debt must not be touched on.' The winning entry depicted the Eagle arriving to fetch Alice. '"Come along, child!"' he tells her, and when Alice asks, '"Won't I be rather home-sick?"' he replies, '"Oh no! . . . You'll have plenty of other English National Treasures to keep you company."' It was a small satirical act of resistance to the fact that Alice was now so popular that the definition of 'our nation' stretched democratically across the world.

*

Forty

The revelation that there had been a real Alice, and that she was still alive, sharpened the desire among critics and journalists to know more about her relationship with the man who had sent her namesake down a rabbit-hole all those years ago. Soon representatives from both families found themselves trying to explain how a lopsided friendship between a little girl and an Oxford don had sparked Wonderland into life. Their approaches to this task differed significantly. When Ina told Florence Becker Lennon in 1930 that Carroll's manner had become 'too affectionate' towards Alice as she grew older, she was attempting to fill a gap in the biographer's knowledge with a new piece of information, or possibly misinformation. By contrast, someone in Carroll's family preferred to leave such gaps exactly where they were. After meeting another biographer, Langford Reed, in February 1932, Carroll's niece Menella boasted in a letter to Falconer Madan, the former Librarian of the Bodleian Library in Oxford, that 'Beyond supplying him with a few actual facts concerning dates & the like, we let him go as ignorant as he came.' It may also have been Menella who created some extra blank spaces in the historical record by removing six pages from his diary. Although exactly what they contained is a matter for conjecture, enough is known about some of the omissions to suggest that the person wielding the razor was unusually sensitive about Carroll's reputation.

Another sentence originally marked for excision came from an entry written in April 1863, after Carroll had visited Alice in the Deanery where she was recovering after a riding accident. An attempt was made to cross it out, but it is still legible: 'Alice was in an unusually imperious and un-gentle mood by no means improved by being an invalid.' It is unlikely that the other censored passages in the diary were any more revealing, but this does not explain why four of the manuscript volumes, including two that dealt with the four-year period April 1858 to May 1862 when Carroll was spending most time with the Liddell children, are also missing. We know that Stuart Dodgson Collingwood had access to all thirteen volumes when he was compiling the *Life and Letters* in 1898, and we also know that by the time Roger Lancelyn Green was asked to edit the diaries in 1953 only nine volumes remained. Were they accidentally lost, deliberately destroyed or quietly tucked into the corner of an attic and left to gather dust? If anybody knows, they aren't telling.

Carroll's relationship with Alice Liddell was again thrust into the spotlight in 1932, when a series of events to mark the centenary of Carroll's birth was organized in both Britain and America, and again it was Mrs Reginald Hargreaves who became the focus of everyone's attention. By now she was spending more of her time at the Breaches, an elegantly proportioned and more manageable three-storey house located in the pretty market town of Westerham, Kent, a mile away from the home of her sister Rhoda, who was one of only three other Liddell siblings still alive. Even here she was not safe from unwelcome attention, although mostly this came in the form of letters, including one from a representative of Sun Life Assurance, who had read her polite comment after the auction of the *Alice* manuscript that 'It is a large sum of money and I do not know what I shall do with it', and helpfully wrote to offer a solution. Other correspondents were equally happy to give her advice: a vicar in Staffordshire suggested a donation that would allow him to build some new toilets, while a 'poor widow' in London asked for 'just a wee bonus of your percentage' to support her 'ailing' mother. Despite all this, with Caryl having married in 1929 and set up home in London, her life was perhaps not as full or purposeful as it had once been, and the opportunity to take a leading role in the centenary celebrations was one she accepted without complaint.

Her main focus was fund-raising. On 12 March 1932, 'An Appeal to all lovers of "Alice" throughout the World' was published in *The Times*, carrying her signature alongside those of leading literary figures such as J. M. Barrie and A. A. Milne and asking for funds to endow a 'Lewis Carroll Ward for Children' at St Mary's Hospital, London. A natural extension of the first appeal in 1898, this time a more ambitious target of £10,000 was set, supported by a Varsity Ball at the Dorchester on 7 July, and an 'All-Star Matinée' at St James's Theatre, where boys' boxing matches and a ballet version of *Through the Looking-Glass* were promised, together with an auction of first editions of both *Alice* books 'autographed by the original "Alice"'. Younger readers were not forgotten: there was a new club, the Helpers of Wonderland League, which sent its members a badge and 'a copy of Secret Rules' in return for a minimum donation of a shilling. Its application form pointed out that 'Your pets or your dolls can also become members in exactly the same way, by sending in an entry form, with a subscription, for each.' The aim of all these fund-raising activities was spelled out in a leaflet, which explained that the plan was to construct 'a Wonderland for children where pain will be lost in happiness, and tears in laughter'. An illustration showed Carroll's Alice directing other characters from the stories as they enthusiastically moved beds into the new ward.

Alice Hargreaves did more than lend her name to this appeal. She also made personal appearances (a flyer for 'Alice's Party' at Church House, Westminster, on 23 and 24 November promised that *'The original "ALICE" Mrs. Hargreaves will be present'*), signed autographs, and in December was photographed meeting the latest stage Alice, a thirteen-year-old named Beryl Laverick. This production at the Little Theatre on the Strand was publicized with 'A Letter from Alice in Wonderland', which pretended to be a real letter sent from Wonderland, handwritten on bright pink paper with faux-authentic blots and crossings-out. In other photographs taken this year Alice Hargreaves looks poised but frail – she now needed two canes to walk – but when she was too tired to fulfil an engagement, Caryl was on hand to make a short speech in her place; on one occasion he apologized for the absence of Alice's 'real self' before going on to talk about her 'mythical self'. An astute and ambitious businessman, he was keenly aware of the marketing opportunities offered by his mother, the living embodiment of the *Alice* brand, and he was not slow to take advantage of them, even if that sometimes came close to taking advantage of her. For the next two years he busied himself seeking endorsements from advertisers, corresponding with the manufacturers of various *Alice*-themed souvenirs, and searching in odd corners of his mother's memory for material he could assemble into articles.

Even when 'the original "Alice"' was not autographing books or shaking hands, journalists on both sides of the Atlantic worked to keep her in the forefront of their readers' minds. Most chose to abandon the usual distinctions between life and art: 'Alice Lives in Wonderland . . . and in Fact', declared the *New York Times* in January, while the *Herald Tribune* introduced her to its readers as 'The Real Alice of "Wonderland"', explaining that despite her 'wise, old, gently smiling eyes', anyone who felt the urge to bow down and say 'Good morning, Alice in Wonderland' would be responding to 'neither fantasy nor a whim, but reality and common sense'. A similar tactic was employed by the minor poet Muriel Fancourt Bell, who used a piece of light verse entitled 'To Alice' to reflect on a meeting with Alice Hargreaves:

> I met a little lady,
>> So sweet and calm of face,
> So quiet in her movements,
>> Her manner full of grace.
>
> Her brow seemed still unclouded,
>> And wistful still her eyes,
> As if she caught from Wonderland
>> Some of its magic guise!
>
> She talked with Humpty Dumpty
>> A sitting on a wall,
> And greeted smiling Cheshire Puss,
>> Who told her where to call.
>
> And with the March Hare feasting,
>> She heard the Dormouse tell
> Its funny little story
>> Of treacle in a well.

The poem continues in similarly glutinous fashion for another four stanzas, and concludes with Bell asking the old lady 'If she could really be | The charming little Alice', but already one word has given her the answer she is secretly hoping for: 'she'. In the ninth line of the poem, the elderly 'she' who is sweet and calm of face becomes the young 'she' who met the fantastic creatures of Wonderland, with only a stanza break to mark the transition from one to the other. It makes the title of the poem unusually ambiguous, because whereas most dedications try to single someone out, 'To Alice' sandwiches together a fictional character and a real person into a seamless composite. The little lady and little Alice are impossible to tell apart.

This widespread fascination with Alice Hargreaves's past life as Alice Liddell reached a climax during her longest engagement in 1932, the fortnight she spent in America. Columbia University had originally invited her to receive an honorary degree in January, offering an all-expenses-paid trip with the razzmatazz usually enjoyed by film stars rather than octogenarian widows, and when that was refused because of her poor health, the event was rescheduled for spring. On Saturday 23 April, accompanied by Caryl and Rhoda, she boarded the Cunard liner *Berengaria* in Southampton and set out for New York. What she discovered over the coming weeks was that American readers shared one important characteristic with their British counterparts: the only event they were really interested in took place on an afternoon almost seventy years earlier. The rest of her life might as well not have happened.

The carefully preserved family records now at Yale show that she and Caryl kept almost everything from their transatlantic adventure: menus, place-cards, invitations, photographs, and even a little pair of British and American flags symbolically tied together with a piece of white ribbon. In her diary Alice records the fortnight in America with her usual reticence, giving away nothing other than neutral information about the weather on their crossing ('lovely day . . . cold rough night') and a list of lunch and dinner engagements. For evidence of just how busy she was it is necessary to turn to Caryl's diary, in which he wrote a detailed account of each day's activities. For although there were a few afternoons when his mother rested in her suite at the Waldorf-Astoria, almost every day a car was waiting to take her somewhere new, where she could see the sights and herself be put on show.

First there was the degree ceremony, which took place on Monday 2 May in the reading room of Columbia University, where Alice was amused to hear the President refer to her in his speech as 'Descendant of John of Gaunt, time-honour'd Lancaster', which made her sound like a character in one of Shakespeare's history plays. At 3 p.m. two days later, on her birthday, there was a grand celebration in the university gymnasium, where 2,000 guests gathered to hear an orchestra and the combined ranks of two glee clubs perform an 'Alice in Wonderland' suite, after which she made a short speech ('rather hesitatingly', according to Caryl) underneath a large painted 'Wonderland' frieze. In addition to these official functions, together she and Caryl travelled to Central Park and the Stock Exchange, up the Empire State Building, and to Philadelphia to meet the Carroll collectors Morris L. Parrish, Dr Rosenbach and Eldridge Johnson, the last of whom still owned the original *Alice* manuscript that was currently being displayed on Carroll's own mahogany table as part of Columbia's centenary exhibition, and who 'had the time of his life showing off the gadget-trimmed, watertight, fireproof, portable, steel safe-deposit box which he had had made to house the precious manuscript so that it would suffer no harm as it travelled on his yacht in the tropical seas while he hunted rare fish'. There was a trip to a cinema to see the newsreel footage of themselves arriving in New York, and also the radio broadcast she made on the WABC-Columbia network; the *New York Times* reported that 'her voice trembled somewhat with the fatigue and excitement of it', as she told listeners, 'America and New York City are such exciting places that they take me back to Wonderland.' In her hotel suite she was photographed, sketched, presented with a copy of *Little Women* and surrounded by numerous bouquets of flowers. And throughout her visit, newspaper reporters were on hand to report her every word. 'REAL ALICE PREFERS THE CHESHIRE CAT . . . LIKES "SOUP AT EVENING" . . . That is Best Rhyme in Volumes She Inspired, Thinks Quaint, Gray-Haired Woman,' announced the *New York Times*, while the *New York American* chose bold print for her comment upon seeing the Statue of Liberty ('**"What is that thing?"**'), as if hoping that upon closer investigation even this apparently inconsequential remark would turn out to be a gnomic piece of wisdom.

The person who took most pleasure in all this fuss was undoubtedly Caryl. He dedicated himself to arranging her diary and protecting her from unwanted callers, but also revelled in the special treatment they received, which began with skipping the queues at passport control and customs ('It is really very nice to be treated like royalty in a democratic country,' he gloated), and was followed by the thrill of a police escort to the hotel, where the express lifts were slowed down especially for his mother. In an unpublished article he sketched out upon his return, 'Visiting America With a Celebrity', he confessed that 'I should like to start doing it as a business', because 'the chief attendant has much more fun than the celebrity!' His diary, to which he gave the title *Alice in America 1932*, fleshes out this idea with a frank account of how much he enjoyed himself once he had safely settled his mother in her suite for the night, visiting everything from illegal speakeasies to nightclubs, including the Cotton Club in Harlem, where he saw 'a quite remarkable show' despite the fact that 'I don't like niggers.'

Compared to his obvious excitement, Alice Hargreaves's response to all the fuss around her was decidedly muted. She simply went where she was told to go, and said what she thought people wanted to hear. Probably the most candid observation she made was in a letter sent to Menella Dodgson on 20 May, the day she returned to Britain, when she confessed that it seemed strange to be so fêted by people whose knowledge of her was almost exclusively drawn from two works of fiction: 'I am very very proud as you will imagine, of being made a D^r L^{tt} – & just through being "Alice" – for it is no merit of my own.'

In a 1932 survey of children's literature, F. J. Harvey Darton singled out *Alice's Adventures in Wonderland* as the book that, more than any of its rivals, had championed 'liberty of thought'. However, it is hard to look at contemporary photographs of Alice Hargreaves in America, in which she appears pleased but also rather bewildered by her reception, and not see someone who had become trapped in a role she had long since outgrown. She wouldn't have been alone in having such thoughts, as she signed more copies of 'her' story, including one to be sent to the young Princess Elizabeth 'From the Original Alice'. On Tuesday 28 June, she opened a new centenary exhibition of Carroll's manuscripts and first editions at the Bumpus bookshop in London's Oxford Street, and there she met a middle-aged publisher, Peter Llewelyn Davies, who had spent the past thirty years carrying his own burden of literary fame.

He was one of the five brothers J. M. Barrie had adopted after the death of their parents, and to whom he had originally told the story of Peter Pan. Barrie later explained to the Llewelyn Davies boys that his hero had been created 'by rubbing the five of you violently together, as savages with two sticks produce a flame', but this was not the conclusion the British press reached. As far as they were concerned, Peter Llewelyn Davies *was* Peter Pan. When a *Daily Express* reporter called on him after the founding of Peter Davies Ltd in 1926, 'not a word would he utter about Peter Pan', but the *Express* still headlined the story 'PETER PAN BECOMES PUBLISHER'. It was as if the usual relationship between fact and fiction

Alice Hargreaves (standing) and Peter Llewelyn Davies (seated to her right) at the opening of the Lewis Carroll Centenary Exhibition (28 June 1932)

had been reversed. No longer was Peter Llewelyn Davies a real person who had become a literary character; he was a literary character trying to cheat fame by disguising himself as a real person. Forever associated with a story he called 'that terrible masterpiece', his life was not his own. 'What's in a name?' he wrote, after suffering relentless teasing at Eton. 'My God, what isn't? If that perennially juvenile lead . . . had only been dubbed George, or Jack, or Michael, or Nicholas, what miseries would have been spared me.'

When Alice met him in Bumpus, inevitably the headline was '"ALICE" MEETS "PETER PAN"'. There is no record of what they said to each other, although John Logan's 2013 play *Peter and Alice* imagines a conversation as they wait in the bookshop's back room. In this version, Alice sees her story as a gift that allows adults to recapture their youth: 'Out of everyone, there's only one Alice. He made me *special*. And that uniqueness has given me a lifetime of people looking back at me, with a growing smile, remembering their better selves, when they were young and life was before them.' Peter counters this by saying that following hard on the smile comes a pain in the eyes, as it slowly dawns on them who they are talking to: '*And then they remember. What growing up really is*: when they've learned that boys can't fly and mermaids don't exist and White Rabbits don't talk and all boys grow old, even Peter Pan, as you've grown old. They've been *deceived*. As if you've somehow been lying to them.' Perhaps Alice Hargreaves's private thoughts came down on one side or the other. All the historical record contains is a letter to Caryl in which she confessed to 'shaking' with tiredness and nerves, and a snatched photograph of her leaving Bumpus, leaning on a stick and looking out shyly from under the brim of a floppy hat.

Compared to the lifelong misery of Peter Llewelyn Davies, Alice Hargreaves's experiences as 'the real Alice' had been largely happy, even if she now found it a more demanding role to play. However, her earlier comment that she had been granted fame through 'no merit of my own' shows that she fully understood the strangeness of being thought of as yourself and someone else at the same time. She would probably have been even more sympathetic to 'the real Peter Pan' if she had known what was later to happen to him. On 5 April 1960, after suffering years of crippling depression, he crossed Sloane Square, walked down into the local tube station and threw himself beneath an oncoming train. 'THE BOY WHO NEVER GREW UP IS DEAD,' announced one headline, while another drew upon a different incident in Barrie's play: 'PETER PAN STOOD ALONE TO DIE.' It was as if his death was merely an unexpected twist to a story everyone thought they knew.

*

Forty-one

Inevitably other events in this centenary year centred more on Carroll. One of the more unusual items acquired by Morris L. Parrish, which he later deposited with the rest of his Carrolliana in Princeton University Library, was a 1931 scrap of 'Alice in Wonderland' chintz from the New York department store Stern Brothers. Advertised as 'Unfadable', it depicted Tenniel's characters in a tight repeating pattern they could never escape. By contrast, Carroll's image was becoming far more uncertain. Two biographies published in 1932 presented significantly different versions of his life. For Walter de la Mare, Carroll was an adult who had never fully outgrown his childhood, and who created Wonderland as an open invitation for readers to join him in a place and 'a state of being' which, until he wrote about it, 'was not only unexplored but undiscovered'. Langford Reed's biography was far more measured in its praise. Although it opened with a poem that was packed with cosy clichés, applauding Carroll as a figure whose writing provided 'fairy charm and mirth', its climax was a chapter on 'The Strange Case of Professor Dodgson and Mr Carroll' that diagnosed him as the victim of a 'dual personality', in which Carroll's cheerful nonsense was engaged in a ceaseless struggle with Dodgson's 'frigid' high seriousness. (Reed left little doubt whose side he was on: one of the summaries he placed at the top of each page was 'The Dullness of Dodgson'.) Yet such competing biographical views probably revealed less about Carroll than they did about the willingness of readers to enlist him in support of their various theories, and by the early 1930s there was no shortage to choose from. Carroll had become the human equivalent of an inkblot in which any number of pictures could be detected.

Many readers enjoyed thinking of him as their friend, which made it hard to argue with them without it seeming like a personal attack, or tried to turn him into a character in a story: in an unpublished tribute of 1930, Ruth H. Dymes, who first met Carroll in Eastbourne when she was seven years old, chose a phrase that Alice Hargreaves would experiment with slightly later, when she remembered him as 'a Fairy Godfather' to her family. Others showed how much they had learned from his example. Writing to *The Times* in 1931, one of his Christ Church pupils pointed out that his 'methods of explaining the elements of Euclid gave me the impression of being extremely lucid', which was exactly the sort of word-play Carroll would have admired, given that 'lucid' requires just one extra letter to become an anagram of 'Euclid', and is already a reshuffled version of 'ludic'.

Yet there were also those who believed that a careful reading of the *Alice* books would severely tarnish Carroll's halo, or at least reveal it to have been tilted at an unexpected angle. The most notorious example was a Freudian analysis by the Balliol College undergraduate Anthony Goldschmidt in 1933, possibly with his tongue wedged in his cheek, which turned the stories into a private psychodrama of forbidden desires battling with repression in the author's mind, making Alice's fall down the rabbit-hole into an obvious 'symbol of coitus', while the little door through which she attempts to pass 'symbolizes a female child; the curtain before it represents the child's clothes'. Even readers who claimed to dislike Carroll's writing found it a source of magnetic attraction. In December 1936, Professor Paul Schilder announced to the annual meeting of the American Psychoanalytic Association at the Waldorf-Astoria Hotel in New York – the hotel Alice Hargreaves had stayed in four years previously – that the *Alice* books were full of fear and 'oral sadistic trends of cannibalism', and Carroll was 'a warped and fearful creature who really wanted to be doing several other things besides sitting on rolling English lawns spinning yarns to open-mouthed children'. The following week, a columnist in the *World Telegram* agreed: 'The average small boy or girl who tackles Lewis Carroll is likely to come away with the impression that it is all very silly,' he observed; nonetheless, the danger of 'emotional instability' posed by these stories was so powerful they should be restricted to adults. His recommendation was only one step away from outright censorship.

This growing uncertainty over Carroll's reputation made him especially interesting to those who viewed ambiguity as an invitation rather than a threat. '"That's a great deal to make one word mean,"' Alice tells Humpty Dumpty after she has heard his long and highly personal definition of 'impenetrability'. The critic William Empson viewed such statements as invitations. In the final chapter of *Some Versions of Pastoral* (1935) he gave a carelessly brilliant assessment of the *Alice* books, in which he made a strong case for seeing them as a tangle of personal and cultural anxieties that had only partially succeeded in disguising themselves as children's stories. Some of his suggestions followed the current fashion for psychoanalysis, on the grounds that 'The books are so frankly about growing up that there is no great discovery in translating them into Freudian terms', and these readings are especially uninhibited, as he points out that when Alice approaches Wonderland, she is 'a father in getting down to the hole, a foetus at the bottom, and can only be born by becoming a mother and producing her own amniotic fluid'. (Empson reportedly told his former Cambridge tutor I. A. Richards, 'There are things in *Alice* that would give Freud the creeps.') What distinguishes this from similar interpretations is Empson's understanding that anxieties about personal development cannot always be separated from other 'ideas of progress', whether these involve evolution or class mobility; for all her obvious social refinement, he points out, Alice 'is often the underdog speaking up for itself'. Yet it was not only in terms of their critical reception that the *Alice* books were developing a reputation as divided as that of their creator. They were equally ambiguous in the way they had started to be represented to a wider public, alternately viewed as a sweet celebration of innocence and a set of dark coded confessions.

Among the most controversial examples of works that tried to exploit this ambiguity were the paintings produced by the French artist Balthus (Balthasar Klossowski), which showed a series of barely pubescent girls being observed by mysteriously smiling cats. Balthus probably hadn't seen Carroll's photographs of Alice Liddell, but greatly admired his writing; as late as 1957, he was working on *Golden Afternoon*, in which a girl is shown asleep in a window-seat with her cat dozing alongside her. His earlier paintings occupied the same imaginative territory. They too are delicately situated on a line dividing the known from the unknown, with their depiction of girls who have abandoned themselves to their dreams and so are unaware of anyone watching them. They are like paintings of Wonderland as seen from the perspective of Alice's sister, because although the cats seem to be in on a private joke, the only thought processes we can access when we look at them are our own.

The uncomplicatedly innocent category of *Alice* representations was especially well stocked with examples from cinema. In 1930, one of the musical numbers in the film *Puttin' on the Ritz* had featured an Alice who walked through an oversized mirror into what had now become generally accepted as Wonderland – a place inhabited by characters from both *Alice* books – where she met dozens of figures, including a high-kicking Hatter and a full chorus line of oysters, who appeared to have danced straight out of Tenniel's illustrations and on to a Broadway stage. The same principle of narrative melding could be seen in the 1933 Paramount film *Alice in Wonderland*. This made a few minor alterations to Carroll's writing, so that when Alice falls down the rabbit-hole she passes a jar that, in keeping with supposed American tastes, is marked 'JAM' rather than 'MARMALADE', but otherwise the film includes the most famous situations from both books. (The studio treated Alice Hargreaves to a special screening in the Breaches, and she loyally responded by telling the magazine *Picturegoer*, 'I cherish the hope that this picture will have a wonderful success.') However, the main difference between these films and Carroll's stories lies not in what happens but how it happens. In each film, as also in a low-budget version produced in 1931 that featured a grinning actress in a platinum blonde wig, Alice is delighted by everything and surprised by nothing; very rarely does she express any frustration or lose her temper. Indeed, in all three films Wonderland turned out to resemble Hollywood itself – somewhere that was just starting to be known as 'a dream factory' – rather than the contents of any particular girl's head.

This was especially true of the 1933 version, in which Alice cannot travel far in any direction without bumping into a major movie star: Cary

Alice in Wonderland (dir. Norman Z. McLeod, 1933)

Grant as the Mock Turtle, W. C. Fields as Humpty Dumpty, Gary Cooper as the White Knight, and several more. Alice was played by an unknown seventeen-year-old actress named Charlotte Henry, who was chosen after an international search in which 7,000 girls were considered for the role, but if her perky performance drained any ambiguity from the finished film, it was probably a deliberate strategy on the part of the studio. She was 'a Nobody', in the view of *Time*'s show business reporter, but she was also an Everybody – the sort of girl whose faithfully reported likes (ham, detective stories, golf) and dislikes (boys who talk too much, spinach) made her seem charmingly ordinary. She later claimed that putting on Alice's costume transformed her into 'the creature people had read about as children. My identity was gone.' But of course that was precisely why she had been chosen. She could only be the centre of the film, or the face of movie tie-ins that included a special book and Wrigley's chewing gum, if her character was more famous than she was. That is what allowed people to believe she was not merely playing Alice but really was Alice.

In this context, with so many rival Alices competing for attention, it is probably not a coincidence that in 1929 the English language expanded slightly to admit a new adjective: 'Alice-ish', meaning 'reminiscent of the character Alice or the books in which she appears'. It was a suitably imprecise word, because if Carroll's *Alice* books continued to be read in the same form that had been familiar for over half a century, what they meant was far less stable. They represented the triumph of innocence, but also everything that threatened it; they revealed a writer skilled in manipulating ideas that were deliberately kept out of view, like a literary version of the sleight of hand he had practised as a boy conjurer, but also one who produced pages of writing that were thought to be windows into his unconscious mind. Indeed, although Alice begins her second adventure by going through a looking-glass, by the end of 1933 it would be equally true to say that she had become a looking-glass in herself. She was a fictional character in whose features readers of every sort saw images of their own hopes and fears, a mirror that captured every passing reflection.

*

Forty-two

On 3 November 1934, the front page of the *Daily Express* announced that 'The Alice who wandered in Wonderland seventy-two years ago is dying.' Now eighty-two years old, Alice Hargreaves had been taken ill while out driving, and lay in a coma in the Breaches, while newspaper reporters gathered outside and waited for news. For the next fortnight they gave regular updates on her health, although little changed from one day to the next: on 5 November, the 'Invalids' column of *The Times* noted that she was 'about the same', and the following day she was again 'about the same'. On Thursday 15 November, she died without ever having regained consciousness. After a cremation at Golders Green, and a separate funeral service at the Church of St Michael and All Angels in Lyndhurst, her ashes were interred in the Hargreaves plot beside those of her husband.

What nobody outside her immediate family seemed entirely sure about was whose life had just ended. While the front of the Order of Service for her funeral referred to her only by the initials A. P. H., the *Times* obituary on 17 November was headed 'MRS. HARGREAVES', and underneath in slightly smaller letters '"ALICE IN WONDERLAND"'. The family tomb already had the severe and simple 'HARGREAVES' chiselled on its headstone, but someone later added a stone slab that announced it as THE GRAVE OF | MRS REGINALD HARGREAVES | THE 'ALICE' IN LEWIS CARROLL'S | 'ALICE IN WONDERLAND.' The *Evening Standard* simply informed its readers that 'ALICE IN WONDERLAND IS DEAD.' Even in death there was a creative confusion of fact and fiction.

While Alice Hargreaves passed into the obituary columns, Alice in Wonderland continued to work her way into new cultural contexts. In

1934 alone she would take on dozens of extra forms. On the page, she was the inspiration for works as diverse as *Frankie in Wonderland*, a fifty-cent American satirical pamphlet lashing out at the New Deal, and Ernest Le Prade's *Alice in Orchestra Land*, in which a girl who is convinced that she must be 'distantly related' to Carroll's character ('third or fourth cousins, perhaps') learns about different musical instruments after disappearing into a winding brass tunnel. Her influence could also be seen in works of far greater literary merit. In Berlin, Nabokov was busy writing *Invitation to a Beheading*, which Brian Boyd has described as a 'comic nightmare' and another 'topsy-turvey world'; meanwhile, in Paris, James Joyce was still adding new layers to *Finnegans Wake* (1939), a dazzlingly complex dream narrative in which numerous versions of Lewis Carroll, Alice Liddell and the characters of the *Alice* books repeatedly rise to the surface of the text before sinking back into a bubbling melting pot of language: 'Dodgfather, Dodgson and Coo', 'Wonderlawn's lost us for ever. Alis, alas, she broke the glass! Liddell locker through the leafery, ours is mistery of pain', 'A liss in hunterland', 'Alicious, twinstreams twinestraines, through alluring glass or alas in jumboland?', 'knives of hearts', 'from tweedledeedumms down to twiddledeedees' and many similar 'loose carolleries'. Joyce claimed to have read only 'bits and scraps' of Carroll until 1927, but in *Finnegans Wake* he set out to prove that the mind too deals principally in bits and scraps. His narrative is one in which anything can bump into anything else, and language is revealed as a jigsaw puzzle with an infinite number of solutions.

The art world was similarly open to Carroll's influence. When Balthus's first solo exhibition opened at Paris's Galerie Pierre in May 1934, it included a large painting in which a Tweedledum or Tweedledee figure could be seen walking mechanically past a small blonde girl playing in the street, and in the following year Carroll would be identified as one of the literary precursors of the Surrealist movement. In his 1928 work *Surrealism and Painting*, André Breton had already praised Picasso's Cubist paintings for showing viewers a new Wonderland, and in 1936 some of Carroll's own drawings would be exhibited alongside Surrealist artworks at a major exhibition in New York.

John Armstrong's Surrealist painting *Dreaming Head* (1938)

Wonderland also continued to be used for radically different political purposes. Michael Fry's book *Hitler's Wonderland* (1934) claimed to approach the subject of Nazi foreign and domestic policy without prejudice but, starting with the swastika printed on its front cover, quickly revealed itself to be a salivating act of hero worship in which Hitler was celebrated as a model political leader, 'his voice charged with the electricity of enthusiasm and unshakeable sincerity – his heart bent on revitalizing the Fatherland'. The idea that Wonderland and the Fatherland shared a common identity was especially chilling. On the other side of the argument, in 1933 a satire entitled 'Alice in Naziland' had appeared in a special issue of the *Jewish Chronicle* on the topic of 'Germany – Silent Voices' that included articles on religious persecution and the plight of refugees seeking safety in Poland.

While such writing demonstrated the dire consequences of certain kinds of utopian dreaming, it was still possible in 1934 to escape into more playful versions of Wonderland. That year saw the release of *Betty in Blunderland*, in which a saucer-eyed Betty Boop passed through a mirror to meet manically inventive cartoon versions of Carroll's characters, and also *Babes in Toyland*, in which Laurel and Hardy, as 'Stanley Dum' and 'Ollie Dee', encountered Bo-Peep, played by the actress (Charlotte Henry) who had previously starred as Alice in the 1933 film. Even opening up a newspaper or theatre programme could reveal unexpected glimpses of

Wonderland. A major Guinness campaign featured dozens of product-related parodies of the *Alice* books, while other advertisements in 1934 included a spoof of 'You are old, Father William' for Seagram's Whisky: '"My boy," quoth the sage, "your mention of age | Reminds me of Seagram's 'V. O.'; | For years it is aged till it reaches a stage | Of perfection – you'll like it, I know!"' Wherever one looked, Carroll's characters were talking and singing, playing and punning, and inevitably Alice was the busiest of them all.

In 1990, an essay on Alice in the *New York Times Book Review* pointed out 'That Girl Is Everywhere', but her slippery cultural presence was hardly a recent phenomenon. By the end of 1934, Alice had long since transcended her original status as an extended private joke in Victorian Oxford to become something more like a modern myth. She represented abstract hopes and fears that could be made comprehensible only by the addition of a human face; she was an empty vessel to which new meanings could be added without any danger of her ever being filled up. The girl was not only everywhere; she was also everyone and everything.

As for the other Alice, who had inspired this global phenomenon and then lived in its shadow for the next seventy years, her part in the story was played out. 'So Mrs Hargreaves has gone,' Menella Dodgson noted in a letter sent on 27 November. 'I wonder how long she will be remembered.'

*   *   *   *

*   *   *

*   *   *   *

EPILOGUE

'To write about the painter David Salle is to be forced into a kind of parody of his melancholy art of fragments, quotations, absences . . .'

JANET MALCOLM, *Forty-One False Starts*

Unknown

Oxford is a city of ghosts. Listen closely, and it's easy to imagine that you can hear the rustle of pages being turned by fingers that have long since turned to dust. In some of the older colleges, there are paving slabs that have become contoured with shallow ridges and valleys over the centuries, tiny man-made landscapes sculpted by generations of passing feet. And everywhere there are traces of Lewis Carroll. Even the road where I live, a quiet Victorian terrace to the east of the city, includes the house to which he once followed a young girl hoping to persuade her to sit for a photograph.

If you retrace his steps from this house back to the church where he first spotted her, after a hundred yards you reach a bar called the Mad Hatter. Carry on across Magdalen Bridge, and you find yourself walking into the heart of the city. On the surface a good deal has changed: the modern High Street is packed with buses and burger vans rather than horses and Velocimans, while orange pools of fluorescent street lighting have replaced the hesitant flicker of gas. But underneath this shiny modern skin Oxford is still recognizably the place Carroll knew. Turn left at the bottom of the High, walk past the Oxford City Museum – where some of Alice Hargreaves's personal belongings are on display, including the ivory case for her visiting cards and a glossy red seal for her letters bearing the initials A. P. H. – and you arrive at Christ Church. Here Tom still peals with eccentric regularity, and opposite the college's gated entrance there still stands the higgledy-piggledy building Carroll included in *Through the Looking-Glass* as a shop run by a sheep. If you choose to turn right at the bottom of the High, however, zigzagging through the narrow streets and passing another Mad Hatter on the way, this time a tour guide costumed like one of Tenniel's illustrations, you eventually arrive at the Museum of Natural History, a place Carroll visited often. And here you encounter the Oxford Dodo.

It isn't a specimen Carroll would have known. The original stuffed dodo was part of the celebrated 'Ark' of curiosities collected by John Tradescant the Elder in the seventeenth century, but over the years it gradually fell apart, and by the time it arrived at the new Museum in 1860 all that remained was a scaly left foot and a mummified head covered in a few scraps of leathery flesh. These fragments were exhibited alongside a painting by Johannes Savery (1650) that depicted a plump living dodo staring nervously into the distance; Victorian viewers were left to fill in the gaps for themselves. What modern visitors see, standing perkily in a glass case, is a new composite skeleton created by taxidermist Derek Frampton in 1998 from bones found in a swamp on Mauritius. It is mostly the colour of milky tea, with some parts that look bashed around the edges, and signs that others have been broken off. But that isn't the dodo your eye is drawn to. Standing next to it, almost beak-to-beak, is a sleek life-size model covered in goose and duck feathers; it looks less like a zoological specimen than a real bird that has paused to cock its head at the museum's visitors before waddling away. The last time I was there, the skeleton was attracting attention from a pair of solemn schoolboys, whose noses were

The dodo in Oxford's Museum of Natural History

pressed up hard against the glass, but the model was drawing the crowds. A beautifully crafted imitation of something that no longer exists, it seemed much more believable than the real thing.

It is tempting to think that biography works in a similar way. The biographer too pieces together fragments of evidence before fleshing them out into a story that will give the illusion of life, while trying to disguise those places where an important bone is missing or a bit of extra stuffing is required. That's an especially difficult task when it comes to the story of Lewis Carroll and his creation of Wonderland. To begin with, the bones of Carroll's life aren't all in one place; like those of many popular writers, his literary remains have been scattered into archives across the world. There are also numerous missing fragments. Many of the manuscripts and photographs he left behind have been lost (the scrap of paper about hunting buffalo he placed under the floorboards of Croft Rectory is just one item that can no longer be located), and others have disappeared into private collections. Indeed, although one of the best modern reworkings of the Alice stories, Jeff Noon's novel *Automated Alice* (1996), shows Alice gathering up the fragments from a 'jigsaw of the past', trying to solve this puzzle is much harder when it involves slotting together the pieces of someone else's life. Even the Dodgson family's jigsaw depicting 'The Life of Christ', now in Guildford Museum just a few yards from the Chestnuts, has a piece missing: the crucifixion scene features a headless Christ. It is what happens to many fragile objects over time, of course, but in this instance the gap might be viewed as more than an historical accident. It is like an emblem of the whole biographical pursuit.

Sometimes the range of materials a biographer has to work from will expand through new discoveries. A box in an attic turns out to contain a dusty bundle of letters; a photograph bought in a junk shop is revealed to be the lost page of an album now kept in a museum vault. In Carroll's case, however, it is not always easy to distinguish real discoveries from wishful thinking. A privately printed 1875 pamphlet entitled *Some Popular Fallacies about Vivisection*, with annotations in purple ink, was widely accepted as one of Carroll's lost works, until it was revealed to be a forgery from the 1920s. Guaranteed 'signed' copies of the *Alice* books are routinely exposed as fakes. Yet still we rummage in libraries and bookshops in the search for a genuine missing piece of the puzzle.

What complicates this search is how unreliable even some of the most popular facts about Carroll's life turn out to be. For example, next to the Oxford Dodo there is another glass case, containing an assortment of books and bones, and a stuffed white rabbit standing on its hind legs and clasping a fob watch. The title of this display is 'The real Alice', and it includes a summary of Carroll's relationship with Alice Liddell, which explains that 'Dodgson brought Alice and her sisters here on rainy afternoons and so incorporated into the wonderful stories he created for them many of the creatures from the displays, including the famous Oxford Dodo, a favourite for Dodgson who had a stammer: Do-do-dodgson.' The assumption that Carroll introduced the Dodo into Wonderland as a rueful private joke is now so widely accepted it has become indistinguishable from fact. '"What I tell you three times must be true,"' says the Bellman in *The Hunting of the Snark*, and the standard explanation of Carroll's nickname has been repeated so often it has acquired an even richer patina of truth. The only problem is that there is practically no evidence to support it. It is certainly the case that in 1886 Carroll gave Robinson Duckworth, his rowing companion on the 'golden afternoon', a copy of the facsimile edition of *Alice's Adventures Under Ground*, which he signed 'The Duck from the Dodo'. But he may have thought of himself as a dodo for many reasons other than his occasional difficulty in releasing words into the open. Perhaps he was joking about his physical ungainliness, or nervously alluding to the fact that if he failed to marry he was in danger of being the last of his line. He may also have recognized how close their names were alphabetically – Jan Morris has pointed out that when Dodgson and the dodo found their way into the *Encyclopaedia Britannica*, 'the two of them were happily placed side by side'. Alternatively, 'Dodo' may have been a small child's attempt at his name that Carroll willingly adopted, thereby becoming an extra member of the family to sit alongside 'Mama' and 'Papa'. Given

Carroll's addiction to wordplay, he might even have been making a shy boast about his work ethic: few people got more done in a day than Do-do-dodgson. But nobody really knows.

The story of 'the real Alice' is similarly littered with inventions masquerading as discoveries. One photograph widely available on the internet purports to show Alice as a little girl reaching up to kiss Carroll passionately on the lips. It is a crude fake made by splicing together a self-portrait Carroll took in 1857, when Ina Liddell assisted him by taking off the lens cap, with a fragment of *Open Your Mouth and Shut Your Eyes*. But its very existence indicates the temptation to create another piece of evidence when the historical record falls silent. Not everyone will notice that photographic manipulation has given Carroll an extra arm, which snakes amorously around Alice's waist, and even if people did notice they might not care. Indeed, some viewers might actually prefer the solidity of a myth to a patchy set of facts, in the same way that many visitors to the Oxford Museum of Natural History prefer an imitation dodo to authentic skeletal remains. Even glass eyes gleam invitingly when compared to empty sockets.

The gaps in Carroll's life have a wide range of causes. Some are the result of deliberate destruction (e.g. Mrs Liddell tearing up his letters to Alice), or accidental loss (e.g. presentation copies of the *Alice* books that were read until they fell apart), and some uncertainly straddle both categories (e.g. the missing volumes of his diary). Then there are all the works he did not live to complete, such as planned editions of a Child's Bible and a Girl's Shakespeare, or a book on religious difficulties that was still at a 'very fragmentary and unarranged' state two years before his death. Add to these the blank spaces in his diary when he forgot to fill in a name or a date, and thoughts that were too private to confide even to himself, and trying to capture his personality in a biography can feel less like reworking raw materials than scooping water with a sieve.

This would not have bothered Carroll in the slightest. 'My constant aim is to remain, personally, unknown to the world,' he told one correspondent, and any letters that were addressed to 'Lewis Carroll' at Christ

Church were returned with 'NOT KNOWN' written firmly across the envelope. This had literary as well as social implications. According to Stuart Dodgson Collingwood, Carroll's first publication, which appeared in the *Richmond School Magazine* in 1845, was a short story called 'The Unknown One' (appropriately, no copy of it survives), and when Collingwood put together an anthology of Carroll's minor writings in 1899 it was later published in America as *The Unknown Lewis Carroll*. It might just as well have been called *Lewis Carroll*, because even today he remains a frustratingly elusive figure.

Some writers have filled these gaps in the record with theories that range from the barely plausible (Carroll as a sufferer of epilepsy) to the ingeniously counterfactual (Carroll as Mrs Liddell's secret lover). Alice has been subjected to equally imaginative speculation, as if her reticence provided a blank page on which anything could be written, such as the series of insults that is thrown at her by the fictional Alice at the end of John Logan's play *Peter and Alice*: 'She took lovers and then grew bored . . . She despises tradesmen and blackies and chinkies and pretty much anyone who's not her . . . She bites into her pillow and cries every night . . . She looks at the bottle of laudanum and wonders.' None of these accusations has any substance, but they do remind us why returning to the *Alice* books can feel like such a relief. For Carroll's stories do not ask us to worry about what *is* true; instead, they entertain us with what we can imagine *as* true, and encourage us to enjoy being puzzled at what we do not know. They are invitations to wonder.

Both *Alice* books are full of questions – there are more than 150 in *Alice's Adventures in Wonderland* alone – and although some of these are straightforward to answer ('"What else have you got in your pocket?"'), others are important because they resist simple responses, such as Alice's '"What *will* become of me?"' That can make them frustrating narratives to read, because they are forever opening up lacunae and refusing to close them, but it is also one of the main reasons for their lasting success. From their first page to their last, they are a celebration of the fact that Carroll never forgot what it was like to be a child. In his preface to the New York Edition of *What Maisie Knew* (1907–8), Henry James noted that there are 'great gaps and voids' in a child's understanding of the world, and to hear Alice asking so many questions puts us firmly in the position of someone for whom life is still an obstacle course of surprises. It is this that makes the *Alice* books more than books for children. As Virginia Woolf argued in a 1939 review of Carroll's collected works, they are rather 'the only books in which we become children'.

As we grow older, many of these gaps and voids are filled in by experience, but some remain unknown territory. Other people's motives continue to be confusingly opaque; love continues to be a mystery that makes much more sense when it is happening to someone else. Here too the *Alice* books turn out to be surprisingly good companions; not because they have anything very useful to say about such matters (they are not Victorian self-help manuals), but because they always seem to be one step ahead of our attempts to explain them away. Not only have they proven to be infinitely elastic since *Alice's Adventures in Wonderland* was first published in 1865, faithfully reflecting every passing cultural trend; they also grow up with us as individuals. My own childhood copies are now sallow and blotchy with age, and a few pages even have wrinkles from the time I accidentally dropped them in the bath, but the most interesting changes are not visible to the naked eye. They are the endlessly moving outlines of each story I carry around inside my head.

I am far from being the only reader who enjoys returning to Alice's reassuringly predictable and endlessly surprising adventures. When Will Brooker set out to analyse their place in contemporary culture, he discovered that they had taken on a dizzying variety of forms, including films, comics, fan fiction, computer games, theme park rides, sculptures and pornography. Since the publication of his book *Alice's Adventures* in 2004, hundreds more *Alices* (and Alices) have been created, many of them online, turning the computer screen into a modern looking-glass through which it is possible to explore an entirely new Wonderland: WWWonderland. But reading Carroll's stories remains the best way of exploring their full creative range. This is partly because Wonderland is an imaginary universe that is still expanding. Francis Spufford has suggested that the great pleasure of reading stories in childhood that begin in the real world, and then take you somewhere else, is that 'once opened, the door would never entirely shut behind you'. The door into Wonderland works like that. Wonderland may exist only in Alice's head, but once we have visited it in her company it exists in our heads too. And because this door never altogether shuts behind us, after we return to the life that exists outside books it never seems quite the same again.

When I came back to Oxford at the end of 2013, after a period spent trying to untangle the secret history of Wonderland, it was clear that very little had changed. The city was still shrouded in fog and drizzle. I had not yet managed to silence the low grumble of advancing middle age. I also had a sadder motive for wanting to retrieve the tatty copy of *Alice's Adventures in Wonderland* that was waiting on a shelf beside my desk. The last time I had discussed the story with a student, during the previous academic year, we had both cracked up at a joke that was so silly it made us laugh at the sheer fact we were laughing. A few months later the student had died, and the joke no longer seemed quite so funny. Now I wondered if the same would be true of the book as a whole. I opened it and began to read.

Afterwards, I looked out through a rain-flecked window, and couldn't help smiling at the power Alice's story still has to change how we think and what we feel.

A trip to Wonderland unpeels the world around us, and makes it seem fresh and new.

*   *   *   *

*   *   *

*   *   *   *

Notes

LIST OF ABBREVIATIONS

Diaries: Edward Wakeling (ed.), *Lewis Carroll's Diaries: The Private Journals of Charles Lutwidge Dodgson*, 10 vols (The Lewis Carroll Society, 1993–2007)

Interviews & Recollections: Morton N. Cohen (ed.), *Lewis Carroll: Interviews and Recollections* (Basingstoke: Macmillan, 1989)

Letters: Morton N. Cohen (ed.), *The Letters of Lewis Carroll*, 2 vols (New York: Oxford University Press, 1979)

Life & Letters: Stuart Dodgson Collingwood, *The Life and Letters of Lewis Carroll (Rev. C. L. Dodgson)* (London: T. Fisher Unwin, 1898)

Macmillan: Morton N. Cohen and Anita Gandolfo (eds), *Lewis Carroll and the House of Macmillan* (Cambridge: Cambridge University Press, 1987)

ARCHIVES

Berg: the Berg Collection, New York Public Library.

Bodleian: the John Johnson Collection of Printed Ephemera, Bodleian Library, Oxford.

Christ Church: the Library and Archives of Christ Church, Oxford.

Dodgson Family Collection: material held at the Surrey History Centre, Woking.

Fales: the Berol Collection held at the Fales Library, New York.

Guildford Museum.

Hargreaves Papers: the Caryl Liddell Hargreaves Papers relating to Alice Liddell Hargreaves and the Lewis Carroll Centenary, held at the Beinecke Library, Yale University.

Harry Ransom Center: the Harry Ransom Center, University of Texas at Austin.

Harvard: the Harcourt Amory Collection held at the Houghton Library, Harvard University.

New Forest Centre: the Christopher Tower New Forest Reference Library, Lyndhurst.

Oxford City Museum.

Oxford Museum of Natural History.

Oxford Museum of Science.

Pierpont Morgan: the Pierpont Morgan Library, New York.

Princeton: the Morton Parrish Collection held at Princeton University Library.

Rosenbach: the Rosenbach Museum and Library, Philadelphia.

Private collections of material relating to Lewis Carroll and Alice Liddell Hargreaves.

Unless otherwise stated, Carroll's published works are quoted from *The Complete Works of Lewis Carroll* (London: Nonesuch Press, 1939), and his unpublished writings from the original manuscripts.

I follow standard practice in referring to Lewis Carroll rather than to Charles Dodgson, although I discuss Alice as Alice Liddell until her marriage and Alice Hargreaves thereafter. Carroll's characters are referred to by their names in the original *Alice* books, e.g. 'the Hatter' rather than 'the Mad Hatter'. The publication date of *Through the Looking-Glass* is given as 1872, as printed in the first edition, although it was actually issued in December 1871.

*

PROLOGUE: SNAP

3   **Alice P. Hargreaves** . . . Hargreaves Papers.

5   **'are extremely rare'** . . . Major Ernie Odell and John Mounsey, 'Sapper Before Sunset: A Period Piece' (unpublished TS, 1977), New Forest Centre, caption to first illustration (n.p.).

5   **'I do get tired'** . . . Private collection.

5   **'Alice in U. S. Land!'** . . . I am grateful to Edward Wakeling for allowing me to view his copy of this rare footage.

6   **'black fur coat'** . . . All quotations from newspaper reports are taken from a scrapbook of clippings in the Hargreaves Papers.

6   **'will be disappointed'** . . . Hargreaves Papers.

7   **'should have asked $1000'** . . . 'Alice in America 1932' (unpublished diary), Hargreaves Papers.

9   **her autograph** . . . Hargreaves Papers.

9   **'Once upon a time'** . . . Hargreaves Papers. 'Fairy Godfather' was also a phrase that had been used in an obituary (signed 'Vera') published in the *Lady's Pictorial* (27 January 1898) under the title 'A Wizard of Wonderland', repr. in August A. Imholtz, Jr and Charlie Lovett (eds), *In Memoriam Charles Lutwidge Dodgson, 1832–1898* (New York: The Lewis Carroll Society of North America, 1998), p. 79.

9   **crossed out in pencil** . . . Hargreaves Papers.

9   **'people prefer books'** . . . Julian Barnes, *Flaubert's Parrot* (London: Picador, 1984), p. 201.

10   **'cast by the'** . . . Hargreaves Papers.

10   **'new-made hayrick'** . . . Letter to Violet Dodgson (12 June 1932), Dodgson Family Collection; *Life & Letters*, p. 96.

10   **'golden afternoon'** . . . '"Alice" on the Stage', *The Theatre*, N.S., 9 (April 1887), pp. 179–80.

11   **temperature of 67.9°F** . . . Cited in Martin Gardner, *The Annotated Alice* (London: Penguin, 2001), pp. 9–10.

11   **'her own memories'** . . . Will Brooker, *Alice's Adventures: Lewis Carroll in Popular Culture* (New York; London: Continuum, 2004), p. 8.

11   **Brooker notes** . . . *Ibid.*, pp. 6–17.

11   **'insects and nettles'** . . . Jo Elwyn Jones and J. Francis Gladstone, *The Alice Companion: A Guide to Lewis Carroll's Alice Books* (Basingstoke: Macmillan, 1998), p. 215.

13   **their original stories** . . . 'Dingley Dell and the Fleet', repr. in W. H. Auden, *Selected Essays* (London: Faber, 1964).

14   **'nobody ever has'** . . . 'Avenging Angel', *The New Yorker* (27 August 2007).

15   **'Lewd's carol'** . . . in *Finnegans Wake*; see Morton Cohen, *Lewis Carroll, Photographer of Children: Four Nude Studies* (New York: Potter, 1978), p. 30.

15   **'a white stone'** . . . *Diaries*, vol. 3, pp. 73, 108.

16   **levels of satisfaction** . . . Pliny the Elder, *Natural History*, 7.40.131; similar stories are told about the Cretans and Scythians.

16   **'super-fastidiousness'** . . . *Letters*, vol. 2, p. 756.

16   **'the Mad Hatter'** . . . *Interviews & Recollections*, p. 18; Derek Hudson, *Lewis Carroll* (London: Constable, 1954, repr. 1995), p. 323.

16   **'unfinished business'** . . . '"In the Midst of his Laughter and Glee": Nonsense and Nothingness in Lewis Carroll', *Soundings: An Interdisciplinary Journal*, 82: 3–4 (Fall–Winter 1999), p. 541.

17   **'will never end'** . . . *Diaries*, vol. 7, p. 382.

17   **'any liking for'** . . . *Letters*, vol. 1, p. 472.

17   **'(to be continued)'** . . . *Letters*, vol. 1, p. 21.

17   **'Finis'** . . . Reproduced in Edward Guiliano (ed.), *Lewis Carroll Observed: A Collection of Unpublished Photographs, Drawings, Poetry, and New Essays* (New York: Clarkson N. Potter, 1976), p. 91.

17   **'never-failing stories'** . . . *Letters*, vol. 1, p. 209n.

18   **'praise of ferrets'** . . . Gardner (ed.), *The Annotated Alice*, pp. 38–9.

21   **'moved beneath mine'** . . . *Alice I Have Been* (New York: Bantam, 2011), pp. 339–40.

21   **'lips clamp shut'** . . . *White Stone: The Alice Poems* (Montreal: Signal, 2005), p. 21.

23   **man and a superman** . . . Joseph Campbell, *The Hero With a Thousand Faces* (1949, repr. Princeton: Princeton University Press, 1968), pp. 318–34. On Superman, see Joseph J. Darowski (ed.), *The Ages of Superman: Essays on the Man of Steel in Changing Times* (Jefferson: McFarland & Co., 2012).

ONE

27   **'to the children'** . . . *Life & Letters*, p. 11.

28   **five and seven** . . . D. V. Glass, *Population Policies and Movements in Europe* (New York: A. M. Kelley, 1967), pp. 70–5.

28   **'very respectable'** . . . Letter from Rev Dodgson to his brother Hassard, cited in *Diaries*, vol. 1, p. 17.

28   **signed a letter** . . . *Letters*, vol. 1, p. 320.

30   **nagging superstition** . . . William E. Jarvis notes that 'Desiccated chickens, domestic cats and well-worn shoes were secreted under floors, thresholds, inside walls, chimney recesses or roofs from the seventeenth through the nineteenth centuries', and offers the example of 'an early seventeenth-century English child's shoe found behind wooden paneling' in a nursery: *Time Capsules: A Cultural History* (Jefferson: McFarland & Co., 2003), pp. 83, 97.

30   **encouraged to assemble** . . . in *On Longing: Narratives of the Miniature, the Gigantic, the Souvenir, the Collection* (Durham; London: Duke University Press, 1993), Susan Stewart quotes a children's guide to collecting, published in 1890, which recommends that 'every house ought to possess a "Museum", even if it is only one shelf in a small cupboard; here, carefully dated and named, should be placed the pretty shells you gather on the seashore, the old fossils you find in the rocks,

the skeleton leaves you pick up from under the hedges, the strange orchids you find on the downs' (p. 162).

30   **'us and them'** . . . Repr. in *The Kenneth Grahame Book* (London: Methuen & Co., 1932), pp. 225–7.

31   **'shower of thimbles'** . . . *Letters*, vol. 1, p. 239.

31   **'in your pocket!'** . . . cited in *Diaries*, vol. 8, p. 513n.

31   **just been delivered** . . . *Letters*, vol. 2, pp. 975–6.

31   **'folks' gloves' or foxgloves** . . . Isa Bowman, *The Story of Lewis Carroll Told for Young People by the Real Alice in Wonderland* (London: J. M. Dent & Co., 1899), p. 70; when another child-friend accidentally carried off one of his gloves, Carroll sent her a mock bill (*Letters*, vol. 1, p. 114).

31   **'chase the Buffalo'** . . . Harding B 11(482), Bodleian.

Two

33   **'cups of tea'** . . . 'Isa's Visit to Oxford' (1888), repr. in Bowman, *The Story of Lewis Carroll*, appendix.

33   **'submission to discipline'** . . . *Diaries*, vol. 3, p. 18.

34   **the same slight pout** . . . Dodgson Family Collection.

34   **'his were very dull'** . . . 'Lewis Carroll as I Knew Him' TS, Dodgson Family Collection.

34   **'fitful flashes of enthusiasm'** . . . *A Sermon Preached in Ripon Minster, at the Ordination Held by the Lord Bishop of Ripon, on Sunday, July 29th, 1838* (Warrington: J. Haddock, 1838), p. 15.

34   **'the poor Clergyman'** . . . *The Providence of God Manifested in the Temporal Condition of the Poorer Clergy: A Sermon Preached in the Collegiate Church of Manchester, on Thursday July 18th, 1839, at the Meeting of the Society for the Relief of the Widows and Orphans of the Clergy of the Archdeaconry of Chester*, cited in Anne Clark, *The Real Alice* (New York: Stein & Day, 1981), p. 23.

34   **'earnest and affectionate wishes'** . . . 21 May 1857 and 12 November 1857, repr. in Anne Clark Amor (ed.), *Letters to Skeffington Dodgson from his Father* (The Lewis Carroll Society, 1990), pp. 16–17.

34   **'destruction of the Town'** . . . *Letters*, vol. 1, p. 4.

35   **hippo dancing in a tutu** . . . Karoline Leach, *In the Shadow of the Dreamchild: The Myth and Reality of Lewis Carroll*, rev. edn (London; Chester Springs, PA: Peter Owen, 2009), pp. 68–9.

35   **notebook kept by his mother** . . . Dodgson Family Collection.

35   **set of biblical texts** . . . Dodgson Family Collection.

35   **'Skeleton Maps CLD'** . . . Dodgson Family Collection.

36   **speckled with unknown worlds** . . . *Diaries*, vol. 7, p. 188.

36   **'family entertainer'** . . . W. H. Auden, 'Lewis Carroll', *Forewords and Afterwords* (London: Faber, 1973), p. 286.

36   **'the most *persevering* way'** . . . 6 July (no year, but after 1843), Dodgson Family Collection.

36   **'behaves badly to prison'** . . . 'Railway Rules' (Harvard).

37   **an agreed set of rules** . . . *The Field of Nonsense* (London: Chatto & Windus, 1952), pp. 27–8.

37   **'tea for the station master'** . . . *The Midland Counties Railway Companion*

(Nottingham; Leicester: R. Allen & E. Allen, 1840), p. xii; '"Love's" Railway Guide' (Harvard).

37   *La Guida di Bragia* . . . The original manuscript is in the Fales Library, and has been reprinted in a modern edition (New York: The Lewis Carroll Society of North America, 2007).

38   **wooden pupils** . . . Both toys are at Guildford Museum.

38   **set of eight tiny tools** . . . The box is now housed in a 'wizard's workshop' in the toy gallery of Hove Museum and Art Gallery.

38   **'collection of micro-photographs'** . . . *Diaries*, vol. 4, p. 95.

39   **'Lilliputian Stationery'** . . . The sales catalogue for Carroll's effects after his death included a collection of very small notepaper and matching envelopes in a larger envelope marked 'Lilliputian Stationery'; see Jeffrey Stern, *Lewis Carroll's Library* (Charlottesville: University Press of Virginia, 1981), p. 79.

39   **'ever so much of my love'** . . . Pierpont Morgan, repr. in *Letters*, vol. 2, p. 828.

39   *Useful and Instructive Poetry* . . . The original manuscript is in Fales, and has been reprinted several times.

39   **'tail of boundless length'** . . . 'Cogitations on Conclusions', *The Rectory Magazine* (Harry Ransom Center).

40   **unless Carroll saw them in manuscript** . . . In *Lewis Carroll: A Biography* (London: J. M. Dent & Sons, 1979), p. 49, Anne Clark speculates that this might have been possible: Knowsley, where Lear had been commissioned by the Earl of Derby to illustrate his zoological specimens, was only a few miles from Daresbury.

41   **'a hard "C"' in a shop** . . . *Letters*, vol. 1, p. 202.

42   **'don't forget Amy's napkin'** . . . *Little Women* (1868–69), ed. Valerie Alderson (Oxford: Oxford University Press, 1994), pp. 98–102; copies of the original *Pickwick Portfolio* are now at Harvard.

42   **'sick families'** . . . See Christine Alexander, 'Play and Apprenticeship: the Culture of Family Magazines', in Christine Alexander and Juliet McMaster (eds), *The Child Writer from Austen to Woolf* (Cambridge: Cambridge University Press, 2010), pp. 31–50.

42   **'"memory, and muchness"'** . . . 'Musings on Milk', in *The Rectory Magazine* (Harry Ransom Center), offers another experiment in 'M' words, beginning 'Marvellously many materials make milk! Much too many to mention.'

43   **a verdict of 'suicide'** . . . 'Crundle Castle' ch. 1, *The Rectory Magazine* (Harry Ransom Center); 'Lays of Sorrow No. 1', *The Rectory Umbrella* (Harvard).

44   **'down, down, down he went'** . . . 'Crundle Castle' ch. 1, and 'Sidney Hamilton' ch. 3, *The Rectory Magazine* (Harry Ransom Center).

44   **'beings of very mixed motives'** . . . *Letters*, vol. 2, p. 769.

44   **'his sleight-of-hand'** . . . *Life & Letters*, p. 20.

44   **destination as 'Bank'** . . . Collingwood reproduces the cartoon in 'Before "Alice" – The Boyhood of Lewis Carroll', *Strand Magazine* (1898).

45   **'the meaning of "Tees"!'** . . . 'The Two Brothers', *Mischmasch* (Harvard).

45   **'wrote down Pine'** . . . Harry Ransom Center.

45   **two 'dissected puzzles'** . . . Guildford Museum.

46   **seating plans** . . . In 1871, Carroll suggested to his publisher that it would be 'a good thing' to publish sets of blank cards, 'with ornamental borders, and with lined rules for names', which could be filled in by the hosts of dinner parties to show their guests where to sit; see *Macmillan*, pp. 95–6.

46   **the snaking appearance he wanted** . . . The proof is now in the archives of Christ Church.

47   **'the end of another day'** . . . Dodgson Family Collection.

48   **in New Zealand it is noon** . . . 'Apparent Course of the Sun'; Anne Clark discusses this example in *Lewis Carroll: A Biography*, p. 17.

48   **midnight in Greenwich** . . . *Diaries*, vol. 8, p. 190.

48   **the time as '6¼'** . . . H. L. Rowell in *Interviews & Recollections*, p. 135.

48   **'inflicting a sudden shock'** . . . *Letters*, vol. 1, p. 159.

49   **'"seven and a half exactly"'** . . . Martin Gardner weighs up the evidence for the age of the fictional Alice in *The Annotated Alice*, p. 144.

THREE

50   **'*But,* please explain!'** . . . *Life & Letters*, pp. 12–13.

50   **'superiority over other boys'** . . . Dodgson Family Collection.

51   **continued Arnold's reforms** . . . J. B. Hope Simpson, *Rugby since Arnold: A History of Rugby School from 1842* (New York: St Martin's Press, 1967), p. 10.

52   **'his daily exercise'** . . . Anthony Trollope, *An Autobiography*, ed. Michael Sadleir and Frederick Page (Oxford: Oxford University Press, 1980), p. 8.

52   **'as if it had been skinned'** . . . Lee Warner, cited in Hope Simpson, *Rugby since Arnold*, pp. 32–3.

52   **'use his fists'** . . . *Life & Letters*, p. 23.

52   **'no tricks now'** . . . *Letters*, vol. 1, p. 5.

52   **'falling down'** . . . *Letters*, vol. 1, p. 7.

52   **copy of Virgil** . . . Harvard.

53   **any given date in history** . . . 'To Find the Day of the Week for Any Given Date', *Nature*, 35 (31 March 1887), p. 517.

53   **the 'calculating boys'** . . . Sally Shuttleworth discusses the phenomenon of the 'calculating boys' in *The Mind of the Child: Child Development in Literature, Science, and Medicine, 1840–1900* (Oxford: Oxford University Press, 2010), pp. 142–4.

53   **'an account to render hereafter'** . . . *A Sermon Preached in the Minster at Ripon on Sunday, Jan. 15, 1837, at the First Ordination held by the Right Rev. Chas. Thomas Longley, D.D., Lord Bishop of Ripon* (Oxford: J. H. Parker, 1837), p. 7.

53   **'Right and Wrong'** . . . *Letters*, vol. 2, p. 746.

53   **dozens of questions** . . . *The Tutor's Assistant: Being a Compendium of Arithmetic, &c.* (York: T. Wilson & Sons, 1842), p. 189 (Harvard). The same narrative impulse would later influence the collection of mathematical puzzles Carroll published in 1885 as *A Tangled Tale*.

54   **the number forty-two** . . . There are many other examples, some of them self-evident (in 'Phantasmagoria' the narrator reveals that he is forty-two years old) and others involving fiendishly clever use of prime numbers and hidden codes, which Edward Wakeling has discussed in two articles in the *Carrollian*, 6: 4 (Autumn 1977) and 17: 1–2 (Winter–Spring 1988); see also Robin Wilson, *Lewis Carroll in Numberland: His Fantastical Mathematical Logical Life* (London: Penguin, 2008), pp. 64–6.

54   **'best shots of his day'** . . . Obituary, cited in *Letters*, vol. 1, p. 32n.

55   **'as far as possible'** . . . Violet Dodgson, 'Lewis Carroll as I Knew Him' TS, Dodgson Family Collection.

55 **'Dodgson is a muff'** . . . Harvard.

55 **'incompetent person'** . . . *OED*, 'muff'.

55 **'young muff'** . . . Thomas Hughes, *Tom Brown's School Days* (1857), ed. Andrew Sanders (Oxford: Oxford University Press, 1989), pp. 128, 222.

55 **delicate new boy** . . . [C. B. Wheeler], *Memoir of John Lang Bickersteth, Late of Rugby School* (London: The Religious Tract Society, 1851), pp. 35–70.

56 **'annoyance at night'** . . . *Life & Letters*, pp. 30–1.

56 **'asleep secure of harm'** . . . Book IV, l. 789.

56 **'petty perversions'** . . . W. D. Arnold et al., *The Book of Rugby School: Its History and its Daily Life* (Rugby: Crossley & Billington, 1856), p. 204.

56 **'"knowing good and evil"'** . . . F. W. Farrar, *Eric; or, Little by Little* (London: S. W. Partridge, 1858), pp. 80, 85. The biblical allusion is to Genesis 3: 5.

FOUR

57 **how rarely mothers feature** . . . See Jenny Woolf, *The Mystery of Lewis Carroll* (London: Haus Publishing, 2010), pp. 29–30.

57 **'missing morning chapel'** . . . *Letters*, vol. 1, p. 13.

57 **'Alarum bedstead'** . . . *A Guide to the Great Exhibition* (London: Cox & Wyman, 1851), p. 80.

57 **Theophilus Carter** . . . See Mark Davies, 'The Mad Hatter on the High', *TLS* (17 May 2013), pp. 14–15; Davies suggests that the real inspiration for the Hatter was indeed a hatter, namely the Oxford tailor Thomas Randall.

58 **'a sort of fairyland'** . . . *Letters*, vol. 1, p. 17.

58 **'To meet the sun'** . . . Thackeray, 'A May Day Ode', *The Times* (1 May 1851).

58 **'Hardware, Class 22'** . . . *Official Catalogue of the Great Exhibition of the Works of Industry of All Nations*, 3 vols (London: Spicer Brothers, 1851), vol. 2, p. 598.

58 **'as you go'** . . . *Letters*, vol. 1, p. 18.

59 **'Wilson the Hosier'** . . . John Keats, unpublished verses contained in a letter (September 1817).

59 **'river-rounded'** . . . G. M. Hopkins, 'Duns Scotus's Oxford' (1879).

59 **'walking publicly in boots'** . . . Clark, *Lewis Carroll: A Biography*, p. 64.

60 **'the Man who Rows'** . . . [S. R. Hole], *Hints to Freshmen, in the University of Oxford* (Oxford: J. Vincent, 1853), p. 18.

60 **'(loud cheers)'** . . . Edward Bradley ('Cuthbert Bede'), *The Adventures of Mr Verdant Green, An Oxford Freshman* (London: Nathaniel Cooke, 1853), pp. 48, 71.

60 **'thy byrthe-day'** . . . *Letters*, vol. 1, p. 15.

60 **'uncommon grandeur'** . . . James Marshall Francis, *A Hand-Book for Oxford; or an Historical and Topographical Guide to the University, City, and Environs* (Oxford: J. & R. Dewe, 1841), p. 135; Anon., *The Oxford University and City Guide, on a New Plan* (Oxford: Henry Slatter, 1842), p. 139.

61 **more general attitudes** . . . Thomas Hughes, *Tom Brown at Oxford* (1861, repr. London: Macmillan, 1897), p. 72.

62 **boiled pelican** . . . *Life & Letters*, p. 442.

62 **'How is your father?'** . . . Christopher Butler (ed.), *Christ Church, Oxford: A Portrait of the House* (London: Third Millennium, 2006), p. 91.

62 **'out walking together'** . . . *Letters*, vol. 1, p. 14; in *Oxford Yesterday: Memoirs of Oxford Seventy Years Ago* (Oxford: Basil Blackwell, 1927), W. E. Sherwood recalls

that this type of undergraduate was 'always with a friend, taking conscientiously his daily "grind" of about two miles or so out along the different rounds round Oxford, and then back to work' (p. 22).

62   **Prime Minister William Gladstone** . . . See Butler, *Christ Church, Oxford: A Portrait of the House*, p. 89.

62   **'winning something good'** . . . Frederick Arnold, *Christ Church Days. An Oxford Story*, 2 vols (London: Richard Bentley, 1867), vol. 1, p. 56.

62   **'steady quiet conduct'** . . . Letter from E. B. Pusey to Revd Dodgson (1851), Dodgson Family Collection.

63   **'do nothing more about it'** . . . *Diaries*, vol. 4, p. 138.

63   **'this Beauty is perceived'** . . . Dodgson Family Collection.

64   **'beauty in any form'** . . . 'Lewis Carroll As I Knew Him', p. 9.

64   **'Pope of Rome next'** . . . *Letters*, vol. 1, p. 29.

65   **'a good Head'** . . . Dodgson Family Collection.

65   **'*may* perhaps compose –'** . . . Dodgson Family Collection.

FIVE

66   **'surviving the year'** . . . *Diaries*, vol. 2, pp. 12–13.

67   **annoyance of real life** . . . See U. C. Knoepflmacher, *Ventures into Childland: Victorians, Fairy Tales, and Femininity* (Chicago; London: University of Chicago Press, 1998), pp. 39–40.

69   **'*Lewis Carroll* was chosen'** . . . *Diaries*, vol. 2, p. 39.

69   **'the past year'** . . . *Life & Letters*, pp. 64–5.

69   **July, August and September** . . . See Seamus Perry, 'Quod Talk', *Oxford Times* (12 September 2013).

69   **'to recommend your son'** . . . Dodgson Family Collection.

69   **rewarding the best-connected** . . . See Henry L. Thompson, *Christ Church* (London: F. E. Robinson, 1900), p. 195; Christ Church's attempts to meet the objections of the commissioners included a decision in 1854 to abolish the ancient system of private nomination to Studentships, although the fact that they agreed to elect men who were 'of irreproachable moral conduct' and only secondly 'of competent learning' might still have raised some eyebrows (p. 197).

70   **'satisfaction in the college'** . . . *Diaries*, vol. 1, p. 101.

70   **'peaceful revolution'** . . . Thompson, *Christ Church*, p. 202.

71   **'a tedious performance'** . . . *Diaries*, vol. 1, p. 50.

71   **'Thoroughly wet day'** . . . Vol. 1, p. 8 (Christ Church MS 536).

72   **'a better and holier life!'** . . . *Diaries*, vol. 4, pp. 158 & 242.

72   **'dry and perfunctory'** . . . *Interviews & Recollections*, pp. 19, 76.

72   **'laughing at *you*, Sir!'** . . . Recorded in Hudson, *Lewis Carroll*, p. 85.

73   **'time and trouble'** . . . *Diaries*, vol. 2, pp. 30–44.

73   **'all this reading'** . . . *Diaries*, vol. 2, pp. 26, 34–5.

73   **'Register of Letters'** . . . This information comes from Stuart Dodgson Collingwood; see 'Lewis Carroll: An Interview with His Biographer', *Westminster Budget*, 12 (9 Dec 1898), p. 23.

74   **Marmion Savage** . . . *Diaries*, vol. 1, pp. 84–90.

74   **'full many a flower'** . . . *Diaries*, vol. 3, p. 41; the sonnet does not appear to have survived.

77   'piece of machinery' . . . *Letters*, vol. 1, p. 19.

77   'attempt that I have seen' . . . *Diaries*, vol. 1, p. 66.

77   **Photography** . . . This summary draws on Roger Taylor's introduction to *Lewis Carroll, Photographer: The Princeton University Library Albums*, ed. Roger Taylor and Edward Wakeling (Princeton: Princeton University Press, 2002), pp. 1–120.

78   **wooden box** . . . Oxford Museum of Science.

79   'my life already' . . . *Diaries*, vol. 1, p. 78.

79   **3,000 photographs** . . . See Edward Wakeling's reconstruction of Carroll's photographic output in *Lewis Carroll, Photographer*, pp. 240–75.

79   'happy *now!*' . . . Carroll told H. L. Rowell that happiness 'was nearly always realized only in retrospect', so that 'the thought was not "I *am* happy now", but rather "I *was* happy then"', cited in Hudson, *Lewis Carroll*, p. 320.

80   **daguerreotypes of Venice** . . . *Praeterita* (1886–87), *The Works of John Ruskin*, ed. E. T. Cook and Alexander Wedderburn, 39 vols (London: George Allen, 1903–12), vol. 35, pp. 372–3.

80   **a young art** . . . See Lindsay Smith, *The Politics of Focus: Women, Children and Nineteenth-Century Photography* (Manchester: Manchester University Press, 1998), pp. 88–92.

80   'if lying down' . . . *Letters*, vol. 2, p. 982.

81   'I ever saw' . . . *Diaries*, vol. 2, p. 48.

82   'white stone' . . . *Diaries*, vol. 2, p. 65.

82   'Allius' . . . Catullus 68.

82   'nonsense poetry' and 'no-nonsense' . . . I am grateful to Matt Bevis for drawing these dates to my attention.

82   **her earliest writings** . . . Oxford City Museum.

83   **reflection of himself** . . . This argument is persuasively put forward by Catherine Robson in *Men in Wonderland: The Lost Girlhood of the Victorian Gentleman* (Princeton: Princeton University Press, 2001), pp. 129–53.

84   'might have been his' . . . Hudson, *Lewis Carroll*, p. 187.

85   'hole in the table' . . . *Letters*, vol. 1, pp. 24–5.

89   'seven different voices' . . . *Diaries*, vol. 2, p. 128.

90   'on the premises long enough' . . . *Diaries*, vol. 2, pp. 79, 113, 116.

90   'undesirable acquaintances for him' . . . *Diaries*, vol. 3, pp. 59–63.

90   'stayed to tea' . . . *Diaries*, vol. 3, p. 55.

90   **Carroll checking his watch** . . . Carroll's fob watch is now owned by Oxford City Museum; it was sold after his death for six shillings.

90   'great deal of waste time' . . . *Diaries*, vol. 2, p. 73; vol. 3, pp. 90, 142–3.

90   'not made much of it yet' . . . *Diaries*, vol. 2, p. 112.

91   'Prose and Poetry' . . . *Diaries*, vol. 3, p. 156.

91   'Scripture reading before chapel' . . . *Diaries*, vol. 3, p. 158.

91   'Hiawatha's Photographing' . . . See Jane M. Rabb (ed.), *Literature and Photography: Interactions 1840–1990* (Albuquerque: University of New Mexico Press, 1995), p. 46.

92   **conventions of Victorian theatre** . . . Michael R. Booth offers a good summary of these staging conventions in *Theatre in the Victorian Age* (Cambridge: Cambridge University Press, 1991), p. 125.

93   **His first album** . . . Album ([A]VI]) dates from 1856 and is now in the Harry Ransom Center. In 1857, Carroll saw Kate Terry playing the part of Ariel in a production he described as 'one of the most beautiful living pictures I ever saw'; see *Diaries*, vol. 3, p. 81, and Roger Taylor's introduction to *Lewis Carroll, Photographer*, p. 29.

93   **'devote much time to sketching'** . . . *Life & Letters*, p. 102.

93   **1862 watercolour** . . . Reproduced as the frontispiece to Charles C. Lovett and Stephanie B. Lovett, *Lewis Carroll's Alice: An Annotated Checklist of the Lovett Collection* (Westport, CT: Meckler, 1990); details of the painting's provenance are given on pp. 485–6.

93   **'entirely ignorant of it!'** . . . *The Gentlewoman* (5 February 1898), repr. in Imholtz and Lovett (eds), *In Memoriam Charles Lutwidge Dodgson*, p. 57.

93   **'the best enamel'** . . . *Diaries*, vol. 2, p. 19.

93   **more artistic** . . . The relationship between painting and photography in the period is expertly discussed in Michael Bartram, *The Pre-Raphaelite Camera: Aspects of Victorian Photography* (London: Weidenfeld & Nicolson, 1985).

93   **'taken from the life'** . . . *Diaries*, vol. 3, p. 174.

94   **'a pleasant sleep'** . . . *Romeo and Juliet*, IV. 1. 108–9.

94   **Little Red Riding-Hood** . . . *Diaries*, vol. 4, p. 120.

95   **more photographs of her** . . . James Alexander provides a helpful comparative table in 'Sentiment and Aesthetics in Victorian Photography: The Child Portraits of C. L. Dodgson', *Carrollian*, 17 (2006), p. 25.

95   **'reserved for grown-ups!'** . . . 'Alice's Recollections of Carrollian Days', *Cornhill Magazine*, 73: 433 (July 1932), p. 6.

96   **'Queen o' the May'** . . . *The Poems of Tennyson*, ed. Christopher Ricks, 3 vols (Harlow: Longman, 1987), vol. 1, p. 456; these lines were inscribed opposite a copy of the photograph (now missing) in one of Carroll's albums, and are mistakenly described as 'probably an original composition by Dodgson' in Taylor and Wakeling (eds), *Lewis Carroll, Photographer*, p. 164.

96   **'Fascination'** . . . See, e.g., Kate Greenaway, *Language of Flowers* (London: n.p., 1884), p. 17.

96   **Victorian educationalists** . . . James R. Kincaid discusses these analogies in *Child-Loving: The Erotic Child and Victorian Culture* (New York: Routledge, 1992), pp. 90–1.

96   **'perfectly overcome'** . . . 'Photographic Exhibition', *Illustrated Times* (28 January 1860), p. 57.

96   **'very fine specimen'** . . . H. M. Stanley, *London Street Arabs* (London: Cassell, 1890), p. 7.

97   **'bare to the knee'** . . . *Diaries*, vol. 3, pp. 94–5.

98   **'Before the king Cophetua'** . . . Ricks (ed.), *The Poems of Tennyson*, vol. 2, pp. 604–5.

EIGHT

100   **memento mori** . . . Michael Wheeler discusses the analogical thinking that compared sleep and death in *Heaven, Hell, and the Victorians* (Cambridge:

Cambridge University Press, 1994); a good selection of these photographs is printed in Jay Ruby, *Secure the Shadow: Death and Photography in America* (Cambridge, Mass.; London: MIT Press, 1995).

101   **'a beautiful photograph'** . . . *Letters*, vol. 1, pp. 44–5.

102   **'72nd birthday'** . . . *Letters*, vol. 1, p. 49.

102   **arrested development** . . . *OED* (T. H. Huxley).

102   **'steady under excitement'** . . . James Hunt, *Stammering and Stuttering, Their Nature and Treatment* (London: Longman, Brown, Green, Longman, & Roberts, 1861), pp. 169–70.

103   **'an eloquent divine'** . . . James Hunt, *A Treatise on the Cure of Stammering* (London: Longman, Brown, Green, & Longmans, 1854), pp. 73–4.

103   **'Training of the Organs of'** . . . James Hunt, *A Manual of the Philosophy of Voice and Speech, Especially in Relation to the English Language and the Art of Public Speaking* (London: Longman, Brown, Green, Longmans, & Roberts, 1859), pp. xi–xiii.

103   **'in the house'** . . . *Letters*, vol. 1, pp. 42, 54.

103   **'a wonderful stage'** . . . Greville MacDonald, *George MacDonald and His Wife* (London: George Allen & Unwin, 1924), p. 343.

103   **'when occasion demanded'** . . . William Raeper, *George MacDonald: Novelist and Victorian Visionary* (Tring: Lion Publishing, 1987), pp. 194, 169.

104   **'Down and down she went . . .'** . . . George MacDonald, *Dealings with the Fairies* (London: Alexander Strahan, 1867), pp. 209, 214. The story was originally published in *Beeton's Christmas Annual* (1862).

104   **'without shame or desire!'** . . . George MacDonald, *Phantastes, and Lilith* (London: Gollancz, 1962), p. 161.

104   **'surprised at nothing'** . . . *Ibid.*, p. 33.

NINE

105   **'parents and their children'** . . . Bourne Hall Draper, *Frank and His Father; or, Conversations on the First Three Chapters of the Book of Genesis* (London: William Darton & Son, n.d.), p. vi.

106   **'I am happy'** . . . Mary Martha Sherwood, *The History of the Fairchild Family; or, The Child's Manual: Being a Collection of Stories Calculated to Shew the Importance and Effects of a Religious Education*, 6th edn (London: J. Hatchard, 1822), pp. 286–93.

106   **'characters of the book'** . . . Lord Frederic Hamilton, *The Days Before Yesterday* (London: Hodder & Stoughton, 1920), p. 34.

107   **'"say very little"'** . . . Susan Warner ('Elizabeth Wetherell'), *Mr Rutherford's Children* (London: George Routledge & Co., 1855), pp. 5, 10, 34, 13.

108   **'Have a life of HOLIDAY'** . . . Repr. in *Letters*, vol. 1, p. 51.

109   **'side of a room'** . . . Catherine Sinclair, *Holiday House: A Book for the Young* (1839, repr. London: Ward, Lock & Co., 1879), pp. 31, 70, 79.

109   **'wax legs and armes'** . . . These letters were sold in 2001, and are cited in the sales catalogue *Lewis Carroll's Alice: The Photographs, Books, Papers and Personal Effects of Alice Liddell and Her Family* (Sotheby's, 2001), pp. 19–20.

109   **'their story books'** . . . Cited in J. S. Bratton, *The Impact of Victorian Children's Fiction* (London: Croom Helm, 1981), p. 178.

110   **actual experiences of children** . . . These examples are drawn from Valerie

Sanders (ed.), *Records of Girlhood: An Anthology of Nineteenth-Century Women's Childhoods* (Aldershot: Ashgate, 2000), pp. 7–11.

110   **'fair hair'** . . . Hughes, *Tom Brown's School Days*, p. 217.

111   **'I ever saw'** . . . *Diaries*, vol. 3, p. 108.

111   **'"Kingdom of heaven"'** . . . Cited in Colin Gordon, *Beyond the Looking Glass: Reflections of Alice and Her Family* (London: Hodder & Stoughton, 1982), pp. 81–2.

111   **'love of his dreams'** . . . Edgar Jepson, *Memories of a Victorian* (London: Victor Gollancz, 1933), pp. 219–20.

112   **'Afterwards – phugh!'** . . . Desmond Flower and Henry Maas (eds), *The Letters of Ernest Dowson* (London: Cassell, 1967), pp. 162, 88.

112   **'three-fourths of my life'** . . . Bowman, *The Story of Lewis Carroll*, p. 57.

112   **'little pictures'** . . . *Diaries*, vol. 4, p. 290.

113   **'kingdom of heaven'** . . . Matthew 18: 3.

113   **'more regular habits'** . . . *Diaries*, vol. 4, pp. 204, 217.

114   **'sweet-relief of girl-society'** . . . *Letters*, vol. 2, pp. 980, 1095.

114   **'photographed or to be photographed'** . . . *Diaries*, vol. 4, pp. 178–81.

114   **'(not *to* us)'** . . . *Interviews & Recollections*, p. 154.

115   **'again quite merry'** . . . *The Old Curiosity Shop* (1840–41), ed. Elizabeth M. Brennan (Oxford: Oxford University Press, 1998), pp. 6, 415–17, 538, 554. John Bowen brilliantly discusses these switches of narrative tone in *Other Dickens: Pickwick to Chuzzlewit* (Oxford: Oxford University Press, 2000), pp. 151–6.

116   **'execrable noise'** . . . *Letters*, vol. 1, pp. 392–3.

TEN

117   **'for Alice'** . . . *Diaries*, vol. 4, pp. 94–5.

119   **'his waste-paper basket'** . . . 'Alice's Recollections of Carrollian Days', p. 5.

119   **shaken out of place** . . . For the idea that picnics involve 'shaking everything up' I am indebted to Katie Roiphe's novel *Still She Haunts Me* (London: Headline, 2001), p. 23.

119   **'what was to happen afterwards'** . . . *Diaries*, vol. 4, p. 94; '"Alice" on the Stage', p. 180.

120   **echoes of these works** . . . See Donald Thomas, *Lewis Carroll: A Portrait with Background* (London: John Murray, 1996), pp. 157–60.

120   **Dante's *Inferno*** . . . In a letter of 1890, Carroll claimed never to have read a word of Dante, but John Docherty makes a good case for thinking that this was just another bit of teasing in 'Dantean Allusions in Wonderland', *Jabberwocky*, 19: 1–2 (Winter–Spring 1990), pp. 13–16.

120   **under our feet** . . . This fictional tradition is expertly mapped out in David Standish, *Hollow Earth* (Cambridge, Mass.: Da Capo Press, 2006).

121   **'passion for dreaming'** . . . John Hollingshead, *Underground London* (London: Groombridge & Sons, 1862), pp. 1–3; some chapters were published earlier in *All the Year Round*.

122   **painting *Work*** . . . *Diaries*, vol. 5, p. 72.

122   **'the lower depths'** . . . Henry L. Thompson, *Henry George Liddell, D.D., Dean of Christ Church, Oxford: A Memoir* (London: John Murray, 1899), p. 196.

122   **risk of drowning underground** . . . For details of the Metropolitan Railway's construction, see Christian Wolmar, *The Subterranean Railway: How the London*

      Underground Was Built and How It Changed the City Forever (London: Atlantic, 2012), pp. 8–40.

122 **'under the earth's surface'** . . . *London: A Pilgrimage* (1872); see Peter Conrad, *The Victorian Treasure-House* (London: Collins, 1973), p. 70.

123 **'revealed till the end'** . . . *Letters*, vol. 1, p. 65.

124 **Macnish's examples** . . . Robert Macnish, *The Philosophy of Sleep* (Glasgow: W. R. McPhun, 1830), pp. 56–82.

124 **'agitation resembling delirium'** . . . 'Frank Seafield' [Alexander Henley Grant], *The Literature and Curiosities of Dreams* (London: Chapman & Hall, 1865), p. 323.

124 **'the bowels, &c.'** . . . [Thomas Stone], 'Dreams', *Household Words* (8 March 1851), p. 567.

124 **'spell of earth's beauty'** . . . James Sully, 'The Dream as a Revelation' (1893), repr. in *Embodied Selves: An Anthology of Psychological Texts 1830–1890*, ed. Sally Shuttleworth and Jenny Bourne Taylor (Oxford: Oxford University Press, 1998), p. 122.

125 **'always crying'** . . . Gardner (ed.), *The Annotated Alice*, pp. 26–31; Jenny Woolf makes this connection in *The Mystery of Lewis Carroll*, p. 217.

125 **'to whom the spoonerisms happened'** . . . William Empson, *Some Versions of Pastoral* (1935, repr. London: The Hogarth Press, 1986), p. 271; Jones and Gladstone (eds), *The Alice Companion*, p. 165. The most influential attempt to prove that Carroll's stories are full of lightly disguised allusions to contemporary academic and religious controversies is Alexander L. Taylor's *The White Knight: A Study of C. L. Dodgson (Lewis Carroll)* (Edinburgh: Oliver & Boyd, 1952).

126 **'difficulty and trouble'** . . . 'Seafield', *The Literature and Curiosities of Dreams* provides a helpful digest, pp. 353ff.

128 **'some evil-disposed person'** . . . *Charley Ross: The Story of his Abduction and the Incidents of the Search for his Recovery* (London: Hodder & Stoughton, 1877); *Letters*, vol. 2, p. 1147.

128 **a falling tree** . . . *Diaries*, vol. 3, p. 36.

Eleven

129 **'parts I couldn't understand'** . . . Francis Spufford, *The Child That Books Built: A Memoir of Childhood and Reading* (London: Faber, 2002), p. 71.

129 **'without design'** . . . *OED*, 'adventure'.

129 **'kept going on, going on'** . . . 'Alice's Recollections of Carrollian Days', p. 8.

129 **some 'headings'** . . . *Diaries*, vol. 4, p. 95.

130 **he should publish it** . . . *Diaries*, vol. 4, pp. 110, 113, 149, 115, 173, 195, 193.

130 **'sixty thousand volumes'** . . . MacDonald, *George MacDonald and His Wife*, p. 342.

130 **'all this term'** . . . *Diaries*, vol. 4, pp. 257, 264.

131 **'Cut Pages in Diary'** . . . An article by Karoline Leach in the *TLS* (3 May 1996) explored some possible reasons for this censoring of the diary; see also *Diaries*, vol. 4, pp. 214–15n., and the articles by Edward Wakeling, 'What Happened to Lewis Carroll's Diaries', *Carrollian*, 8 (Autumn 2001), pp. 51–64, and Will Brooker, 'The Cut Pages in Lewis Carroll's Diaries', *Carrollian*, 15 (Spring 2005), pp. 58–60.

131 **'courting Ina –'** . . . Dodgson Family Collection; it also summarizes the contents of two other cut pages.

132   'renewed his games' . . . Jane Morris (ed.), *The Oxford Book of Oxford* (Oxford: Oxford University Press, 1978), p. 189.

132   'all intercourse ceasing' . . . Edward Wakeling, 'Two Letters from Lorina to Alice', *Jabberwocky*, 80 (Autumn 1992), pp. 91–3.

132   'intercourse between them ceased' . . . Margaret Woods, 'Oxford in the 'Seventies' (1941), repr. in *Interviews & Recollections*, p. 198.

133   'It looks like it' . . . Cited in Morton Cohen, *Lewis Carroll: A Biography* (London: Macmillan, 1995), p. 101.

133   'calling at the house' . . . *Diaries*, vol. 7, pp. 472–3.

133   'when I was a little girl' . . . 'Alice's Recollections of Carrollian Days', p. 9.

133   'I was stupid' . . . Cited in Gordon, *Beyond the Looking Glass*, p. 120.

133   'very pleasant conclusion' . . . *Diaries*, vol. 4, p. 213.

134   she turned eighteen . . . David Williams, *Genesis and Exodus: A Portrait of the Benson Family* (London: Hamish Hamilton, 1979), pp. 10–19.

134   'St. Crumpet' . . . Ruskin, *Praeterita*, *Works*, vol. 35, p. 525.

134   'conjugal embrace' . . . Andrew Lycett, *Wilkie Collins: A Life of Sensation* (London: Hutchinson, 2013), pp. 395–6.

134   'virtuous attachment' . . . See Hugues Lebailly, 'C. L. Dodgson and the Victorian Cult of the Child', *Carrollian*, 4 (Autumn 1999), p. 16.

136   'a very anxious subject' . . . *Diaries*, vol. 5, p. 180; Edward Wakeling has suggested that 'A. L.' may have been a mistake on Carroll's part ('he probably meant to write "A. D."', vol. 5, p. 180n.).

136   'I second fiddle' . . . Attributed to C. A. Spring-Rice (*c.* 1880) in Morris (ed.), *The Oxford Book of Oxford*, p. 289.

136   'the beauty line' . . . Gordon N. Ray (ed.), *The Letters and Private Papers of William Makepeace Thackeray*, 4 vols (London: Oxford University Press, 1945–46), vol. 2, pp. 641–2.

136   'ever been written' . . . 'The Lewis Carroll That Alice Recalls', *New York Times*, 81 (1 May 1932), p. 15.

136   'poor C. L. D. would have been' . . . Private collection.

136   'no present likelihood' . . . *Diaries*, vol. 3, p. 84.

137   'far less for *life*!' . . . *Letters*, vol. 2, p. 730.

137   'in love with her' . . . Letter to Menella Dodgson (3 February 1932), Dodgson Family Collection.

137   'over the age of ten' . . . *Interviews & Recollections*, p. 240.

137   'poor thing!' . . . *Diaries*, vol. 7, p. 15.

137   'Ellen Terry's hair!' . . . Cited in Langford Reed, *The Life of Lewis Carroll* (London: W. & G. Foyle, 1932), p. 90.

137   'almost unique' . . . *Letters*, vol. 2, p. 1073.

138   'in this connection' . . . Hudson, *Lewis Carroll*, pp. 200–1.

138   '"Louisa Caroline"' . . . Robert S. Phillips (ed.), *Aspects of Alice: Lewis Carroll's Dreamchild as Seen Through the Critics' Looking-Glasses, 1865–1971* (London: Gollancz, 1972), p. 317; the poem ('The Vulture and the Husbandman', a parody of 'The Walrus and the Carpenter') was originally published in the first issue of the satirical magazine *The Light Green* (1872), and is repr. in S. D. Collingwood (ed.), *The Lewis Carroll Picture Book* (London; Glasgow: Collins, 1899), pp. 263–5. The copy Vere Bayne pasted into one of his scrapbooks (now at Christ Church)

includes a pen addition that names the author as Arthur Clement Hilton of Cambridge.

138 **violet ink** . . . 'Roughly speaking, Carroll used black ink (often faded to brownish) until and including October 10, 1870: then purple ink until about the end of 1890: and then black again until his death': Warren Weaver, 'Ink (and Pen) Used by Lewis Carroll', *Jabberwocky*, 4 (Winter 1975), pp. 3–4.

138 **'rather superfluous caution'** . . . *Letters*, vol. 1, p. 67; *Diaries*, vol. 4, p. 299.

138 **true sexual preferences** . . . The fullest arguments in support of the idea that Carroll used his child-friendships as a form of cover for adult sexual activity have been made by Leach, *In The Shadow of the Dreamchild*.

138 **'normal temptations'** . . . Hudson, *Lewis Carroll*, p. 208.

139 **'the picture'** . . . *Diaries*, vol. 5, p. 89; the photograph has not been traced.

TWELVE

141 **'during the day'** . . . *Letters*, vol. 1, p. 68.

141 **Carroll's surviving sketches** . . . Christ Church.

144 **'"a mere child!"'** . . . The cartoon is reproduced by Michael Hancher in *The Tenniel Illustrations to the 'Alice' Books* (Columbus: Ohio State University Press, 1985), p. 116.

144 **sitting up a tree** . . . *Ibid.*, p. 8.

145 **'a pervading bad smell'** . . . Empson, *Some Versions of Pastoral*, p. 254.

145 **an earlier sketch** . . . Christ Church.

146 **'Struggle for Life'** . . . *The Origin of Species* (1859), ed. Gillian Beer (Oxford: Oxford University Press, 1996), pp. 396–7.

146 **'the art of survival'** . . . John Bayley, 'Alice, or The Art of Survival', *The New York Review of Books* (15 February 1996), p. 12.

146 **'*came of itself*'** . . . '"Alice" on the Stage', p. 180 (Carroll's italics).

147 ***Oxford English Dictionary*** . . . At the time Henry Liddell was one of the Delegates to Oxford University Press, the committee of academics that was responsible for recommending the publication of the *OED*; see Simon Winchester, *The Meaning of Everything: The Story of the Oxford English Dictionary* (Oxford: Oxford University Press, 2003), p. 91.

149 **'new-born idea from perishing'** . . . '"Alice" on the Stage', p. 180.

THIRTEEN

151 **'awkward stage of transition'** . . . *Diaries*, vol. 5, p. 74.

151 **'best likeness of the three'** . . . *Diaries*, vol. 5, p. 60; Carroll photographed the painting in July 1876.

151 **'can do justice'** . . . A. M. W. Stirling, *The Richmond Papers, From the Correspondence of George Richmond, R.A. and his Son, Sir William Richmond, R.A., K.C.B.* (London: W. Heinemann, 1926), p. 193.

151 **'charming'** . . . See Clark, *The Real Alice*, p. 102.

152 **'bower of chintz'** . . . Margaret Oliphant, 'The Great Unrepresented', *Blackwood's*, 100 (1866), p. 374. This paragraph draws on Sarah Bilston's excellent discussion in *The Awkward Age in Women's Popular Fiction, 1850–1900* (Oxford: Clarendon Press, 2004), pp. 61–95.

152 **'childish eyes'** . . . See Macmillan, p. 35.

153   'the printing of the pictures' . . . *Diaries*, vol. 5, p. 97.

153   'superior to the old' . . . *Diaries*, vol. 5, p. 115.

154   'something sensational' . . . *Letters*, vol. 1, p. 65.

155   'living Wonder-land' . . . John William Jackson, 'My Lady-Love', *Echoes from My Youth, and Other Poems* (London: Trübner & Co., 1864), p. 44; Sarah Helen Whitman, 'Hours of Life', *Hours of Life, and Other Poems* (Providence: George H. Whitney, 1853), p. 8; [Vernon Lushington], 'Carlyle', *The Oxford and Cambridge Magazine* (May 1856), p. 300.

155   'Down into wonderland go!' . . . 'Peter Pindar' [John Wolcot], 'A Complimentary Epistle to James Bruce, Esq.' (1816), *The Works of Peter Pindar, Esq.* (Philadelphia: M. Wallis Woodward & Co. 1835), p. 226; J. G. Holland, *The Mistress of the Manse* (New York: Scribner, Armstrong & Co., 1877), p. 278. Further examples include Karl Oppel, *Das alte Wunderland der Pyramiden* (Leipzig: Verlag von Otto Spamer, 1863), and Edmund Evans, *The Sydenham Sinbad: A Narrative of his Seven Journeys to Wonder-Land* (London: J. & C. Brown & Co., 1860).

155   'a beautiful photograph' . . . *Diaries*, vol. 3, p. 88. In *Lewis Carroll Among His Books: A Descriptive Catalogue of the Private Library of Charles L. Dodgson* (Jefferson, NC; London: McFarland, 2005), p. 230, Charlie Lovett interprets the brief description 'Palgrave's Poems' in Carroll's auction catalogue to mean a copy of *Lyrical Poems* (1871), but the sonnet to Agnes Grace was printed in *Idyls and Songs* (London: John W. Parker & Son, 1854), p. 110.

156   'All maidenhood in miniature' . . . Palgrave, *Idyls and Songs*, pp. 100–5.

FOURTEEN

158   'such a place as Wonderland!' . . . *Letters*, vol. 1, p. 124.

158   'a sort of wonderland' . . . W. M. Rossetti (ed.), *The Poetical Works of Christina Georgina Rossetti* (London: Macmillan, 1904), p. lxiv.

159   olive-green scrapbook . . . Harvard.

159   'ought to know better?' . . . The early reviews are gathered together in *Jabberwocky*, 9: 1–4 (Winter 1979/1980–Autumn 1980) and discussed by Elizabeth A. Cripps in '*Alice* and the Reviewers', *Children's Literature: Annual of the Modern Language Association Division on Children's Literature and The Children's Literature Association*, 11 (1983), pp. 32–48.

159   'read every word' . . . Berg; *The Correspondence of Dante Gabriel Rossetti*, ed. William E. Fredeman, 9 vols (Cambridge: D. S. Brewer, 2002–10), vol. 3, p. 384; *Macmillan*, p. 40n.

160   a single six-month period . . . *Diaries*, vol. 5, p. 173; vol. 6, p. 75.

160   '*very bad*' . . . *Diaries*, vol. 5, p. 192; vol. 6, p. 72; vol. 5, p. 91.

160   'a staunch Conservative' . . . *Life & Letters*, p. 91.

160   for Carroll politics was a matter . . . Jean Gattégno provides a helpful summary of Carroll's views in *Lewis Carroll: Fragments of a Looking-Glass* (London: George Allen & Unwin, 1977), pp. 202–10.

160   'still swarming about' . . . *Diaries*, vol. 5, p. 166.

161   'window-breaking, etc.' . . . *Diaries*, vol. 5, p. 168.

161   'little child, Constance' . . . *Diaries*, vol. 1, p. 130.

161   'will go at trees' . . . *Diaries*, vol. 6, pp. 64–5.

161   *Dreaming of Fairy-Land* . . . *Diaries*, vol. 6, pp. 14–15, 71.

161   'the two Alices' . . . *Diaries*, vol. 5, pp. 144, 149.

162   '"her life?"' . . . Jerrold M. Packard, *Victoria's Daughters* (New York: St Martin's Griffin, 1998), p. 26.

163   Edith Jebb . . . *Diaries*, vol. 5, p. 177.

163   'second edition of the mother' . . . *Diaries*, vol. 2, p. 74; on the idea that a book can be viewed as a metaphorical baby (regardless of the writer's gender) see *inter alia* Douglas A. Brooks (ed.), *Printing and Parenting in Early Modern England* (Aldershot: Ashgate, 2005), and Tom MacFaul, *Poetry and Paternity in Renaissance England* (Cambridge: Cambridge University Press, 2010).

164   an 'eyesore' . . . *Macmillan*, pp. 40, 44, 47, 54, 59, 72, 65, 79.

164   'a dozen of the pictures!' . . . *Ibid.*, p. 47.

164   '(the Human Species?)' . . . *Letters*, vol. 1, p. 133.

165   'a stranger to himself' . . . Frederik Paludan-Müller, *The Fountain of Youth*, trans. H. W. Freeland (London: Macmillan & Co., 1867), pp. 16, 23, 109.

165   'I'll ne'er grow cold' . . . *Letters*, vol. 1, pp. 110–12.

166   'so distressing!' . . . Harry Ransom Center.

FIFTEEN

167   'I ever met' . . . *Mark Twain's Autobiography*, 2 vols (New York; London: Harper & Bros, 1924), vol. 2, p. 232; *Diaries*, vol. 7, p. 195.

167   Meetings between writers . . . Richard Ellmann gives details of these and other records of their conversation in *James Joyce* (New York: Oxford University Press, 1959), pp. 523–4.

168   'a corkscrew leg' . . . I draw these examples from Elizabeth Sewell's discussion of the writers' shared preoccupations in *The Field of Nonsense* (London: Chatto & Windus, 1952), pp. 7–16.

168   a stopping place or a room . . . *OED*, 'stanza'.

168   Holland, Italy, Jerusalem . . . . . . The best discussion of Lear's wanderlust is Vivien Noakes, *Edward Lear: The Life of a Wanderer*, rev. edn (Stroud: Sutton Publishing, 2004).

169   'travelling on the Continent' . . . Rosenbach.

169   'much taken by the idea' . . . Morton N. Cohen (ed.), *The Russian Journal – II: A Record Kept by Henry Parry Liddon of a Tour Taken with C. L. Dodgson in the Summer of 1867* (New York: The Lewis Carroll Society of North America, 1979), p. xiii.

169   'never yet left England' . . . *Diaries*, vol. 5, p. 253.

169   'Alpine slippers' . . . John Pudney, *The Thomas Cook Story* (London: Michael Joseph, 1953), p. 136.

169   new breed of Victorian tourist . . . Both of these Mrs Brown books were written in 1869; in 1874, Rose published *Mrs Brown on the Royal Russian Marriage* (London: George Routledge), but this is largely a comic monologue about foreigners ('Not as I believe the Rooshuns come from bears, any more than that feller as wants to make out as we was all original monkeys', p. 39) rather than a travel book.

170   'the other end of Russia' . . . *Letters*, vol. 1, p. 74.

170   'a glorious wonder-land' . . . George Augustus Sala, *A Journey Due North; Being Notes of a Residence in Russia, in the Summer of 1856* (London: Richard Bentley, 1858), p. 30.

170   'sparkling, surprising thing' . . . Cohen (ed.), *The Russian Journal – II*, p. xix.

170   '*The Times*' . . .*Ibid.*, p. ix.

170   '**Disgusted**' . . . J. O. Johnston, *Life and Letters of Henry Parry Liddon* (London: Longmans, Green, & Co., 1904), pp. 5, 282, 8.

171   **rousing tales of heroism** . . . See Anthony G. Cross, *The Russian Theme in English Literature from the Sixteenth Century to 1980* (Oxford: Willem A. Meeuws, 1980).

171   '**a piece of life**' . . . 'Count Leo Tolstoi', *Fortnightly Review* (December 1887), repr. in *Essays in Criticism: Second Series* (1888, repr. London: Macmillan, 1913), p. 260.

171   '**living story-books in themselves**' . . . Sala, *A Journey Due North*, pp. 30, 202, 140.

172   '**boots and hat**' . . . W. H. G. Kingston, *Fred Markham in Russia; or, The Boy Travellers in the Land of the Czar* (London: Griffith & Farran, 1858), p. 5.

172   '**on the way**' . . . Bowman, *The Story of Lewis Carroll*, p. 36.

173   '**Telegraph-forms & 6d stamps**' . . . Princeton.

173   **key words of vocabulary** . . . Fales.

173   **smaller geographical niches** . . . C. P. Brand, *Italy and the English Romantics: The Italianate Fashion in Early Nineteenth-Century England* (Cambridge: Cambridge University Press, 1957), p. 16; the best survey of this phenomenon is provided by James Buzard in *The Beaten Track: European Tourism, Literature, and the Ways to 'Culture' 1800–1918* (Oxford: Oxford University Press, 1993), pp. 156–72.

173   '**of persons defending themselves**' . . . *Diaries*, vol. 5, pp. 266, 282, 283.

174   '**a brilliant story-teller**' . . . Cohen (ed.), *The Russian Journal – II*, p. xix.

174   '**the Park of Brussels**' . . . *Diaries*, vol. 5, p. 259; Cohen (ed.), *The Russian Journal – II*, p. 2.

174   *the Wonderful Lamp* . . . *Diaries*, vol. 5, pp. 309–11.

175   '**verifying their Murray**' . . . Buzard, *The Beaten Track*, pp. 75–6.

175   '**dirty wenches!**' . . . *Notes of a Journey from Cornhill to Grand Cairo* (1846), cited in Buzard, *The Beaten Track*, p. 127.

176   '**almost like a dream**' . . . *Diaries*, vol. 5, pp. 283, 289, 291, 299, 284, 328–30.

176   '**not a single person was ill**' . . . *Diaries*, vol. 5, p. 369; Cohen (ed.), *The Russian Journal – II*, p. 46.

176   '**A Russian's Day in England**' . . . Harry Ransom Center; the poem was written for Gwendolyn Cecil, the teenage daughter of Lord Salisbury.

176   **invested considerable sums** . . . See Edward Wakeling, 'Lewis Carroll's Investments in Steamships', *Princeton University Library Chronicle*, 60: 3 (Spring 1999), pp. 443–58.

176   '**greatest blow**' . . . *Life & Letters*, p. 131.

177   **new set of rooms** . . . Full details are given in Edward Wakeling, 'Lewis Carroll's Rooms at Christ Church, Oxford', *Jabberwocky*, 12: 3 (Spring 1983), pp. 51–61.

177   '**neatly labelled**' . . . *Life & Letters*, p. 135.

177   '**in North America**' . . . 'Panorama of the Falls of Niagara', *Morning Post* (15 June 1833).

177   '**very wonderful**' . . . Collingwood (ed.), *The Lewis Carroll Picture Book*, p. 233.

178   '**would take you next**' . . . Lionel A. Tollemache, 'Reminiscences of "Lewis Carroll"' (1898), repr. in *Interviews & Recollections*, p. 47.

Sixteen

179   '**my gracious reception**' . . . *Diaries*, vol. 6, p. 120.

179   '**a Continental sale**' . . . *Macmillan*, p. 44.

179   **the French edition** . . . *Exercises on Translation from English into French* (Oxford:

J. H. & Jas. Parker, 1857); see Claude Romney, 'The First French Translator of Alice: Henri Bué', *Jabberwocky*, 10: 4 (Autumn 1981), pp. 89–94.

180   **'(easy translation)'** . . . Donald Rackin, *Alice's Adventures in Wonderland and Through the Looking-Glass: Nonsense, Sense, and Meaning* (New York: Twayne Publishers, 1991), p. 68.

180   **'"fiddle-de-dee"'** . . . The first citation in the *OED* is from Boswell's *Life of Samuel Johnson* (1791): 'All he said was "Fiddle-de-dee, my dear".'

181   **'unintelligible'** . . . *Macmillan*, pp. 46, 50.

181   **'Les chats mangent-ils les chauves-souris?'** . . . This is pointed out in the *Spectator*'s review 'Alice Translated' (7 August 1869).

182   **'as much as that!'** . . . Letter from Lady Augusta Stanley, cited in *Diaries*, vol. 5, p. 122; story cited in Rodney Engen, *Sir John Tenniel: Alice's White Knight* (Aldershot: Scolar, 1991), p. 84.

183   **'you send out'** . . . *Macmillan*, p. 76.

183   **'phantasmagoria'** . . . See Stephen Prickett, *Victorian Fantasy*, rev. edn (Waco: Baylor University Press, 2005), pp. 31–4.

184   **'curious' to know more** . . . *Macmillan*, p. 44.

184   **'anything pretty and graceful'** . . . *Ibid.*, p. 63.

184   **'Alice II'** . . . *Diaries*, vol. 6, p. 37; *Macmillan*, p. 63.

SEVENTEEN

186   **enchanted Venetian looking-glass** . . . William Gilbert, *The Magic Mirror: A Round of Tales for Young and Old* (London; New York: Alexander Strahan, 1866), reviewed in *The Times* (26 December 1865), p. 4.

186   **'looking-glass curtain'** . . . See *The New Monthly Magazine and Literary Journal*, 6 (1822), p. 61, and Isobel Armstrong, *Victorian Glassworlds: Glass Culture and the Imagination, 1830–1880* (Oxford: Oxford University Press, 2008), pp. 98–9; George Rowell gives a history of the curtain's demise in *The Old Vic Theatre: A History* (Cambridge: Cambridge University Press, 1993), pp. 13–14.

186   **'if only I could get into it'** . . . *Phantastes*, ch. 10.

186   **'standing on its head'** . . . Bowman, *The Story of Lewis Carroll*, p. 21.

187   **included mirrors** . . . The mirror was also a prop used by other Victorian photographers such as Lady Clementina Hawarden; see Bartram, *The Pre-Raphaelite Camera*, pp. 143–4.

187   **'the mirror with a memory'** . . . 'The Stereoscope and the Stereograph', *The Atlantic* (1 June 1859).

189   **'"feather our oars" properly'** . . . 'Alice's Recollections of Carrollian Days', p. 8.

190   **'no plot to speak of'** . . . *The Examiner* (15 December 1866).

190   **he had taught Alice Liddell** . . . 'Alice's Recollections of Carrollian Days', p. 4.

191   **internal stitching** . . . Compare an unexpectedly witty section on 'The Dash' in John Wilson's *A Treatise on Grammatical Punctuation* (Manchester, n.p., 1844), which points out that 'the dash is used where a sentence breaks off abruptly, and the subject is changed; – where the sense is suspended, and is continued after a short interruption; – where a significant or long pause is required; – or where there is an unexpected turn in the sentiment' (p. 71).

193   **'it was about "malice"'** . . . *Letters*, vol. 1, pp. 107–8.

193   **most powerful woman in the world** . . . See Bilston, *The Awkward Age*, p. 23.

193 **a form of disguised autobiography** . . . The most persuasive of such readings is
Morton N. Cohen's in *Lewis Carroll: A Biography*, pp. 216–17.

Eighteen

195 **'so much crinoline'** . . . *Life & Letters*, p. 130.

195 **working man's paper cap** . . . See Hancher, *The Tenniel Illustrations to the 'Alice'
Books*, pp. 3–26.

196 **imitated Egg's viewpoint** . . . Tom Lubbock discusses how 'the dream world of
Alice [casts] its spell, and its fame, over Egg's social realism' in his analysis of the
painting in *The Independent* (16 March 2007).

196 **losing oneself in a book** . . . The original illustration plan is in Christ Church, and
has been analysed by Edward Wakeling in *Jabberwocky*, 21: 2 (Spring 1992), pp. 27–38.

196 **'postponed to midsummer'** . . . *Macmillan*, p. 90.

196 **'taking imaginary journeys'** . . . Bedford Pollard, *Elsie's Adventures in Fairyland*
(London: Elliott Stock, 1898), pp. 3–4.

197 **'rather inexperienced editor'** . . . *Macmillan*, pp. 86–7.

197 *plagiarius* . . . OED, 'plagiary'; the word was also applied to slaves.

197 **'copyright be infringed'** . . . *Macmillan*, p. 86.

197 **'the brim of a hat'** . . . William Boyd, *The Songs from 'Alice's Adventures in
Wonderland'* (London: Weekes & Co., 1870), p. 9.

198 **'"my right hand?"'** . . . Letter to *The Times* (15 January 1932).

198 **'his child Alice'** . . . *Diaries*, vol. 6, pp. 92, 109.

198 **'wonderful thing occurred'** . . . *Diaries*, vol. 6, p. 121.

199 **Longfellow's lines were widely quoted** . . . See Bilston, *The Awkward Age*, p. 5.

199 **'where brook and river meet'** . . . Ricks (ed.), *The Poems of Tennyson*, vol. 2, p. 500.

199 **'"the stream and river meet"'** . . . *Letters*, vol. 1, p. 595. Carroll owned at least two
editions of Longfellow's poems, and his misquotation of 'stream' for 'brook' was
not uncommon: compare 'Mrs J. H. Riddell' [Charlotte Eliza Riddell], *Austin
Friars: A Novel*, 3 vols (London: Tinsley Brothers, 1870): 'a young girl at the point
"where the stream and river meet" – a girl with her feet just on the very threshold
of existence, looking with wistful eyes on life' (vol. 1, p. 49).

200 **'a new life in me'** . . . *Diaries*, vol. 6, p. 139.

200 **'more trouble than the first'** . . . *Diaries*, vol. 6, p. 140.

200 **trial pages** . . . Harvard.

200 **'my life now'** . . . *Diaries*, vol. 6, pp. 146–8.

201 **'"To 'Alice'"'** . . . *Diaries*, vol. 6, pp. 146, 189.

201 **'before many weeks are over'** . . . Unpublished letter to Hassard Dodgson (29
November 1871). Private collection.

201 **'children of all ages'** . . . *Athenaeum* (16 December 1871).

201 **'that enchanted afternoon'** . . . M. Vivian Hughes, *A London Child of the Seventies*
(London: Oxford University Press, 1934), p. 60.

201 **print of *The Beggar Maid*** . . . *Lewis Carroll's Alice* (Sotheby's catalogue), p. 52.

Twenty

206 **'very strange'** . . . Henry Liddell's journal (1837), cited in Gordon, *Beyond the
Looking Glass*, p. 48.

206 **'& other skies'** . . . Cited in Clark, *The Real Alice*, pp. 120–1.

207 **'so like a dream now'** . . . *Praeterita*, 3 vols (London: George Allen, 1907), vol. 3, pp. 53–5.

208 **'Mignonette'** . . . Pierpont Morgan.

208 **'a quadrille'** . . . Cited in Gordon, *Beyond the Looking Glass*, p. 111.

208 **'Get married'** . . . *Essays on the Pursuits of Women* (London: Emily Faithfull, 1863), p. 26.

209 **'tiresome prig'** . . . Cited in Gordon, *Beyond the Looking Glass*, p. 136.

209 **'fumbling at his braces'** . . . 'Viator Verax', *Cautions for the First Tour . . .*, 2nd edn (London: W. Ridgway, 1863), cited in Buzard, *The Beaten Track*, p. 150.

210 **'too excitable'** . . . Letter to Caryl Hargreaves (8 February 1934). Private collection.

212 **'S' before her name** . . . 'Sexy' is first recorded in 1896 (*OED*); most of the early examples are American.

212 **'Chinese dress (2 positions)'** . . . *Diaries*, vol. 6, pp. 124, 273, 276, 279, 282.

213 **'it would take in'** . . . *Letters*, vol. 1, p. 174.

213 **'if it rained'** . . . *The Academy* (1899), p. 741.

213 **'living lay figures'** . . . *Daily News*, cited in 'On Composition Photographs', in *Journal of the Photographic Society*, 8: 130 (16 February 1863), p. 234.

214 **'*second childhood* comes'** . . . *Letters*, vol. 2, p. 689.

214 **'"Papa" and "Mamma"'** . . . Evelyn M. Hatch (ed.), *A Selection from the Letters of Lewis Carroll to His Child-Friends* (London: Macmillan & Co., 1933), pp. 83–4.

214 **'beginning to melt'** . . . *Letters*, vol. 1, pp. 196–7.

215 **'back to my rooms'** . . . *Letters*, vol. 1, p. 196.

Twenty-one

217 **'mere comic writer'** . . . *Letters*, vol. 1, p. 168.

217 **'calls you child'** . . . *Letters*, vol. 1, p. 580.

217 **a new advertisement** . . . *Macmillan*, p. 57n.

217 **'Think of the postmen'** . . . *Macmillan*, p. 85.

218 **'made themselves known'** . . . These examples are drawn from Bradley Deane's chapter on literary friendship in *The Making of the Victorian Novelist: Anxieties of Authorship in the Mass Market* (New York; London: Routledge, 2003).

218 **'(would be appreciated)'** . . . *Macmillan*, p. 77.

219 **'Plate Dancing extraordinary'** . . . *Chemical News* (16 June 1876), p. 252.

219 **'child of about 10'** . . . *Diaries*, vol. 6, p. 457.

219 **'painfully out of tune'** . . . *Macmillan*, p. 142; *Diaries*, vol. 7, p. 138.

220 **'wonderful things'** . . . *Puss-Cat Mew, and Other Stories for My Children* (New York: Harper & Brothers, 1871), pp. 75, 79, 83, 86; Knatchbull-Hugessen returned to the *Alice* books in *Whispers From Fairyland* (London: Longmans, Green, & Co., 1875).

220 **'"to play with"'** . . . Jean Ingelow, *Mopsa the Fairy* (London: Longmans, Green, & Co., 1869), pp. 102, 135; here I follow U. C. Knoepflmacher's fine reading of the story in *Ventures into Childland*, pp. 270–311.

221 **'a motherless orphan's lot'** . . . M. C. Pyle, *Minna in Wonder-land and Roland and His Friend* (Philadelphia: Porter & Coates, 1871), p. 3.

221 **'new line of fairy-lore'** . . . '"Alice"' on the Stage', p. 180.

222 **'swallows up Light'** . . . Mary Dummett Nauman, *Eva's Adventures in Shadow-Land* (Philadelphia: J. P. Lippincott & Co., 1872), p. 95.

222 '"scrub themselves white!"' . . . Clara Bradford, *Ethel's Adventures in the Doll Country* (London: John F. Shaw & Co., 1880), p. 55.

223 **slammed shut again** . . . Alice Corkran, *Down the Snow Stairs; or, From Good-night to Good-morning* (London: Blackie & Son, 1887), p. 54.

224 **'unusually clever'** . . . Repr. in Juliana Horatia Ewing, *The Brownies and Other Tales* (London: SPCK, 1871), pp. 198, 202, 237–8. The volume also contains 'The Land of Lost Toys', another of Ewing's responses to the first *Alice* book.

224 **capering in the margins** . . . See Knoepflmacher, *Ventures into Childland*, p. 408.

224 **'Mr. Punch'** . . . *Punch*, 62 (20 April 1872), p. 160.

225 **'Alice in Wonderland, etc.'** . . . *Lewis Carroll and His Illustrators: Collaborations and Correspondence, 1865–1898*, ed. Morton N. Cohen and Edward Wakeling (London: Macmillan, 2003), p. 17; a parody of 'Jabberwocky' entitled 'The Waggawock' had appeared in *Punch* on 16 March 1872.

225 **'we think we know it'** . . . Elizabeth Sewell, 'The Nonsense System in Lewis Carroll's Work and in Today's World', in Guiliano (ed.), *Lewis Carroll Observed*, p. 64.

225 **'tame'** . . . *Diaries*, vol. 5, p. 215.

225 **'ground of insanity'** . . . *Diaries*, vol. 5, p. 118.

226 **'Alice in Blunderland'** . . . *Punch*, 78 (30 October 1880), pp. 197–8.

227 **'tied together with tape'** . . . 'Jean Jambon', *Our Trip to Blunderland; or Grand Excursion to Blundertown and Back* (Edinburgh; London: William Blackwood & Sons, 1877), p. 105.

228 **'mix up or mingle'** . . . *OED*, 'blunder'.

228 **swastikas** . . . John Kendrick Bangs, *Alice in Blunderland: An Iridescent Dream* (London: Doubleday, Page & Co., 1907), p. 50; James Dyrenforth and Max Kester, *Adolf in Blunderland* (London: Frederick Muller Ltd., 1939), p. 22.

229 **version of Alice herself** . . . See, e.g., 'B. T.', 'Critics in Wonderland', *Fraser's Magazine*, 13: 73 (1876), pp. 13–21, a satire on the flowery language of Aestheticism.

TWENTY-TWO

230 **'preserved her youth'** . . . Cited in Gordon, *Beyond the Looking Glass*, p. 96.

230 **beauty treatments** . . . See Helen Rappaport, *Beautiful for Ever* (Ebrington: Long Barn Books, 2010).

231 **eccentric amateur photographer** . . . A good outline of her career is provided in Helmut Gernsheim, *Julia Margaret Cameron: Her Life and Photographic Work* (London: The Fountain Press, 1948).

232 **'taken out of focus'** . . . *Diaries*, vol. 4, p. 315.

233 **'literature of dreams'** . . . *Diaries*, vol. 7, pp. 175–6.

233 **'the same child'** . . . *Diaries*, vol. 6, p. 473.

233 **'a perfect child'** . . . *Diaries*, vol. 6, p. 353; *Letters*, vol. 1, p. 380; *Diaries*, vol. 6, pp. 376, 443.

233 **'as a general rule'** . . . *Letters*, vol. 1, p. 370.

233 **'has an engagement'** . . . Dodgson Family Collection, cited in *Diaries*, vol. 7, p. 83.

234 **'merely refined animal'** . . . *Diaries*, vol. 2, p. 12. Carroll was less keen on pets, coolly noting in 1882 that a friend's dog with rabies had attacked the family's cat, which ended with the dog being shot while someone else 'finished the cat with Prussic acid' (*Diaries*, vol. 7, p. 439).

234   **'sulphurous acid'** . . . *Diaries*, vol. 7, pp. 105, 491.

234   **'in rags'** . . . *Diaries*, vol. 7, p. 286.

234   **'to be photographed'** . . . *Diaries*, vol. 6, p. 266.

234   **'she seemed to be . . .'** . . . *Letters*, vol. 1, p. 248.

234   **'a copy of *Alice*'** . . . *Diaries*, vol. 7, p. 66.

234   **Frederick Morgan's sentimental painting** . . . Carroll called on the artist in April 1878.

235   **aped adult fashions** . . . See *Interviews & Recollections*, p. 190.

236   **types of 'grown-up' child** . . . See Malcolm Andrews, *Dickens and the Grown-Up Child* (Basingstoke: Macmillan, 1994).

236   **'young, and beautiful'** . . . As with all traditional folk tales there are different variations on the same plot; this example is taken from a book Carroll owned, W. R. S. Ralston's *Russian Folk-Tales* (London: Smith, Elder, & Co., 1873), p. 59, where it is entitled 'The Smith and the Demon'.

237   **'door swings open'** . . . Cited in *Letters*, vol. 1, p. 209n.

237   **'sheep did their trick'** . . . *Interviews & Recollections*, p. 153.

237   **'Oh, Mamma! Mamma!'** . . . *Letters*, vol. 1, p. 187.

237   **'some Bible-readings'** . . . *Diaries*, vol. 9, p. 15.

237   **'kissed me passionately'** . . . Bowman, *The Story of Lewis Carroll*, p. 18.

237   **'a very subdued "Uncle"'** . . . *Life & Letters*, p. 402.

238   **'wonderful bag'** . . . *Interviews & Recollections*, p. 167

238   **'the wire puzzle'** . . . *Diaries*, vol. 6, pp. 477, 483.

238   **'responsible for her actions'** . . . *Letters*, vol. 1, p. 246.

238   **his uncle Skeffington** . . . For Skeffington's contributions to legislative reform, see Sarah Wise, *Inconvenient People: Lunacy, Liberty and the Mad-Doctors in Victorian England* (London: The Bodley Head, 2012), pp. 80–2.

239   **'sits up every night'** . . . *Diaries*, vol. 6, p. 347.

239   **Charlie's sickroom** . . . Fernando Soto argues (in a more intricate way) that the poem is an allegory of tuberculosis, in 'The Consumption of the Snark and the Decline of Nonsense: A Medico-Linguistic Reading of Carroll's Fitful Agony', *Carrollian*, 8 (Autumn 2001), pp. 9–50.

239   **'search for the Absolute'** . . . A summary of these interpretations is contained in Martin Gardner's Preface to *The Annotated Hunting of the Snark: The Definitive Edition* (New York: W. W. Norton, 2006), pp. xxxiv–xxxvi.

239   **'the Pursuit of Happiness'** . . . *Letters*, vol. 2, p. 1113.

239   **enjoy on the way** . . . On the poem as 'a grotesque celebration of the things we do as death-substitutes', see Bayley, 'Alice, or The Art of Survival', p. 13.

240   **'to match *Alice*'** . . . *Macmillan*, p. 117; although the first edition was produced in a buff-coloured cloth, Carroll had a hundred presentation copies bound in red.

Twenty-three

242   **'Through the Looking-Glass'** . . . *Macmillan*, pp. 107–8.

242   **without having to be there in person** . . . Carroll gave away a large number of copies to hospitals, recording those that had accepted his gifts in a printed catalogue (1890); see *Letters*, vol. 1, p. 150.

243   **'freely criticised'** . . . Louisa M. Alcott, *Jo's Boys, and How They Turned Out* (Boston: Roberts Brothers, 1891), p. 48.

243 '"anonym" would give him' . . . *Letters*, vol. 1, p. 446.

243 'grave, repellent face' . . . *Letters*, vol. 1, p. 466; *Macmillan*, p. 150; Rev
W. Tuckwell, *Reminiscences of Oxford* (London: Cassell & Co., 1900), p. 161.

243 'not wholesome reading' . . . Private collection, published in *Carrollian*, 13 (Spring
2004), p. 45.

243 'known to strangers' . . . *Diaries*, vol. 6, p. 447; Ward's mother later remembered
that 'he was so exceptionally modest that if anyone mentioned *Alice in Wonderland*
or any other of his works he would frown, fidget, and disappear as soon as he
could' (*Interviews & Recollections*, p. 239).

244 '"*Alice in Wonderland!*"' . . . *Interviews & Recollections*, p. 120; Carroll rejected an
invitation to a party in 1879 for the same reason: 'I fear in such an assembly it
would be almost impossible to preserve an incognito. I cannot of course help
there being many people who know the connection between my real name and
my "alias", but the fewer there are who are able to connect my *face* with the name
"Lewis Carroll" the happier for me' (*Letters*, vol. 1, p. 337).

244 'serious request' . . . *Diaries*, vol. 8, p. 148n.

244 'distasteful and annoying' . . . *Letters*, vol. 1, p. 395 (a similar letter was sent to
another dictionary compiler in 1883); vol. 1, p. 554.

244 tremble with rage . . . Lucasta Miller, *The Brontë Myth* (London: Jonathan Cape,
2001), p. 21.

244 '*how many* know it' . . . *Letters*, vol. 1, p. 433. See Denis Crutch, 'Dodgson v.
Carroll', *TLS* (19 July 1974) for more on Carroll's struggles against such
publications.

244 'we know it well' . . . See Edward Wakeling, 'C. L. Dodgson and the Shotover
Papers', *Bandersnatch,* 161 (December 2013), p. 16.

246 'from the mountains' . . . Travis Elborough, *Wish You Were Here: England on Sea*
(London: Sceptre, 2010), p. 43.

246 'propelled by real Italians' . . . John K. Walton, *The English Seaside Resort: A Social
History 1750–1914* (Leicester: Leicester University Press, 1983), pp. 180, 176.

246 'healthiest town in England' . . . T. S. Gowland, *The Guide to East Bourne and its
Environs*, 6th edn (n.p., 1863), p. 3.

246 'bedroom adjoining' . . . *Diaries*, vol. 7, p. 51.

247 'just above the waist' . . . *Diaries*, vol. 8, pp. 529, 146.

247 'youthful town' . . . *Powell's Popular Eastbourne Guide, Lodging-House Keepers'
Directory, and Tradesmen's Advertiser* (n.p., 1863), p. v.

247 'except on worms' . . . *Parsons and Towers' Shilling Guide to Eastbourne and its
Environs*, rev. edn (n.p.); *Abel Haywood's Penny Guide to Eastbourne* (n.p., 1886).

247 'thick ankles' . . . *Letters*, vol. 2, p. 981.

247 'I pick and choose . . .' . . . *Letters*, vol. 2, p. 781.

248 'a few minutes' . . . *Diaries*, vol. 7, pp. 52–63.

248 two surviving sketchbooks . . . Dodgson Family Collection and Harvard.

248 'a veritable "Alice"' . . . *Diaries*, vol. 7, p. 206; another girl recalled her cousin
being invited to stay 'as one of a number of similar "Alices", at some sort of
holiday-home over which the Rev. Mr Dodgson presided' (*Interviews &
Recollections*, p. 196).

249 'a child's love' . . . *Letters*, vol. 1, p. 441.

250 'with her *fiancé*' . . . *Letters*, vol. 1, pp. 565–6.

250 'young-lady-friends' . . . *Letters*, vol. 1, pp. 572, 325.

250 the latest fashions . . . For more on this 'permanently childlike' model, see Deborah Gorham, *The Victorian Girl and the Feminine Ideal* (Bloomington: Indiana University Press, 1992), p. 6.

250 'past eight, I am' . . . *London Labour and the London Poor*, 4 vols (London: Griffin, Bohn, & Co., 1861), vol. 1, p. 152.

251 visit her often . . . [Valentine Durrant], *His Child Friend* (London: Vizetelly & Co., 1886), pp. 58, 68–9, 212–17, 140–3, 221–4.

251 'sadist' and 'masochist' . . . The *OED*'s first citation in English is attributed to Havelock Ellis's *Studies in the Psychology of Sex* (1906).

252 'a little child' . . . *Letters*, vol. 1, pp. 381, 267.

252 'quite exquisite' . . . *Diaries*, vol. 6, p. 314.

252 'to photograph' . . . *Letters*, vol. 1, p. 364.

252 'stockings – and then –' . . . Rodney Engen, *Kate Greenaway* (New York: Schocken, 1981), pp. 93–4.

252 total photographic output . . . I derive this figure from Edward Wakeling, who has made the fullest analysis of Carroll's photographic output. James Alexander offers a slightly higher figure of 'at least twenty-four and perhaps as many as thirty-seven', 'Sentiment and Aesthetics in Victorian Photography: the Child Portraits of C. L. Dodgson', *Carrollian*, 17 (Spring 2006), p. 50.

253 'see such purity' . . . *Diaries*, vol. 9, p. 99.

253 'suggestive of impropriety' . . . *Letters*, vol. 2, p. 1027.

253 'getting into other hands' . . . Harvard.

253 'to be run again' . . . *Letters*, vol. 2, p. 987.

253 'their host' . . . *Letters*, vol. 1, p. 346n.

253 'were not ashamed' . . . Genesis 2: 25.

254 'any nudities at all' . . . *Letters*, vol. 1, pp. 340–1.

254 '*de rigueur*' . . . *Diaries*, vol. 6, p. 102; *Letters*, vol. 1, pp. 347, 253; *Diaries*, vol. 7, pp. 192–3, vol. 5, p. 244; *Letters*, vol. 1, pp. 272–3.

254 possibility of redemption . . . See Marina Warner, *Monuments and Maidens: the Allegory of the Female Form* (Berkeley: University of California Press, 1985, repr. 2000), pp. 294–328.

254 commercially produced Christmas cards . . . Harry Ransom Center. For a discussion of the publisher (De La Rue) see George Buday, *The History of the Christmas Card* (London: Spring Books, 1954).

255 'Morality of the Nude' . . . 'Indecent Photographs', *British Journal of Photography* (3 February 1871); 'Alleged Immorality of Photographers', *British Journal of Photography* (1 January 1869); 'The Morality of the Nude', *British Journal of Photography* (5 February 1869). I draw here on Roger Taylor's introduction to *Lewis Carroll, Photographer*, pp. 101–5.

255 two more Alices . . . The photograph of Beatrice only survives as a watercolour painted by Anne Lydia Bond in 1873, 'probably achieved by placing a translucent piece of paper over Carroll's print' (Morton N. Cohen, *Reflections in a Looking Glass: A Centennial Celebration of Lewis Carroll, Photographer* (New York: Aperture, 1998, p. 74).

256   **'children of nature'** . . . *Letters*, vol. 1, p. 346. A third surviving image is similar, depicting Annie and Frances Henderson as the survivors of a shipwreck, although in this case their modesty has been preserved by a painted loincloth and a strategically placed sprig of vegetation.

256   **'nothing to hide'** . . . Warner, *Monuments and Maidens*, p. 315.

256   **'any way you like'** . . . *Letters*, vol. 1, p. 348.

256   **'this letter!'** . . . *Letters*, vol. 1, p. 354.

256   **'You are very cruel'** . . . *Letters*, vol. 1, p. 354.

257   **a test of his nerve** . . . *Diaries*, vol. 3, pp. 138–39.

Twenty-five

258   **'in her books'** . . . Jowett, cited in Clark, *The Real Alice*, p. 170.

259   **'to be beheaded'** . . . Cited in Gordon, *Beyond the Looking Glass*, p. 172.

259   **waspish theatrical sketch** . . . The satire exists in two equally rare forms: *Apollo and Diana* (Oxford: T. Shrimpton & Son, 1874) and *Cakeless* (Oxford: Mowbray, 1874). Citations here are from the copy of *Apollo and Diana* in Pierpont Morgan.

260   **seed, weed, WEEP** . . . *Interviews & Recollections*, pp. 190–1; this solution adopts Denis Crutch's suggestion in *Bandersnatch* (July 1976).

261   **'C. L. Dodgson'** . . . *Diaries*, vol. 7, p. 486; *Letters*, vol. 1, p. 480.

261   **'such a message'** . . . *Letters*, vol. 1, p. 379.

261   **'60° to 75°'** . . . *Letters*, vol. 1, p. 444.

263   **'resists verbal representation'** . . . *On Kissing, Tickling and Being Bored* (London: Faber, 1993), p. 102.

263   **'*kiss the signature*'** . . . *Letters*, vol. 2, p. 983.

263   **'better than nothing'** . . . *Letters*, vol. 1, p. 555; in another letter he explains that 'as for *kissing* [your letters] when I get them, why, I'd just as soon kiss – kiss – kiss *you*, you tiresome thing!' (vol. 2, p. 786).

263   **'1,0000000 kisses'** . . . *Letters*, vol. 1, pp. 255, 307.

263   **'a kiss to yourself'** . . . *Life & Letters*, p. 386; *Letters*, vol. 2, p. 786.

264   **'kisses from me'** . . . *Life & Letters*, p. 14.

264   **'false, false lips'** . . . 'Madrigal'; 'Stolen Waters'.

264   **'the sexual act'** . . . *Introductory Lectures on Psycho-Analysis*, cited in Phillips, *On Kissing, Tickling, and Being Bored*, p. 104.

264   **'my nightie'** . . . *Interviews & Recollections*, p. 192.

264   **'give me a kiss'** . . . *Letters*, vol. 2, p. 1006; Cohen discusses 'the ritual of friendship' in *Lewis Carroll: A Biography*, p. 184.

264   **'I counted'** . . . 'To Me He Was Mr. Dodgson', *Harper's Magazine* (February 1943).

264   **'under 12 is "kissable"'** . . . *Letters*, vol. 2, p. 826.

264   **'kisses was sexual'** . . . Cohen, *Lewis Carroll: A Biography*, p. 228, summarizing a conversation with Agnes Hull's son.

264   **Victorian conduct manuals** . . . See, e.g., Florence Hartley, *The Ladies' Book of Etiquette, and Manual of Politeness* (Boston: G. W. Cottrell, 1860): 'Do not make any display of affection for even your dearest friend; kissing in public, or embracing, are in bad taste' (p. 56).

265   **the adult world** . . . The moment this occurred could be determined as much by attitude as by history; in 1884 Carroll wrote to tell Ethel Hatch's mother, 'You

would do a good service for old bachelors like me, if you would invent a symbol (say a locket or ribbon) which should indicate, as to any young lady, whether one is expected to kiss or shake hands . . . The difficulty is constantly occurring to me, and I ca'n't discover *any* rule among my friends. Even in the Oxford High School I have 2 young friends, aged 15 and 17, who expect me to kiss them: and outside it the same law prevails with friends up to 19, and even up to 24 or so!' (cited in *Diaries*, vol. 8, p. 87n.).

266 **'*in the least* hurt'** . . . *Letters*, vol. 2, p. 1063.

266 **his last recorded photographs** . . . In a letter he sent in 1881, Carroll claimed that 'the last photograph I took was in August, 1880', although there is no other record of this (cited in *Diaries*, vol. 7, p. 280n.).

266 **'a few shillings'** . . . Morton N. Cohen (ed.), *Lewis Carroll and the Kitchins* (New York: The Lewis Carroll Society of North America, 1980), p. 37; *Diaries*, vol. 7, p. 280n.

266 **'"nothing to wear"'** . . . *Diaries*, vol. 7, p. 273.

266 **'"Mrs. Sidney Owen"!'** . . . Cohen (ed.), *Lewis Carroll and the Kitchins*, p. 43.

267 **'to be rumpled, to be kissed'** . . . Preface, *The Nursery "Alice"* (London: Macmillan, 1890).

267 **'Full to the brim with childish glee'** . . . 'A Nursery "Darling"', *The Nursery "Alice"*.

TWENTY-SIX

268 **'I drew *her* too'** . . . *Diaries*, vol. 7, pp. 291–2.

268 **ink drawings** . . . Private collection (Christ Church).

269 **a social type** . . . The following paragraphs draw on private collections of family papers, supplemented by Gordon, *Beyond the Looking Glass*.

270 **a silver looking-glass** . . . The full list of gifts is repr. as an appendix in Clark, *The Real Alice*, pp. 253–5.

270 **travelling to 'Wonderland'** . . . George T. Chapman, *The Natural Wonders of New Zealand (The Wonderland of the Pacific): its boiling lakes, steam holes, mud volcanoes, sulphur baths, medicinal springs, and burning mountains*, 2nd edn (London: E. Stanford, 1881); D. C. Angus, *The Eastern Wonderland* (London: Cassell, Petter, Galpin & Co., 1881).

270 **'stage of their existence'** . . . Mrs Brassey, *A Voyage in the 'Sunbeam', Our Home on the Ocean for Eleven Months* (London: Longmans, Green, & Co., 1879), p. 318.

270 **beyond Dover** . . . Reginald Hargreaves's travel journal: private collection.

271 **'smooth to tameness'** . . . Private collection.

272 **'care for me'** . . . Private collection.

TWENTY-SEVEN

273 **'dessert and ices'** . . . 'The Art of Fiction' (1884), repr. in Roger Gard (ed.), *The Critical Muse: Selected Literary Criticism* (London: Penguin, 1987), p. 190.

274 **'radiant idleness'** . . . 'Charles Dickens', *Inside the Whale* (London: Victor Gollancz, 1940), pp. 63–6.

274 **'splendid lofty conservatory'** . . . New Forest Centre.

274 **monogrammed ivory case** . . . Oxford City Museum.

275 **the housemaid's wages** . . . Cohen, *Lewis Carroll: A Biography*, pp. 523–4.

276 **the diaries of Maria Hibbert** . . . New Forest Centre.

276 **'dresses, flags, &c.'** . . . *Hampshire Advertiser*, 3981 (9 August 1884), p. 7.

277 **Alice's watercolours** . . . Princeton.

277 **miniature** . . . Pierpont Morgan; the miniature is entitled *Lewis Carroll* rather than *Charles Dodgson*.

278 **'the outer world diminishes'** . . . Ethel M. Arnold, 'Social Life in Oxford', *Harper's New Monthly Magazine*, 81: 482 (July 1890), pp. 246–6.

278 **'"irons in the fire"'** . . . *Letters*, vol. 1, p. 513.

279 **'work until bed'** . . . This schedule is a summary of the information given in a letter repr. in *Diaries*, vol. 7, pp. 406–9.

279 **'original in your work'** . . . Mason Currey, *Daily Rituals: How Great Minds Make Time, Find Inspiration, and Get to Work* (London: Picador, 2013), pp. xiv, 144.

279 **shave in cold water** . . . See *Interviews & Recollections*, p. 25.

279 **'more regular habits'** . . . *Diaries*, vol. 7, p. 482.

280 **'and so on . . .'** . . . *Interviews & Recollections*, p. 59.

281 **'tops of the flowers'** . . . *Letters*, vol. 2, pp. 674–5.

281 **'Orange Marmalade'** . . . Christ Church.

281 **'odd corners and shelves'** . . . *Letters*, vol. 2, p. 688.

282 **'bread-and-butter'** . . . Christ Church.

282 **Common Room resolutions** . . . Christ Church.

TWENTY-EIGHT

283 **'a fine baby-brother'** . . . 'M. M. D.', 'Alice in Wonderland', *St Nicholas; An Illustrated Magazine for Young Folks*, 8: 2 (September 1881), p. 875.

283 **'dazzled eyes'** . . . 'Wonderland', *Sylvia's Home Journal* (Christmas 1885), p. 549.

284 **'useful moral lessons'** . . . Alfonzo Gardiner (ed.), *Tales and Stories from Wonderland* (London: John Heywood, 1894), Preface.

284 **'Believing Voyage'** . . . Charles E. Carryl, *Davy and the Goblin; or What Followed Reading 'Alice's Adventures in Wonderland'* (Boston: Tichnor & Co., 1885), p. 14.

284 **'surname to "Carroll"'** . . . Humphrey Carpenter, *Secret Gardens: A Study of the Golden Age of Children's Literature* (1985, repr. London: Faber, 2009), p. 226n.

285 **space for each day** . . . E. Stanley Leathes (ed.), *Alice's Wonderland Birthday Book* (London: Griffith & Farran, 1884).

285 **their own eyes** . . . W. Percival Westell, *Nature's Wonderland* (London: The Pilgrim Press, 1915); Wood Smith, *Wonderland; or, Curiosities of Nature and Art* (London: Thomas Nelson & Sons, 1897).

285 **the butterfly** . . . Constance M. Foot, *Insect Wonderland* (London: Methuen & Co., 1910), pp. 26–34.

285 **'made everything possible'** . . . John Ingold, 'The King of Diamonds', *Glimpses from Wonderland* (London: John Long, 1900), p. 66.

286 **'set it in motion'** . . . Albert and George Gresswell, *The Wonderland of Evolution* (London: Field & Tuer, 1884), pp. 3, 132.

286 **'wisdom of GOD'** . . . Rev John Isabell, *Wonderland Wonders* (London: Home Words Office, 1897), pp. 7–9.

287 **'in six years'** . . . *Diaries*, vol. 7, p. 357.

287 **'brain can act on brain'** . . . *Letters*, vol. 1, p. 471.

288 **'phenomena under discussion'** . . . Renée Haynes, *The Society for Psychical Research, 1882–1982: A History* (London: Macdonald, 1982), p. xiv.

288 **'Bible of British Spiritualism'** . . . Alan Gauld, *The Founders of Psychical Research* (London: Routledge & Kegan Paul, 1968), p. 78.

288 **teenage girls** . . . According to the Rev C. M. Davies in 1875, 'the time seems to have gone by for portly matrons . . . or elderly spinsters . . . and we anxious investigators can scarcely complain of the change which brings us face to face with fair young maidens in their teens', cited in Janet Oppenheim, *The Other World: Spiritualism and Psychical Research in England, 1850–1914* (Cambridge: Cambridge University Press, 1988), p. 19.

289 **delicate tuning rods** . . . Sally Shuttleworth points out that the records of the SPR contain 'numerous examples of times when spirits had either appeared to, or spoken through, children', *The Mind of the Child*, pp. 214–15.

289 **'an angel *might* be'** . . . *Letters*, vol. 1, p. 607.

289 **'positive electricity'** . . . *Letters*, vol. 1, p. 467.

290 **'"such is the fact!"'** . . . *Light: A Journal of Psychical, Occult and Mystical Research*, 4 (1884), p. 472.

290 **'the White Knight?'** . . . *Light*, 5 (1885), p. 588.

290 **'"the thing is called"'** . . . *Borderland: A Quarterly Review and Index*, 4 (1897), p. 8.

290 **'a veritable wonderland'** . . . *Phantasms of the Living*, 1 (1886), p. 11.

TWENTY-NINE

291 **'never have written at all'** . . . *Lewis Carroll's Alice* (Sotheby's catalogue), p. 133.

291 **'ancient times'** . . . *Letters*, vol. 1, pp. 520–1.

292 **'a different thing'** . . . *Letters*, vol. 1, pp. 560–1.

292 **'120,000 copies'** . . . *Lewis Carroll's Alice* (Sotheby's catalogue), p. 134.

292 **'reproducing the photograph'** . . . *Letters*, vol. 1, p. 561.

293 **'"He's gone *mad!*"'** . . . *Letters*, vol. 1, p. 579; a similar story is told in *Interviews & Recollections*, p. 206.

293 **King Herod** . . . *Diaries*, vol. 8, p. 197.

294 **'studies of his children'** . . . *Diaries*, vol. 8, pp. 199, 204.

294 **'inveterate child-fancier'** . . . *Letters*, vol. 1, p. 499.

295 **a particular chord with Carroll** . . . I draw these examples from Sally Shuttleworth's discussion of Victorian psychiatry in *The Mind of the Child*, pp. 190–2; the paraphrase of Maudsley's case study (which he borrows from J. E. D. Esquirol) is her own (p. 191).

295 **'real and ghastly'** . . . *Diaries*, vol. 7, pp. 121–3.

295 **'restoration of fallen women'** . . . *Letters*, vol. 1, p. 184.

295 **investigative journalism** . . . 'The Maiden Tribute of Modern Babylon' was published in four parts, on 6, 7, 8 and 10 July 1885 (*Pall Mall Gazette*, 42: 6336–8, 6340), from which all quotations are taken unless otherwise indicated.

296 **'Gothic fairy tale'** . . . Judith R. Walkowitz, *City of Dreadful Delight: Narratives of Sexual Danger in Late-Victorian London* (London: Virago, 1992), p. 85.

297 **'inverted fairy tale'** . . . *Ibid.*, p. 102.

297 **'icepack on his head'** . . . A. J. Milner, cited *ibid.*, p. 96.

298 **'noble and Royal'** . . . *Pall Mall Gazette* (8 July 1885), p. 1.

298 **'conducive to public morality'** . . . *Letters*, vol. 1, p. 597.

299 'thrust upon them' . . . *Diaries*, vol. 8, pp. 222–4.

299 'quoting pungent sentences' . . . Cited in Walkowitz, *City of Dreadful Delight*, p. 122.

299 'the bitter fruit' . . . *A Letter to the Editor of the Pall Mall Gazette*, by an Oxford M.A. (London: Jackson Gaskill, n.d.), p. 5.

299 'serpent in Eden' . . . William McGlashan, *England on her Defence! Being a Reply to 'The Maiden Tribute of Modern Bablylon'* (Newcastle: John B. Barnes, 1885), p. 4.

299 'evil desire' . . . *Diaries*, vol. 8, p. 225; Carroll is quoting from a sermon by Rev E. Munro published in 1850.

299 'new experience in Art' . . . *Diaries*, vol. 8, p. 217.

300 'consent' . . . Lindsay Smith discusses Carroll's understanding of 'consent' in *The Politics of Focus*, pp. 98–101.

300 'some Liddells as companions' . . . *Letters*, vol. 1, p. 63.

300 'understands by it' . . . 'The Stage and the Spirit of Reverence', *The Theatre* (June 1888), repr. in Collingwood (ed.), *The Lewis Carroll Picture Book*, p. 136.

300 'best goods he can' . . . *Letters*, vol. 2, p. 771.

300 '"the fireworks"' . . . 'Walter', *My Secret Life* (1888–92, repr. London: Arrow, 1994), vol. 1, p. 254.

300 'a sense of beauty' . . . *Diaries*, vol. 8, p. 377.

301 'honi soit' . . . James Alexander, 'Sentiment and Aesthetics in Victorian Photography', *Carrollian*, 17 (Spring 2006), p. 50.

301 'escaped my memory' . . . Letter to Walter Watson (15 March 1886) cited in *Diaries*, vol. 8, pp. 262–3.

302 '*Under it!*' . . . *Letters*, vol. 2, p. 647.

302 'the one before' . . . Edward Bulwer-Lytton to Lady Blessington (23 October 1834), repr. in *The Life of Edward Bulwer First Lord Lytton*, 2 vols (London: Macmillan & Co., 1913), vol. 1, p. 458.

THIRTY

303 'nature of the incident' . . . *Letters*, vol. 1, p. 540.

303 'to consider it' . . . *Diaries*, vol. 5, p. 46.

304 'like *The Mikado*' . . . *Letters*, vol. 2, p. 637.

304 'forgive me?' . . . *Letters*, vol. 2, p. 681; Ellen Terry records the incident in *Ellen Terry's Memoirs* (London: V. Gollancz, 1933), pp. 141–2.

304 'pure and good' . . . 'The Stage and the Spirit of Reverence', *The Theatre* (June 1888), repr. in Collingwood (ed.), *The Lewis Carroll Picture Book*, p. 134.

304 'ennoble its aims' . . . *Life & Letters*, p. 181. In addition to sending out over a hundred copies of the school's prospectus with a covering letter, in 1882 Carroll published two letters on 'Education for the Stage' in the *St James's Gazette*.

305 'sinful feelings roused' . . . Harvard.

305 'a thousand times better' . . . *Letters*, vol. 1, p. 335.

305 'no longer little' . . . *Diaries*, vol. 3, p. 77.

305 'orange receiving' . . . Cited in S. L. Kotar and J. E. Gessler, *The Rise of the American Circus, 1716–1899* (Jefferson: McFarland & Co., 2011), p. 90.

305 'looks about 8' . . . *Diaries*, vol. 5, p. 127.

306 'subject for the camera' . . . *Diaries*, vol. 6, p. 86.

306 'Children in Theatres' . . . 'Stage Children' . . . Published respectively in the *St James's Gazette* (19 July 1887) and the *Sunday Times* (4 August 1889).

307   **'the baby *Pinafore*'** . . . Clement William Scott, *The Theatre* (1 January 1880), p. 39.

307   **'pretty as a whole'** . . . *Diaries*, vol. 7, p. 316. Carroll's particular objection was to a 'sweet bevy of little girls' chorusing the word 'damme'; his full reaction is recorded in 'The Stage and the Spirit of Reverence'.

307   **'into a pantomime'** . . . *Diaries*, vol. 5, pp. 201–5; *Letters*, vol. 1, pp. 99–102.

307   **'kind permission'** . . . *Alice and Other Fairy Plays for Children* (London: George Bell & Sons, 1878), Preface; *Alice Through the Looking-Glass and Other Fairy Plays for Children* (London: W. Swan Sonnenschein, 1882), Preface.

307   **'should ever be dramatised'** . . . *Diaries*, vol. 6, p. 236; Lebailly quotes some of the reviews Lydia Howard attracted in 1872, including one in *The Times*, which described her as 'a perfect little genius' ('C. L. Dodgson and the Victorian Cult of the Child', p. 29).

308   **'exhibit it'** . . . *Letters*, vol. 1, p. 180.

308   **'surpassing prettiness'** . . . *Diaries*, vol. 6, p. 260; *Letters*, vol. 1, p. 183n.

308   **'absurdly extravagant'** . . . *Letters*, vol. 1, pp. 274n., 278n.

308   **'needful constructive talent'** . . . *Diaries*, vol. 8, p. 105.

308   **'a drama on *Alice*'** . . . *Diaries*, vol. 8, p. 183.

308   **she made a guest appearance** . . . See Charles C. Lovett, *Alice on Stage* (Westport, Conn; London: Meckler, 1989), p. 35.

309   **'coarseness or vulgarity'** . . . *Ibid.*, p. 36.

309   **sheets of gauze** . . . Henry Morley pointed out in his *Examiner* review that the Sadler's Wells production of *A Midsummer Night's Dream* in 1853 successfully used green gauze to capture the play's unearthly atmosphere: 'as in a dream, one scene [was] made to glide insensibly into another' (repr. in *Journal of a London Playgoer*, ed. Michael Booth (Leicester: Leicester University Press, 1974), p. 57).

309   **'men in the Gallery'** . . . *Letters*, vol. 2, pp. 636–8.

309   **'as if half-asleep'** . . . *Letters*, vol. 2, p. 644.

310   **'dear little friend'** . . . Fales.

310   **should be 'sacrificed'** . . . Fales.

310   **'a new *name*'** . . . Fales.

311   **'all the time it lasted'** . . . *Diaries*, vol. 1, pp. 105–6.

311   **three-act drama *Claudian*** . . . *Diaries*, vol. 8, pp. 80–1.

311   **'*broken loose . . .*'** . . . Joseph Hatton, *The Lyceum 'Faust'* (London: Virtue, 1894), p. 23. Michael R. Booth discusses the context of such productions in *Victorian Spectacular Theatre, 1850–1910* (London: Routledge, 1981).

312   **a sandwich board** . . . Lucien Besché's original costume designs for the 1886 production are in the Harry Ransom Center.

313   **'utterly lost'** . . . See Lovett, *Alice on Stage*, pp. 60–3.

313   **'on any account!'** . . . *Letters*, vol. 2, p. 768.

313   **'clever little school paper'** . . . Newspaper clipping, cited in *Letters*, vol. 2, p. 696n.

313   ***Humorous Poems of the Century*** . . . *Letters*, vol. 2, p. 720.

314   **'7 year-old maiden'** . . . *Diaries*, vol. 8, p. 432.

THIRTY-ONE

316   **Nyctograph** . . . *Diaries*, vol. 8, p. 582.

316   **'sell the article'** . . . Cited in Cohen, *Lewis Carroll: A Biography*, p. 287.

316   **'how I manage with mine'** . . . *Diaries*, vol. 9, pp. 248–50n.

317 'filled the teapot' . . . Edith Olivier in *Interviews & Recollections*, p. 183.

317 'exactly ten minutes' . . . Bowman, *The Story of Lewis Carroll*, p. 34.

317 'in its perfect form' . . . *Diaries*, vol. 8, p. 524.

317 'clearness and range' . . . Advertisement, *The Graphic* (25 October 1884).

317 'scientific physical training' . . . Advertisement contained in *Oxonian Cycles*, a pamphlet issued by the Oxford Cycle Company in 1897 (Bodleian). Collingwood reports that 'He was so pleased with the "Exerciser", that he bought several more of them, and made presents of them to his friends' (*Life & Letters*, p. 339).

317 'on a hill' . . . *Diaries*, vol. 7, p. 435.

317 'a tricycle' . . . *Life & Letters*, pp. 219–20.

317 'walking would have been' . . . *Diaries*, vol. 8, pp. 221–2.

318 'ink your fingers' . . . *Letters*, vol. 2, p. 627.

318 'ridges in cylinder' . . . *Diaries*, vol. 8, p. 396.

318 'were commonplace' . . . *Patent Inventions: Intellectual Property and the Victorian Novel* (Oxford: Oxford University Press, 2004), p. 5.

319 'for fastening envelopes' . . . *Diaries*, vol. 9, pp. 191, 263.

319 'use in the invention' . . . Letter from G. L. Craik, cited in *Macmillan*, p. 275n.

320 'uses no other' . . . *Eight or Nine Wise Words About Letter-Writing* (Oxford: Emberlin & Son, 1890), pp. 12, 15, 7.

320 gauze-and-wire flying contraption . . . Bowman, *The Story of Lewis Carroll*, p. 22.

321 carved ivory parasol handle . . . *Letters*, vol. 2, p. 883; Carroll had previously allowed individuals to use his characters for decorative purposes, including one to whom he gave permission in 1880 'to reproduce the "Mad Tea Party" on a tablecloth' (*Macmillan*, p. 161).

321 '*Beau—ootiful So—oap!*' . . . Bodleian. Thomas Richards points out that similar images were used in advertising from the 1870s onwards to sell a wide range of products, including Cadbury's Cocoa, Beecham's ointments, Chichester Brand Potted Meats and Y&N Diagonal Seam Corsets; see *The Commodity Culture of Victorian Britain: Advertising and Spectacle, 1851–1914* (Stanford: Stanford University Press, 1990), ch. 5: 'Those Lovely Seaside Girls'.

321 'germs collecting at night' . . . Bodleian.

321 'The Fosco Gallop' . . . See Andrew Lycett, *Wilkie Collins: A Life of Sensation* (London: Hutchinson, 2013), p. 215.

322 'a children's tin' . . . *Letters*, vol. 2, p. 832.

322 'considerable artistic merit' . . . *Letters*, vol. 2, p. 835.

323 'to go out *empty*' . . . *Letters*, vol. 2, pp. 927, 938.

323 special packets . . . Dodgson Family Collection.

323 'biscuit tins were empty!' . . . *Interviews & Recollections*, p. 144.

324 'Mrs and the Masters Hargreaves' . . . Dodgson Family Collection.

324 Caryl (1887) . . . When one of the Hargreaves family tins came up for auction in 2001, it was revealed to be as battered as a well-loved toy (*Lewis Carroll's Alice* (Sotheby's catalogue), p. 149).

324 'the total number is 364!' . . . *Letters*, vol. 2, p. 930.

324 'to go through you' . . . Dodgson Family Collection.

324 'to get into it' . . . *Letters*, vol. 2, p. 924&n.

324 'toy animals in it' . . . *Letters*, vol. 2, p. 924n.

325   **a new *Alice* industry** . . . I adopt here the term '*Alice* industry' from Jan Susina, *The Place of Lewis Carroll in Children's Literature* (London; New York: Routledge, 2011), ch. 4: 'Multiple *Wonderlands*: Lewis Carroll and the Creation of the *Alice* Industry'.

325   **'my new friend'** . . . *Letters*, vol. 2, p. 1101; *Diaries*, vol. 8, p. 625.

325   **Daisy, Edith, Florence** . . . . . . Some of Carroll's 'new friends' from October 1890 to the end of 1891, *Diaries*, vol. 8, pp. 633–4.

326   **'"Alice" books put together'** . . . Addendum slip inserted into the 1890 edition of *The Nursery "Alice"* (Fales).

326   **'a consecutive story'** . . . Preface to *Sylvie and Bruno*.

327   **'a plot'** . . . *Letters*, vol. 2, p. 776; for a bold attempt to defend Carroll's stylistic unevenness as the result of 'a carefully articulated plan', see Edmund Miller, 'The *Sylvie and Bruno* Books as Victorian Novel', in Guiliano (ed.), *Lewis Carroll Observed*, pp. 132–44 (p. 132).

327   **'another new path'** . . . Preface to *Sylvie and Bruno*.

327   **'embodiment of Purity'** . . . *Letters*, vol. 2, p. 653.

327   **'graver thoughts of human life'** . . . Preface to *Sylvie and Bruno*.

328   **'much in sympathy'** . . . Preface to *Sylvie and Bruno Concluded*.

329   **'I'm twite tired'** . . . *Letters*, vol. 1, p. 3; on the commercial appeal of baby talk in late-Victorian fiction, see Carpenter, *Secret Gardens*, p. 106.

329   **shot his first birds** . . . Letters sent 22 June 1890, n.d. (*c.* 1891), 29 May 1891 and 11 February 1900 (private collection).

329   **'she could reach'** . . . Sir John Martin-Harvey, *Autobiography* (1933), cited in *Letters*, vol. 2, p. 1029.

330   **'weird and unearthly'** . . . 'Children and Modern Literature', *The National Review*, 18 (December 1891), pp. 507, 515. For more on Dickens's gnome-like child characters, see John Carey, *The Violent Effigy* (London: Faber, 1973), p. 137.

330   **new field of child development** . . . Sally Shuttleworth points out that 'By the 1890s one finds a deluge of scientific, education, and literary texts with titles like *The Children*, *The Mind of a Child*, *Child and Child Nature*, or *The Development of a Child*' (*The Mind of the Child*, p. 271).

330   **'enchanted ground'** . . . 'Aunt Em', 'Christmas', *Woman's Exponent*, 13: 17 (1888), p. 99.

331   **'"where had I got to?"'** . . . Kenneth Grahame, *The Golden Age* (New York; London: John Lane, 1899), p. 67.

331   **'beasts moving unseen'** . . . *Ibid.*, p. 65.

331   **'a little child'** . . . *Letters*, vol. 2, p. 738.

331   **Alice appeared in colour** . . . An earlier Dutch abridgement, *Lize's Avonturen in 't Wonderland*, had featured several hand-coloured versions of Tenniel's illustrations. Carroll owned a copy by 1881, and it may have given him the idea for his own colour version (see *Letters*, vol. 1, p. 419).

332   **'7 year-old maiden'** . . . 'Began text of Nursery "Alice"', *Diaries*, vol. 8, p. 439 (28 December 1889).

332   **'enormous tangles'** . . . *Letters*, vol. 1, p. 418n.; Selwyn H. Goodacre provides a helpful outline in *Jabberwocky*, 4: 4 (Autumn 1975).

333   **'bright and gaudy'** . . . *Macmillan*, p. 259.

334   **fireplace tiles in Christ Church** . . . *Letters*, vol. 1, p. 520n.

334 **magic lantern slides** . . . Perken, Son & Rayment's set of forty-two slides is advertised in their book *The Magic Lantern: its Construction and Use* (London: n.p., *c.* 1889), p. 123; Carroll had previously explored the possibility of a Leeds manufacturer (W. L. Breare) producing a set of slides (*Macmillan*, p. 122).

335 **an individual** . . . I owe this observation to Beverly Lyon Clark, 'What Went Wrong With Alice?' in Donald E. Morse (ed.), *The Fantastic in World Literature and the Arts* (Westport, Conn.; London: Greenwood Press, 1984), pp. 98–9.

335 **'certainly appear to him'** . . . *Diaries*, vol. 8, p. 596n.

335 **'all the way from Wonderland!'** . . . *Diaries*, vol. 8, p. 514n.

335 **'the lady-in-waiting'** . . . Princess Alice, Countess of Athlone, *For My Grandchildren* (1966), cited in *Letters*, vol. 2, p. 749n.

Thirty-three

336 **'from the Author'** . . . Fales.

336 **'the Author's sincere regards'** . . . Fales.

336 **'"Alice in Wonderland"'** . . . Copy of the seventh edition (1886), sold at auction in 2001, *Lewis Carroll's Alice* (Sotheby's catalogue), p. 175.

337 **'totally inexperienced'** . . . E. M. Rowell, 'To Me He Was Mr. Dodgson', *Harper's Magazine*, 186 (February 1943), pp. 321–2.

337 **'WITH HER FEET'** . . . Harry Ransom Center. 'Wonderland' was also a popular generic title for magic shows: a flyer advertising the debut performance of 'The Great Egyptian Sphinx' on 18 December 1878 promised that his routine would begin with an illusion known as 'The Shawl of Wonderland' (Johnson Collection), while in 1905 an American magician known as 'The Mystifier' announced that he was launching a new touring show to be called 'An Evening in Wonderland', *The Sphinx: A Monthly Magazine for Magicians and Illusionists*, 4 (1905–06), p. 88.

338 **put on display** . . . For details of Edison's talking dolls, see Gaby Wood, *Living Dolls: a Magical History of the Quest for Mechanical Life* (London: Faber, 2002), pp. 107–54.

338 **'the Wonderland is hiding'** . . . Amy C. Morant, 'Wonderland: a Woman's Answer', *The Adult: The Journal of Sex*, 1: 2 (1898), p. 19.

339 **'most of them broken'** . . . Anna M. Richards, *A New Alice in the Old Wonderland* (Philadelphia: J. B. Lippincott, 1895), pp. 14, 33, 44–5, 55. See Carolyn Sigler, 'Brave New Alice: Anna Matlack Richards's Maternal Wonderland', *Children's Literature*, 24 (1996), pp. 55–73, for the argument that Richards's 'subversive impulse' lies in her 'matriarchal re-creation of Wonderland' (even the Cheshire Cat has kittens) and her 'transformation of Carroll's anxiously polite Alice into [a] courageous "new Alice"' who shares many qualities with the turn-of-the-century New Woman (pp. 61–2).

339 **'"She is she"'** . . . Cited in *Letters*, vol. 2, p. 860n.

340 ***From Nowhere to the North Pole*** . . . See Selwyn H. Goodacre and Jeffrey Stern, 'The Land of Idleness – An Enquiry', *Jabberwocky*, 13: 1 (Winter 1984–85), p. 19. Jan Susina discusses the context of this warning in *The Place of Lewis Carroll in Children's Literature*, ch. 5.

340 **invitation to tea** . . . *Letters*, vol. 2, p. 876.

340   '7 years old!' . . . Private collection; the version printed in *Letters* contains the final sentence without Carroll's underlining of '*husband*'.

341   'in the afternoon' . . . *Diaries*, vol. 8, p. 598.

341   'that mountainous maiden' . . . *Letters*, vol. 2, p. 785.

341   'shame and misery' . . . *Letters*, vol. 2, p. 919.

342   seasonal 'adventures' . . . *Letters*, vol. 2, p. 973.

342   'sofa, so good' . . . Letter cited in *Diaries*, vol. 8, p. 393n.

342   'the common metals' . . . *Letters*, vol. 2, p. 966.

342   'failed to find elsewhere' . . . *Letters*, vol. 2, p. 1113.

342   'broken-hearted hopeless old bachelor' . . . *Letters*, vol. 2, pp. 964, 862.

342   'out of my life' . . . *Letters*, vol. 2, p. 873.

342   'My darling' . . . *Letters*, vol. 2, p. 1121.

343   'in the sight of God' . . . *Letters*, vol. 2, p. 977.

343   'old-new friend' . . . Cited in *Diaries*, vol. 9, p. 354n.

343   a 'charming' girl . . . *Letters*, vol. 2, p. 1111 (compare vol. 2, p. 1121, in which he signs himself 'Your very loving antique'); *Diaries*, vol. 9, p. 304.

344   'ca'n't' and 'wo'n't' . . . Selwyn H. Goodacre discusses revisions to the 1897 six shilling editions of *Alice's Adventures in Wonderland* and *Through the Looking-Glass*, in *Jabberwocky*, 51 (Summer 1982), pp. 67–76, and *Carrollian*, 22 (Autumn 2008), pp. 12–24.

344   'Damn the Dons' . . . *Diaries*, vol. 8, p. 544; vol. 9, p. 109.

344   'vanishing world' . . . *Interviews & Recollections*, pp. 68–9.

345   'excessive brain-stimulation' . . . *Letters*, vol. 1, pp. 557–8n, 572.

345   'a vision of topsyturvydom' . . . Charlotte Smith, 'Mr Besant's Riddle', *The Woman's Herald*, 41: 8 (1893), p. 653.

346   weeping and blushing . . . 'Petticoats for Men' [presented as a translation from a German journal], *The Woman Patriot: dedicated to the defense of womanhood, motherhood, the family and the state, against suffragism, feminism, and socialism*, 6: 3 (1919), p. 5.

346   'no places to live in' . . . W. H. Auden, 'Lewis Carroll', *Forewords and Afterwords*, p. 291.

THIRTY-FOUR

347   'less and less of a shock' . . . *Letters*, vol. 2, p. 1100.

347   central tenets of his religious faith . . . In his preface to *Sylvie and Bruno*, Carroll observed that the possibility of sudden death was 'one of the best possible tests as to our going to any scene of amusement being right or wrong'.

347   'last year and a half' . . . *Letters*, vol. 2, p. 1100.

348   '"Thy will be done"' . . . Hymn 264 in *Hymns Ancient and Modern*, rev. edn (London: William Clowes & Sons, 1877), p. 73.

348   'I shall need them no more' . . . *Life & Letters*, pp. 347–8.

348   'a small plain head-stone' . . . 'Directions regarding my Funeral &c', Harvard.

348   a short will . . . Princeton.

348   'prettiest parts of the cemetery' . . . Private collection.

348   100,000 *Looking-Glasses* . . . Selwyn H. Goodacre, 'Lewis Carroll's 1887 Corrections to *Alice*', *Library* (June 1973), cited in Cohen, *Lewis Carroll: A Biography*, p. 134.

349   **'a solitary vote'** . . . 'What Children Like to Read: The Verdict', *Pall Mall Gazette*, 10378 (1 July 1898), pp. 1–2.

349   **'your brother looks!'** . . . *Life & Letters*, p. 364.

THIRTY-FIVE

350   **'mass of papers &c'** . . . Christ Church.

351   **'all he held most dear'** . . . Frederick York Powell's poem was first published in Oliver Elton, *Frederick York Powell* (1906), and is repr. in Denis Crutch (ed.), *The Lewis Carroll Handbook*, rev. edn (Dawson: Archon, 1979), p. 259.

351   **'photographic purposes'** . . . Sales catalogue (Oxford: Hall & Son, 1898), pp. 7–10.

351   **'spirited competition'** . . . 'The Sale of "Lewis Carroll's" Effects', local newspaper report in Dodgson Family Collection.

351   **auctioned by Christie's** . . . *New York Times* (11 December 1998).

352   **such a daunting task** . . . Repr. in Imholtz and Lovett (eds), *In Memoriam Charles Lutwidge Dodgson*, p. 86.

352   **'anecdotes about him, &c.'** . . . *Ibid.*, p. xix.

352   **'unnecessary weed'** . . . *Life & Letters*, pp. 302–3.

352   **'in three volumes'** . . . Cited in Ian Hamilton, *Keepers of the Flame: Literary Estates and the Rise of Biography* (London: Pimlico, 1993), p. 144.

353   **'the scrubbing of marble'** . . . *Ibid.*

353   **'as much as possible'** . . . *Ibid.*, p. 89.

353   **'if you saw him?'** . . . *Interviews & Recollections*, p. 142.

353   **'not speaking to "Lewis Carroll"'** . . . *Edward Bok: An Autobiography* (London: Butterworth, 1921), p. 200.

354   **'his own name'** . . . Crutch (ed.), *The Lewis Carroll Handbook*, p. 168.

354   **Lewis Carroll and Charles Dodgson** . . . Oxford's Bodleian Library, on the other hand, refused his request to separate the two names, and instead followed standard cataloguing procedures by linking them; see *Letters*, vol. 1, p. 457.

354   **'Lewis Carroll and C. L. Dodgson'** . . . *Letters*, vol. 1, p. 237.

354   **Jekyll and Hyde** . . . The most influential example of this approach is Langford Reed's *The Life of Lewis Carroll* (1932), which I discuss in chapter 41.

355   **'"There are two of them"'** . . . Henry James, *The Aspern Papers and Other Stories*, ed. Adrian Poole (Oxford: Oxford's World's Classics, 1983), p. 117.

355   **spinning a coin** . . . *Life & Letters*, pp. 331–5.

355   **'the imperishable kingdom is!'** . . . 'Lewis Carroll', repr. in Imholtz and Lovett (eds), *In Memoriam Charles Lutwidge Dodgson*, p. 130.

355   **'Miss Mite'** . . . *Life & Letters*, pp. 99, 101, 110.

356   **'his little friend also'** . . . Alice Meynell, 'The "Lewis Carroll" Cot', *St James's Gazette* (16 February 1898), repr. in Imholtz and Lovett (eds), *In Memoriam Charles Lutwidge Dodgson*, p. 181.

356   **the Mock Turtle** . . . For details, see Imholtz and Lovett (eds), *In Memoriam Charles Lutwidge Dodgson*, pp. xiv–xvii.

356   **'as might have been expected'** . . . 'The Sale of "Lewis Carroll's" Effects'.

356   **'small pieces of pipe'** . . . *Life & Letters*, pp. 11–12.

356   **'our dreams and hopes'** . . . Imholtz and Lovett (eds), *In Memoriam Charles Lutwidge Dodgson*, pp. 12, 349.

357 '"Alice in Wonderland"' . . . Letter to A. W. Mackenzie (12 November 1899), Harry Ransom Center.

357 'a personal loss' . . . Obituary repr. in Imholtz and Lovett (eds), *In Memoriam Charles Lutwidge Dodgson*, p. 77.

358 **almost all of these were generous** . . . See, e.g., the obituary in *Good-Will* (March 1898): '"Lewis Carroll" had been really lost to us for some time; the magic wand was broken, and it was certain that he would never again reach the level of his best work' (Imholtz and Lovett (eds), *In Memoriam Charles Lutwidge Dodgson*, p. 65).

358 'a sick child' . . . Imholtz and Lovett (eds), *In Memoriam Charles Lutwidge Dodgson*, pp. 26, 32, 21, 35, 155, 82.

358 'so well known' . . . Ibid., p. 64.

358 '"Tell us a story"' . . . *Life & Letters*, p. 96.

358 'I am the real Alice' . . . *Theatre News*, I: 1 (4 February 1899), p. 2.

359 'always will be' . . . *The Academy* (22 January 1898), repr. in Imholtz and Lovett (eds), *In Memoriam Charles Lutwidge Dodgson*, p. 8.

359 **all "Alices" more or less** . . . 'Lewis Carroll, the Children's Writer', *Child Life*, 3: 10 (15 April 1901), pp. 94–5.

THIRTY-SIX

360 **reached as many minds** . . . Rev Francis Paget, 'The Virtue of Simplicity' (sermon preached on 23 January 1898), repr. in Imholtz and Lovett (eds), *In Memoriam Charles Lutwidge Dodgson*, p. 176.

360 **the *Discovery*** . . . The books were brought back by the physician and geologist Reginald Koettlitz, and auctioned at Bonham's on 4 December 2012 (source: *Daily Telegraph*, 20 November 2012).

360 'books of the *Alice* type' . . . *Diaries*, vol. 8, p. 579.

360 '"Wonderland for themselves!"' . . . Walter Burges Smith, *Looking for Alice* (London: Gay & Bird, 1904), pp. 9, 194.

361 'a little time' . . . Ibid., p. 196.

361 **Wonderland Co., Buenos Aires** . . . *Proceedings of the Central Criminal Court* (14 December 1896), p. 42.

361 *Pinocchio's Adventures in Wonderland* . . . For the full sequence of events, see Richard Wunderlich and Thomas J. Morrisey, *Pinocchio Goes Postmodern: Perils of a Puppet in the United States* (New York; London: Routledge, 2002), pp. 31–2.

361 **advertising gimmick** . . . *Publisher's Weekly* (1 October 1898), p. 520.

362 '"Dwindle, dwindle, little war"' . . . Hector H. Munro ('Saki'), *The Westminster Alice* (London: The Westminster Gazette Office, 1902), pp. 36–7.

362 '"An arrow escape"' . . . John Rae, *New Adventures of 'Alice'* (Chicago: P. F. Volland Co., 1917), pp. 11, 14, 43.

363 **almost getting impaled** . . . Winsor McCay, *The Complete Little Nemo in Slumberland, Volume I: 1905–1907*, ed. Richard Marschall, 2nd edn (London: Titan, 1990), pp. 17–19.

363 **children's anthologies** . . . *Days in Wonderland: A Story Book for Boys and Girls* (London: Cassell & Co., 1910), n.p.

364 '"the way to Wonderland!"' . . . Mary Stewart, *The Way to Wonderland* (London: Hodder & Stoughton, 1920), pp. 43, 147.

364 **breeding ground for typhoid** . . . Miller, *The Brontë Myth*, pp. 100–8.

365 'A wonderland by the waves' . . . *Woman's Life* (4 July 1903), p. 213.

365   **new editions** . . . John Davis points out that a number of rival American editions had been published earlier; see *The Illustrators of Alice*, ed. Graham Ovenden (London: Academy Editions, 1972), p. 10. For a full discussion of editions of both *Alice* books before and after 1907, see Zoe Jaques and Eugene Giddens, *Lewis Carroll's Alice's Adventures in Wonderland and Through the Looking-Glass: A Publishing History* (Farnham: Ashgate, 2013).

366   **Tenniel's figures** . . . The cartoon is reproduced in Guiliano (ed.), *Lewis Carroll Observed*, pp. 32–3.

366   **the Hatter actually wears a hat** . . . I owe this example to Brooker, *Alice's Adventures*, p. 130.

368   **another Alice in another Wonderland** . . . For the best recent account of the Cottingley fairies, see Douglas Kerr, *Conan Doyle: Writing, Profession, and Practice* (Oxford: Oxford University Press, 2013), pp. 233–9.

Thirty-seven

369   **'wholesomely repressed'** . . . *The Saturday Review* (22 January 1898), repr. in Imholtz and Lovett (eds), *In Memoriam Charles Lutwidge Dodgson*, p. 142.

369   **'all-accomplished, wise'** . . . 'Dedication' to *Idylls of the King*, in Ricks (ed.), *The Poems of Tennyson*, vol. 3, p. 264.

370   **'"to be Comrades"'** . . . Henry T. Schnittkind, *Alice and the Stork: A Fairy Tale for Workingmen's Children* (Boston: Richard G. Badger, 1915), pp. 69, 35–6.

370   **'the everyday world'** . . . Carpenter, *Secret Gardens*, pp. 16–17.

371   **'"Calloo, callay!"'** . . . Rudyard Kipling, *The Complete Stalky & Co.*, ed. Isabel Quigly (Oxford: Oxford University Press, 1987, repr. 2009), pp. 72, 81.

371   **'rambling and incoherent'** . . . 'Modern Fairy Tales', *The Advance* (19 August 1909), cited in *The Annotated Wizard of Oz*, ed. Michael Patrick Hearn (New York; London: W. W. Norton, 2000), p. 12.

372   **'for the most part, avoid'** . . . 'An Historical Essayist', *Instigations of Ezra Pound: Together With an Essay on the Chinese Written Character* (New York: Boni & Liveright, 1920), p. 224.

373   **'tired out with life'** . . . Willa Cather, 'The Prodigies', *The Home Monthly*, 6 (July 1897), pp. 9–11.

373   **'sense of wonder'** . . . G. K. Chesterton, 'A Defence of Nonsense' (1901), repr. in *Stories, Essays, and Poems* (London: Dent, 1939), pp. 123–7.

373   **'and mad at that'** . . . *The Letters of Virginia Woolf*, ed. Nigel Nicolson and Joanne Trautmann, 6 vols (London: The Hogarth Press, 1975–80), vol. 4, pp. 128–9; I owe this example to Juliet Dusinberre, *Alice to the Lighthouse: Children's Books and Radical Experiments in Art*, 2nd edn (Basingstoke: Macmillan, 1999).

373   **'mawkish sentimental drivel'** . . . Roger Fry, *Reflections on British Painting* (London: Faber, 1934), p. 107; Dusinberre points out that 'a very old copy of *Alice in Wonderland* was among the Fry children's books' (*Alice to the Lighthouse*, p. 280n.)

374   **'(à la Alice in Wonderland)'** . . . *The Selected Letters of Ezra Pound to John Quinn 1915–1924*, ed. Timothy Materer (Durham; London: Duke University Press, 1991), p. 103.

374   **'"near this table"'** . . . *The Collected Letters of Katherine Mansfield, Vol. 1: 1903–1917*, ed. Vincent O'Sullivan and Margaret Scott (Oxford: Clarendon Press, 1984), p. 267.

374   **'excellent book I think'** . . . Cited in Humphrey Carpenter, *The Brideshead Generation: Evelyn Waugh and His Friends* (London: Faber, 1989), p. 157.

374 **standard narrative templates** . . . I owe some of these examples to Carpenter, *ibid.*, e.g. *'Decline and Fall* is a modern *Alice'* (p. 159).

375 **'enclosed and enchanted garden'** . . . Evelyn Waugh, *Brideshead Revisited* (Harmondsworth: Penguin, 1986), p. 40.

375 **nine *Dr Jekyll and Mr Hydes*** . . . Matthew Sweet, *Inventing the Victorians* (London: Faber, 2001), p. 25.

THIRTY-EIGHT

378 **a short train ride away** . . . F. W. Martindale, *Alice in Holidayland* (n.p., c. 1914).

379 **everything changed** . . . Ernie Odell's reminiscences are cited from *Odell and Mounsey, Sapper Before Sunset*, pp. 1–10.

379 **'coming to any harm'** . . . (2 January 1909), private collection.

380 **'careful eye of Nanny'** . . . (n.d.), private collection.

380 **special commemorative medal** . . . Oxford City Museum.

380 **'not dangerous Alan'** . . . Telegram (14 October 1914), private collection.

380 **'to avoid haemorrhage'** . . . Letter from Alan Hargreaves (13 October 1914), private collection.

381 **'about 4 a.m.'** . . . Private collection.

381 **'in hospital'** . . . Letter from R. B. Stephens (20 May 1915), private collection.

381 **'wounded & subsequent death'** . . . Private collection.

381 **photograph of his grave** . . . Private collection.

381 **'their men in attack'** . . . Letter from Neville Henderson (28 September 1916), private collection.

381 **'ever come across'** . . . Private collection; Rudyard Kipling, *The Irish Guards and the Great War*, 2 vols (London: Macmillan & Co., 1923), vol. 1, pp. 185–6.

381 **'friendly fire'** . . . *OED*.

382 **'You *are* a funny chap!'** . . . R. C. Sherriff, *Journey's End* (1929, repr. London: Penguin, 1983), pp. 61–3.

383 **'a stick o' chocolate'** . . . *Ibid.*, 24, 70, 75.

383 **'darkness in the dugout'** . . . *Ibid.*, p. 95.

384 **'a sad, enchanted region'** . . . 'War Fever', *The Red Feather (The Regimental Magazine of the 6th (Service) Battalion of the Duke of Cornwall's Light Infantry)* (December 1915), pp. 9–10.

384 **'Back to Wonderland'** . . . *Chronicles of the N.Z.E.F.* (17 January 1917), p. 229.

384 **'Alas: In Wonderland'** . . . *Aussie: The Australian Soldiers' Magazine* (June 1918), p. 15.

384 **'The Quartermaster in Wonderland'** . . . *1918 Souvenir of The Welsh Division* (January 1918), p. 9.

384 **'the authors [sic] of "Alice in Wonderland"'** . . . 'The O. C. and the Adjutant', *Chronicles of the N.Z.E.F.* (29 November 1916), p. 152.

384 **'"You're a bun"'** . . . Frank Birch and Dilly Knox, *Alice in I.D. 25*, ed. Mavis Batey and Edward Wakeling (London: Aznet Publishing, 2007), pp. 51–2.

THIRTY-NINE

386 **'part of the wreckage'** . . . Cited in Gordon, *Beyond the Looking Glass*, p. 223. An official obituary appeared in *The Times* on 14 February 1926.

386 **'what you have been to me'** . . . *Ibid.*

386 **'as you think'** . . . Private collection.

387 **the value of land** . . . See Giles Worsley, *England's Lost Houses* (London: Aurum Press, 2002), p. 11.

387 **'glutted and shrinking'** . . . *Ibid.*

387 **the Women's Institute** . . . An engraved key presented to Alice Hargreaves to commemorate her term of office is at Oxford City Museum.

387 **draughty main rooms** . . . I draw this information from Clark, *The Real Alice*, p. 232, who interviewed Mary Gailor, a fifteen-year-old housemaid taken on at Cuffnells in 1928.

387 **'1 ft square'** . . . Private collection.

388 **distant parts of the British Empire** . . . The tradition of topographical wonderlands was not completely dead; in a boys' adventure story published in 1896, the two heroes spend an afternoon bathing in an 'enchanting' natural spring, and decide that they would like 'to spend at least a month in this wonderland', J. Macdonald Oxley, *Two Boy Tramps* (London; Edinburgh: W. & R. Chambers, 1896), p. 237.

388 **'perfect them'** . . . 'Alice', repr. in Phillips (ed.), *Aspects of Alice*, pp. 114–15.

388 **'stepping with Alice in Wonderland'** . . . Alexander Davis, *The Native Problem in South Africa* (London: Chapman & Hall, 1903), p. 33; Mary Gaunt, *Alone in West Africa* (London: T. Werner Laurie, 1911), p. 186.

389 **'a flutter of playing-cards'** . . . Evelyn Waugh, *Remote People* (London: Duckworth, 1931), p. 29. I am grateful to John Bowen for drawing this example to my attention.

389 **new *Alice* translations** . . . These and other translations are listed in Warren Weaver, *Alice in Many Tongues: The Translations of Alice in Wonderland* (Madison: University of Wisconsin Press, 1964).

389 **'a Russian nursery'** . . . *Vladimir Nabokov: The Russian Years* (London: Chatto & Windus, 1990), p. 197.

389 **'Anglo-Saxon civilisation'** . . . Cited in Nina Demurova, 'Vladimir Nabokov, Translator of Lewis Carroll's *Alice in Wonderland*', in *Nabokov at Cornell*, ed. Gavriel Shapiro (Ithaca; London: Cornell University Press, 2003), p. 182.

390 **victim of a show trial** . . . I owe this insight to Victor Fet, 'Beheading First: On Nabokov's Translation of Lewis Carroll', *The Nabokovian*, 63 (2009), pp. 55–63.

390 **'"that kid's book, 'Alice in Wonderland'"'** . . . Francis Durham Grierson, *The Mad Hatter Mystery* (London: Eyre & Spottiswoode, 1941), p. 8.

390 **'begin at the beginning'** . . . Dorothy L. Sayers, *The Unpleasantness at the Bellona Club* (1928, repr. London: Hodder & Stoughton, 2003), pp. 45, 61.

391 **'arsenic into tea'** . . . Agatha Christie Mallowan, *Come, Tell Me How You Live* (London: Collins, 1946), pp. 9–10.

391 **'"r's and l's"'** . . . Florence Scott Bernard, *Through the Cloud Mountain* (Philadelphia; London: J. B. Lippincott Co., 1922), p. 34.

391 **'"it makes them happy"'** . . . *Ibid.*

391 **Other characters** . . . For example, in both versions of Tod Browning's crime thriller *The Unholy Three*, a 1925 silent film that was remade as a talkie in 1930, the dwarf actor Harry Earles played a thief named Tweedledee, who discovers where valuable jewels are hidden by disguising himself as a baby in a pram, and

celebrates a successful raid by strutting around in a sharp suit and lighting up a fat cigar.

392   **'animated cartoons!'** . . . Neal Gabler, *Walt Disney: The Triumph of the American Imagination* (New York: Alfred A. Knopf, 2007), p. 70.

393   **ancestor of Mickey Mouse** . . . Gabler lists a whole cartoonist's nest of other mice and rats who featured in the later *Alice* comedies, *ibid.*, p. 113.

393   **'imaginations of the night'** . . . Emile Cammaerts, *The Poetry of Nonsense* (London: George Routledge & Sons, 1926), p. 32.

393   **Ficolax** . . . *Alice in Fi-co-land* (published by Ficolax, London, 1919), p. 4.

394   **£400 per year** . . . Particulars printed by Hampton & Sons estate agents, dated 1928 and addressed 'To Captain C. L. Hargreaves' (Beinecke).

394   **a record for a book sold at auction** . . . Selwyn H. Goodacre, 'The "Alice" Manuscript – From 1928', *Jabberwocky*, 36 (Autumn 1978), p. 86.

394   **'she, too, vanishes'** . . . Cited in Gordon, *Beyond the Looking Glass*, p. 233.

396   **'wonderful'** . . . Private collection.

396   **'the little volume'** . . . Goodacre, 'The "Alice" Manuscript – From 1928', p. 86.

396   **'a long period single-handed'** . . . Cited in Gordon, *Beyond the Looking Glass*, p. 234.

396   **pieces of Carrolliana** . . . See Peter C. Bunnell's introduction to Taylor and Wakeling, *Lewis Carroll, Photographer*, p. xii.

397   **'bitterly regret'** . . . *The Times* (22 March 1928), p. 17.

397   **'his bulgy pockets'** . . . Edward Hope, *Alice in the Delighted States* (London: George Routledge & Sons Ltd, 1928), p. 284.

397   **'"to keep you company"'** . . . Dodgson Family Collection.

FORTY

398   **'as ignorant as he came'** . . . To Falconer Madan (14 February 1932), Princeton.

398   **removing six pages from his diary** . . . Morton Cohen's article 'Who Censored Lewis Carroll?' in *The Times* (23 January 1982) points the finger firmly at Menella, noting that a collector who visited her in 1957 was shown the diaries in a small brown cardboard box, and was told that 'some sections had been cut out' and 'Miss Dodgson said she was going to cut out more before she died' (p. 9).

398   **'being an invalid'** . . . *Diaries*, vol. 4, p. 193.

399   **her 'ailing' mother** . . . I draw these examples from Gordon, *Beyond the Looking Glass*, p. 235.

400   **'tears in laughter'** . . . Dodgson Family Collection.

400   **blots and crossings-out** . . . Dodgson Family Collection; Harry Ransom Center.

400   **'mythical self'** . . . Speech made by Caryl Hargreaves at 'Alice's Party' in the Central Hall, Westminster on 23 November 1932 (private collection).

401   **'reality and common sense'** . . . Hargreaves Papers.

402   **'charming little Alice'** . . . Muriel Fancourt Bell, 'To Alice (On meeting Mrs. Reginald Hargreaves, the original Alice in Wonderland)', *The Kashmir Valley and Others* (London: Poetry of To-day, 1935), pp. 12–13.

402   **'cold rough night'** . . . Private collection.

403   **'hunted rare fish'** . . . Edwin Wolf 2nd & John F. Fleming, *Rosenbach: A Biography* (London: Weidenfeld & Nicolson, 1960), p. 371.

403 'take me back to Wonderland' . . . 1 May 1932.

404 '"What is that thing?"' . . . *New York Times* (30 April 1932); *New York American* (30 April 1932) (Hargreaves Papers).

404 'more fun than the celebrity!' . . . Hargreaves Papers.

404 illegal speakeasies to nightclubs . . . Hargreaves Papers.

404 'no merit of my own' . . . Dodgson Family Collection.

404 'liberty of thought' . . . F. J. Harvey Darton, *Children's Books in England: Five Centuries of Social Life* (1932; 2nd edn, Cambridge: Cambridge University Press, 1958), p. 260.

405 'PETER PAN BECOMES PUBLISHER' . . . Andrew Birkin, *J. M. Barrie and the Lost Boys* (London: Constable, 1979), pp. 1–2.

406 'what miseries would have been spared me' . . . *Ibid.*, p. 196.

406 '"ALICE" MEETS "PETER PAN"' . . . *News Chronicle* (29 June 1932) (Hargreaves Papers).

406 'lying to them' . . . John Logan, *Peter and Alice* (London: Oberon Books, 2013), pp. 14–15.

406 'shaking' . . . Private collection.

406 'ALONE TO DIE' . . . Birkin, *J. M. Barrie and the Lost Boys*, p. 1.

FORTY-ONE

408 'unexplored but undiscovered' . . . Walter de la Mare, *Lewis Carroll* (London: Faber, 1932), p. 45.

408 'The Dullness of Dodgson' . . . Reed, *The Life of Lewis Carroll*, pp. 7, 126–33.

409 'a Fairy Godfather' . . . Harry Ransom Center.

409 'being extremely lucid' . . . John H. Pearson, letter to *The Times* (22 December 1931), repr. in *Interviews & Recollections*, pp. 76–7.

409 'the child's clothes' . . . A. M. E. Goldschmidt, '"Alice in Wonderland" Psychoanalyzed', *New Oxford Outlook* (May 1933), pp. 69–70.

409 'open-mouthed children' . . . Summary in the *New York Times* (30 December 1936).

409 outright censorship . . . Heywood Broun, 'It Seems to Me', *World Telegram* (6 January 1933).

410 'give Freud the creeps' . . . Cited in Stanley Edgar Hyman, *The Armed Vision* (New York: Vintage, 1955), p. 264.

410 'speaking up for itself' . . . Empson, *Some Versions of Pastoral*, pp. 253, 272–3, 260. F. R. Leavis was prepared to publish part of Empson's book in *Scrutiny*, praising his chapter on 'Proletarian Literature' as 'a good thing', but refused point-blank to print the chapter on *Alice*, which he viewed only as a source of 'mild amusement'; see Ian MacKillop, *F. R. Leavis: A Life in Criticism* (London: Allen Lane, 1995), p. 206.

410 *Golden Afternoon* . . . The parallels between Balthus and Carroll are outlined in Sabine Rewald's introduction to *Balthus: Cats and Girls* (New York: Metropolitan Museum of Art, 2013).

411 'a wonderful success' . . . Cited in Clark, *The Real Alice*, p. 248.

411 'a dream factory' . . . The *OED*'s first examples of 'dream factory' in reference to the film industry are from 1935 and 1936.

412 'a Nobody' . . . *Time*, 22: 26 (25 December 1933), p. 20.

412 'My identity was gone' . . . Cited in Gordon, *Beyond the Looking Glass*, p. 246.

412 'Alice-ish' . . . *OED*.

414   **'is dying'** . . . *Daily Express* (3 November 1934).

414   **'about the same'** . . . *The Times* (5–6 November 1934).

414   **Order of Service** . . . Private collection.

414   **'"ALICE IN WONDERLAND"'** . . . *The Times* (17 November 1934).

414   **'ALICE IN WONDERLAND IS DEAD'** . . . *Evening Standard* (16 November 1934).

415   **American satirical pamphlet** . . . *Frankie in Wonderland* (New York: E. P. Dutton & Co., 1934).

415   **winding brass tunnel** . . . Ernest La Prade, *Alice in Orchestra Land* (London: Cobden-Sanderson, 1934), pp. 16–17.

415   **'topsy-turvy world'** . . . Boyd, *Vladimir Nabokov: The Russian Years*, pp. 414–15.

415   **'loose carolleries'** . . . James Joyce, *Finnegans Wake* (London: Faber, 1939, repr. 1975), pp. 482, 270, 276, 528, 405, 258, 294. Ann McGarrity Buki discusses Carroll's pervasive presence in Joyce's 'nightynovel' in *Lewis Carroll: A Celebration*, ed. Edward Guiliano (New York: Clarkson Potter, 1982), pp. 154–66; see too Hugh Kenner, *Dublin's Joyce* (London: Chatto & Windus, 1955), pp. 276–300.

415   **'bits and scraps'** . . . Letter to Harriet Weaver (31 May 1927), cited in James A. Atherton, *The Books at the Wake: A Study of Literary Allusions in James Joyce's 'Finnegans Wake'* (New York: Viking, 1960), p. 127.

415   **the Surrealist movement** . . . David Gascoyne, *A Short Survey of Surrealism* (1935, repr. London: Enitharmon Press, 2000), p. 94.

415   **a new Wonderland** . . . André Breton, *Surrealism and Painting* (1928), trans. Simon Watson Taylor (Boston: MFA Publishing, 2002), p. 6.

415   **a major exhibition in New York** . . . Fantastic Art, Dada, Surrealism at the Museum of Modern Art; Carroll's influence on the work of artists such as René Magritte and Max Ernst is helpfully outlined in Christoph Benjamin Schulz, 'Down the Rabbit Hole and Into the Museum: Alice and the Visual Arts', in *Alice in Wonderland Through the Visual Arts*, ed. Gavin Delahunty and Christoph Benjamin Schulz (London: Tate Publishing, 2011), pp. 14–17.

416   **'revitalizing the Fatherland'** . . . Michael Fry, *Hitler's Wonderland* (London: John Murray, 1934), p. 213.

416   **'Germany – Silent Voices'** . . . *The Jewish Chronicle* (22 September 1933).

417   **'"you'll like it, I know!"'** . . . Playbill for Sean O'Casey's *Within the Gates* (National Theatre, New York), which opened on 12 November 1934, p. 9.

417   **'That Girl Is Everywhere'** . . . See Beverly Lyon Clark, *Kiddie Lit: The Cultural Construction of Children's Literature in America* (Baltimore; London: Johns Hopkins University Press, 2003), p. 151.

417   **'she will be remembered'** . . . Princeton.

EPILOGUE

421   **sit for a photograph** . . . I discuss this episode in chapter 14.

423   **fragments of evidence** . . . See Hermione Lee, *Body Parts: Essays on Life-writing* (London: Chatto & Windus, 2005) on 'the parts and bits and gaps which are left over after [a] life has ended', and the biographical challenge of 'trying to make a solid figure, embodied on the page, out of what is gone' (p. 5).

423   'a jigsaw of the past' . . . Jeff Noon, *Automated Alice* (1996, repr. London: Corgi, 1997), p. 128.

424   one of Carroll's lost works . . . See Selwyn H. Goodacre, 'An Enquiry into the Nature of a Certain Lewis Carroll Pamphlet', *The Book Collector*, 27: 3 (Autumn 1978), pp. 325–72.

424   Carroll's nickname . . . See, e.g., Gardner (ed.), *The Annotated Alice*: 'Carroll's Dodo was intended as caricature of himself – his stammer is said to have made him pronounce his name "Dodo-Dodgson"' (p. 28n.).

424   'side by side' . . . Jan Morris, *Oxford*, 3rd edn (Oxford: Oxford University Press, 2001), p. 86.

425   'very fragmentary and unarranged' . . . *Letters*, vol. 2, p. 1100.

425   'unknown to the world' . . . Letter to Mrs Heurtley (11 May 1883), cited in *Diaries*, vol. 7, p. 534n.

426   'The Unknown One' . . . *Life & Letters*, p. 24.

426   'the bottle of laudanum and wonders' . . . Logan, *Peter and Alice*, pp. 54–5.

427   'great gaps and voids' . . . Henry James, *What Maisie Knew*, ed. Paul Theroux (Harmondsworth: Penguin, 1985), p. 27.

427   'we become children' . . . Phillips (ed.), *Aspects of Alice*, p. 48.

427   place in contemporary culture . . . Brooker, *Alice's Adventures*, pp. 151–264.

428   'shut behind you' . . . Spufford, *The Child That Books Built*, p. 85.

Acknowledgements

Writing any book is a collaborative enterprise, but this one in particular would have remained a patchwork of scribbled notes and half-formed hunches without the generous assistance of many people.

Alice Liddell Hargreaves's great-granddaughter Vanessa Tait supported it from the beginning, lending me many unpublished family papers, while I am also indebted to other private collectors who allowed me access to the material in their keeping. The editor of Carroll's diaries, Edward Wakeling, deserves special mention: not only did he allow me to view his extraordinarily rich collection of Carrolliana, offering hospitality and answering questions with equal generosity, but he also read an early draft of the whole book, picking up many errors in the process. (Of course, any that remain are my responsibility alone.) I am also lucky to have met many people whose immediate response, when contacted by someone who pestered them with bizarre queries, was not to slam down the phone but to go out of their way to help. Peter and Jane Atkinson kindly invited me to stay in Carroll's old home in Croft-on-Tees, and showed me the hoard of treasures that had been discovered under the floorboards; Derek Frampton explained how he reconstructed the Oxford Dodo; Peter Jewitt took me up the Thames to the picnic spot where Carroll first introduced Alice to Wonderland; Catriona Smellie, collections officer at the Guildford Museum, volunteered to complete one of the Dodgson family's jigsaw puzzles and discovered that it had a piece missing; Patrick J. Rodgers sent me photographs of Carroll's Russian passport from its new home in the Rosenbach Museum and Library, Philadelphia.

My Oxford colleagues Felix Budelmann, Gregory Hutchinson and Antony Smith explained to me the significance of white stones in classical literature, while Laurie Maguire was a tigress in protecting me from all the things that would otherwise have prevented me from being as single-minded as I needed to be in order to get this book completed during a period of research leave. The exception was a BBC documentary on which I worked as a consultant in 2014, and I am indebted to Clare Beavan, Neil Crombie, Martha Kearney and Jonathan Parker for asking the sort of questions that helped me get my own thoughts a little better in focus.

I am also grateful to the many librarians and archivists who uncomplainingly unlocked glass cases and fetched boxes as I briskly filleted their collections, especially those at the Surrey History Centre, New Forest Centre Reference Library, Museum of Oxford, Oxford Museum of Science, Oxford Museum of Natural History, Princeton University Library, Houghton Library, Beinecke Library, Pierpont Morgan Library, Fales Library, Harry Ransom Research Center, Christ Church Oxford (where I am particularly grateful to the Librarian Janet McMullin and Archivist Judith Corthoys for their assistance) and the Bodleian Library. This is not the first time Alice Liddell Hargreaves's story has been told, and although I record specific borrowings in my notes, I am happy to acknowledge a more general debt to Colin Gordon and Anne Clark, whose earlier biographies introduced me to several areas of enquiry I might not otherwise have considered.

Sam Plumb and Sophie Ratcliffe generously read earlier drafts of this book and made a number of perceptive suggestions that greatly improved what I originally sent to them, while Ushashi Dasgupta – a young scholar so efficient I suspect she may actually be twins or triplets in disguise – was not only a superb research assistant, digging up quirky literary odds and ends that I would almost certainly have missed otherwise, but also helped me to tame the results.

I am very fortunate in having had editors – Michal Shavit and Ellie Steel at Harvill Secker, and John Kulka at Harvard University Press – who were actually willing to edit, and together with my hawk-eyed copy-editor Beth Humphries worked with me to tighten up a flabby initial draft with such enthusiasm it barely felt like work at all. I am also thankful for the outstanding design and publicity team behind this book, particularly Suzanne Dean, Fiona Murphy and Simon Rhodes. Before and behind everything else, my agent Peter Straus believed in *The Story of Alice* from the moment I first tentatively broached the idea to him, and Mac Castro showed his usual tireless patience in letting me get on with it, even when all he could hear coming from my study was a steady stream of expletives.

On the day before I was due to fly to America to visit a number of Carroll archives, something happened that made my writing take a rather different turn. Conor Robinson, one of my students at Magdalen College, died after an accidental fall. He was a hugely talented young man, who managed to combine a sophisticated critical mind with a childlike capacity for wonder at the everyday, and his smile haunted me through the following months of research and writing. This book is dedicated to his memory.

Credits

Image credits: **p. 2**: held in the Beinecke Rare Book and Manuscript Library; **p. 29**: private collection/author's photo; **p. 47**: The Governing Body of Christ Church, Oxford; **p. 64**: private collection/Bridgeman Images; **p. 75**: MS Eng 718.1 (pages 14–15), Houghton Library, Harvard University; **p. 81**: © National Media Museum/Science & Society Picture Library; **p.97**: Princeton University Library; **p. 100**: © National Media Museum/Science & Society Picture Library; **p. 114**: Scottish National Portrait Gallery; **p. 127**: © The British Library Board; **p. 135**: private collection/The Stapleton Collection/Bridgeman Images; **p. 142**: The Governing Body of Christ Church, Oxford; **p. 152**: private collection/Bridgeman Images; **p. 162**: Harry Ransom Center, The University of Texas at Austin; **p. 172**: Princeton University Library; **p. 183**: The Governing Body of Christ Church, Oxford; **p. 187**: reproduced by permission of Vanessa Tait; **p. 199**: © National Media Museum/Science & Society Picture Library; **p. 212**: photo © The Metropolitan Museum of Art/Art Resource/Scala, Florence; **p. 226**: Mary Evans Picture Library; **p. 232**: © Royal Photographic Society/National Media Museum/Science & Society Picture Library; **p. 248**: MS Eng 718.11 (page 14), Houghton Library, Harvard University; **p. 255**: Harry Ransom Center, The University of Texas at Austin; **pp. 262–3**: facsimile of a letter reproduced in Isa Bowman's 1899 memoir *The Story of Lewis Carroll* © The British Library Board; **p. 272**: reproduced in E. W. Brayley and J. Britton's *The Beauties of England and Wales*, vol. 6 (1805) © The British Library Board; **p. 277**: photo © Pierpont Morgan Library/Art Resource/Scala, Florence; **p. 284**: Royal Pavilion, Libraries & Museums, Brighton & Hove/Bridgeman Images; **p. 293**: © Fine Art Photographic Library/Corbis; **p. 310**: © National Portrait Gallery, London; **p. 319**: © The British Library Board; **p. 332**: © The British Library Board; **p. 337**:

Harry Ransom Center, The University of Texas at Austin; **p. 350**: reproduced in Stuart Dodgson Collingwood's *The Life and Letters of Lewis Carroll* (1898) © The British Library Board; **p. 368**: © National Media Museum/Science & Society Picture Library; **p. 376**: courtesy of BFI National Archive; **p. 380**: private collection; **p. 395**: © The British Library Board; Daily Sketch/Associated Newspapers Ltd; **p. 405**: Topfoto; **p. 412**: courtesy of BFI National Archive; **p. 416**: photo © Tate, London 2015; **p. 422**: Oxford University Images/Greg Smolonski.

Quotations: **p. 21**: 'Thames' from Stephanie Bolster, *White Stone: The Alice Poems*, Signal Editions/Véhicule Press; **p. 25**: *Copenhagen* © Michael Frayn, 1998, Bloomsbury Methuen Drama, an imprint of Bloomsbury Publishing Plc.; **p. 382**: *Journey's End* © R. C. Sherriff, 1929 (first published 1929, Penguin Books 1983, Penguin Classics 2000); **pp. 406** and **426**: *Peter and Alice* © John Logan, 2013. Reprinted by permission of Oberon Books; **p. 419**: *Forty-One False Starts: Essays on Artists and Writers* © Janet Malcolm, 2013. Reprinted by permission of Granta Publications and Farrar, Straus and Giroux, LLC.

Excerpts from Lewis Carroll's letters reprinted by permission of AP Watt *at* United Agents on behalf of the Executors of the C. L. Dodgson Estate, Morton Cohen and Scirard Lancelyn Green; Lewis Carroll's diaries by permission of AP Watt *at* United Agents on behalf of the Executors of the C. L. Dodgson Estate and Scirard Lancelyn Green; and archive documents in the Dodgson Family Collection by permission of AP Watt *at* United Agents on behalf of the Executors of the C. L. Dodgson Estate. While permission has been granted, the Executors of the C. L. Dodgson Estate may not necessarily agree with the ideas put forward in this book.

Index

All works are by Lewis Carroll unless otherwise stated.

479